Shards Of Divinities

Whispers From The Semantic Spaces Within The Soul

Nissim Levy

Shards Of Divinities Copyright © 2016 by Third Age Communications

Cover art copyright © Reborn by Tomasz Alen Kopera www.alenkopera.com

All rights reserved. No part of this book may be reproduced or transmitted for financial gain in any form or by any means without written permission from the author. However, the author encourages spreading the teachings of this novel, through any medium, if the motives are not for financial gain and instead are for the noble purpose of enlightening the collective soul.

ISBN-13: 978-1532783159

ISBN-10: 1532783159

Dedicated To my father

Shmuel (Samuel) Levy

He was a citizen of a different realm

Milestones

The First Age: A Quest For Divinities
- 2   The Yeast That Leavens Empires
- 12   Childhood Musings
- 20   Maturity
- 39   Dancing With My Fears
- 53   Worlds Within Worlds
- 67   Address to the Examining Reader

The Second Age: A Quest For The ONE
- 70   The Semantic Spaces Within The Soul
- 75   The Four Corners
- 98   The Moon Reflects Our Soul
- 107   The Breeze of Yahvah: The Desert Beckons At Night
- 116   The Navel Of Creation: A Loop In Eternity
- 145   The Curtains Open: The Second Act

The Third Age: A Quest For En Sof
- 151   The First Iteration
- 166   A Leitmotif In The Final Key
- 170   Crossing Over To New Realms
- 178   The Early Years: Why Are All Bachelors Unmarried?
- 210   Beyond the Shadows: Existential Whiplash
- 245   Gödel And Chaos: The Tree Of Creation
- 272   I AM Ready
- 283   My Manifesto
- 318   The Dancer And The Wrestler
- 332   The Story Unfolds
- 350   I AM Writing Gödel And Chaos: The Tree Of Creation
- 362   I AM Not An Island
- 372   I AM Writing My Manifesto
- 390   I AM Done
- 412   The Curtains Open: The Third Act

The First Age: A Quest For Divinities

The Yeast That Leavens Empires

Ever since I was a child I always felt like a citizen of a different realm. I have sown the seeds of that realm in my childhood, but I can only know the fruits of the reaping once I cross over into that other realm. I was born at home in the city of Ur, in the shadow of the great Ziggurat of Ur-Nammu. The ziggurat was, by far, the tallest edifice in the city. It was taller than fifteen men all together, and two hundred men with arms connected and outstretched could not enclose it.

I was born a Habiru and we are at best tolerated and at worst despised. This has always been the case and will continue to be so until the highest god sees fit otherwise. As a child, I felt stigmatized by society. I felt like an outsider. This is not to say the Habiru never had it tougher than during my childhood years. There are more severe scars in our collective psyche. When I was a child my father Terah would captivate my brothers and me with tales of great woe. He never tired of telling the story of King Sargon.

"Let me tell you about the butcher-king Sargon who reigned with a mighty grip over all of Sumer four hundred years ago." He paused and ran his large, rough hands through his long, coarse beard. His beard was still mostly dark in those days.

"Pa, hurry up and tell us the story," my brother Haran said. "You always start this story with the exact same words and make us wait forever before you continue."

"Hardly forever my boy, but is it not worth the wait? Do I not add more to the story each time I tell it? Don't rush me my boy. I need to draw inspiration from the gods."

The Habiru will always remember King Sargon as a heartless tyrant and a bloodthirsty butcher. During his reign he summarily expelled all Habiru living throughout Sumer. Most gravitated to the distant eastern lands, but overall were scattered in all directions - as far west as Erev, the land of the setting sun, as far north as Or Layla, the lands of the midnight sun, and as far south as the great bottomless ocean. Many died in transit from dehydration, from exhaustion, from hunger and disease. It is at once ironic and disturbing the Habiru, known as ontological nomads since time immemorial, should perish in great numbers while in transit. They had become too soft, too urbanized. They had betrayed their cultural zeitgeist. I am ashamed to admit we have made the same mistakes in our own generation. The sins of the father are forgotten by the child.

A few breaths later my father nodded his head in contentment. He had settled on the story for the day. "Today I will enthrall you all with the tale of Elshor the Bull."

Our eyes widened in anticipation.

"As you all already know, Sargon expelled all the Habiru from Sumer shortly after he gained the throne. That much they teach you in school, but what those damned purebreds won't teach you is that we were hardly kicked out of our homes without putting up a spirited fight." He pursed his lips and squinted his eyes while nodding his head.

"Some say in the hundreds of years since the great expulsion the story I'm about to tell you was invented. Some say it's merely a legend that has been artfully spun like golden silk at the hands of a master yarn spinner. But let me tell you all here and now it is nothing of the sort. Every word is as authentic and true as the sun setting in the West."

My father had a lyrical way with words. In many ways I am my father's son more so than any of my brothers. I also have the gift of poetic expression and an almost mystical way with words.

My father continued: "What they won't teach you in school is that we, the Habiru, have a great tenacity and strength of character. We revolted shortly after Sargon decreed the expulsion."

"Damn right we did," Haran said while clenching his fists and swinging his right arm upwards. "No one kicks a Habiru around without getting the end of our sword up his butt."

All my brothers laughed and nodded in enthusiastic agreement.

My father laughed along with my brothers. "Yes Haran, you're always the mob leader, aren't you?"

As my father continued with the tale of Elshor The Bull we were all transported to that far away time, and it was no longer our father telling the story; we were experiencing it firsthand.

Imagine a king who reigns over his subjects as a god does over his creation. This man is more than a king because he has conquered the lands and kingdoms of other peoples and has subjugated them and broken their will. This man is a king of kings and a godlike tyrant. This man is a merciless butcher of those who challenge his claims of divinity. Such a man was Sargon the Great, also known as Sargon of Akkad, and to the Habiru known above all else as Sargon the Butcher. My father was an evocative storyteller and my brothers and I were drawn into the story as if we were witnessing it firsthand. We were witnessing Elshor preparing himself for the onslaught surely to come. We could no longer hear our father's voice; we could only hear the voices of Elshor and his cohorts.

"Elshor, Elshor, I've been searching for you all day. Thank the gods I've

found you. I've heard you arrived from your travels in the land of Lagash and I rushed to find you."

"Yes Lugal. I returned just yesterday. I learned much in Lagash."

"Are our fears true? Will Sargon decree our expulsion?"

"It is certain, Lugal. I received the word directly from Sargon's ministry offices the day I embarked on my voyage back to Ur. Even now, as we speak, Sargon's ambassadors are on their way here to formally announce the decree."

"And I'm certain not far behind his ambassadors are his merciless hordes and assassins. How long are we given to vacate our homes and lands?" Lugal's voice trembled with fear and the grief of impending loss.

"I can't say for sure. I've heard rumors that from the time of the decree we have no more than sixty days to completely vacate Ur."

As my father continued telling the story of the great expulsion, I drifted in and out of those legendary times. My consciousness was a skipping stone briefly skimming over the waters of legend and myth.

"When Sargon's ambassadors entered Ur they ordered the Habiru population to evacuate within sixty days."

"And that's when we smashed their faces in, right pa?"

"Well, we did put up a valiant struggle. We started the great revolt in those days. Elshor the Bull hastily recruited one thousand of the strongest and bravest Habiru and trained them to be deadly warriors. Some say ordinarily it would take months or years of training, but he achieved it in mere days. When his great warriors were ready, Elshor led them against Sargon's government buildings. They stormed those buildings like wild jackals sinking their glistening fangs into their prey. We Habiru have a notorious reputation as brigands and thieves, but we are no such things. We are the proud spawn of clans who roamed the earth during times so ancient they predate myths. But I digress, back to my tale. When Sargon heard of the attack on the government buildings his rage knew no bounds."

"He wasn't in the government buildings when the revolt happened?"

"No Abram, he was far away in the North, conquering the lands of Urkesh. It wasn't long before word reached him of the Habiru revolt, and he dispatched two hundred chariots and two thousand foot soldiers to squash the revolt."

"And we showed him that two hundred chariots and even two thousand soldiers are no match for one thousand angry Habiru, fighting for their homes and lands, right pa?"

"Haran, do you have any idea of the power of a full military chariot?

The Yeast That Leavens Empires

Have you ever stood next to a Sumerian chariot commandeered by soldiers in full battle-armor and armed with the most advanced swords, spears and military grade bows? It's the most frightening military machine ever devised by the human mind. Perhaps mankind will never see a more potent military killing machine."

My father paused briefly, letting our vivid imaginations grasp his words.

"Tell us, tell us, what's it like to come up close to a full military chariot?" I said.

"Great armies trembled at the sight of Sargon's approaching chariots. From a great distance one could hear the ominous thunder of Sargon's chariots, numbering in the hundreds, as they raced towards their unfortunate prey. And upon reaching their prey, they pounced on it and engulfed it as do the masses of enraged Army ants when they swarm their prey and then engulf it and tear its flesh from its bones. They tear and devour the flesh of their prey without a shred of mercy. They are oblivious to shrill, soul-piercing screams of agony of their victims because they do not possess the capacity for mercy and compassion. As are the Army ants so were Sargon's legions of chariots."

We soaked in every word of our father's tale. We sat on the ground facing our father, our limp arms slung over our thighs, shoulders and necks slumped forward and mouths gaping in awe.

Our father was satisfied at the shock his tale inspired. He continued: "This motley group of Habiru makeshift warriors fought as lions and, against great odds, almost succeeded in defeating Sargon's charioteers. Sargon's response to the uprising was swift and brutal. Thousands of Habiru were rounded up and executed in unimaginably barbaric ways. Habiru children and infants were fodder at the sacrificial altar of the sun-god Shamash."

My brothers and I listened in a hypnotic stupor as my father described, in morbid detail, the disembowelment of young children, while still alive, at the foot of the statue of Shamash. He described how young children vibrated and twitched with screams of agony as Sargon's soldiers sliced and gutted them like fattened rams while their parents were forced to watch. My father then turned his head and jabbed his right arm in the direction of the gates of Ur. As he pointed towards the gates he spoke in a too dramatic way: "To this day, the statue of Shamash stands at the outskirts of Ur, like a great monolith and reminder to Habiru about their place in a society that may tolerate them at times but will never consider them as true heirs of the great social experiment that is Ur."

My father paused again for a few breaths, licked his lips and then continued: "There is a positive and more encouraging side to this story. Legend has it Sargon ordered his charioteers to capture Elshor the Bull and bring him alive to the imperial compound. Sargon's imperial guards cast Elshor at Sargon's feet, naked and bound in chains. He then asked all to leave his quarters and that's precisely when Elshor, in an explosive feat of divine strength, burst his chains and was transformed by Annu, the chief god of the heavens, into a massive and enraged bull. Upon witnessing this miracle, Sargon collapsed to the floor and begged the transformed Elshor for forgiveness."

"But pa," I said, "why would Sargon punish the Habiru so brutally because they revolted against him if he witnessed firsthand how the gods themselves are obviously on the side of the leader of the Habiru? Why would he ask Elshor for forgiveness and then banish his people from Ur?" My father did not respond, or maybe I have forgotten his response because it did not ring true to my ears.

In the four hundred years since Sargon's reign, a great influx of Habiru have again made Ur their home. Some are descendants of those expelled by Sargon so long ago. Many others do not trace their genealogies at all to Ur or even to Sumer in general. Many Habiru have roots in other modern empires such as the Egyptian empire. When I was a child a Habiru family of Egyptian ancestry moved next door to me. I trace my ancestry to Ur as far back as the time of the great expulsion. However, before that time and into the murky depths of the past, I am not certain of the origin of my people. I once did genealogical research at the Library of Annan Sin and discovered evidence my ancestors possibly originate from the lands of India many hundreds of years ago. I learned of the great Indian priestly class called the Brahmin. The similarities between the Brahmin and the Habiru are very compelling. My name Abram, a common Habiru name, probably points to my ancestry from the Brahmin priestly class. Perhaps that explains my compulsion to understand the nature of divinity and all you will learn about my character and my passions as you continue reading. Another stunning similarity is while the Brahmin worship the cow, my own people regard the bull with divine undertones. This is a recurring theme with my people - a leitmotif. Indeed, the legend of Elshor the Bull is a great example of this. I am not certain, however, if the Habiru descend from the Brahmin or the other way around. Did god create the chicken or the egg first?

My family's existence in Ur was urbane. This is not a surprise, Ur is one of the world's most developed and sophisticated cities. I enjoyed the privileges that come with calling Ur my home even if in many other ways my life in Ur had its discontent and disappointments. I enjoyed one of the world's most well stocked libraries. I studied the great mathematical works of Sumer and Egypt. I was knowledgeable about history, religion, astronomy, music theory and many other subjects. I was always musing about what I had learned and the implications of such provocative things filled my head with delicious mystery and an overwhelming hunger for the truth.

My two favorite areas of study were religion and Egyptian astronomy. Sumerian astronomy is cut from a different piece of cloth. Egyptian astronomy details the behaviors of the heavenly bodies while simultaneously appreciating their divine attributes. However, Sumerian astronomy is purely religious and does not concern itself at all with the more physical aspects of the heavenly bodies. My own proclivities were for Egyptian astronomy. I saw the fingerprints of the gods in the heavens and earth, but I also craved to discover the details of how the gods created and set in motion the heavenly bodies. Initially, my world view connected the actions of divine beings with the actions of nature. I believed in systematic principles pointing to the gods. I searched hungrily for logical motivations leading to a belief in divine beings, rather than assuming their existence as an a priori or as simply an article of faith.

When I was seven my father enrolled me in Ur's school system. I was one of the few Habiru pupils swimming in a sea of proper purebred children of Ur. That is how they fancy themselves. From the very beginning I demonstrated a love for learning and a real talent too. I took first place in mathematics during my first year in school and every year thereafter. This nurtured a great resentment amongst my purebred peers and I was rarely included in the great tapestry of childhood friendships and the nascent bonds forming the foundation of an adult's psyche. Even as a young child I had a nose for the festering bowels of discrimination and I realized that, at a fundamental level, I was ostracized because I am Habiru. If I were not Habiru my penchant for learning and my adeptness at my studies would not have evoked such a visceral response from my peers. A Habiru is not supposed to outshine the proper purebred children of Ur and the fact many Habiru often did evoked a great cognitive dissonance its purebred sufferers only understood subconsciously and which manifested itself consciously in the crassness and banality of prejudice.

The Egyptian Habiru family living next door to me has three sons and four daughters. Their youngest is my age and he is my classmate and only true friend. His name is Khaferu. We are both Habiru and this has cemented our friendship and our bond. Despite being a third generation Sumerian, his name is distinctly Egyptian. I mention he is my classmate as a lead into a discussion of Ur's compulsory school system. The law requires all citizens of Ur, from the ages of seven to seventeen, to attend school. Ur is unique in this respect. I have never known of any other city to implement such a requirement.

Back in the old days, and down to these times, Ur is still a political powerhouse of Sumer and this is why its citizens are, overall, urbane, educated and overachieving. This is in contrast to the areas in the immediate vicinity which are populated by uneducated nomads who would not know the difference between thirty-six and thirty-six hundred. Most of these nomads have, throughout the ages, been Habiru who have never been urbane and cultured. Indeed, most Habiru live as nomads to this day, pitching their tents as the winds blow. Most are poor, subsisting day to day off their meager flocks of livestock and the lean bounty of the land. However, my father has told me stories of Habiru nomads who had done very well for themselves, owning huge herds, slaves numbering many times sixty, a bountiful harem of wives and sixty and sixty-fold of children. My father, who has a gift for speculation, had an interesting idea. He speculated that great empires and cities emerged from such affluent nomadic clans of Habiru through a process of accretion. The Habiru can then be understood as the yeast leavening empires. If this is true then modern cities such as Ur, and even current civilizations such as the Egyptians, Sumerians and Hittites, are the fruits of wealthy Habiru clans who roamed the Earth during times so ancient that legend is blurred into fact. Society's stigmatization of the Habiru may indeed derive from a source deep down in its collective soul, very much like a son who has done well for himself and is ashamed of and distances himself from his unworldly and rustic family.

I introduced my only childhood friend Khaferu. I have a tendency to veer off topic. I must seem to you like a housefly, forever whimsically zigzagging hitherto and fro towards some unfathomable and unthinking goal. However, I believe my madness has a method whose flavor, texture and identity will emerge as you read on. I promise you that.

I have many fond memories of my childhood. Some of these are of my friendship with Khaferu, while others are of my relationship with my family, particularly my father. This is despite the many rocky patches in our relationship. Khaferu's family is more affluent than mine. His father owns a large shop selling fine fabrics. Four days per week, since our first year in school, we have walked together to school and from school back home. The walks to school were mostly brisk and uninspiring, but our walks back home were more relaxed and playful. I will always savor bittersweet nostalgia for these after-school walks, often through a thick, sweltering heat like a steaming silk robe caressing our souls. We inhaled deeply the enticing aromas wafting in the air from the food markets - aromas of exotic spices, roasted goat and lamb mixing harmoniously with the musky pungency of the Euphrates river snaking its way nearby, beyond the city walls. The competing shouts and supplications of the merchants advertising their wares resonated almost rhythmically with the metallic hums and shrieks of bull, horse and ox-pulled wagons meandering through the congested streets and back-alleys.

Khaferu was a decent enough student, but he hated mathematics and I often coached him before exams and assignments. He was thin, of average height, and with straight and silky black hair that kissed his shoulders. He had an effeminate tendency to engage in girlish games such as hopscotch and rope-skipping. In contrast, I had a wild head of brown curls, a sturdy, almost muscular build, was tall for my age and was very masculine in my play preferences. Because I had few other playmates, and none I could truly call friend, I was compelled to mold Khaferu in my image. Khaferu had few playmates himself, and I am sure he would have wanted to engage me in his favorite games, but he was far too placid to force his way. I, on the other hand, had a very forceful personality and I succeeded mostly in getting my way. Looking back, I see I must have been quite an overbearing child.

My favorite game was Angle Ball, also known as Pinot. Khaferu would stand across the road from me and throw a bouncy leather ball towards me. Most roads in Ur have raised embankments on either side. These embankments are only for pedestrians. The road itself is only for horse, ass or cattle-pulled traffic. While standing across from each other, Khaferu and I would throw a ball of toughened goat leather that we tightly pumped with air until our arms burned with fatigue. This type of ball bounces with great force when it hits a hard surface. The object of the game is to hit the corner of the embankment on the opposite side of the street precisely in a way that would direct it back to you. If you are then able to catch the ball, without stepping off the embankment, as it bounces back to you then you earn a point, and you continue bouncing the ball against the opposite embankment until you fail to catch it. Your opponent then has his turn. The first player to reach thirty-six points is the winner. Countless generations of Habiru boys have played Pinot. The street on which we lived was about twenty paces wide. At this distance Pinot is a difficult game to master. Compounding the difficulty were the uneven embankment corners. They changed from day to day due to the constant pedestrian traffic and the carriage wheels and animals that often scraped and deformed them. Consequently, the leather ball would often bounce in unpredictable trajectories from throw to throw. The trick was to find a patch of embankment that was reasonably even for about an arm's length or two, and on both sides of the road. If we could only find an even patch on one side of the road then we would switch sides every eighteen points. Khaferu and I played this game almost every day after school. He even started liking the game after a while and I did not have to twist his arm to play it.

Following our games we each headed to our respective homes for supper and then often reconvened, in Khaferu's home or mine, for our school studies. By the time we reached the fourth or fifth years of our studies I had become a budding philosopher, and Khaferu and I spent hours discussing my favorite subject - the creation of the world. At school, starting from the first year, we learned about the great pantheon of gods and goddesses, each controlling a unique aspect of the world. We learned this pantheon has a hierarchical structure headed by the four primary gods: Anu, Bel, Ea and Enlil. Anu is the sky god, the creator of the heavenly objects and the judge of people's misdeeds. Enlil is the god of wind and the life force of flowers, shrubs, trees and grasses. Bel is the god of the earth, the bringer of order and life. Ea is god of the waters, the bringer of Chaos, and yet without whom Bel, the granter of order, could not accomplish his divine fiat.

Additionally, we learned of the minor gods and goddesses. These minor deities exhibit the pettiness and weaknesses of human beings. In giving their gods human characteristics, the Sumerians projected unto them the conflicts they found amongst themselves. For example, I learned in school of the dispute between the god of cattle Lahar and his sister Ashnan, the goddess of grain. Like many other gods, these gods were vain and self-absorbed and hungered for praise and validation from Anu, the god of the heavens. Each of the two sibling gods extolled his or her achievements and ridiculed the achievements of the other.

Despite such petty characteristics of the gods and goddesses, religion always fascinated me because it aims to answer the big questions. Even before my school years, I felt drawn to thinking of such things. Perhaps this inclination is the result of my father who owned a small shop selling, amongst other things, statues and figurines of deities. Let me lead you on a journey into the labyrinth of my young mind. This will give you a better appreciation of what motivated me then and perhaps to this very day. The following dialog is really a compendium of various memorable dreams or imaginary dialogs that I had with the idols in my father's shop over the years. I present this dialog from the perspective of my young mind as if it had occurred in the real world, but the perceptive reader, having the benefit of transcending the story of this dialog, can fathom otherwise.

Childhood Musings

My father Terah was a shopkeeper and he sold the most exquisite figurines. Some stood taller than a man by a head and others were no bigger than my pinky. Some were colorful like a breathtaking rainbow cutting through a springtime sky, others were the color of granite and as hoary looking as the mountains to the east. I remember being four years of age and running through my father's shop, running circles and circles within circles between those ominous idols. Yes, they were idols. I did not grasp that reality at first. I was but an innocent child and those lumbering hunks of clay and stone, of marble and precious metals, were my trusted companions. Each morning my father and I would wake up at sunrise and get ready for the day's work. My dear mother Amathlaah would prepare our breakfast, usually of some freshly hatched eggs - fried to a golden perfection, a smattering of goat cheese on some freshly baked pita and some dates or maybe some honey, if we were lucky and we could find some at the markets. My brother Haran would then get ready for school while I helped my mother clean up. Finally, my father and I would head off into town to the shop. Of course, once I started school myself I could not visit my father's shop every day, but only two or three times a week. I lived right in the center of Ur, which is to this day a bustling and lively city, dense with people, shops, and markets of all kinds.

During those early years I had a wild imagination and I lived more in my head than in the real world. Some say things have not changed much to this day. By the time I reached the age of seven my imagination had grown even richer. I vividly remember one of the idols in my father's shop. His name was Orofus the fertility idol. He was a magnificent creature made of the finest Phoenician marble. He was the tallest idol in the shop, standing a head taller than my father and his rippling muscles bulged as if they would explode at any time. He was naked and his turgid penis was as thick as my ankle and as long as a cat's tail. It pointed straight towards the sky and there was a thick, ropy vein on its underside. He was a suitably equipped fertility idol. Orofus had a very disdainful sneer and his eyes looked crazy, like he was perpetually spitting on your grandmother's grave. His skin was a deep earthy red and he appeared as if covered in crusted blood. His features were rough and ugly but that elicited my awe and respect. I could not imagine such a villainous and disrespectful brute being at all pleasant looking. Orofus was not the type to care for the niceties of polite society, I imagined. I would engage him in conversation when my father was away from the shop, tending to some unknown matter or other.

Childhood Musings

"What is it that you do at night," I asked, "when I'm home and there's no one here to keep you company?"

Orofus sneered and replied in a very throaty and deep voice: "I am the master of your father's shop. I shackle all the other gods and demons and I then make my way into the night."

"And where do you go when you make your way into the night?"

"I gallop across the desert floor and all the pretty virgins run away from me in delightful terror."

I did not understand his words. Please remember I was only seven years old. "Orofus, what's a virgin?"

Orofus sneered again and replied: "You are but a little boy and you don't know of such things. A man goes through three stages while he is on this earth. The first stage is the stage of ignorance. It is a stage of innocence. The second stage is a stage of physical and intellectual maturity while the third is a stage of the spirit, a stage of wisdom. You are but in your first stage and you are not ready to know what a virgin is until you reach the second stage."

I thought for a few minutes about his teachings and I decided to not let him get away with waxing so philosophically without answering my question.

"But Orofus, can't you just tell me what a virgin means anyway? I promise I will listen really hard and maybe I'll understand."

"You are a persistent little bugger. There is a big difference between knowing the details of something and understanding its full implications. A man meandering through the forest knows of the trees around him, but only when he climbs atop a mountain does he appreciate these trees border a river sustaining them. No, I will not explain what a virgin is because you are not in the stage of life where your limbs can carry you atop the mountain. So let me-"

"But Orofus please-"

"Quiet little boy. I was telling a tale of what it is I do at night, when you and your father Terah are home, so I will continue my story without your childish interruptions."

I resigned myself to not knowing what a virgin is until my second stage in life, even though I didn't even have a clue what a second stage in life is. I figured I had to be in this mysterious second stage of life not just to understand what a virgin is but even to understand what a second stage of life is.

"So here I am out at night, naked and wild and I've sent the virgins off to the hills in delightful terror. I then steal and pillage from the townspeople

Childhood Musings

and there is none who can stand in my way. I then gallop to a far away hole in the desert, as deep into the ground as the sky is high, and I jump in with all my misbegotten bounty. Do you know what exists down in that hole, little boy?"

My imagination was now running wild as only a child's could. I had forgotten about that virgin thing. "Tell me, tell me, what's in the hole?" I shrieked, hardly able to contain my excitement.

Orofus seemed satisfied with my deep interest in his tale and he replied: "There are all manner of serpents in that hole. The deeper you descend into the hole the bigger are the serpents. At first you will barely notice them for they are no larger than a maggot and a tiny maggot at that, but there are as many of them as the stars in the sky. Very gradually, as you descend deeper into the pit, they get larger and larger yet fewer and fewer in number, and before you know it they are as thick as a eucalyptus tree and as long as it is tall, but at that point there are only as many serpents as there are fingers on my hands."

I looked at his hands. I was amazed because I had only ever seen his fists but now I saw his outstretched fingers, and for the first time I noticed his long and slender bejeweled fingers, in stark contrast to his brutish and hulking face and body.

Orofus continued: "These magnificent serpents are talking serpents and-"

"Wow, what do they say Orofus. What do they tell you?"

"Well I was about to tell you. Don't interrupt me little boy or I will heave you into the serpent hole my next outing."

Orofus looked even meaner than usual and I imagined him clenching his ornate fists as an engorged bluish vein pulsated on the left side of his thick brow.

"They have the gift of the oracle. They speak for the gods. When I first climb into the serpent hole all I can hear are muted whispers and these whispers are repeated from a great jumble of little serpents in all directions around me. It truly is a cacophony. I cannot understand what they are saying because each serpent speaks a different language from all other serpents. As I climb deeper, and the serpents get larger and fewer in number, the cacophony slowly dissipates and I start to understand what it is they are saying because they are speaking with a more common voice."

Orofus paused and I seized my opportunity to ask him a question without risking being tossed into that mysterious serpent hole.

"Orofus, how deep down do you have to go into the serpent hole before you can start to understand what the serpents are saying?"

Childhood Musings

Orofus' perpetually pissed off expression morphed into a look of complete bewilderment. He looked like he had been sucker-punched hard in his powerful gut. He was silent for several minutes, diligently pondering my question. I had no idea I had posed such a deep and meaningful question. I could not imagine what must have been going on in his unfathomable mind. Finally, after a timeless eternity, he snapped out of his haze of bewilderment and his countenance assumed a look of deep wisdom. I had never seen that either. He did not look his usual pissed-off-at-the-world self and he no longer looked bewildered. I had never seen so many sides to him. I guess he was not just another gruesome face. When he next spoke he posed many strange questions.

"Where does the ocean's shore end and the ocean begin?"

He paused briefly. This was his cue I should answer. I contemplated his question but could not answer it. The question seemed very odd to me. It was not just that I did not know the answer but the very question itself seemed like it had something wrong with it.

"I don't know, Orofus. I've never been to the ocean in my whole life."

"How old is the oldest young person?"

At that my mind became tied in knots. Not only did I not know the answer, but I could not even understand the question. The first question tied my head in knots when trying to answer it, but this question tied my head in knots just trying to understand what in blazes the question was asking. Orofus saw what must have been a look of painful perplexity on my face. I think my eyes were crossed and my mouth was hanging open, inviting any passing by fly to use it as a perch.

"Look at it this way: are you young Abram?"

Finally, a question I could easily understand and answer.

"I'm just a boy. Yes, I'm very young."

"Will you be young when you're one hundred years old?"

Orofus seemed to have gone into a different mode of questioning. All the questions were now so easy I did not even need to give them a second thought. I liked this new Orofus.

"Ha ha Orofus, of course I won't be young. I'll be a very old man, probably with a long, white beard like my grandfather Nahor. He talks with a really squeaky voice like one of the sheep at home and-"

"Quiet, you annoying, snot-faced little boy. Just answer my questions."

"No Orofus, I will not be a young man when I'm one hundred years old," I answered obediently.

"That's correct Abram. Now answer this: If you are a fresh-faced young boy right now and you will be a crusty-faced old man when you are one

Childhood Musings

hundred, does that not mean somewhere between the age of seven and the age of one hundred you will be making this inevitable metamorphosis?"

This seemed perfectly reasonable to me so I answered immediately: "Yes, you are right." That's when Orofus lowered the hammer on me again.

"Great, I'm glad you understand that. Tell me Abram, at what age will you be making this transformation?"

I realized I was in trouble again. Orofus surreptitiously guided me into a knotted cognitive maze again. At least I now understood the initial question, the one about the young old man or the old young man or something like that. Gradually it dawned on me what the implications of his questions were. Oh by the way, I know what you are thinking and if you ask me exactly when I went from not understanding these implications to understanding these implications than I will gladly and non apologetically smack you on the head. I feigned ignorance. "Huh? What age? What?"

Orofus barked his response: "You know perfectly well what I am talking about, you little twerp. Now answer my question."

Frankly I do not know why I so enjoyed these conversations with Orofus. He was always rude and threatening and unbearable. I always wrestled with his ridiculous questions and crazy tales of serpents, virgins and holes in the ground. "I dunno, how about seventy? Yeah, when you're seventy you're an old man." I answered with no conviction, pretending I had just settled the matter once and for all.

"So a man who is sixty-nine is not an old man?" Orofus was playing along with my little game of make believe I had just settled the matter once and for all.

"Yes, a man who is sixty-nine is an old man," I answered dryly, knowing what his next question would be. I did not want to seal the exclamation mark on our crazy discussion. If my father had heard this discussion, he would have ordered me to get my head out of the clouds and start polishing Ardus, another idol in the shop, the one with an eagle's head, the lithe and buxom body of a naked young woman, and the tail of a goat. A priest from the city of Larsa had just bought Ardus the previous week and my father had entrusted me that day to prepare him for delivery.

Orofus continued: "Abram, I think you now understand what I am getting at, right?"

I was at first bewildered but the answer dawned on me. "Yes Orofus, I think I understand. Some things are clearly true and some are true but we can't really pinpoint it to a definite place or time. There's no place where you go from saying something is completely false to saying something is completely true."

Orofus nodded his head while giving me a look that betrayed how impressed he was with my perceptiveness.

"That's exactly right Abram. The gods designed reality in a topsy-turvy manner. I think the gods are having a rip-roaring laugh seeing you backward mortals wrapping your feeble intellects around the nature of the world. The gods have designed the world in such a way that the ultimate building blocks are not well defined. The ultimate building blocks appear to be ephemeral and ill defined, like a fine gossamer spider's web that appears fleetingly when the sunlight shines off it from just the right angle."

Orofus paused and looked at me appreciatively. "When you asked me that question, that's when it occurred to me. You know what they say Abram - children ask the darnedest questions."

"My father also says that sometimes out of the mouth of babes comes wisdom."

"He's absolutely right."

"But Orofus, didn't you say before that I had to be in my third stage of life in order to be wise?"

Orofus scratched his alabaster head. "Well yes I did say that but...but, well you see Abram, do not be so literal minded all the time. Remember what you just observed. Sometimes there are no sharp borders between truth and falsehood. You have to consider many factors and variables before you evaluate an issue such as this. You see Abram, there is also another universal principle at play here: opposites are, at a fundamental level, just two sides of the same coin. A tension exists between opposites, like a serpent eating its own tail, but I digress. I'm going to continue now with my adventures at the bottom of the serpent hole."

I had already forgotten about the serpent hole. My conversations with Orofus always took many layered and unpredictable turns. Here we were, discussing some story or other, and we always found a way to recursively drill down into various nooks and crannies of the story and to discover interesting things to talk about and to ponder.

"So where did we leave off... oh yes, I remember. I finally reach the bottom of the hole and the voices who were such a cacophony when I first entered the serpent hole, way up at the opening on the desert floor, are now crystal clear."

Orofus paused for what seemed like four or five minutes and he gazed at me. I was too afraid to speak; I certainly did not want him to chuck me into that mysterious and awful serpent hole. I gazed back at him, trying to win our staring contest, but realized the futility of my attempt. I could not win a staring contest against a magnificent marbled creature like Orofus. I finally

Childhood Musings

averted my gaze and that is when he continued his tale.

"Well Abram, when I finally reach the bottom of the serpent hole do you know what I find there?"

Orofus paused as if testing my sophistication and intelligence. I considered his question for a long time, enough for the walk from my home to the shop. Orofus was always a very patient sort. He could wait without flinching a muscle for ages while I formulated my answers. I then had an epiphany and I leaped like a startled goat.

"I know, I know," I yelled, "if the number of serpents goes down as you go down the hole but each serpent gets bigger then when you reach the bottom there's just one huge serpent and he speaks with a very loud and clear voice." I gazed at Orofus with self pride. He erupted to life again.

"You are a smart boy Abram. You are close but the truth is even more startling. You see, when I reach the bottom of the serpent hole I do not see anything at all. There is a big void, a foreboding emptiness. However, I somehow realize all the serpents immediately above this void and all the smaller serpents above those serpents and all the yet smaller serpents above those serpents and on and on until the surface of the desert above, all of these serpents are somehow originating from the bottom of the hole."

"You mean they climbed up from the bottom and that all the serpents will after a while come out of the hole and into the desert?"

"No Abram, each serpent will always be at the same level down the hole."

"You mean that they climbed from the bottom of the hole until they reached the level where they are now and they stayed there?"

"No Abram, they didn't climb from the bottom. They have been at the same level eternally."

"I don't get it. So where did they come from?"

"They are all a part of the giant serpent, don't you see? The giant serpent you expected to find at the very bottom of the pit is not there as you expected him to be. The giant serpent is the totality of the hole itself. The giant serpent is not isolated at the bottom of the hole, it is all the serpents, at all levels, as One and also as None. It is the ground of being from which all the serpents of all sizes and from all levels down the pit are a part of."

He was doing it to me again. My head was in knots.

"Orofus, I don't get it. Is this one of those things I have to be in the second stage of life before I understand it, just like understanding what a virgin means?"

"No Abram, I'm afraid to understand this you will have to be in your third stage of life."

"So Orofus, why are you telling me this story now?"

"I am blowing the winds of transition within you Abram. I am planting within your soul the seeds of wisdom and one day you will reap their fruit handsomely, Abram. I promise you that."

This is the end of the dialog. I engaged in these types of dialogs with Orofus from my early childhood until my fifth year of school. I hope you are slowly developing a feel for who I am, how I think, what excites me and what gets my juices flowing. If you know the boy then you will get a glimpse of the man he will become. My life story is about the search for a deep understanding of Creation. The context of this search has always been a quest for a synthesis between the divine and the earthly, between the compelling nature of mathematics and logic, the beauty of music and the humbling experience of kneeling at the foot of divinity.

Maturity

By our eighth year in school Khaferu and I, while still very much two red-blooded growing boys engaged in the rough physical play that is the hallmark of boys that age, had been spending more and more time in deep conversations of an epistemological nature. These were conversations about my main interests, the nature of Creation and the role of the gods within it.

Once, around the beginning of our eighth school year, Khaferu solemnly remarked: "You know what's really fascinating about you Abram?"

"No, what? My dashing good looks and charm with the ladies?"

"Ha, you wish. No really, I mean you have many academic interests, not even my older brothers or even my father can match your knowledge of mathematics, astronomy and other stuff like that. But what's really fascinating about you is no matter what subject we talk about, or anyone talks about, you always find a way to connect it somehow to the big picture, to the big questions."

"Sure, but isn't that really the essence, the basic principle, of how the world works. I mean, look at music and mathematics. We learned in school that the gods have a deep relationship with numbers and these are the numbers encoding the primary ratios of music. The physical world is…well how can I explain this, yeah here it is…I mean it's basically described as something arising out of this deep relationship between numbers and divinity. That's why mathematics is so good at describing all that exists."

I paused and then continued because Khaferu was listening without interrupting.

"And it's all kinda expressed through musical relationships and by extension through the musicality of poetry and storytelling. Don't you see? The whole of Creation is but a lover's overture to the objects of its infatuation, the gods."

Khaferu was deep in thought for a few seconds and reflected on my words. He then pointed his right hand index finger sharply into the air. What I said seemed to have triggered memories of long ago. He had buried these memories in the recesses of his mind but they were now brought to the fore.

"That's true now that you mention it. I mean, from grade one in religious studies they constantly drilled into our heads this relationship between numbers and music and between music and the gods. But then later we started taking all these practical math courses, you know… all those math for finance or math in architecture courses and I kinda stopped thinking about those abstract types of mathematical notions."

"That's exactly right. You see, what happened to us in school is exactly paralleled by what happened to civilization itself. Thousands of years ago the gods revealed to us their dance with numbers, but since those times humans, being the cunning and clever creatures we are, noticed the divine nature of numbers also has a very practical use in managing our finances, in building our great cities, in annihilating our enemies. And you know what? We've forgotten the big picture."

I paused, chuckled and continued: "We're so busy serving our petty desires that we have stripped the most beautiful gift the gods have given us of its divinity. You see, the fool can ask Annu himself any question he fancies and come away from the experience with just practical tools for managing the mundane affairs of his life, but he that loves the truth sees further. He sees the divine foundation underlying the whole convoluted edifice."

"Abram, are you sure you're just thirteen?"

"Why, do I come across older?"

"You come across like you should be growing a white flowing beard and be sitting cross-legged in the holy room atop the ziggurat."

"Really? I hope I don't come across as a know-it-all."

"You can't help it Abram. Your only option is to actually know it all."

"Bite your lip, don't say that. Only the gods can know it all."

Throughout my school years my teachers were impressed with my curiosity and my quick wit.

"Abram has a good head on his shoulders," they would tell my father whenever they had occasioned to meet.

"Abram is a pious child and he nurtures a rare love for knowledge."

"Abram has the originality of mind and spirit that will get him far in life."

At the beginning of my last school year, my religious studies teacher recommended to my father I apply to the seminaries in hopes of studying for the priesthood after my compulsory schooling is completed. My father was particularly shocked by that recommendation because there had never been a Habiru who was admitted to the patrician inner society of the priesthood.

Originality of mind and spirit is as unpredictable as the bouncy ball in the game of Pinot. If you play against an uneven embankment you are hard-pressed to predict the ball's trajectory. Fortunately, if you look hard enough, you can find an even patch of embankment and the ball's path as it bounces back to you is more predictable. Unfortunately, the great quest for fundamental truth must always be played against an uneven embankment. The search for an even patch of embankment in the fundamental fabric of Creation is a fool's errand.

By my last year of school, my hitherto praised originality of mind and spirit had sent me on a trajectory quickly diverging from my teachers' world view and the very paradigm, the zeitgeist, of Sumerian civilization. My teachers could no longer catch the ball they threw towards my side of the embankment. They had to leap off the comfort and security of the embankment on which they stood and they were not willing to make that paradigm shift. To my dismay, and due to my naïveté, they met my hunger for the truth, no matter where it may lead, with a suspicion and fear that betrayed the existence of an educational bureaucracy steeped in a rigid tradition of thought that had made an idol out of idolatry. I gradually realized idolatry was not self-sustaining. I realized the falsehood of idolatry contains the seeds of its own destruction.

Sometime halfway through my last school year I experienced an epiphany both exhilarating and frightening. I came to realize the religious tradition I had learned and long cherished, the pantheon of gods and goddesses - both major and minor - inextricably woven into the fabric of Sumerian society, is a falsehood.

My new-found realization caused me to become intoxicated with a sudden intellectual and spiritual freedom that need not serve any institution, that bows to no tradition, and is unencumbered with the artificial constraints of a paradigm constructed by man and which serves only man and not the divine. I realized I could heartily drink from this overflowing cup of Truth without following the customs and etiquette of a society steeped in the stinking garbage heap of idolatry. A heap composed of the rotting bodies of a pantheon of gods and goddesses I once cherished as the fundamental, indivisible principle of Creation but which I now realized could not possibly be at the root of the magnificent beauty and unity of this edifice.

This epiphany was an unexpected visitor, and when it came knocking on my door I greeted it as a lover I had only ever known in the recesses of my soul and who now appeared before me as flesh and blood. This epiphany was a rose bush whose seed I planted long ago, and which now burst the earth after a long and arduous winter in the unknowing, white-eyed womb of Creation. And when I reached for its tempting yet thorny flower I felt a piercing pain shooting through my soul, and I came face to face with the awe-full one, the great El-Shaddai, the principle of Creation, the great veiled One, the Truth overflowing my cup. Deep in my soul an unspeaking voice woke from an eternal slumber, and I at once came to know that land for which I had always felt a kinship, that realm of which I am a citizen, always will be and always have been.

"Abram, I have been waiting for you. Abram, I have been yearning for you. Come and suckle at my bosom. Come and savor from my abundance."

"Oh lord, are you my salvation? Oh lord, are you what I have always thirsted for? Can I now lie at your feet, sated and satisfied? Can I now rest from my burden, my unquenchable yearning for understanding?"

"Abram, from this day I shall always be with you and your generations to come. From this day I shall be your companion, I shall be your comfort and I shall be your master. Abram, you will walk humbly with me and you shall be my everlasting friend. Abram, I AM the way, I AM the Truth. I AM the One, and there are no others before me. You shall abandon your idolatry because it does not speak for me. Look in the eyes of your idols and you will no longer see me. You shall forsake your idolatry and you shall cleave unto me as a betrothed cleaves unto his bride."

"Lord, where will I see you? How may I serve you? How shall I worship you?"

"Abram, you have already taken the first step in a journey leading to me. From this day your life is in servitude to me. You shall be my humble messenger and my plan for you shall unfold as the most exquisite poetry, as the most beautiful yet poignant melody."

The voice deep within me receded into its veiled embrace and I was standing in the middle of my room, drenched in a cold sweat, the milky-white of the full moon streaming in like an uninvited yet welcomed guest. I heard my mother's voice calling me for dinner. I quickly stripped off my sweat-drenched tunic, wiped my body with a fresh towel and slipped into a clean tunic. As I took my place around the family meal I noticed all my brothers and sisters were already sitting and looking hungrily at a meal they were forbidden to taste until I arrived. My father gave me a fishy look.

"Abram, thank you for finally gracing us with your presence. What in blazes were you doing in there?"

I tried to act cool and collected. I really did not have much of an appetite. Would you have an appetite after having a conversation with god?

"I'm not very hungry. May I be excused to go back to my room? I'd like to do some homework."

My father barked in protest: "You certainly may not. Why did your mother-"

He paused mid-sentence and looked me over from my feet to the top of my head.

"Why is your face so flush? And your hair looks like it hasn't seen a comb forever. Are you feeling alright?"

"Yes, I'm just fine. You don't have to fuss over me like that, I-"

"Why did your mother have to call you five, maybe six times, before you decided to join us. Are you going deaf Abram, or do you just not think you need to bother with your family anymore?"

"Look, I said I'm fine. I was just daydreaming about something and I didn't notice you were calling me. No big deal. Not the end of humanity as we know it."

My brother Haran barked in protest: "Can we start eating already? I'm so hungry I could eat an ass."

My father gave a sweeping gesture with both hands. "Yes, go ahead everybody, eat." He then turned his focus on me again. "Have you started your composition yet?"

Ever since my religious studies teacher had said I have potential for the priesthood, my father had been strutting like a peacock. He had told all his friends and business associates I would be the first Habiru anointed to the priesthood. To be honest, until that night I was excited about the prospect of entering the priesthood. Not because of its elitism but rather because of the depth and breadth of a priest's education. Sumerian society regards priests with respect and reverence. They are the intellectual elite. The education of a priest is both lengthy and intense. A freshly minted priest is adept in higher mathematics, music, theology, history, astronomy and the list goes on. Every year thousands of eager graduates of the Foundation schools apply to the seminaries but few are accepted. In a society where religion is its lifeblood, the priesthood is reserved for the best and the brightest. My father was a good man, a hard working man. He was also a man cut out for greater things. I'm not alluding to a vapid and pedestrian longing for wealth or power but rather to something more refined, more spiritual and noble. My father had a charisma that flowed and bubbled freely from within. The sole reason he had not ascended the ladder of greatness is that he was, through the caprice of fate, born a Habiru. A Habiru's greatness will always be overshadowed by the mediocrity of a purebred child of Ur. Being a perceptive child, from an early age I could smell my father's resignation to a lot in life that could not measure up to his ontological loftiness. My father was like a king without his throne, like a lover in a world devoid of his beloved, like a great warrior living in the cradle of peace.

You may now appreciate how thrilled he was my religious studies teacher recommended me for the priesthood. He would repeat with glee, and with a whisper he did not intend for others to hear, but all overheard: "My son the seminarian". He was living vicariously through his son. I was his deliverance by proxy. I was not ascending to the priesthood, it was he. I was not overcoming the stigma of being Habiru, it was he. Do not take this the wrong way; he was not stealing my thunder, he just blurred the distinction between father and son. A father beaten up by the vagaries of life surely has that prerogative.

The first step in applying for a spot at a seminary is for a student in the last year of Foundation school to write a composition about any theological topic. The seminaries of the student's choice then evaluate the composition. To be invited to submit a composition is a great honor; a student has to be on the honor roll and be recommended by at least two teachers, one of which must be a religious studies teacher. I was ecstatic to be invited to submit a composition, but now I was very conflicted. I still could not fully digest the experience I had in my room. It was like a rug had been yanked from under my feet. My faith in the gods had been shattered into a thousand little pieces and from those shards of divinities something emerged that ran a chill through my spine and made the hairs at the back of my neck stand up. Intellectually and spiritually I knew I had to leave behind the old ways and step intrepidly into a new age of divine consciousness. But I had not yet processed all this emotionally. The last thing I wanted to do was have this conversation with my father. I needed some alone time. I needed to gather my thoughts. I needed to recover from my existential whiplash.

I replied to my father: "Um...eh well not yet. I've been giving it a lot of thought really and I'm still kinda trying to get a bird's eye view of the whole thing."

"Abram, I don't know what's going on with you. You seem different. Just yesterday you were hardly contained in your own skin. You were so excited about all this. And now, well I don't know, you seem like you're not really into this at all."

"I'm fine, really. I'm just in a funk right now, I don't know why but I'll be fine, really. I just need some alone time so I can really get a feel for what I want to write about."

My father mulled over my defense and then seemed to reach some kind of understanding putting him at ease.

"Well, maybe I'm just misinterpreting all this. I guess the magnitude of all this can be a little overwhelming for a seventeen year old at the cusp of adulthood. Even one as gifted as yourself, eh Abram?"

He did not know the half of it. I chuckled to myself. My father turned to my siblings and my mother and asked: "Are you all fine with Abram excusing himself from the meal?"

My brother Haran replied: "That's fine with me, more food for me. Abram can have his theology and mathematics and all that boring stuff that turns on geeks like him. Can I have his lentil stew?"

My father gave Haran a look that could kill and then turned his gaze to me. "That's great Abram, you're excused if you wish. Go to your room and do whatever it takes to get back your groove. This composition isn't going to write itself, you know? Give your mother a hug and thank her for this wonderful meal she prepared and then off you go."

I excused myself and retired to my room. The moonlight was streaming in and I did not bother lighting the lamp. I collapsed on my bed face down, my arms radiating out like an unwanted part of my humanity. I lay motionless thinking through my confusion. I needed to confide in someone not in a position of authority over me. I needed to reveal this experience to someone who would understand and even sympathize. I had to talk to Khaferu. I knew were I to reveal my thoughts to my father or, worse yet, to my teachers, I would incur a wrath woven into a society that cherishes its religious paradigm above all else and has no place for anyone rejecting or even questioning it. I knew I had to make a decision between keeping all this to myself or being non-apologetically on fire for the truth. I called out for the one god but got no reply. I demanded he give me guidance but he was silent. Deep down I feared I could no longer write the kind of composition that would be my ticket to a posh life in the priesthood. I tried to rationalize that realization away. Why Could I not teach the truth from the inside? Why could I not change society's erroneous religious beliefs as a priest? Would that not be the most efficient means to that end? I could luxuriate in my priestly splendor all the while teaching society deep and valuable lessons about the true nature of the divine. A smile cracked my solemn face. I imagined being adored by a society longing and hungry for the truth. I imagined throngs of people at my feet, enchanted and mesmerized by my great revelations to the world…and then I woke up.

"Abram, Abram, for goodness sake, Abram wake up."

I could not make out who or what was barking at me. "Uh? What? Who there?" I was in the twilight zone separating the eternal dream world from the jagged reality of space and time. My earthly senses whooshed towards me as a genie's animus whooshes out of a bottle that is its primordial home but is compelled towards a locus of flesh and blood. It was my mother's concerned face that emerged from the fog of my sleep.

"Abram, wake up. Do you realize you fell asleep in your clothes? You've never done that before."

"Sorry ma. Is it time to get ready for school yet?"

"Yes, get up and put on a fresh tunic. I have it laid out over there by your tablets."

I stumbled out of bed. The sun was screaming through the window and I covered my eyes. The last thing I remembered before dozing off was mulling over my options for the composition. I could not remember if I had arrived at a satisfactory solution. My mind was still emerging from the fog. My mother was not done with her questioning. She sensed my anxiety, but I imagine it did not require much perceptiveness. I remembered my yearning to confide in Khaferu. I could confide in no other. I rushed through my morning rituals. My father reminded me he was expecting a new shipment at the shop the next day and he needed my help. I did not want to return to the shop. How would I react to the miasma of its idols? I had always found great comfort in my father's idol shop. How would I feel now? But I then realized I did want to be back at the shop as an experiment. I wondered if the echoes of my conversations with Orofus would reverberate within its once hallowed walls.

Khaferu was waiting for me by his front door.

"You're ten minutes late. What's up?"

He looked me up and down. "Your left sandal is undone, your hair looks like I barfed on it and your belt is loose around your waist. You look like shit."

I tied my sandal, tightened my tunic belt and ran my fingers through my hair.

"You look like you got up from the wrong side of your bed. What's up?"

I ignored his questions. "Let's hurry and get to class. We'll be late."

Khaferu sensed I was not in a conversational mood and he did not press me on the issue. We hurried to school, not exchanging a word until we were at the door to our class. Before we entered I put a hand on Khaferu's shoulder and we stopped.

"I need to talk to you about something after school."

"Is everything OK? I mean, is anything wrong?"

"I don't know. I need to talk to you first and see what you think?"

"About what?"

Khaferu gave me a squinty look and I could tell I was planting in him a seed of concern.

"I don't have time now to go into it. We'll talk later."

"Hey you Nimrod," Khaferu shot back, "we had all the time in the world while we were walking to school and you choose just now to dump this on me?"

"Look, just drop it now or I won't even tell you later. Why are you being such a demanding ass?"

"Fine, we'll talk later if that'll make you happy, OK?"

Throughout the day I could not focus on my classes. I realized more than ever I needed to confide in Khaferu before I explode.

My last class of the day was Astronomy and when the bell rang I ran towards the other side of the school to intercept Khaferu. Khaferu's last class was religious studies. In our last two years of Foundation school our schedules diverged, unlike our early school years when we always attended the same classes. This was partly due to the more varied curriculum of the upper grades, but also because I was on an advanced academic track while Khaferu was a bird of a different feather. He was a decent enough student, but his passion was art. He had a talent for sculpting and an eye for color and form. When I was within sight of his classroom I saw him exit it and head down the long hallway with his back to me.

"Hey Khaferu, hold on, let me catch up with you," I shouted. Khaferu heard me and swiveled to face me.

"Hey, I was just about to go get you, you wanna head home?"

"Yeah, let's go home. My mom's making some lentil soup with spiced lamb. And for desert she's making your favorite, hon-"

Khaferu enthusiastically filled in my words. "Honeyed marzipan, way to go buddy, I love your mom. Your brother Haran, on the other hand, I could do without. I swear that annoying dipshit gets pleasure from making my life miserable and probably torturing little animals too."

"Yeah, he's a real piece of work, but anyway, let's head to my place. I want to run some things by you."

"You're being very mysterious, what's up?"

"Let's get out of this hell hole first. It's humid as hell in here and it smells like some people don't believe in bathing."

We headed out of the school building. The sun was shining through a perfectly clear-blue sky and a sweet aromatic breeze was blowing from the west. Summer was coming to an end; fall would soon arrive. The temperature had plummeted the last week and it was now pleasantly warm. We headed down the main road leading to our apartment complex. Here we were, two longtime friends, even soul mates, inseparable since we were knee high to a grasshopper. We were beginning our last year of Foundation school and we both knew the unbroken bond we had shared might soon be breached. After graduation Khaferu had plans to attend the Kartum Salash academy for the arts while I, at least until recently, had plans to enroll in one of the seminaries. All the best seminaries had long ago been relocated to the city of Larsa which is several weeks of travel away. Of course, I now doubted ever enrolling in a seminary. What to do? I was confused as I had ever been. My path towards my destiny now seemed to be an obstacle course. The voice within was whispering to me that the stairway to heaven lies elsewhere.

We were ten minutes into our walk home and did not yet speak a word. Unlike earlier that day, Khaferu did not needle me for information. He knew I would soon dump on him everything weighing on my mind and he allowed me the opportunity to find the perfect moment, the perfect piece of embankment to throw my ball of existential angst against. When ready, I halted, turned to him and put my right hand on his left shoulder.

"God talked to me last night," I blurted.

Khaferu gave me a puzzled look, like a turkey cocking its head towards the ground, all the while keeping its gaze on the horizon.

"Excuse me?"

"You heard me. God talked to me last night when I was in my room getting ready for dinner."

"I didn't know you kept any idols in your room."

"I don't."

"Then how could a god talk to you without going through the vessel of an idol? Come on Abram, you're the religious studies genius. We've always been taught the gods communicate to the mortal plane by being channeled through an idol, and only to a high priest at that, and only during special ceremonies and high holidays."

"I didn't say a god talked to me. I said god talked to me."

"You mean the big guy himself, Annu the chief god?"

"No, not Annu, not Balal, not Shamash, not any of these so-called gods."

"So who?"

"The one and only god, I didn't catch his name so don't ask me."

"The one and only god? What are you talking about Abram? How can there be only one god? Where are all the other ones?"

"I no longer believe all of these gods we've learned about exist at all."

"Excuse me? Don't let your mom hear you say that, she'll make you brush your teeth with pepper and gargle with goat fat."

I shot him an exasperated glance. "Khaferu, listen to me. I mean it. I no longer believe in anything we've ever learned about the gods."

Khaferu studied my face and it finally dawned on him I was serious.

"What are you talking about Abram? You, the teacher's pet, the religious studies guru, the..." He paused for a few seconds and then raised his voice a notch. "You, the future priest, you don't believe in the gods? You mean you don't think they even exist?"

I felt a sudden pang of guilt for my new found paradigm shift. I felt guilty for having all these years guided and reinforced Khaferu's world view in one direction and now yanking it all from under his feet. I was already the first victim of this intellectual and spiritual shift and perhaps now Khaferu would be the second. How would society in general react to it? I had not felt this sense of guilt until that time and the sudden onset of this feeling took me by surprise. I so wanted to explore this feeling as a shaper of gold figurines explores the orchestra of light bouncing off his creations, or as an artist explores the rainbow of emotions evoked by her art. I made a mental note to do this later.

"Look Khaferu, I know this doesn't sound like anything I've ever said, or anything I would ever say, but this has been coming for a long time. I've been thinking about all this for a long time."

"You mean you've had these doubts about the gods for a long time? Since when, and why haven't you ever clued me in?"

"No, no, it's not like that. I stopped believing in the gods suddenly. I had this sudden euphoric epiphany, but it was the result of years of thinking, years of trying to connect the dots. What I mean is I've always been the sort to dwell on the nature of the gods. I'm ontologically a mystic. Religious Studies was not just something I did well in because I'm a good student. There's always been something in me compelling me to understand reality, to understand nature. I'm sure you know what I mean."

Khaferu seemed unsure of where this was all heading. He had a perplexed look on his face that betrayed his struggle to understand how what I had reminded him of myself was connected to all this new-found rejection of standard Sumerian theology. But then a look of understanding rippled across his face.

"Yes Abram, I know exactly what you mean and I've always admired that in you. I always sensed something in you that was so much at the foundation of truth it seemed completely alien." He chuckled. "Now I see exactly how alien it really is."

"Let's get going home," I said, "we've been standing here with my hand on your shoulder for about ten minutes already, oblivious to everything around us, and people are starting to wonder what the hell we're talking about that's so absorbing."

"Fine Abram, let's get going, but I'm still far from sure what you're talking about."

"We'll have dinner and then I'll tell my father I need to go to your place and help you with your upcoming quadratic equation algorithms test. We'll then have all the time we need to sort this out."

Khaferu's face lit up with enthusiasm. "Oh yeah, I forgot, honeyed marzipan. Yum!"

We all had dinner and my father was demanding to know what topic I chose for my composition. I did my best to be non-committal but his questioning was relentless. I blurted something about writing a composition regarding the monster of the deep, the Tiamat, and the composition being an analysis of this creature's existence before the gods created the heavens and the earth. My father seemed satisfied with my response and commented this was a question he himself had, from time to time, pondered and he was indeed pleased I showed the same affinity for the big questions. I muttered under my breath: "If you only knew the half of it. If you only realized what I was struggling with made the scope of the Tiamat monster pale in comparison." I then realized he would soon know my struggle and I cringed when I imagined his anger.

Khaferu ate my mother's cooking like a man who had not eaten for days. We then made our escape before my father could regroup and launch another assault on me. We were soon in Khaferu's apartment, just two buildings south from where I lived and across the street. I greeted his mother and a few of his siblings, and we then retreated to his room.

"Hey, I think the topic you chose for your paper is kinda cool."

I shook my head in annoyance. "No you moron, I just blurted that out to keep him from leaning on me like that."

"So you're going to write about something else? Like what?"

I shot him an exasperated look. "What do you think? Man, you're out of it. After everything I've already told you so far, you don't know what I'm gonna write about?"

"Oh yeah, that's right, I forgot...about this one and only god business and how Sumerian theology is all a buncha crap."

Khaferu paused and appeared to reflect on what he had just said.

"Hey hold on a second - about how Sumerian theology is all a bunch of crap? You're gonna write a composition about that and present it to the Examining Reader of the seminary? Are you out of your stinking mind? Have you lost it? They won't just reject you, they'll present your balls as an offering to the fertility goddess."

"So what do you think I should do, Khaferu?"

That was not a rhetorical question. I honestly needed Khaferu's advice

Maturity

and he picked up on that.

"Before I can honestly give you advice, I need to really understand what you're saying about this one and only god and how he talked to you in your room before dinner."

I realized Khaferu was mixing in some sarcasm in his cup of advice but I chose to overlook that.

"Khaferu, look at it this way: according to the religion we studied in school, every natural phenomenon has a god or goddess pulling its strings, right?"

"Sure, that makes sense. For example, how could the crops of the field grow without a god or goddess orchestrating this growth? You think the grass just grows on its own? That would be like saying that tunic you're wearing just weaved itself, ha ha."

"Yeah, you're a real joker. Anyway, so we have a deity for the growth of the crops and another deity for the falling rain and another deity for the falling snow and another deity for fire and another deity for the sun, right?"

"Sure, all those things you mentioned are distinct attributes of Creation and each is the domain of one deity. So what's your point?"

Khaferu sounded like he was monotonously reciting a religious studies lesson.

"I'm getting to it, listen. Let's take the deities of rain and snow. Both of these things fall to the ground, right? OK, so now we have to postulate there must exist a deity of fallingness."

Khaferu gave me another one of his patented turkey cocking its head towards the ground look while keeping its gaze on the horizon.

"Huh? Excuse me? A deity of fallingness? Abram, have you been drinking from your father's wine cache?"

I chose to ignore Khaferu's mocking tone. "Khaferu, think about it. Let's take two more of the examples I just mentioned. Both fire and the sun emit heat, so now we have to postulate a deity of heat."

Khaferu quickly replied: "But why do we have to postulate a deity for heat? Why can't we just say the god of fire created fire and the god of the sun created the sun and both these things emit heat?"

"OK, let's run with that, so we have to conclude heat is something pre existent, that it's not a result of any god having created it."

"Sure, just like the Tiamat monster. What's wrong with supposing that?"

"Remember we have gods and goddesses of love, of war and so on, so deities are not just for material creations like the sun and the rain but also for intangibles like war, love and so on. So how come heat is an intangible pre existent, but the intangible abstraction of love does have a god that created it? There's no rhyme or reason in all this. It all seems so arbitrary."

"Oh, I see where you're going with this. You want religion to make sense. Good luck with that, buddy. Listen, I haven't been able to make sense of it since the first day in Religious Studies class."

Khaferu laughed and then squinted his black as a moonless night eyes for a few seconds and cocked his head slightly to his right. He seemed deep in thought. When he seemed to reach some understanding he replied sharply: "Fine, then let's suppose we have a god of heat and a god that makes things fall to the ground. Do you agree we now don't have a problem anymore?"

I replied confidently and quickly because I anticipated such objections: "Well, not really. First of all, there is no god of heat or of making things fall to the ground in our religion, so even if we agree that would solve the problem, we have a deficiency in our theology. Secondly, there is still a problem even if we add these gods to our pantheon."

"Like what?"

"Well, both the god of the sun and the god of fire would be dependent on the god of heat in order to create fire and the sun. So we have a hierarchical dependency between the gods of tangible things and the gods of abstract things. Have you ever learned any such thing in religion class?"

"No, not really.

"It gets more convoluted, just wait. The goddess of plants and herbs needs water, does she not?"

"Of course."

"So now the hierarchy gets deeper because we don't just have a dependency between the gods of abstract things and the gods of tangible things, but also between gods of tangible things and gods of other tangible things like plants, herbs and water."

"OK, I see where you're going with this. So it looks like we have a hierarchy of gods with those at the top dispensing their services to lower level gods and so on down the hierarchy. Just like a tree with its trunk and then branches coming off that trunk and then yet smaller branches coming off these branches all the way until we get to the leaves."

"Wait, it gets worse. There are things in nature that are codependent. For example, you have the clouds that are formed when rainwater evaporates from lakes, so you will say the god of lakes is the parent to the god of the clouds. But the lakes are formed because of the rain falling from the clouds. So now you have a hierarchy of gods and goddesses that sometimes loops back unto itself and creates two way loops. The leaf can be the father of the tree."

Maturity

"Abram, I'm starting to get dizzy. All these hierarchies and interrelationships and loops inside loops are starting to confuse me."

"That's exactly right, we are forced to do all kinds of uncomfortable intellectual gyrations and convolutions in order to make this whole damned theological edifice stand."

"Why can't we just conclude these kinds of convolutions and gyrations, as you put it, are the way things are and just leave it at that?"

"Khaferu, do you remember when we first learned how to manipulate those algorithms in order to solve quadratic equations?"

"Sure, what's your point?"

"Do you remember how it always came out that of all the possible approaches it was always the simplest algorithm that yielded the best solution?"

"Yeah I remember, it took me awhile to get the hang of all that. You know math and me - I suck at it. So again, what's your point?"

"What I'm saying is the correct solution will be the simplest solution. If you're forced to start creating all kinds of weird systems and assumptions in order to make sense of something then it's time to step back, take a deep breath and tear down the whole damned, convoluted, rotten system. I realized that one day when I was looking at my father shaving."

"Fine, I see where you're going with this. You're saying the simplest explanation to the creation of the world is that it was created by one god."

"Exactly, now you got it. Let's abandon all this unworkable nonsense about a god for this and a goddess for that and the convoluted relationships between these gods that I showed must exist if they are the creators of all Reality, and own up to an inescapable conclusion: Reality is an organic, indivisible whole created by one and only one supreme being."

"Tell me something Abram, you told me this morning this supreme being talked to you last night while you were getting ready for dinner. Now it seems to me you've arrived at the realization of this supreme being's existence not because he revealed this to you but simply because you've used logical arguments to arrive at this conclusion. So I'm kinda confused. Did this one and only god reveal these logical arguments to you or did you come up with them by yourself?"

Khaferu had an incisive point. I never dissected my new found relationship with the one god in this way. It never occurred to me to make a distinction between logical argumentation and direct revelation from god.

"Well... I mean ...well, I'm not sure how to answer this so bear with me. When I say god talked to me last night I'm not really saying I heard a voice as I do now when I talk to you. It was something that came from within me

34

but still not like a voice, more like a feeling or... well, more like a sudden euphoric feeling I was now seeing some deep truth I had never seen before. It wasn't really an intellectual thing like following a quadratic equation algorithm. I'm not sure really how to explain it. Get it?"

Khaferu seemed to be immersed in what I was saying and my clumsy attempts to elucidate my divine experience seemed to have sparked an understanding within him.

"I got it Abram. I think I got it. Wow, I understand what you're trying to explain. It's like a person's breathing. You don't have to consciously control the act of breathing. It's like you are not breathing but the breathing is being done for you. So it's like when you had your experience with god, you were not thinking those thoughts, you were being thoughted, so to speak."

"Wow Khaferu, that's exactly right. That's exactly what it felt like. That's an excellent analogy with breathing. Way to go, I couldn't have found a better way to explain it."

Khaferu had a grin on his face from ear to ear; the kind of grin that, on the surface, imparts an air of pride and ego but is clearly just meant in jest.

"I'm not just another silky-haired, pretty face you know? So tell me Abram, what else did this nameless one and only god tell you? What does he want from you?"

"God told me I'm to forsake all idolatry and that he has a plan for me."

"What did he mean exactly by idolatry? Did he mean the worship of clay and stone statues for example?"

"It goes much deeper than that. Idolatry means the worship of multiple gods. Idolatry is the belief that the lowest common denominator, the finest granularity of Reality, is the plurality of the gods. Idolatry is the belief in this irreducible complexity."

"I get it, idolatry is a system of thought. It's a way of seeing the world. Idolatry is the belief that Reality can only be explained in terms of multiple gods. That it cannot be reduced to one creative principle."

"Exactly, idolatry is a state of mind which is an illegitimate relationship with the divine."

"You said god has a plan for you. What is it?"

"I'm not sure. He said this plan would unfold before me, kind of like on a need-to-know basis I suppose. He did say from this day my life would be in servitude to him and I will walk humbly with him and I will be his everlasting friend."

"This god is a male god then, right? You keep referring to a Him when you talk of this god."

"I think so, although I'm not really sure what that would mean. I don't think god needs a penis, it's not like there's a young woman with whom he will father a child. I haven't asked him what form he takes. I'm not sure what he looks like so I'm not really sure what I mean when I use the word Him."

"Well, like you said, he will reveal himself to you on a need-to-know basis."

"Exactly, I think I still have much to learn about all this."

"Great, so now comes the defining moment. Are you going to write your composition about your revelation from god?"

I sighed in despair. "I honestly don't know what to do. If I write about all this then I definitely will not be admitted to a seminary."

"That's putting it mildly Abram. You will not just not be admitted to study for the priesthood; you'll probably be expelled from school. You will not be able to even complete Foundation school."

"I know, I know. I had this thought that I can just fake it. I can pretend to be a good, pious student, full of love and reverence for the gods. I can write some bullshit composition about the Tiamat monster and eventually become a priest, and then watch out brother. I will be working from the inside and I will smash their idolatry and change their outlook. Don't you think working from a position of power can be more effective in steering society towards the one true god?"

"I have to think about that one. Perhaps it's not from a position of power that you can change the hearts of people but from a position of influence. Get the difference? I can say one thing right now."

Khaferu paused for a few breaths while trying to formulate his thoughts. He focused on an ant crawling on the floor.

"What's on your mind?" I asked.

Khaferu looked up again into my eyes. He had a look as if he did not want to upset me by what he had to say, but the right thing to do would be to say it.

"All I have to say right now about this plan of shattering idols from the inside is you have to look deep into your heart and make sure this is not just an excuse to become a priest after all; kind of like having your cake and eating it too. Make sure you are not lying to yourself is what I'm trying to say."

I could not deny Khaferu's wisdom. Of course, the same notion had already occurred to me, but in not mentioning that to Khaferu I had hoped I was mistaken, that working from the inside had nothing to do with, as Khaferu eloquently put it, having my cake and eating it too.

"I like that expression, having my cake and eating it too. That's brilliant. I've never heard that before. I understand exactly what you mean by that. It's the opposite of being stuck between a rock and a hard place, wouldn't you say?"

"Why that's right Abram. That's very insightful and quick thinking of you. Feel free to use my new expression. Maybe one day I'll become famous for coining it."

"Anyway, the sad thing is you might be right. If I'm honest with myself I have to admit I don't really believe the best way to change society's theology is by working from the inside. I have to admit there's a side of me that doesn't want to give up the privileges the priesthood offers. There's another side of me that's just plain terrified of disappointing my father. I think this side is stronger than the first one."

"Well, if you say so. I just wanted you to make sure of your true motives. The rest is up to you. Of course, this suggests the question, even if joining the priesthood is not a part of some grand divine plan, are you sure it's worth it to sacrifice so much for this god of yours? Are you willing to become a social pariah?"

"Actually yes, it is and I am."

These words forced themselves out of my mouth. I again had the impression I was being thoughted. I now recognized this to be a passion with the force of a military chariot at full gallop.

"Yes, I feel god in me and I will do anything for him. Yes, I will write the composition exactly in this way. I will say what's on my mind. I won't move away from the truth, not to appease my father or society."

"You know all hell will break loose when you submit this composition. I'm afraid of losing you as a friend. You've been like a real brother to me. I'm afraid I'll never see you again after this."

"Why? What do you think will happen to me?"

"Well, after they expel you from school, they'll probably strike some deal with your father. You do realize your father will suffer from this also, don't you?"

"Yes I know. He'll be deeply hurt by this. He was so excited I would become a priest. Make no mistake; he has complete confidence I will write a composition that will wow and amaze them."

"That too, but when I say he will be hurt by this I don't just mean in that way. I mean that the Religious Tribunal might take action against your father in some way."

I raised my voice in surprise. "Like what?"

"Don't be so naive Abram. They might pull your father's business license for this."

"But he has nothing to do with this. The composition is not allowed to be read by anyone except the writer and the Examining Reader. I can always say my father knew nothing of this. That's actually the truth. I even lied to him about my topic choice."

"That doesn't matter Abram. Don't expect to change their minds with the force of your logic."

I realized he was right. They have too much of a vested interest to be swayed by logic. They will not allow an inconvenient truth to get in the way of their interests.

"Oh great. So here I am thinking I'm doing the ethical thing by giving up the posh life of a priest and now you're telling me I may actually be doing the selfish thing by giving up the posh life of a priest."

"No, no, I'm not saying any such thing. All I'm saying are the facts. You make of it as you wish, but believe me Abram, not once did it cross my mind you are selfish or in any way unethical. You are the most ethical and just person I've ever met, almost to a fault."

"You know what I'll do. I'm going to write this composition in a way that will reveal not just my new found ideas but will also reveal my innermost self. I will not just talk about my ideas but also about my thoughts, my fears, you know… who and what I am. Maybe if I do that they'll realize I'm not just some apostate out to destroy the fabric of their society. Maybe then they'll empathize with me."

"What do you mean? You'll not just talk about why it makes no sense to believe in multiple gods, but you'll also talk about this kind of conversation we're having right now? About your feelings and stuff like that?"

"Exactly, I'll write the composition as a story, a self-reflecting narrative. Maybe then they'll see my full humanity and not just see me as someone who is a one dimensional person only motivated to disrespect their beliefs."

"When is the composition deadline?"

"It needs to be in the hands of the Examining Reader no later than the beginning of spring, so that gives me about five months to write it. That's lots of time."

"Sure, that's lots of time for you to be stewing about this. I don't envy you Abram. I pray to your god he doesn't find favor in me. The repercussions are too grave."

Dancing With My Fears

I had a dream last night. I was seven years old in my dream and I was at my father's shop late at night. I had never been at my father's shop so late and I feared I would interrupt the secret lives of the idols. I dismissed my concerns because my eyes had recently been opened to the truth that these idols were inert objects with a divinity only imagined. I was on a mission to confront my father about his polytheistic idolatry. In my dream I had already adopted a monotheistic world view by the age of seven. I do not know if there is a meaningful interpretation of why I became a monotheist at such an early age in my dream.

I was holding a large bronze rod that should have been too heavy and thick for a seven year old to yield. The dreamer seldom allows the sensibilities of the word of the awake to interfere with the dream's unfolding. As I looked at each of the dozens of idols, great and small, I was puzzled at how society could attribute divinity to such lifeless chunks of clay, rock and metal. I was strong in my resolve to lead my father to the truth. I swung, with great difficulty, the heavy rod to my right side as I sealed my eyes, gritted my teeth, and reached deep into my psyche, desperately searching for a source of rage. I swung the rod and smashed the idols with almost no discrimination. I was timid at first but I soon felt rewarded because once I found my rage it flowed without effort. When my rage subsided I opened my eyes wide, despite fearing the repercussions of my rage's handiwork. The shop was in shambles. Shards of divinities were strewn and intermingled across the floor.

At the center of the shop was the greatest of these idols. Orofus the fertility idol was the only one to escape my almost indiscriminate rage. That was in my plan. I did not want to shatter him. I inserted the bronze rod firmly in his grasp. I intended to frame him. I knew that the next day my father would accuse me of the havoc in the shop. But why would he suspect me when I have never been at the shop at that late hour? I imagined in my dream that when my father accuses me of the crime, I would calmly show him the heavy bronze rod in Orofus' grasp and with a straight face explain that clearly Orofus must be the culprit. How could my father deny that? Would such a denial not betray his lack of belief in these idols? Better yet, would my outrageous accusation of Orofus force my father to confront the truth? These idols are not divine, they are lifeless and spiritually inert.

The next day I was at my father's shop. That had been my first time at the shop since my divine experience, my existential whiplash, and I was curious how I would feel in that shop surrounded by the idols. A new shipment of assorted bronze and silver figurines was coming in and my job was to polish and arrange them on display. These were an assorted collection of gods and goddesses, ranging from the size of my pinky finger to the size of a small child. These figurines were meant for private household use. It is very fashionable in Ur households to devote a whole room, or a section of the main living space for the less affluent, to religious symbols and artifacts. In reality, most buy such symbols and artifacts simply as decorations and for insincere bragging rights as in: "look at me, I'm so pious."

To be perfectly honest, and as one is to expect, my relationship with the idols in my father's shop had evolved over the years. As a small child they fascinated me not strictly due to their theological connotations but also due to a small child's propensity to experience awe for such things as a rainbow, the clap of distant thunder, or dew embracing the ground during a crisp early spring morning. A young child often cannot distinguish between the genuine truth and beauty of Creation and the lie of that which is made by man's hand. The ability to marvel at the beauty of Creation is an affectation of childhood often lost with the onset of intellectual maturity. As I matured, I understood more deeply the purpose of these idols and my innocent awe was replaced with a deep and misguided religiosity. A poor man is easy prey to those who are crafty as a fox and are inclined to entice him with fool's gold. A man denied a woman's sexual love will succumb to those who do not honor humanity's soul and instead are merchants of its flesh. Likewise, a man hungry for the divine is susceptible to the charms of idolatry as is a serpent to the enticing melody seeping freely from the charmer's flute.

My eyes had now opened and I was no longer susceptible to the alluring lie of idolatry. A man who tries to satiate his appetite for the truth with idolatry will forever feel the pangs of spiritual hunger, but he that forsakes idolatry and reaches out to the one and only true god of Creation will be immediately satiated.

I entered my father's shop and once I passed the administrative area and entered the large display area I felt at once a foreboding emptiness I had never felt before. What was once filled with the sweet aroma of humanity's prostration at the foot of divinity now had the stench of a tragic comedy of errors. A beam of sunlight pierced the shop at an oblique angle through the iron bars comprising the upper portion of the east facing wall. The display room was dusty and within the beam of sunlight a myriad dust particles danced chaotically to a silent melody. If not for the beam of light the dust particles would have danced an anonymous dance. The light revealed a dance hitherto hidden from my eyes as god's light of truth had revealed to me his eternal dance with his creation. The foreboding feeling of emptiness I felt when I entered the shop was due to the absence of this dance within its walls. I remembered what god had taught me when he revealed himself to me. He said that from then on when I look into the eyes of an idol I will not see him. When I entered my father's shop of idols I no longer felt the eternal dance. I realized my days in that shop were numbered.

As the days passed my resolve to proclaim the truth strengthened. I started working on my composition the week after my divine experience and when my father realized I had begun he was pleased and ceased his incessant interrogations. Fortunately, it is standard policy that before a composition for entrance to a seminary is completed and submitted to the Examining Reader, only the applicant is permitted to see it. Had that not been the case my father would have insisted he read my work in progress. I would then have had to write two compositions: one for his prying eyes and the other for submission. I would have to hide the real composition from his almost omniscient reach. I would also have to find my own supply of fresh clay, probably from the river banks beyond the city walls.

Fall turned to winter and winter turned to spring. I kept my focus on writing my composition, and as the days passed and the weeks turned to months, it took a life that seemed distinct from me. When I first began to write, my inexperience led me to revealing all my thoughts at once. I soon realized the art of storytelling and a coherent elucidation of ideas must follow a tempo that cannot be rushed. A beautiful melody when performed at too quick or too slow a tempo will lose its charm. Playing it six times faster will not afford you the opportunity to compress the same enjoyment and enlightenment into a time six times shorter. All things are to be experienced on their own terms and will only then, with no effort, engage you in the dance. I was not a proficient Pinot player until I learned to dance with the ball instead of trying to bend it to my will. One cannot master a discipline as a slave owner masters his slaves. Proficiency in any discipline only comes when you cease aspiring for control and instead engage in the dance without pretension. I applied this lesson to my fear and unease with the certainty of my father's anger and disappointment when he discovers the message of my composition. I feared him for my own sake but I also deeply empathized with him for the disappointment he will surely experience once I've eliminated any possibility of his son being admitted to the lofty and respected position of a priest. At a more abstract level, I felt guilty for not following through on becoming the first Habiru to join the priesthood. At some level I felt I would be branded a failed messiah of my people, as one who rejected the key that had been handed him to the heart and soul of Ur, Sumer, and in the eyes of many Habiru, the gods themselves. When I ceased struggling with these notions and engaged them in the Divine Dance, I at once lost my trepidations and I felt a deep and satisfying peace. While engaging in the dance I gazed deeply into my partner's eyes and recognized the face of god. I now understood his promise to always walk with me.

This wisdom is the Received Wisdom from god and it will allow anyone to achieve spiritual contentment. To dance with your adversary is to accept your adversary as simply the complement of your binary whole. Just as the tail side of a coin must embrace its heads side, so must one resonate with adversity rather than create discord.

Each day after school, and on many off days, I walked to my father's shop and took a fresh loaf of light-brown clay from the back-room. My father uses clay to record accounting information but he always had enough to spare for my needs. After dinner, while the clay was still warm and moist and malleable, I cut a slice about the thickness of my wrist and then kneaded it with a marble roller until I fashioned it into a roughly rectangular tablet the thickness of half my pinky finger and the width and length of a man's face. Sweat rolled down my brow for it was hard work but it was a work of love. I then worked quickly with the stylus to etch my thoughts on the tablet before it hardens. A thin tablet of clay loses its moisture and malleability much quicker than a thick loaf. That is why I only fashioned another thin tablet after I had finished etching my thoughts on the previous one. Most evenings three tablets sufficed but during rare times I could not find inspiration and I stared with futility at the clay loaf and all I could see was its monolithic lifelessness and inertness. On other rare evenings I became a geyser erupting with inspiration and I could no longer see an inert loaf of clay in front of me but instead I could only see it as infinite forms superimposed one on the other and forming its body, and I then cut a slice from its effervescent body and I inhaled deeply from its pungency and consummated our relationship.

I adore the pungent aroma of fresh clay. I have come to associate it with a work of passion in progress. But I also adore, with equal measure, the subtle aroma of clay tablets after they've been sun-baked into a permanent hardness. Each day, before I departed for school, I laid the previous night's tablets on a table in my room and let the sun's searing light, through my west facing window bare and bright, bake my tablets and give my thoughts permanence. It was during that fateful night, when I let in the moon's milky-white through that same window, that the whispers emanated from within the recesses of the soul. But it is the sun's strong light that baked these eternal whispers onto my clay tablets.

One fine day, during the springtime fertility festival, I put down my etching stylus. I had finished my composition and it was everything I had hoped it would be. When the Examining Reader reads my work I knew I would be at a point of no return and I would never again be afforded the opportunity to join the priesthood. I was in my last year of Foundation School, with only five weeks remaining to graduation, and I was unsure if I would be permitted to graduate. Would I be forever stigmatized? Would I become a pariah?

I found my father brewing a pot of tea in the kitchen. He heard me behind him and swiveled to face me. When he saw the look on my face he knew.

"You've finished your composition, haven't you Abram?"

I wasn't surprised at his perceptiveness and I didn't feign surprise.

"Yes I have."

"Congratulations Abram."

My father had a proud smile on his face and he hugged me too tightly.

"I'm sure you're going to wow them with your brilliance."

He looked at me with pride in his eyes. "You know Abram, you will make Habiru from all walks of life proud."

"I haven't even submitted my composition yet. You sound like not only has my composition been approved for entrance to the seminary but I'm already a priest, and a senior priest at that."

"Abram, let me indulge will you? I have all the confidence in you, son. Your teachers all agree you've got a great intellect, a gift from the gods, and you have the potential to contribute greatly to society. I think you were born to be a priest, to be a great spiritual teacher. How better to do that than to enter the priesthood?"

He was inundating me with praise. I cringed every time he expressed his trust in me. From an early age my head was humming, but god had other plans for me, and my path to heaven was in sharing with humanity his whispers to me.

He paused for a few breaths and then dropped his voice a notch. "Abram, these last few months I've seen you diligently apply yourself to writing this composition, and despite having to carry on with your regular schoolwork you've managed to devote the kind of time to this composition that it deserves."

"Well, letting me off the hook with my duties at the shop really helped. I couldn't possibly have done that too while writing the composition and taking care of my school work."

"What, you think I would jeopardize your brilliant future in the priesthood for that? No Abram, one day you will be the first Habiru priest. Do you realize what an honor that is? Are you even aware of the repercussions of this? You will be in a position one day to open doors for your people. We are to this day still considered second class citizens. When you ascend to the priesthood, I have a feeling the floodgates will be opened and that will be the beginning of full assimilation and genuine acceptance into society for all Habiru. You, Abram, will be remembered for a long time to come as a seminal figure."

"But will we still be Habiru once we're assimilated?"

"Whatever do you mean, Abram?"

"Never mind. I just wish you wouldn't say things like that. It's hard to feel I'm taking on the responsibility not just for myself or my family but for all my people as well. Maybe I don't want to be a messiah."

"You will be what the gods want you to be. Just keep your nose to the grindstone and great things will happen. Where are your composition tablets?"

"They're in my room. I've wrapped them in cloth and I've tied them securely. They're ready for being submitted."

"Great, I'll give you a ride to school tomorrow morning. How many tablets did you use?"

"Seventy-two."

My father wrinkled his forehead and cocked his head forward with surprise. "Are you serious? Your religious studies teacher tells me most compositions for admittance to the priesthood are about forty tablets maximum. Did you fashion yours to standard size and standard words per tablet?"

"Yes, yes. It's all quite standard in that way. You see, I wrote my composition in a kind of unique way. I wrote it in a kind of self-reflecting way. It's talking about itself."

My father gave me a puzzled look. "That's a mouthful of words Abram. Care to explain?"

"It's the telling of a story, so in that sense it's a fictional narrative, like story telling is, but on the other hand it's also a work of non-fiction because it's about something really happening in the real world. And that thing happening in the real world is my writing of the composition. So the composition is talking about itself. It's a story of how and why I wrote the composition and what was happening in my life as I was writing it."

My father grimaced. He squinted his eyes and cocked his head back.

"Let me see if I get this. The composition is about you writing the composition? Why did you choose to use this strange format?"

"Well, I didn't just want to explain to the Examining Reader my point of view regarding my basic theme, but also to have him see my humanity and how these notions I've come up with have affected me as a citizen of our great society. I want the Examining Reader to get an idea of how I see my place in our society."

"So you are yourself one of the characters in your narrative?"

"Of course, like I said, it's about me writing the composition. But I don't think I should say more. Don't you remember you're not supposed to read my composition before the Examining Reader has read it?"

"I haven't read one word of it."

"If you pry anymore into it then you might as well have."

"Fine Abram. Point taken. Go wash for supper and remember I'm helping you to get the composition tablets to school tomorrow before I open up the shop, so you'll be getting to school about an hour earlier than usual."

"Sure, I'll get up earlier."

"As soon as I get you to school we'll be meeting with three people: a recruitment priest Ananu of Agasher, your head master and your religious studies teacher Levy."

"They've got a full house I see."

"Don't be a smart-ass, Abram. This is standard procedure for all priesthood hopefuls submitting their composition. This year you're the only one from your graduating class who's been invited to submit."

My father gave me an approving wink.

"Yeah, I know. I think last year's graduating class had two people who were invited to submit a composition and one of them actually got accepted."

"Well, your school is going to be graced this year with another success story. Not many Foundation Schools have sent students to study for the priesthood two years in a row. That's quite a feather in the cap for your school. Just think about it. From all across Sumer, all the major cities with school systems, and your school will have it two years in a row."

That night I tossed and turned and I could not sleep well. I knew my life would now take a turn into uncharted territory, and for the first time since I resolved to write this composition I was once again afraid. I never questioned my decision, but I was plagued with demons of fear. During the months I had been writing my composition I managed to exorcise these demons, but now I realized their exorcism was tenuous at best, they dwelt just beyond the horizon of my psyche. They now popped into view once more and I again felt compelled to reflect on the Received Wisdom: "Do not strive for mastery of friend nor foe, but rather for a communion that can only be achieved through the Divine Dance."

During the months I wrote my composition I danced with my demons at my bosom and, because my rhythm was perfect, I resonated with their destructiveness and they could do no harm. A discordant ripple now breached my dance and I lost my step. It did not take much, just a slight misstep allowing destructive vibrations to feed upon themselves, and the dance came crashing down. I once again stood on the mountain top overlooking my destiny and I was unprotected before my demons of fear.

In the twilight hour just before sunrise a beautiful young woman appeared before me. She offered me her right hand in a sweeping motion. I took her right hand in mine and danced with her. Our dance was a lover's dance and we became one flesh.

"Look into my eyes, Abram."

I felt unworthy but I looked into my woman's enchanting gaze as does a man who feels unworthy of a lady's embrace. I could hear her voice but it was etched in the silences between the sounds. I could see her ravishing beauty and yet could see no color nor form.

"What is your name?" I asked.

"I am the Bat Kol."

"What does that name mean? I don't understand."

"Abram, I am the daughter of the Voice. I am the feminine emanation from the white-eyed womb of Creation."

"I didn't know god was female. I don't know who you are. I don't understand you."

"Abram, have you forgotten all that has already been revealed to you? Have you forgotten the Received Wisdom? Do you not know god's holiest name?"

"Yes, I know now God's name. Khaferu and I figured it out. The name is YHVH."

"Abram, all of Creation is in the image of the H in YHVH. All of Creation flows tautologically when the H, the white-eyed womb of Creation, reflects upon itself. And when he curves back on himself, he creates and creates. This white-eyed womb of Creation is neither male nor female, neither mighty nor weak, neither up nor down, neither this nor that."

I dared to ask: "Then what is the essence of the H. If it is neither male nor female and neither any one thing nor its polar opposite? And how can a feminine Bat Kol exist then?"

"Abram, the essence of the H, the white-eyed womb of Creation, is the superposition of all things into NONE. All of Creation simultaneously exists in the H. Within the H the two polar opposites, the Divine Dancers, share an intimate dance, the Dance of the Void. To understand YHVH you had to shatter idols but when you shatter the H you breach the intimacy of the Dance of the Void and Existence then explodes out. The H is a vessel restraining the Waters of Creation and when the vessel is shattered then Creation flows freely. The H is a vessel for Creation's void and when the vessel is broken then Creation's first light veils the void. Do you see your demon, Abram?"

"Oh yes, I see my demon and I am once again afraid."

The Bat Kol broke our embrace but not our dance, all the while seamlessly joining my right hand with my demon's left hand.

"Your dance is not complete, Abram. Descend from the mountain top Abram for you are destined to walk the holy land."

Before I knew it I was once again fully engaged with my demon at my bosom, the Bat Kol vanished and I was no longer afraid.

Sunlight was again screaming through my east window and I awoke to see my father at the foot of my bed.

"Wake up, Abram. You promised you would be up early, remember?"

I quickly gained my wits and I was fully awake. I had managed to fall into a deep slumber about an hour before sunrise. I tried to clear the cobwebs of my memory and then I remembered the fear I had felt for most of the night and the welcoming relief I felt when I finally managed to once again dance with my demons.

"Sorry pa. I didn't have a good sleep last night."

"Why? Are you feeling a few butterflies in your stomach?"

"Yeah, something like that."

"Don't worry, Abram, you'll do great. I have all the confidence in you, son."

I wished my father stopped repeating how confident he is in me. It is like a mantra legitimizing a truth he doubted at a fundamental level. I wanted to teach him that truth must be legitimized from within one's soul and not by an external principality. But can the child teach the father? Can a leaf heal a sick tree?

"I'm fine now, pa. It's just that for most of the night I was tossing and turning, but I think I've got it under control now."

"Great, get ready quickly and we're off to school. I've already packed your tablets on the cart so just get ready, have a bite to eat and we're off."

The ride to school was silent. My father gave airs of extreme pride. His head was held high and proud as he commandeered the team of donkeys that pulled our rickety carriage and cut our path towards an illustrious destiny that was more his dream than mine. Along the way Habiru shopkeepers and tradesmen cheered for us.

"Go get 'em Abram. You're our champion."

My father had spread the word about my completed composition far and wide. Once we arrived at the school we headed to the headmaster's administrative chamber. On the way there, several of my classmates, the purebred children of Ur, gazed at us and I could see their jealousy burning in their eyes. Their souls ached with resentment for a lowly Habiru that was to become a priest and yet not them. And in that moment I could see into their diseased minds and I knew they attributed all their ills and failures to the Habiru - the Other - in their midst.

As expected, we were greeted by three men: my school headmaster, my religious studies teacher and an impressively tall, thin and elegant looking man I had never seen before. He was dressed in a sparkling long, red and golden silk robe that hid his feet. The robe was meticulously stitched with images of Enki, god of wisdom and of the waters. The stitched images portrayed Enki with streams of water gushing from his shoulders. The man's face was a compendium of strong, aquiline features and long narrow eyes the color of pure coal. His thin eyebrows were also the color of pure coal and were tweezed and arched. He sported a groomed, short-cropped beard whose pure blackness and sharp lines further accentuated his bony features. He looked to be in his middle years but with a youthful blush. However, his face radiated an energy emoting an ancient wisdom privy only to the inner sanctum of the priesthood. He appeared to be a living contradiction. His elaborate appearance inspired reverence from one perspective, but from another perspective looked pompous.

He was the first to speak. "So, this is the young man I've heard so much about?"

His baritone voice was mellifluous and calming. He stepped forward and grasped both my shoulders with his long, slender and bejeweled fingers. He then let go his grip, took a step back and waited for my reaction. He was testing me. I was expected to greet him as any citizen of Ur is expected to greet a priest. I knew the drill perfectly and decided to play along with customs my composition would soon break into shards of divinities. Without any hesitation I curtsied onto my left knee and kissed the ring on the middle finger of his right hand.

Dancing With My Fears

"It is an honor to be in your presence, your holiness."

He smiled, nodded his head then he spoke to my father. "Do you give your son the blessings to enter the life of the priesthood?"

This was strictly a formality. In reality, once the priesthood sets its eyes on a candidate, the candidate's father has no say in the matter. However, I cannot imagine any father had ever objected to his son becoming a holy man and an exalted priest.

My father replied immediately. "Yes your holiness. I approve without a shred of reservation."

The priest appeared to approve, not because my father had given his permission but rather because my father had done what was expected of him. He then turned his gaze on me.

"Do you, Abram, aspire to the priesthood with all of your soul and with every fiber of your being?"

"Yes your holiness," I lied. I did not reveal my true inclinations at this point because it was too early to do so. The rhythm of my dance with my fears would have been disrupted.

The priest formally inquired: "What is the topic for your composition?"

My father interjected before I had a chance to reply. "Your holiness, my son has shown great ambition in writing a dissertation concerning issues of the Tiamat monster and its a priori existence before the creation of the heavens and the earth."

The priest turned his intense gaze on me. "That is indeed an ambitious topic, Abram."

I briefly gazed into my father's eyes and then averted my gaze towards the priest. Did my father understand my trepidation? I was not sure. "Your holiness, I must say that I have not written my paper about the Tiamat monster as I told my father."

My father's expression went from that of a proud peacock to one of sheer confusion.

"What do you mean, Abram? You've told me months ago that was your composition topic?"

The priest glanced at both my religious studies teacher and the school's headmaster. They had not said a word since I was introduced to the priest. The headmaster commented that the choice of composition topic was entirely up to the candidate and that no one is to know of the topic until the composition is submitted, not even the candidate's father.

"Father, it is true I initially planned on this topic, but shortly after I revealed to you my topic of choice I remembered I am not permitted to release any information until the day of submission, so I changed my topic without your knowledge."

The priest said: "You are a sneaky one Abram. You are most certainly correct about that. So what is your topic of choice? Now is the time to reveal it."

My father had an uneasy look on his face. He realized something was up. He realized the explanation I had given as to why I did not write about the Tiamat monster was somewhat suspect.

"My topic of choice concerns the hierarchical structure of the gods. I have written an analysis of this hierarchical structure based on the principles of deductive logic."

"That's certainly an ambitious topic for a youngster barely out of Foundation School," the priest said. "Are you sure you are worthy of dissecting such a venerable body of wisdom and revealed truth?"

"I believe I have something of value to add," I responded, standing my ground almost with defiance.

"My dear boy," continued the priest, "can the nature of the gods be deduced through our fallible intellectual faculties? Is it not a truth revealed by the gods rather than deduced by humanity?"

I shot a quick, short glance at my father. A bead of sweat was slithering down his brow. He did not utter a word. He was fidgeting as he listened to my exchange with the high priest.

"Your holiness, are not our intellectual faculties gifted to us by the gods? When we use our minds to glean these eternal truths, is it not the gods that are to be given the credit? Is it not the gods that are in effect deducing their own reality?"

My father appeared anxious as he cranked his head towards the high priest. He waited for his response. The high priest closed his eyes in deep contemplation and then when he opened them he said: "I see Abram. You have cleverly leveraged my objection in your favor. You show great cleverness, young man. Perhaps your composition is not just about the hierarchical nature of the gods but also about the essence of what is divine revelation?"

I again shot a furtive glance at my father. A smile rippled across his face and he nodded. I responded to the priest: "Your holiness, is it not the measure of a man that he helps himself and his family rather than passively wait for morsels of charity? Should I not use the faculties of my intellect to glean divine truths rather than beg for them of the gods as a pauper begs for morsels of bread?"

I danced with the high priest rather than resist his spirit. The high priest responded: "Abram, do you always answer a question with another?"

"Your holiness, as you have already wisely remarked, our intellectual faculties are limited. We cannot hope to have all the answers. Is there not more wisdom in our questions than in our answers?" My question reflected the priest's question. The medium is the message.

The high priest did not respond but appeared in deep thought. My father held his breath. I kept my mouth shut in order to afford the high priest the opportunity to break the silence at his convenience. But the silence persisted. I decided to humble myself rather than trumpet my cleverness. A master dancer does not always take the lead.

"Your holiness, I realize the topic I have chosen for myself is very ambitious, but I like to challenge myself. If I fail then at least I know I've stretched myself to the limit. I am not one to take the path of least resistance."

My father finally broke his silence and addressed the priest. "Your holiness, my son has done the right thing in keeping me in the dark about his composition subject. I should not have been so presumptuous. I can overreach sometimes, and that is a failing I must conquer."

My father was clearly uncomfortable with the situation and he was most certainly angry at me for exposing his infraction. However, in my defense, it was he who revealed I led him to believe my composition was about the Tiamat monster. He, most likely, unthinkingly uttered that because of his shock that I did not write the composition he anticipated.

"I do not believe for a second your son had initially intended to write about the Tiamat monster. I think I see much of myself in your son. He knows where his path lies and he will not deviate from it. Neither for gain nor for glory." The priest turned towards me and winked knowingly. "Isn't that right Abram?"

I did not respond. I sensed the priest only intended his question to highlight his perceptiveness.

After the priest took my composition and left the school, my father exchanged some pleasantries with my religious studies teacher and the headmaster. He did not ask me any questions, and once he had left for work I settled in to a full day of my classes. During the lunch hour I spied Khaferu sitting under what he and I affectionately called the "grand lady". This was a massive eucalyptus tree that was part of our memories as far back as our first day in Foundation School. Khaferu was very curious about my meeting with the high priest and I recounted in vivid detail all that had happened that morning. He would periodically interrupt my recounting of what was said with exclamations of "Wow, you really said that?" or "And how did you respond to that?" Once I finished my tale, told with great aplomb and enthusiasm, Khaferu said: "Wow Abram. I can't wait to actually read your composition. I think you'll hear back from the Examining Reader in a couple of weeks, right?"

"Well yeah, I mean like usually it takes a couple of weeks but we're in uncharted territory here. It's not like my composition is your typical composition. Once all hell breaks loose, well then I don't know. Will they even give me back my tablets?"

"Damn it Abram, I never thought of that. What if you never see those tablets again? All that work and it'll be gone forever."

The school day raced by, and after my last class Khaferu and I took our usual path home. We continued our lively conversation.

One full month passed since I had submitted my composition and I had not yet heard a word. One fine day when I arrived at school I was intercepted by the school headmaster. He had an officious look on his face. The kind of look I used to get from my father when I was much younger and I would occasionally break one of the idol figurines he was selling in his shop.

"Please come with me Abram. There are some people who are very interested in having a chat with you in my office."

"I guess the Examining Reader has finished reading my composition, hasn't he?"

He ignored my remark and yanked me by my left shoulder and guided me towards his office. As I walked down that long hallway to the headmaster's office I danced with the fears within and they had no power against me. I remembered a day years ago when I asked Khaferu for the name of the god most invulnerable to harm. He guessed it was Anu, the creator of the heavens and the earth, simply because Anu is the chief god. I explained that Nergal, the god of death, is the most invulnerable to harm because the powers that do harm can have no dominion over the dead. Engril dances flawlessly with Ereshkigal, the violent goddess of the Land Of No Return, and her violence is harnessed for the good, as is the power of a ferocious wind dancing with the sails of a great ship.

I danced down that long hallway, cheek-to-cheek with my fears, welcoming my destiny.

Worlds Within Worlds

We had come back from school several hours earlier, and when I announced to Khaferu that I had finished writing my composition he insisted on reading it. While he read it I retreated to the kitchen for a bite of lamb stew my mother was simmering on the fire. My father was still at work and would not be back for several hours.

My mother asked: "What's he doing in your room for so long?"

I did not want to divulge Khaferu was reading my composition. "I'm helping him with his math homework. We have a difficult quiz tomorrow."

"Well, be a good host Abram. Don't abandon him like this for so long. Is he hungry?"

"Don't worry mom, he needs some time alone to read something. Sure, make a bowl of stew for him. He'll never say no to your cooking."

"I don't think he'll say no to anyone's cooking." My mother laughed. "He might as well be one of my own sons, considering the amount of food he eats here."

I delivered the bowl of stew to Khaferu. He put down the tablet he was reading and his eyes lit up when he saw the steaming plate. Khaferu can eat quantities of food that would choke a large man. I do not know where he puts it. He is thin like an arrow.

"Man, that smells so good. My mouth is already watering. Do you have any pita bread with that? I love to mop up the gravy." Khaferu grinned.

I groaned and went to the kitchen to get him pita bread. An hour later, when I was out in the courtyard below our apartment, bouncing a ball against a wall, my mother stuck her head out the living-room window and shrieked: "Abram, Abram...Khaferu says he's finished reading. He wants your help now."

I bolted up the two flights of stairs and burst into my room. "So, what's the verdict?"

Khaferu put down the tablet and looked at me with admiration and delight. "This is amazing, Abram. I couldn't bring myself to stop reading it from the first tablet to the last."

"Really, you really liked it? There's not much more time to make any changes; I have to submit it early next week."

"Of course I loved it, Abram. Your writing is both beautifully lyrical in many passages and powerful, even haunting. I just love the way the seminary entrance composition your story refers to is the seminary composition itself you will be submitting. What a brain bender. I also love the way you capture our early childhood years: playing Pinot, eating your mom's awesome cooking, and the awesome philosophical discussions we had all the time. What made you think of using this self-referential style? Oh wait, you already explained that to your father in your composition itself."

The plate I had delivered to him earlier was on the table by my bed. Khaferu had mopped it clean and he surgically picked all the meat off the bones, they were now naked and shiny. I answered his question nevertheless: "Well, you know how I described the pantheon of gods and goddesses as a lie because it describes Creation as a sort of web of irreducible complexity? So basically, as you know, I just don't accept the idea that each phenomenon in nature is self-contained with its own god or goddess as its creator, and having no connection or operating commonality with any other aspect of nature."

I paused for a short while, allowing Khaferu to fully process my words. "You know how I discuss that thing about abstract concepts like heat, the force that makes things fall to the ground, and so on...how it's not even represented in our pantheon? Their very omission implicitly points to a belief in separateness where not everything is unified into one explanatory system."

Khaferu shot me a quizzical look and asked: "So what does that have to do with choosing a self-referential structure to your composition?"

"Well fine, let me continue. As I explain in my composition, I've come to the conclusion Creation shouldn't be divided into multiple deities but rather there is one comprehensive god that is manifest in nature. If there is nothing separate from this one god then that means everything in nature must be in his image. It means everything that exists is manifest from god's very template of being."

Khaferu mulled my words. "I see, so you're saying the principle of creation in nature is a template that copies itself over and over again, and god is this template?"

"Exactly, god is somehow able to make copies of himself, and these copies are things we see in nature that are manifest as thunder or heat or the sun and all other phenomena. Creation is a recursive hierarchy of the images of god. By recursive, I mean that not only does god make a copy of himself, but the copy is then a piece of god that makes a copy of itself and this process is repeated."

A perfectly illustrative image popped into my head as I was explaining to Khaferu my idea of god as a self-referential phenomenon. I paused briefly in order to organize my thoughts. "Hey Khaferu, I just thought of a perfect example. You know those polished copper mirrors? Well, have you ever seen this effect where you see a mirror appearing within a mirror, and that inner mirror containing another mirror, and so on and so on?"

Khaferu performed his usual tilting his head to his right side while shutting his left eye. That was a sure sign he was in deep contemplation. I did not interrupt and he soon spoke.

"So you're saying in your example the initial mirrors represent god and all the subsequent mirrors within a mirror, within another mirror and so on...that they represent the phenomena in nature such as thunder, the sun and all other things?"

"Exactly, this mirror feedback loop system represents everything in Creation, the Earth itself and the canopy of stars and the moon, as well as abstract things like heat, the propensity of things to fall, love, mathematical constructs and so on. God is the original two mirror system that creates all the subsequent mirrors that are images of god."

Khaferu's eyes opened wide in excitement. He thrust out his right arm while pointing his index finger out and his thumb up. He looked as if he was preparing to pull back the string of a bow. He always had that mannerism whenever he finally understood some thorny concept, or had what he believed to be an alternate way to illustrate what he had learned.

"How about an echo?" Khaferu said. "That's another way to imagine this god of Creation you're proposing. I mean, the original sound that generates the echo is analogous to god, and all the subsequent copies of this original sound are analogous to the various phenomena in nature like thunder, the sun, and all others. Do you see what I'm kinda trying to get at? It's like this amazingly intricate sculpture made from sound instead of clay."

His idea was very compelling and I could see how he believed this analogy is equivalent to the principle of creation I had proposed. However, I immediately realized the flaw in his analogy.

"That image I have now in my head of a sculpture made of sound is so uplifting, and it makes me almost wish it represents god - but no, it's not like that at all. When I say nature is in the image of god, that the phenomena in nature are copies of god, I mean god is a template which is the foundation and all the phenomena in nature are produced recursively from this foundation. The process is based on feedback loops. In my mirror example the image of mirrors within mirrors is created when the first two original mirrors produce a feedback loop with each other."

"I don't understand. How is my echo analogy flawed? The original sound spawns copies of itself as it bounces against the walls of tall cliffs, for example. Doesn't the original sound represent god while the copies of this sound are like the copies of god you mentioned?"

I replied without hesitation: "There is one big, big difference between my mirrors analogy and your echo analogy. The image that is produced by showing the reflection of one mirror in the second mirror is actually a composite. That's what I mean by recursive. The resulting overall system is actually composed of copies of the original mirror as well as the recursive copies. You see? With your echo example you simply have a new sound which is a copy of the original sound, it's not a composite. If you were to just hear the echoed sound there will be no way to know it's actually an echo and not the original. In other words, there are no echoes inside an echo. The echoes are external and independent of the original sound.

"I see your point. My example would be more accurate if, instead of bouncing off a cliff, the echo is produced by the original sound bouncing against itself and producing echoes within echoes, within echoes and so on. I don't know if that would happen, but that's besides the point."

Khaferu shut his eyes and reflected further on our discussion. When he next opened his eyes he had a look of deep understanding.

"Wow Abram, I get it now completely. It's like a tree where each branch contains sub branches and each of these sub branches themselves contain sub branches and so on. That's what you mean by recursion, right?"

"Exactly. Each image contains within it copies of itself."

"Yes. The entire tree represents all of god's creation, where god is the original branch that copies itself over and over again, and in the process the entire tree is constructed. Come to think of it, that could be a new art form of shapes produced in this way."

Khaferu was onto something. Of course, being the consummate artist, he could not help but extend these ideas to his artistic passions. After a brief contemplation I saw a way to refine his idea. "Khaferu, tell me what you think of this idea. God is not a specific branch on the tree that has copied itself recursively. God is the abstract idea of a tree branch along with the rule of how to copy itself. You might say god is the abstract essence of a recursively generated tree. That abstract construction principle is the soul of the tree in a way."

"Yes, yes, I like that idea on so many levels. If you try to locate the branch on the tree which is the god-branch which copies itself indefinitely to produce the whole tree then you're not gonna find it. Can I say you'd be barking up the wrong tree?" Khaferu flinched away from me in mock fear. He had a big grin on his face.

"Oh man, that's corny Khaferu." I laughed and then abruptly resumed my serious contemplation. "Notice also this principle of creation is also very simple. All you have to start with is one simple shape, and by repeating its basic template you get a more complex composite shape, without resorting to any other complexity. That's why I say the notion of the Pantheon of gods and goddesses as being the foundation of nature is fundamentally flawed because this notion leads to multiple irreducible complexities. However, the complexity of nature is produced from lesser complexity, and this lesser complexity is itself produced from lesser complexity, and so on and so on until we get to the foundation of nature which is the one and only god himself, the one abstract branch which is the essence of the tree. The belief in irreducible complexity is flawed, it does not prove divinity but rather denies it."

"Yes Abram, I understand now, but let's get back to the recursive mirrors. Your mirror analogy is not perfect because nature is produced from one god but your mirror analogy starts out with two mirrors. So we have two irreducible essences."

"Well, it's not meant to be a perfect analogy, it's just meant to give you a good understanding of what I'm trying to get across. But my analogy is not as imperfect as you might think, it gives you a good visual of my idea that everything in nature is created through a feedback loop process where the one god is curving back on himself and then he creates and creates. Think of the two mirrors as this feedback loop process between god and himself."

Khaferu shut his eyes and thought about this.

"What are you thinking so hard about?"

Without opening his eyes, Khaferu held up his right hand index finger as if saying: "Give me a moment." I let him ponder his thoughts without interruption. A minute later he snapped out of his intense contemplation.

"Abram, you know how every letter in our alphabet has a meaning associated to it, right? A kind of spiritual or religious meaning?"

I remembered learning in school about the history of written language and the evolution of the alphabet. The letters of the alphabet were initially simply pictures representing actual objects in nature. So, for example, the letter D actually looked like a doorway and the letter A represented an ox head. As humanity matured it secured dependable food sources through agriculture and the domestication of animals and also was freed from constant fear of predators. This afforded the luxury of time spent in spiritual contemplation. The letters were then also assigned meanings that were abstractions of their simple meanings. For example, the letter D now also represented the more abstract meaning of a doorway into a spiritual realm. The letter A now also had the abstract meaning of power or strong leadership.

Now days, very few are aware of these intricacies of the origin of written language. They just think of the letters as imparting a particular sound to speech. I suspected Khaferu had something really groundbreaking to add to our discussion.

"Yes, we learned about that in religion class. What about it?"

"So bear with me now. When we write anything, we usually don't really care what is the spiritual or abstract meaning of each of the letters in a word. We're just using the letters for the way they sound in building our words. My idea is to create a new word where the reason we are using each letter is not for its sound but for its abstract meaning. The resulting word imparts the idea we are conveying through its letters rather than because of some arbitrary meaning we give it. It's kinda like when you wrote in your composition about how the medium is the message. Remember when you were speaking to the high priest about answers compared to questions?"

"OK, let's pretend I know what you're talking about for a moment. The obvious first question is: what's the idea you're conveying that you're capturing in this new word?"

Khaferu crinkled his forehead and stretched out both his hands with his palms facing up. "Abram, what have we been discussing the last hour or so? Try to sum it up in one short sentence."

I sensed his exasperation. "Well, I've been explaining to you my idea of how all of Creation comes about when the one true god references himself like those two mirrors do. Does that sum it up well enough?"

Khaferu's exasperation evaporated. "Yup, sure does. You've summed it up better than I thought you would. So that's actually the idea I'm trying to capture with one new word."

"Why should we do this? What will it accomplish?"

Khaferu shot me a piercing glance. I couldn't determine if he was focusing on me or if he was in deep thought and just had the appearance of focusing on me.

"Well, Abram, what is the name of this one and only god who revealed himself to you?"

"I don't know, I didn't catch his name. Maybe he doesn't have a name."

Khaferu continued, apparently satisfied I would now begin to appreciate his agenda: "This new word we'll be creating will be the name of this one god. Everything we've discussed about your god will be baked into this new name. We'll be using the abstract meaning of the letters instead of their sounds. Let's start constructing this new word, the name of the one true god, shall we?"

I was excited about Khaferu's vision of naming god. The artist in him was again taking over and he was constructing his greatest sculpture yet, but it was an abstract sculpture shaped out of ideas instead of clay, stone and metal. It was a methodology to construct a name that is not arbitrary, like the word 'god', but is very meaningful and organic. It would be a name pregnant with meaning. It would be the name of god that embodies the nature of god. I nodded for him to continue.

"Are you ready for this? The idea is that Creation is a result of god referencing himself like a feedback loop, so let's-"

I slapped my forehead with my right hand. "I get it now, let's find a letter where its abstract meaning is Creation, another that means god in its abstract sense and another that has an abstract meaning of referencing something or doing a loop back into yourself."

Khaferu snapped his fingers. "You got it buddy. Let's do it. Now, about Creation, which letter has that abstract meaning?"

"Khaferu, before we dive into the details, let's first get an idea of what basic template or pattern this name of god has. Not that it's any great resolution of this problem, but I just like to have a clear visual of what I'm trying to solve first, or what the final solution should look like. It's like working backwards from a solution to a problem, get it?"

"It reminds me, for some strange reason, of answering a question with another question, like you wrote in your composition. Well, maybe not exactly but it just reminds me of that."

"So let's represent with the letter G the word we're trying to build, as in G for god. The meaning of the word we're going to build is the same as the sentence 'Creation results from god referencing god'. Now, let's say X = Creation, Y = God and Z = References. The word G now looks like the template XYZY, and is read as 'Creation God References God'. It's really a formula but I'm not including the equals sign. Now, we simply need to substitute X, Y and Z with the letters in the alphabet that have the corresponding abstract or spiritual meanings."

"Sure, that gives a good visual," Khaferu replied, seeming a bit underwhelmed. "I do like your idea though, that this is a mathematical formula. I just thought of it as a shape or a word. So now let's try to find the correct letters for our substitutions. Let's start by finding a letter whose meaning is something like Creation, any ideas?"

"Well, I do remember vaguely learning all the abstract meanings of the letters back in grade two or three and...well, give me a few seconds. We also covered this kind of stuff other times throughout the years in our religion classes. But let's put the word Creation aside for now. I definitely know which letter we can use to represent the concept of referencing something."

Khaferu leaned forwards with great interest. "Which one? I should know this I guess but...well, I wasn't always the most attentive student in religious studies, as you know."

"The letter V actually has the abstract meaning of nailing or hooking two things together. Isn't that very close to the concept of referencing something, as in taking concept A and hooking it with concept B, which is equivalent to saying A is referencing B?"

"Absolutely, you've hit the nail on the head with that one. No pun intended, ha ha. So now we have to find two other letters. One letter should have a meaning which is close to the idea of god and the other to the idea of Creation."

For the next hour we discussed this and considered various letters. We dug deep into our collective memories of all the religion studies classes we had ever taken, and of all the lessons and homework assignments we ever had to suffer through. We had two good candidates for a letter whose abstract meaning is god, but had no idea which letter had the abstract meaning of Creation.

The next day, after school, we headed to the library of Annan Sin in the town square and made a beeline for the religion section. The librarian on duty was particularly alert to our presence because of our bubbling, noisy exuberance. We pored through hundreds of tablets. It wasn't until after sunset that we finally had our three letters. There was no doubt or ambiguity about which three letters best suited our agenda.

The concept of Creation is best represented by the letter Y, which represents a quantity of work or energy. It also represents the initial point of emergence. This is not the same Y we used initially, which was just a placeholder for whichever letter we would eventually decide to substitute.

The letter which best signifies god is the letter H, which is used to denote something of great wonder, or it can also mean the breath of life, as in that which breathes life into the lifeless or the created from the uncreated.

I summarized our findings. "Awesome Khaferu, we now have our word G which encapsulates the essence of god. The name of god we've constructed is YHVH, and is the totality of Creation which springs forth spontaneously when this one god that revealed himself to me feeds back on himself. Or you can say he bootstraps himself. This is similar to the two mirrors referencing themselves and bringing forth all of these subsequent mirrors within mirrors. The mirrors within mirrors are the Creation that springs forth. The feedback loop portion, the HVH part, is analogous to the two initial mirrors. But in this case, the two mirrors are the same mirror referencing itself."

"But there's something that bothers me," Khaferu said.

"What?"

"Well, we said we're constructing a word which is the name of god, right?"

"Yeah, so?"

"You said it's the equation G = YHVH. But we also said H is god. So which is it? Is god H or YHVH?"

"Don't you see Khaferu? Your question is perfect because it highlights the fundamental nature of god."

"How's that?"

"That god is a recursive principle. God is both H and YHVH in the same way the mirror is both the top level mirror and all the nested mirrors within. The nested mirrors are not different mirrors."

Khaferu opened his mouth as if about to speak but then closed it and appeared to be in deep thought. He spoke soon thereafter. "That's brilliant. I forgot the power of the word we constructed. It's so simple yet also so complex. YHVH is Creation itself but Creation is literally made from the innermost essence of god, it's not outside of god. It recurses within god."

"Absolutely."

"That's so mind blowing, Abram. I can't believe I had this idea to name your god like this. Maybe he's speaking to me as well? I like that."

"Or maybe he's speaking to me through you. YHVH will be the holiest name of the one god from now and into the countless generations to come. How do you pronounce that, by the way? Why does it have to be so hard to pronounce?"

"Ha ha Abram, there is a method to this madness. You don't want the name of the one god, the ground of being of all that exists, to be so easily and unambiguously pronounceable, do you? Let's not nail down the pronunciation. Let's leave it with a bit of an ineffable mystery."

"Well, let me take a stab at it anyway. Let's pronounce it something like Yehovah or Jehovah, because in some cultures the Y is pronounced as a J. But maybe I shouldn't do this. Maybe this name is too holy to be uttered. This is great Khaferu. I'm realizing now there's more I want to say in my composition."

"Personally, I prefer the name Yahvah," Khaferu said, "because it just replaces the H with AH, and this keeps the symmetry. That's an important part of how we arrived at the word YHVH. Oh yes Abram, I now understand why you chose this self-referential story telling style for your composition. The very self-referential structure of your story mirrors the message of your teachings. The medium is the message, as you say. I love it when everything falls into place."

"To be honest Khaferu, I didn't really think it through to that extent. True, I had some notion of recursive self-reference, but it's just now we've really nailed this concept of god so precisely."

"So it's pretty interesting how you chose your self-referencing story structure then. Maybe you had these ideas in the back of your head and didn't really realize it?"

"Or maybe it was YHVH who inspired me. Do you remember I wrote about being thoughted? Maybe there's much more truth to this than even I realized. Well, that was your idea, remember?"

"This self-referencing business is starting to make me dizzy. That conversation about you being thoughted is one we really had in real life, so what makes me dizzy is to decide at what level of reality to place that conversation. Is it at the level of when it happened in real life, or at the level where you mention it in your composition, or is this level right now, as we speak, a part of some container iteration? If this recursive methodology is how god created everything then he must be pretty dizzy by now, ha ha."

"You got that right, Khaferu, it's pretty confusing. It's giving me a feeling of nausea, but not in a bad way, in a really breathtaking and exhilarating kind of way. It's like we're inside the mind of god and we are observing how god thinks."

"Well, according to these ideas, we really are."

"I need to add all that we've discussed today to my composition. I thought I explained my ideas clearly enough, but I didn't. I also want to rewrite a passage in an earlier chapter and include the name YHVH. You know the passage where I talk to the Bat Kol? She asks me if I know the name of god and I answer that I don't. I'll change it by answering her with the name YHVH that we just figured out."

Later that night, when we were in my room, Khaferu looked through my tablets and located this passage and read it to me: *"Abram, have you forgotten all that has already been revealed to you? Have you forgotten the Received Wisdom? Do you not know god's holiest name?" I dropped my gaze from the Bat Kol because I was ashamed of my ignorance. "I do not know God's name. He never revealed that to me."*

"Yes, that's the passage. I'm going to change it. I'm going to have it say you and I have figured it out using deductive logic."

While we were still in the library, I said to Khaferu: "I'm going to scramble and spend all my free time the next couple of days adding everything we've come up with today. I also haven't yet written the final part that's supposed to be addressed to the Examining Reader."

The librarian shushed us. Apparently we were too loud. Khaferu whispered: "Well, you better get to it. By the way Abram, where do you think all this is going? If this YHVH god you say revealed himself to you is real then I must ask why he revealed himself to you and what is his agenda."

"I've given this a lot of thought," I whispered, "obviously there's a reason for his revealing himself to me. I think I'm just an actor in a grand play. This new god consciousness, this realization of the true nature of the divine, is the next act in his grand play. Actually, it's the second act. During the first act humanity perceives the divine as a plurality of gods and goddesses. Humanity is currently polytheistic. The theme of the second act is that the divine is One. There are no multiple gods. There's only one holy god who created everything in his image. And I do mean in his image literally, as we've explained using the mirrors metaphor. We will soon enter the second act of the grand play where humanity develops a great monotheistic way of thinking. There's a repeating pattern to humanity's relationship with the divine - a leitmotif."

"That's a big word, Abram. What does it mean?"

"A leitmotif is literally a repeating pattern in a musical composition. It's the same theme played in different keys or at different speeds. I'm extending its meaning. There are repeating patterns in civilization just as there are repeating patterns in the mirrors within mirrors. There will be a paradigm shift in humanity's understanding of the divine. I'm sure there will be more in the future too, new keys by which to play the grand symphony of the Civilization of Man."

We meandered our way out of the library while deeply engaged in our conversation. Khaferu said: "That's very deep and interesting, but you haven't completely answered my question. Why did he reveal this to you? What is your role in this grand divine play?"

"That's kind of a difficult question. I mean there could be so many reasons. I guess he could have picked anybody."

"Well Abram, to be fair to you, you did always have a gift and a real yearning for understanding the divine. I remember when I was reading your composition and you wrote near the beginning how you always had a yearning to understand the divine and how you always felt you were a citizen of a different realm."

Once we were back in my room Khaferu turned his attention to my composition tablets which lay scattered on the floor. He located the second tablet and grasped it firmly. "Here is the passage I was referring to." He read the passage to me: *"My family's existence in Ur was urbane. This is not a surprise; Ur is one of the world's most developed and sophisticated cities. I enjoyed the privileges that come with calling Ur my home even if in many other ways my life in Ur had its dissatisfactions and disappointments. I enjoyed some of the world's most well stocked libraries. I studied the great mathematical works of Sumer and Egypt. I was knowledgeable about history, religion, astronomy, music theory and many other subjects. I was always musing about what I had learned and the implications of such provocative things filled my head with delicious mystery and an overwhelming hunger for the truth.."*

Khaferu lifted his eyes and put down the tablet. "Do you see?"

"So that's the reason god has chosen me. I have an inclination to be a mystic and I live in the midst of a city that can nurture my yearning and hunger for learning. I also live during an age that's ripe for spiritual change. These times are reaching out for a person who will shatter idols, and from these shards of divinities will rise but one god. A new zeitgeist will form and change the world."

"There's something else I remember from reading your composition." Khaferu looked through my composition tablets trying to find the choice paragraph.

"Here it is and I quote." He started slowly and deliberately reading from my composition. *"I was born a Habiru and we are at best tolerated and at worst despised. This has always been the case and will continue to be so until the highest god sees fit otherwise. As a child, I felt socially stigmatized. I felt like an outsider."*

He put down the tablet and slowly lifted his gaze towards me.

"Abram, your composition is a finely woven tapestry of themes and ideas. One of the themes is of the plight of your people, the Habiru. You lament the powerlessness of the Habiru living in a sea of the proper purebred children of Ur. You aspire to elevate the station of the Habiru. Your father definitely aspires to having you join the priesthood because he feels it will not only bring glory to him, but more importantly to all Habiru."

I sensed YHVH talking to me through this dear friend who has been more like a brother to me. I remembered god telling me he would always be by my side and will always be my friend.

"Well Abram, your destiny is so much greater than what even your father is anticipating. Your mission in life is for sure of a spiritual nature.

You'll elevate the Habiru to great prominence, but not immediately as your father hopes, and not because you're the first Habiru to join the religious institution of our times. You'll certainly not do that. You'll glorify the Habiru because you'll usher in a new god-consciousness, and the Habiru will forevermore be the beneficiaries of this legacy."

"Or perhaps the Habiru will suffer the burden of this great commission. Very much as I am soon to suffer the consequences of submitting this composition."

"What do you think will happen to you after the Examining Reader reads your composition?"

"Just to me or to my family in general? Do you still think the repercussions will extend to my father too? I mean, I know we discussed this several times already in the past but still...what do you think?"

"Well, obviously you're not going to be admitted to a seminary with this composition, so let's get the obvious out of the way first. Also obviously, your father will be angry and disappointed."

I was at peace with that because I had danced with that fear many times before.

"The real unknown here is will anything sinister happen to me and my family beyond just not being accepted to the seminary?" I paused, letting that question sink in. Khaferu remained silent. "Are they going to execute us? I don't think so. I've studied the code of Ur-Nammu and it's kind of silent about this situation."

"You're lucky the modern code of Ur-Nammu exists. I remember in our law classes how we learned about the complete anarchy that existed before. So tell me Abram, would your composition be classified as a blasphemy?"

"I don't think so. Not technically as a blasphemy because of the circumstances around my composition. First, there's my age. At just seventeen years old I don't fall under the jurisdiction of the code that deals with crimes committed by adults."

"What are the other circumstances?"

I replied with some hesitation and after some thought: "I can't say for sure. I'll need to do some law research at the library. I don't think there's anything in the blasphemy laws that are applicable to a composition for entrance to a seminary."

"Even if there's nothing in the code that deals specifically with this situation, you must realize at the very least there'll be a lot of stigma you'll suffer because of this."

"I know, I know, but let's put it this way: Perhaps we need a kick in the ass. Maybe this is Yahvah's way to get us all out of Ur and out from under the thumb of Sumer. We are Habiru. We are ontological nomads. It's in our collective blood. I wouldn't be at all surprised if my destiny is to go out into the desert and when I get there I will know Yahvah is waiting for me. That will be a fresh start. What do you think?"

"Yeah, I see your point. Go out into the great desert looking for your god. I know you will find him there, Abram."

"Yes, I can become a rancher and shepherd. I can teach my entire family the Received Wisdom of YHVH, the one true god. I will teach that to my children and they will teach that to their own children and many generations after that. Is this what Yahvah has in store for me, to shatter idols? From these shards of divinities a new order shall rise."

Address to the Examining Reader

At last I have completed my composition to the best of my abilities. I have never met you personally so I cannot appeal to your individualistic sense of right and wrong. I cannot know your spiritual orientation based on a direct experiences of who you are. Yes, I know you are a priest, but even within the priesthood there are a multitude of world-views, most of which are private to one's soul and never revealed to any other. I am appealing to this root of your soul rather than to the veneer you might show the world. I do believe the undertone of each person's soul is a collective soul. I am appealing to the collective soul.

The composition which you have read in the preceding pages is my sincere attempt to convey to you my innermost thoughts and feelings concerning the nature of divinity and its role in all our lives. A pursuit for understanding divinity is at the heart of our great civilization, and while the thoughts and convictions I speak of are unconventional and may be perceived as deeply irreverent, that is not my intent.

We are all spiritual creatures in an adversarial relationship with our physicality. Or perhaps it is our physical self which is more the culprit. I will not coddle one perspective over the other. This adversarial relationship is responsible for the great ills of the human condition. The Received Wisdom teaches our physicality must dance with our spirituality rather than deny it. One is not greater than the other. That is the secret to communion with the one I name YHVH.

In the preceding pages I explained my vision of the nature of divinity. I realize that much of what I believe is at odds with the notions of divinity you cherish, but divine consciousness must always be transformed through periodic paradigm shifts. I believe these modern times are ripe for such a paradigm shift. The composition you see before you is just the first part of what will be my life's work. My life, and I hope my legacy, will be devoted to revealing more about the nature of the divine as it is revealed to me. The paradigm shift at hand will cause an existential whiplash of such a magnitude that humanity will be forever transformed.

The nature of divinity should not be left to unchallenged faith but can be established using our intellectual faculties. Indeed, during the section of my composition titled "Worlds Within Worlds" you have witnessed how I derive the name of god using logic rather than direct revelation. Indeed, the line between receiving the divine through direct revelation or laborious perspiration is a blurry line. Where does the ocean begin and the sandy shore end?

Address to the Examining Reader

Thousands of years ago humanity looked up at the starry sky and at the bounty beneath its feet and it speculated about what might be responsible for such splendid things. We have come a long way since then, but in many ways we have lost that sense of sincere and honest wonder at the great edifice of Creation. We have encapsulated our once sincere spirituality within a religious hierarchy that has made a business out of divinity.

Dear Examining Reader, I reiterate I probably do not know who you are personally, but I sincerely hope you have received something positive out of reading this composition. You will not agree with much of what I have written but I accept that respectfully. Only time will tell if the great cataclysmic paradigm shift of which I speak will be the legacy of these modern times.

Sincerely,

Abram, your humble seeker of truth.

The Second Age: A Quest For The ONE

The Semantic Spaces Within The Soul

The old man climbed the steep, rocky terrain. He had made this climb countless times in years past but with advancing age his limbs protested and ached. The scorching sun felt like arrows impaling his flesh during a fierce battle as he climbed up the terrain, step by step, slowly but surely gaining ground against the onslaught of an invisible enemy. His body yearned for the invigorating coolness of the early evening. His soul yearned for his distant youth. Upon reaching the flat land on top of the valley he sat cross-legged on a small patch of dry, sun-baked grass. The lush green valley below provided a sharp contrast to the arid land above. He had spent the day working alongside his shepherds and laborers. His hands were earth-stained and calloused, his muscles knotted and fatigued and his brow drenched with a sweat earned by the hard physical labor of shepherds and common workmen. But his spirit soared and he felt exhilarated and satisfied to the marrow of his every bone.

He arched his back in defiance of his advanced years and rested his arms on his lap. He gazed at the valley below which was the depth of fifty men standing one on top of another. The valley was carpeted with lush grazing fields dotted with uncountable heads of sheep and cattle. These were his fields and his grazing animals and the shepherds and laborers tending to them belonged to his household. To the south he could see in the distance his own household which was near the great oaks by the towns of Mamre and Hebron. To the east, beyond the horizon, his nephew Lot had established his household with a considerable wealth of sheep, cattle, servants and precious metals. Before that time, Lot's shepherds and his own were grazing their sheep and cattle on the same land and that resulted in much conflict. After a few years of turbulent coexistence the conflict became unbearable and he approached Lot and proposed their households should separate.

"If you go west then I will go east. If you go east then I will go west. It's your prerogative my dear nephew and I will not protest your choice."

Lot chose the more fertile lands in the east and, true to his word, the old man did not resist.

"How can you be such a pushover?" Sarai said. "How can you allow Lot to pluck the choicest lands without any regard to your own well being and the well being of your household?"

Sitting now high above his lands he reflected on his life. "Yahvah has blessed my household beyond my wildest dreams. When I lived in the city which I named after my dear brother Haran I was never wanting for anything, but since Yahvah had commanded me to uproot my household and move to Canaan my wealth has multiplied beyond anything I ever imagined possible."

But he was not fully content. His considerable wealth could not fill the void of Sarai's childlessness. It had been thirteen years since his and Sarai's desperation over their childlessness finally compelled them to seek the surrogacy of Sarai's Egyptian handmaiden. Her name was Hagar and she bore him a beautiful and healthy boy which he named Ishmael - meaning Yahvah heard his cries for a son. He loved Ishmael as he would have loved Sarai's own but Sarai was desperately jealous and resentful of Hagar. Hagar was far from blameless, she developed an arrogance of which he was all too well aware. "I prayed for many years Yahvah will bless Sarai with a son but it's too late now," he thought. "I'm far past my middle years and Sarai is far past her child-bearing years and will never bear me a son now. I will learn to be content with what Yahvah has provided. I will dance with my disappointments and adversities as Yahvah has taught me since I was a fresh-faced young lad."

He was long lost in his thoughts when he remembered he should hurry and make his way back home or it would be dark before his return. The moon would be full but he nevertheless preferred to travel the desert by day rather than night. The route back home was a well traveled path known to be frequented at night by brigands and cutthroats. His trusted camel was tethered nearby and laden with a day's worth of food and water. The trip back home would last the afternoon and if he returned immediately he would reach home before darkness. Abram gazed out towards the horizon and he saw the multitudes of towering sand dunes, each one following another, undulating towards the horizon like towering ocean waves frozen during an indivisible instance in a desert devoid of time.

The sun was setting behind the hills to the west when the old man returned to the compound. He had left at dawn that day. He seldom ventured so far from home these days. With advancing years he became less involved in the day to day management of his shepherds and his household affairs in general.

He reflected: "Soon Ishmael will take over all my affairs and I will fully retire and spend the rest of my days at Yahvah's bosom, listening to the silences within the soul for his voice."

Until such time that Ishmael would assume the stewardship of his considerable estate it was Eliezer of Damascus who was his right-hand man. But that was not in the normal course of affairs because it should have been his adult, first-born son to assume that responsibility. But alas, he was past his middle years when he had his first son and Ishmael was now only thirteen years old. Eliezer was tasked with the role of interim household steward.

"Sarai, Sarai," one of Sarai's maidservants shouted with joy when she saw the old man in the distance, "Abram has returned from the fields."

Sarai sprinted out of her tent and scanned the landscape until she also saw Abram in the distance. She had grown accustomed to having Abram by her side every day, and the full day away from him left her yearning for the sight of his rugged, crease-lined face, the feel of his rough, gray beard snuggled against her face, and the sensation of his large, strong hands squeezing her waist. That made her feel safe and content. Abram had dismounted his camel and approached Sarai. She could now see the exhaustion on his face but his head was held high and his erect posture veiled his exhaustion. Sarai caught a glimpse of Hagar inside her own tent. Hagar did not exit her tent but stood at its entrance and waited to catch a glimpse of Abram as he passes by. Sarai's and Hagar's gazes locked fleetingly and then Hagar looked away and scurried back to the dark confines of her tent.

Sarai darted towards Abram. She was too impatient to wait for him to make his way to her. When Abram first caught sight of Sarai, as she rushed towards him, contentment rippled across his face. She threw her arms around him in a long and silent embrace. She then tilted her head back and gazed into his blood-shot eyes while maintaining her tight embrace.

"I've missed you so much today, Abram. I was starting to get worried. How was your day in the fields with your crew?"

"It was exhausting and exhilarating at the same time. It brought back wonderful memories of when I used to do this every day. Sarai, there is nothing quite like a grueling, honest day's work."

They made their way to their tent. Abram settled himself comfortably inside the cavernous interior. He was in dire need of bathing but his exhaustion was paramount.

"Did you hear Yahvah out there?" Sarai said. "Has he finally spoken to you again after all these long years?"

Abram's expression morphed into a look of deep reflection. "No, I didn't hear his voice. But I know he hasn't abandoned us. He commanded me to move my household to Canaan for a reason. We left Ur and then Haran for a reason. Yahvah is subtle but he is not malicious."

"But that's really the reason you set out early this morning after all these years of retirement, isn't it? You thought maybe a return to the old ways might establish the rapport you once had with Yahvah."

Abram cocked his head and furrowed his brow. "Sarai, let me make it clear once and for all if I haven't already. I have not lost my rapport with Yahvah. He is still by my side wherever I go. Has he not blessed us with great wealth? Has he not protected this great household from marauders and brigands, from mighty kings and clansmen? Do you think we would have been better off staying in Ur or Haran?"

"Abram, your reaction startles me. I did not mean to offend you. whatever made you think I resented you for our leaving Ur? That was Yahvah's doing. He compelled you to defy those purebreds in Ur. It was his plan for you to force the hand of fate as you did."

Abram relaxed his muscles. He was surprised at how unaware he had been of the tension in his body. "I'm sorry Sarai. Forgive my outburst. That was so long ago when we lived in Ur. It's like a lifetime away it seems. Perhaps after all these years I still carry the guilt of what happened. But you are right. I was but a vessel in the hands of Yahvah."

Sarai embraced him and gazed into his eyes. Her expressive multi-colored eyes sang her love for him. "Abram, I don't believe we are just inert lumps of clay that Yahvah shapes. Just as Yahvah reaches deep into his being and then from his bosom Creation flows, then so must you reach deep into your own soul and then your own creations shall flow. Yahvah's Creation is like a bubbling stew cooking atop a fire. Each ingredient offers up its flavor to the others and is rewarded with its essence flavored by the others and mirrored back. Each ingredient perceives its Self only as it is perceived by the others. Each ingredient perceives another only as that other perceives its Self-reflected off all the others."

Abram pondered Sarai's wisdom and he reflected it back to her flavored with his own. "Once again we must bow to the Divine Dance. There is an infinite regression when each flavor mirrors all the others and what emerges is a collective Self which emanates from the parts and yet is a new entity not known by the parts."

"Yes, Abram," Sarai said, "the whole of Creation is greater than its parts because the whole is not known by the parts but the parts are known by the whole. There are no ingredients in the stew that receive yet never give. There are none that perceive themselves other than how they are perceived by the others. There is but a grand unified wholeness, an interrelated participatory web. Like a serpent consuming its own tail. That's Yahvah's Divine Dance you have taught your household so well these many decades since we left Ur. That's the essence of Yahvah's Received Wisdom."

The Semantic Spaces Within The Soul

Abram returned Sarai's embrace and mirrored her gaze. "Sarai, you haven't lost an iota of your beauty across the arc of time. When we left Ur you were a radiant young woman and your beauty still shines through the veneer of the decades. Yahvah shines through you."

"I don't think Hagar thinks as kindly of me," Sarai said.

"Please try to understand Hagar. She knows my heart is with you. That must be a great sorrow to her. How she must feel rejected and how her heart must ache for the sake of Ishmael. She has but one weapon in her arsenal and that's Ishmael's role as my inheritor. It's the only leverage she knows and which she uses to win my attentions. Please Sarai, try to see her as only she sees her Self reflected from your eyes."

Sarai wept. Only now, through Abram's words, did she really know Hagar. But Abram's words were only her own words, flavored by Abram and reflected back to her. "Yes Abram, I know, " she lamented. "I can sympathize during moments of reflection but often her prideful attitude overpowers my empathy. She too must try to see me as only I see my Self reflected from her eyes. I need her as my dance partner but she will not abide because she knows I will never bear you an heir. She sprinkles that sharply bitter seasoning into the stew."

"Sarai, don't be so quick at dismissal. You will bear me an heir, a son. I just know it."

Sarai retreated from Abram's embrace. She laughed at him but it was a laugh tainted by hopelessness and dismay. "At my age you think I will bear you a son? Have you lost your senses, Abram?"

"Don't laugh, Sarai. Nothing is impossible for Yahvah." Abram veiled his own doubts.

"Abram, go into the depths of the desert and try to hear the voice of Yahvah once more. He will shout from the summit of the highest cliff that he has not destined for me to bear you an inheritor. That is Hagar's prerogative and I must accept that. You must accept that. Even now as we speak, Hagar is plotting the day Ishmael will be the steward of your household. I am laughing now that I will bear you a son but she will one day have the last laugh at my expense. I saw her at the entrance to her tent when you returned. She appeared as a vulture waiting to feast not upon life's bubbling stew but instead upon the putrid dish of death."

The Four Corners

The desert is freedom and the freedom is pregnant with potential.
The desert is the white-eyed womb of humanity's chaotic congregation.
The desert is a blank mirror, pregnant with its reflections.

Great civilizations and empires are the fruits of Habiru clans that roamed the desert during times so ancient that legend is blurred into fact.

In the desert a soul can turn its back on a civilization rooted in the here and now and roam the idyllic space of the eternal, the formless, the creative and yet uncreated.

In the desert a soul can dwell in the eternal void between the formed and unformed, ocean and shore, youth and senescence.

In the desert humanity can fleetingly forsake the fruit of the Tree of Knowledge of Good and Evil and return to the eternal garden of the formless, white-eyed void.

In the desert walks Yahvah, shrouded in the formless void, far from his Creation but yet intimately close.

Abram was the founder of Yahvahism and he sailed the ship of Yahvah in the desert amongst the multitudes of others. Each ship was the master of its own passions and affairs. Each ship freely worshiped whomever and whatever called it to do the bidding of its soul. Each ship was aware of the others and sailed its way around the others, like the great whales in the oceans who dance happily around each other. Each whale dances a solo dance, and also dances with the others in the eternal dance of dances.

Abram ruminated: "In Ur I fought fiercely against the errors of idolatry and the fight left me scarred and my household was cast out into the wilderness of the desert. But in the desert I can command the ship of Yahvah peacefully and contently amongst the others."

"Yahvah forced the hand of destiny to cast my household from the lush comforts of Ur and take it into the void of the desert," Abram thought. "I have sailed the ship of Yahvah in the desert as well as I could manage, but yet I haven't heard his voice for many years. I have called out to Yahvah but got no reply. I have demanded he give me guidance, but he has been silent. I have opened myself to the semantic spaces in the soul, but its silent whispers I have not heard."

Abram was convinced the final act between his household and Yahvah was yet to come. "There must be more to this saga of my life than what has so far transpired," He thought. "My household has wealth beyond my wildest dreams, but I feel empty within. Yahvah promised me, when I was a boy, that he would always walk by my side and be my everlasting friend. Have I already visited the convergence of his promises? Have I already experienced my journey's climax?"

***

Abram wept when he left Ur. He knew he would dearly miss the land. Shortly after he submitted his composition for entrance to the priesthood, the Ministry for the Propagation of Virtue and Heresy Investigation, also known informally as the Religious Police, charged Abram and Terah with second degree heresy. They were fortunate not to be charged with first degree heresy because it carried an automatic death sentence. Their heresy was classified as second degree because Abram did not expose the general public to his blasphemy.

The judge presiding over the tribunal presented Terah with two options: "Vacate Ur with your family immediately, or release Abram to the authorities and they will discipline him to the full extent of the law's righteousness." Terah chose to protect his son despite his sharp disappointment and feelings of betrayal.

The tribunal judge forced Terah to read from Abram's heretical composition. Terah and Abram were seated together at a table in front of the podium, where the tribunal judge was presiding from above. The tablets were stacked on the table in front of Terah and he was ordered to read the entire composition. When he read particularly incendiary portions his voice quivered and he would wipe his brow with a handkerchief. For the duration of his reading he never glanced at Abram. The presiding judge often questioned Terah about the meaning of passages he was reading, and if Terah could not answer to the judge's satisfaction then Abram was asked to shed light on what he had intended.

In the chapter named Maturity Terah read the following passage:

"My new-found realization caused me to become intoxicated with a sudden intellectual and spiritual freedom that need not serve any institution, that bows to no tradition, and is unencumbered with the artificial constraints of a paradigm constructed by man and which serves only man and not the divine. I realized I could heartily drink from this overflowing cup of Truth without following the customs and etiquette of a society steeped in the stinking garbage heap of idolatry."

When Terah read the last sentence in that passage he again wiped his glistening brow, and he mumbled inaudibly when he forced out the last five words.

"Speak up. What did you say?"

"Stinking garbage heap of idolatry," Terah said.

"Stinking garbage heap?" The judge shouted. "Stinking garbage heap?"

Terah looked up at the ceiling. Abram glanced at him and then averted his gaze when Terah again turned his focus at the tablet he was reading.

"Abram," the judge said, "you sully the name of the true gods, and what do you call a god in their place? This incomprehensible abstraction you named YHVH? You are free to roam the abstract realms, but you are not free to redefine at your whim the fundamental meaning of divinity and to deny the existence of the true gods. If you had merely proposed this YHVH as just another god, perhaps the god of abstract things I propose, then perhaps our just society might have offered you a sympathetic ear - perhaps I say. You might have assumed the mantle of patron theologian within the priesthood. But instead, you altogether deny the true gods and you wish to install your heretical redefinition of divinity in their place. There cannot be just one god. That is a contradiction of the term."

When Terah finished reading from Abram's composition he glanced at Abram and said: "Why Abram? Why did you do this thing? You had the world at your feet. You would have been the first Habiru priest."

Abram could not look his father in the eyes.

"Who is," Terah asked, "this Yahvah you write about? Is he worth the great sacrifice you have made? A sacrifice not just of your future, but also of your mother's, your brothers' and mine? And why do you portray your dear brother Haran with such contempt? He has been nothing but a sympathetic brother to you."

The judge interrupted Terah. "Abram, you said you have not exposed anyone to the blasphemy of your composition?"

"No, I haven't your most high."

"Who is this Khaferu you mention in your composition? For if he lives then he must also be charged with blasphemy by association."

"He is but a figment of my imagination, your most high."

"Do you not associate with any Habiru classmates?"

"There are only a handful of Habiru pupils in my Foundation school, and none are named Khaferu, nor do I have a strong friendship with any of them."

"Are you protecting someone else with whom you confided? For if you did then you must reveal his identity or face even harsher penalties."

"No, your most high. I confided in no one."

The judge's questioning regarding Abram's accomplices lead him nowhere and he abandoned this interrogation.

When the proceedings were completed, and the judge was ready to pronounce his judgment, he quoted from memory the opening lines of the composition:

"Ever since I was a child I always felt like a citizen of a different realm. I've sown the seeds of that realm in my childhood but I can only know the fruits of the reaping once I cross into the new realm."

"I will now reveal to you," the judge said, "the fruit you shall reap in your new realm. Abram, you have betrayed your people the Habiru. You have betrayed your household. But above all, you have betrayed this noble society which was prepared to assimilate you as if you were one of its own. You were offered the keys to the realm of the gods but you mocked it. You could have brought glory to your people but they shall now recede into the forgotten annals of history. You have forced my hand to cast you and your household into the harsh, inhospitable desert. In Ur you were protected from this harsh desert mistress, but your household shall now be cast into its unforgiving clutches. For the rest of your and your household's existence you shall live by the sweat of your brow, away from the greatness of Ur and, above all, away from the realm of the gods. The desert of ignominy is the realm of which you and your household shall be citizens forevermore."

When Terah and his family were banished from Ur they left behind all their worldly possessions, but Terah also left behind his soul. He became a broken man after that, never again a man with a charisma that flowed and bubbled freely from within, but instead an impervious hollow shell not allowing any spark of yearning or hope to penetrate within. Abram's grief was inconsolable and his guilt unassailable. Abram grieved for the loss of the land of his youth, but he mostly grieved for his father's losses. Not just a loss of land and worldly possessions, but also the loss of a pride in his son's brilliant legacy.

When they rode out of Ur, Terah sobbed as he saw the only home he had ever known recede behind him in the distance. The last thing of Ur he ever saw was the great Ziggurat peeking at him, mocking him, high above the city walls, like a foreboding and fiery sentinel blocking his entry back lest his son convince the citizens of Ur to also eat from the forbidden fruit. It was Terah's soul that climbed atop the Ziggurat, bidding him a final farewell. Abram devoured Terah's grief and craved to embrace him and comfort him, but his guilt was an unbreachable wall.

The Four Corners

Many years later, when Yahvah compelled Abram to take his household out of Haran, Abram thought: "Now, once more, I must forsake my home. Haran has been my home since I left Ur, and that was during the distant days of my youth. I must again uproot my household and my spirit from a land I've grown to love. When I left Ur I was forced to do so, but now I must leave Haran by my own volition, and that commands so much more strength of character and faith in Yahvah. How will I compel Sarai towards the same conviction?"

***

In the middle of the compound was Abram's and Sarai's tent. It was by far the tallest structure in the compound. It was taller than five men all together, and so wide that fifty men with arms connected and outstretched could not enclose it. Abram built four paths, made of small white pebbles, equally spaced around the compound's perimeter and snaking their way into the compound, towards his and Sarai's tent. Each path connected to one of the four doors of the tent: east, west, north and south. Each door had a flap Abram and Sarai always kept open during the waking hours. Above each door was a stitching of a young ram and the words: "Welcome to the thirsty, hungry and weary." Most desert nomads were illiterate, but Abram trusted the power of these words would transcend their syntax and vibrate within the silences of the soul.

The desert was alive and swarming with Habiru nomads pitching their tents as the winds blow. Most were poor, subsisting day to day off their meager flocks of livestock and the lean bounty of the land. However, Abram had done very well for himself, owning huge herds, servants numbering many times sixty, two beautiful wives, precious metals and stones and lush fabrics and leathers.

Abram instructed every member of his household to welcome, with open arms, strangers passing by.

"If anyone unknown to you enters the compound," Abram said to all, "then do not call me out to meet them, but instead welcome them and accompany them to meet Sarai and me at our tent. If you have them wait for me to come out and meet them they will know you consider them suspicious and a threat. When they are outside my tent then again I say, do not call me out to meet them lest they will also suspect I do not trust them and see them as a threat. Have them come into our tent unaccompanied to meet me and Sarai."

By way of explanation, Abram said: "Genuine hospitality is not just in feeding the body but also the soul. I will make no stranger feel like an imposition nor a threat. My tent's four corners will always be open to the east, west, south and north. Just as our compound is not protected by walls, neither will my hospitality be adulterated by the walls of suspicion and distrust."

There came a day, at the height of summer, when the heat peaked beyond anything experienced before. Everyone in the compound sought refuge within their tents, protected from the savage sun. Sarai was safely cocooned within the deepest confines of the tent, perfuming her skin and brushing her long, wavy hair. She hummed a Habiru spiritual song composed many generations before. Abram sat inside the tent, right by the north facing door, facing the great oaks of Mamre in the distance. He gazed at the desolation of the desert. There was not a bird in the sky nor a creature visible on the ground as far as he could see. The desert appeared frozen within a slice of time too fleeting to measure.

Abram was lost in a reverie, listening to Sarai's soul-uplifting rendition wafting from the confines of the tent. She hummed at first, but when she transitioned to song a smile cracked Abram's solemn face. Sarai's comforting voice, singing that ancient Habiru spiritual, stirred memories of his early childhood. His mother also sang that song to him at bedtime, when he was frightened of the stillness and darkness of the night:

I want to touch your heart
I want to uplift your soul
Into an idyllic flight
Where silence and darkness
Are louder and brighter
Than sound and light.

Abram woke from his reverie when he noticed a movement in the distance. It was on top of a small mound of earth and rock, a shade beyond the distance at which he could determine if it is man, woman, beast or other. He had not seen it before that moment because it had appeared from within the patch of oaks in the distance. He wasn't sure at first of the direction of its movement, but after tracking it for a short time he determined it was heading directly towards the compound.

When it got a little closer Abram spied more detail. The blurry, monolithic movement resolved into the shapes of three men. Their legs were shaking under the burden of their bodies. They appeared to be in great distress.

"Sarai, Sarai, come quick. Come see this."

"Into that idyl-" Sarai's singing stopped in mid-word. She rushed out from the inner tent's embrace.

She asked: "What's happening Abram?" She feared they were under attack again, as they were years ago when Lot was kidnapped by the marauding kings. But after regaining her composure she thought: "But no one would be attacking us in such sweltering heat and in the full light of day."

"Come Sarai, come. What do you see in the distance?"

Sarai rushed towards Abram. When she reached the entrance to the tent she squinted her eyes, unaccustomed to the piercing sunlight, and she felt a blast of desert heat, like a bonfire around which she huddled with Abram during cold desert nights.

Once Sarai's eyes became accustomed to the light she said: "Yes, I do see something. Three men are approaching us. They don't seem well. I'm sure they're exhausted and parched to the bone."

"Go Sarai, have food and more water brought to the tent. Bring bread baked today and olives and a spiced root soup, and have the cooks prepare a young ram for us too. I will go out to help them before they enter the compound."

Abram wrapped his head in a protective cotton scarf, a common sight in the desert during the heat of day. He grabbed three flasks of water and braved his way into the desert heat, towards the three men. As he ran towards them he yelled for help and many, in various states of undress, emerged from their tents, curious about the commotion.

Abram called out to three sheep herders who emerged from the tent nearest to his. "Go dress yourselves quickly and meet me back here. There are three men out there close to the compound. They're in dire need of rescue and I will need your help to carry them to my tent."

Abram shot a glance towards the distance and saw one of the men had collapsed and the other two were crouched around him trying to revive him. But they did not have the strength. The three men were now within two or three stone throws from the compound. The sheep herders were soon ready and Abram set out with them towards the strangers.

When they reached them they saw the extent of their distress. The strangers suffered from the suffocating heat and were bloodied and battered. Crusted blood, mixed with sand, painted their faces and they appeared like grotesque chimeras of humanity. Their robes were tattered and their heads unprotected from the sun's aggression. The only barriers between their feet and the blistering desert sand were wrappings of the coarse, white-haired leaves of the perennials that were common in this part of the desert. Their gazes were unfocused and their speech was slurred, as if intoxicated.

"They're delirious from the sun's heat and in dire need of water," Abram said. He uncorked his water flask and poured a thin stream of water into the mouth of one of the men. The man uttered a feeble moan as he drank, he did not have the energy to utter a sound any louder. The sheep herders offered water to the other men. Thereafter, Abram removed his head covering and wrapped it around the head of the man he had watered.

"I need two of you," Abram said, "to remove your head covering and do as I did. These men need it more than we do. They're close to death."

The sheep herders hoisted the three men to their feet and helped them to the compound. It was back-breaking work and the trip in was threefold of the trip out.

Sarai and her maidens nursed the men back to health the following three days. They cleaned their bruises and bumps and cured them with a thick paste made of aromatic medicinal desert herbs. Sarai applied cold compresses to their foreheads while singing sweet Habiru lullabies. The strangers slept well each night. On the third day Sarai had her maidens bathe them with aromatic oils and perfumes and dress them with fine robes and with belts and sandals made of Sarai's finest skins.

During the early evening of the third day Sarai and Abram dined with them. The three men devoured heaping servings of spice-rubbed, roasted ram and root stew cooked in sour milk. The taste of stew was never so sublime to them as now, so sublime their spirits soared like an angel in full flight. It was Abram and Sarai's hospitality that flavored the root stew; as much as did meat, milk, vegetable, lentil, fennel or the root stew as a collective whole. It was infused with a flavor more of the fabric of the soul than of stew's whole.

Some say it is only when one gives to another without a return that two souls connect as one. But what of the other side of the offering? What of the taker who offers nothing in return? Can he too connect with the giver's soul as the giver connects in turn? Yes, because divine symmetry is not in the giving and taking but in the healing of a wound where divinity, neither giver nor taker but two souls as One, eternally rests.

The three men, now gleaming, rested and healing, were not recognizable as the three who were at deaths door just three days before. They were tall, sinewy and strong. They were younger than the mid-years and had the strong, even features, the pale skin, now sunburned, and soulful blue eyes characteristic of the sea-faring Phoenicians of yore. They were handsomely bearded and with loose ebony curls that kissed their shoulders.

Near meal's end Abram said to the men: "It's my salvation to have welcomed you in this time of need. I know nothing of the journey that brought you to one of my tent's corners, seeking solace."

The three men sat across the rug from Abram and Sarai. The middle man spoke and Abram sensed it was not due to seniority or position but as one voice for all. "We are coming from far off, in the lands across from your ocean shores. We are sea faring traders of fabrics, and we were transporting bundles of wild silk from the lands of the East, by way of three trading ships. The three of us you see before you, we departed our ship two nights before we came to your household. We were making our way through the northern desert trade route when our journey was interrupted just a half day by camel from here. We were ambushed by a horde of thieves. They beat us and took our bundles of silk, our food, our water, our pieces of gold, our camels, even our sandals."

"And you were exposed in your precarious condition to the elements of the desert since then?" Abram said. "How could you have survived? The journey is only half a day by camel, but two days by foot."

"Yes, we weren't helped by a soul. We came across wanderers like us, but they were not willing to part with their food or water because we had no means of payment. The next day we happened upon an island of water and lush trees in the midst of the desert's sandy sea, and we drank from it. Our lives were saved that way."

"But I gather you had no container of any sort, "Sarai said, "and you couldn't gather more of the water for the rest of your journey."

"Yes, those thieves came close to stealing our bones. It's a wonder they allowed us the robes on our backs, useless as they were in their state of abuse."

"Where were you transporting your silk bundles?"

"It was destined for merchants in the city of Hebron, a day by camel from here. We decided to continue on our path, instead of returning to our ships, because we were too far from them."

"Were you hoping of reaching Hebron and seeking help there?"

"That was our secondary plan. We didn't trust to receive any help from Hebron. We came empty handed, devoid of our silk bundles destined for the merchants. We would only have raised anger and suspicion within their merchant hearts."

Abram straightened his back. He had been sitting for far too long and his body ached. He longed for a breath of desert air. At this time, the day's heat was subdued and a breeze flowed through the mighty oaks in the distance.

"Come my friends," Abram said, "the heat is no more and a heavenly breeze gallops across the desert floor. It is coming from the garden of the tall oaks from where you emerged when I first saw you. The breeze walks in the garden and asks me where I have hidden you. It yearns to brush by your cheeks and embrace you. I ask it if I am your keeper. I ask how it knows you are my guests."

The men smiled. The mystery in their gaze somehow assured Abram of their sincerity and a wisdom older than time.

"The breeze knows your charitable heart Abram," they said. But it was again only the man in the middle speaking as three voices in one. Abram saw that the man in the middle now speaking was not the same man speaking before. It was always the man in the middle speaking as one voice for all. But it was a middle like on a circle's boundary rather than a straight edge. "Your household's reputation as a mighty clan is known throughout this region. But you are, above all, known for your hospitality. I knew of you Abram. It is not by happy chance we stumbled upon your compound in our time of need."

Abram and the three men rode two camels towards the nearest oaks. Sarai accompanied them until the perimeter of the compound. She had a pressing task and she intended to rejoin them later. She would not reveal the nature of her task, but Abram suspected she intended to confront Hagar for calling out to him earlier in the day, craving to spend more time with him.

"You knew of my location well enough to find me?"

"We are traders and we have criss-crossed this region many times before. Last winter we traded at a small town to the southeast of here, just over there beyond the hills."

"But you never visited us during those times. You only come in your time of need?" Abram's body shuddered with laughter and fine spittle sprayed from the corners of his bearded mouth. Sarai was taken aback by the vivacity of his laughter. He grasped the left shoulder of the man in the middle, the man forever in the middle. But it was as the middle of Eternity and not a day's time.

When they reached the nearest oaks of Mamre, Abram stood facing the three men. They stood under the tallest and widest oak, as the breeze rustled its leaves and the branches above slowly swayed and undulated. It was to this thousand year old tree the breeze had compelled them.

And it was under the tall oaks of Mamre the three men told Abram they knew of his nephew Lot and how Lot's household had come to live amongst the people of Sodom.

"Why do you discuss this with me?" Abram said. "What is the relevance of Lot to you?"

"Abram, the thieves who ambushed us were Sodomites."

"And of what consequence is that? What do you know of the thieves who ambushed you? How do you know they were Sodomites?"

Abram raised his eyebrows and approached the men almost imperceptibly. They noticed Abram's unease.

"They didn't admit that openly," the man in the middle said, "but we heard the words they spoke amongst themselves. They thought foreigners would not understand their language but we have traded in this area many times before and we are not vulnerable to a confusion of tongues."

"What is your intention now? I assume you will be returning to your ships and then to your kingdom? I will, of course, provide for the necessities of your journey. You will have food, water and blazing chariots pulled by my strongest and fieriest camels. I will have four of my servants attend to your safety and comforts as you make your way in the chariots towards your kingdom."

"Your hospitality is without equal. But Abram, the breeze that knows the magnanimity of your heart also knows the darkness within the heart of the Sodomites. They are without hospitality or compassion. They are known throughout the desert as bands of thieves and murderers. The misfortune they have inflicted on us, they have also inflicted on many others."

"Yes, I am well aware of the plague the Sodomites have been to the desert's people. I warned Lot and his household to keep a distance from them, but they are compelled to fraternize with them. They have become intoxicated by them."

"Before we crossed the void of the sea we were commissioned by our king to evaluate the threat posed by the Sodomites. A threat not just to their immediate victims but also to the well-being of the commerce carried out throughout the trade route. Too many times the Sodomites have cut the lifeblood of the desert's trade route, and the world is unraveling beyond. The commerce between small communities is this lifeblood. It binds them together into an interrelated web of dependencies. And from this self-aware web emanates a new entity known as the Civilization of Man."

"You appear to be as much philosophers and wise men as you are traders of fabrics."

Abram did not concern himself with the wisdom of these men, nor their philosophical proclivities. He cared more for their current motives, be they born of heaven or hell.

"To what end are you evaluating the threats of Sodom?" Abram said. "What will your king do with your report? Will you be putting forward a judgment for a course of action?"

"If I may again impose on your hospitality," the man in the middle said, "my others to my left and to my right shall make their way to Sodom to see for themselves its depravity. Abram, may I bask by the light of your hospitality for yet another night? I pledge to you I shall honor your hospitality from the doors at all four corners of your tent at once."

Abram sensed the three men were evading his concerns. He feared for Lot's household swimming to no avail in a turbulent sea. For emphasis he repeated his three questions, word for word. But his tone was now more anguished. His arms were thrust half forwards. His hands opened, palms facing up. "To what end are you evaluating the threats of Sodom? What will your king do with your report? Will you be putting forward a judgment for a course of action?"

"Abram, your concerns are in plain sight. Please forgive us for what you know we must do if our judgment goes against the Sodomites."

"But you hold the lives of so many in your hands," Abram said. "Surely your judgment must not be so harsh if not everyone is guilty of the crimes you judge."

"Abram, there are so very many in Sodom guilty of our charge. Finding a good man there is like finding an untouched man in a lion's den."

Abram approached the three men. "But my lord, I am certain your good king can protect a loyal man from the jaws of a lion. What if there are fifty men such as that, still living in the lion's den amongst the Sodomites. Should you kill them too and say the lions feasted on their flesh?"

"Abram, your concern for the life of others has touched us. If there are fifty such as that we will plead with our king to spare Sodom. We must then meet them on the battlefield instead of taking the conflict to their homes. But by doing so more innocent lives will be shattered out in the open desert and the world beyond."

Abram shut his eyes and contemplated the words of the men. "I understand that my lord. But should peace be left to its own devices or should it be won by the tip of the sword? Should peace alone not be the arbitrator of who lives and who dies, or should the dance of life and death be left to an external principality? Should peace set its own timetable or should it be forced out of the womb, grasping at its mother's umbilical, before it is ready for the world? Please forgive me my lord if I have overstepped my boundary."

The men were unprepared for Abram's tenacity. But they admired his resolve. "I have longed to wrestle with a man such as you Abram. You have danced with your adversities before and they could do you no harm. Now you must wrestle with them."

"How do you know so much about me?" Abram said. "And does dancing with my adversities differ from wrestling with them? Yes, I have danced with them before, during my younger years and to this day. I have reaped much peace of mind and courage from my dance."

"I will tell you of a wonder we experienced many years ago during one of our trading expeditions to the lands of the Far East, by the Ocean of Calm. We were lost in the jungles of the Malay people. We could not find the ocean shore and darkness enveloped us. The jungle's foliage was thick and we could barely hack a path by sword or hatchet. The trees were near me all around. I could touch two trees at once with arms outstretched to my sides. Abram, look at the great oaks above and around. If you think these are dense, you are wrong. You can drive a battle chariot at full gallop and scarcely be concerned of collision."

Abram had never experienced a dense growth of trees as the man had described. He shut his eyes and tried to picture it in his mind's eye. But he sensed the image he conjured was but a shadow of the light of truth.

"We had, step by tormented step, cut a path to a clearing within the jungle. The night was moonless but I knew we had reached a large area devoid of foliage and trees. I knew it for one simple yet breathtaking reason."

"How could you know in the pitch darkness? Perhaps your outstretched arms could no longer touch any tree, or the dense foliage was no longer in your way and you could advance freely? But how could you know that it was a large clearing if you could not see it?"

"Abram, we did say the night was moonless, that much is true. But sprawling on the ground before us, for what seemed in the darkness to be as far as the eye could see in the light of day, were bright pinpoints of light, blinking without any pattern or rhythm we could discern. It was truly a visual cacophony of pinprick lights. And we at once knew the sight before us was a wonder of which we had learned but never expected to see by our own eyes. Before us was a clearing dotted with uncountable blinking fireflies."

Abram's eyes widened and he cocked his head forwards. "Fireflies you say? But I haven't asked you, of what relevance is this tale to our earlier discussions? Yet your tale fascinates me and I want to hear its unfolding if for no other reason than the tale itself. But I do suspect your tale has a

The Four Corners

meaning transcending the details of its circumstances." Abram smiled a brief crooked, closed-mouth smile.

The men continued the tale without reacting to Abram's interruption. But Abram trusted these men now and he knew it was not a rebuke but rather implicit confirmation.

"The spectacle of blinking lights absorbed me and I became one with it. It was no longer sprawled in front of me. It was within me. It was the broken shards of divinities in the soul yearning to become whole. Yearning for the Chaos of the blinking to be no more."

Abram was again puzzled by the intimate knowledge these three men had of him. He had used the expression 'Shards Of Divinities' in his composition for the priesthood so long ago.

"These men before me," Abram thought, "I can no longer think of as anything but a reflection of myself and myself as a reflection of them. When I look into their eyes I see them as they see themselves reflected off mine. And they, in turn, see the mirror image. This reflection repeats forever, eternally. Has Yahvah sent these men to me? Is this the soul curving back unto itself?"

And Abram opened the four corners of his soul and invited the three men in. Not just to his tent's embrace but to the embrace of the soul. And he came to know the three men as never before. Each a reflection of the others, like the mirror within a mirror within another, and to his eyes they became One.

"I don't know why it has never occurred to me before," Abram said to the man before him, "I never asked your name."

"I am Ram, son of Elshor the Bull, father to be of Mayim who is to become a fisherman and then more."

Abram was puzzled. "When I was but a child my father Terah enthralled my brothers and me with tales of wonder about Elshor the Bull. What connection do you have with these Habiru tales of yore?"

"Perhaps my people and yours," Ram said, "share a common origin during times of old."

Just then Sarai returned from the compound. She was on camelback. As she dismounted the camel, Abram said: "Come Sarai, Ram has been enthralling me with tales of his wondrous voyages."

"You know his name? It's of the man in the middle I am sure."

"But there is but one man before me, Sarai. Of who else would it be a name?"

"Abram, have you lost your senses? I see three men before me, but as always the man in the middle speaks for all."

Abram realized only for him the three men appeared as one. Abram told Sarai of Ram's tale of the fireflies exactly as Ram had told it to him, and when done he said to Sarai: "And we must offer Ram, the man you see in the middle, our heartfelt congratulations. His wife is with child and his name shall be Mayim, and he will be a fisherman I'm told." And then Abram regretted telling Sarai of this.

"Yes, he will be a fisherman as he enters physical and intellectual maturity," Ram said, "but that shall not be his final vocation. I will groom him to be a great spiritual teacher during the third phase of his life."

"I offer you heartfelt congratulations on your son to be," Sarai said. "I am sad to say I am destined for no such blessing myself." Sarai paused and looked down at her feet. She then slowly raised her head and looked into Ram's eyes. "I am barren and cracked like bone-dry land during a drought. Yahvah has chosen Hagar above me as the mother of Abram's legacy."

"Don't be without hope Sarai," the man said, "Abram walks humbly with Yahvah and you will not be forgotten. You will have a son, I know it."

Sarai and Abram exchanged puzzled looks.

"What? You also say I will be with child? Abram has told me this and I laughed at him. But I did not expect these words from any other." Sarai laughed at what she thought to be the man's preposterous promise.

Sarai cut short her laughter. "I apologize for my cynicism, but my laughter escaped through cracks in my fractured soul, and I could not restrain it."

"No offense taken, Sarai. We understand your sense of hopelessness. But I will tell you this: We will visit you this time next year and we will be bearing gifts of fine fabrics, do you know why?"

"I suppose you think I will have a baby boy at that time?" Sarai said.

"I just know it Sarai," the man said. "Yahvah will grant you this precious gift."

"But you have not finished your tale of the fireflies," Abram said, trying to change the topic. He also doubted Ram's promise. "Please Ram, continue your spellbinding tale of the fireflies."

"Well, I seem to have lost my place...where was I last?...Oh yes, I do remember now. Gradually, almost imperceptibly at first, I could feel the cacophony dissipating within my core. The multitudes of blinking lights spoke to me with an increasingly common voice. Each firefly's light bounced off all the other fireflies, and they did the same in return. Each firefly now saw each other firefly as that other firefly saw itself reflected from the eyes of the others. This created an interrelated web of dependencies that wrestled each firefly's light towards a common voice. It was like a strange attracting influence pulling each firefly's light into the rhythm of a divine resonance. But this was a resonance without a choreographer. This was an organic resonance and it emanated from a dark and silent place that knows nothing of the resonance it has compelled. Yet it knows of the wrestling match between the chaotic cacophony of lights."

"Are you implying," Abram said, "that the uncountable fireflies began to blink their lights all in unison without the providence of an external guide? I have never seen sheep follow a common path without a shepherd, nor serpents dance without a piper."

"That's precisely the wonder I saw Abram, but there was no shepherd, unseen or otherwise. It was a sight within my being like I never beheld before, and I was silenced by the divine majesty of it all. I was awed by the yearning within the Chaos, a yearning and a struggle for a common voice. The yearning was powerful and poignant and tragic. The yearning voice reached out to me, grasping at the reeds of the soul, kicking and screaming at the Chaos below and seeking even the slightest foothold, lest it plummet back into the unknowing white-eyed sea of turbulence that would consume it once and for all."

Ram stood with Abram, as did the three men with Sarai, under the great oaks of Mamre. The leafy branches, great and small, fluttered and waved in the breeze, hitherto and fro. Ram was silent at his tale's conclusion, patiently waiting for Abram's ruminations, as did the three men for Sarai.

"The tale you've told me," Sarai said, "would have been fascinating even had you not exposed me to the vantage point of your soul. But the manner you described the synchronization process transcends the world of the fireflies and speaks to me, and to Abram I'm sure, from the depths of Creation. It appears as a principle of Creation transcending just the domain of the fireflies and extending to all."

Through Sarai's words, Abram now knew Yahvah sent Ram to be a messenger to them. Abram thought: "But Ram is just a man. Yahvah has revealed himself to me in different ways throughout my life. Through visions and dreams he revealed himself to me, and now through an angelic agency that speaks through Ram. I now see that an angel is like a skipping stone, moving through an eternal space devoid of the waters of time, and occasionally bouncing off the waters of a human soul. The resulting ripples of divinity emanate from soul's source and wash upon all those who are in its vicinity."

"During those estranged distant days when I lived in that magnificent city of Ur," Abram said to Ram, "there came a day when god whispered to me his magnanimous name. I pronounce it Yahvah. His name is YHVH.

The Four Corners

When you first came to me you were as three. I see now the one who was to your left and the one who was to your right are as the H curving back unto itself and they coalesce into the middle V - now known as Ram. It is the void of Existence pregnant with polarities. For every up there must be a down, for every good an evil, for every give a take. It is the H wrestling with itself, and the beauty and rhythm of Creation explodes outwards like light born from the Chaos of the void."

I asked you before," Abram continued, "what is the difference between wrestling and dance? Your tale has triggered in me an upheaval of thoughts that themselves are as the blinking fireflies in the jungle of the Malay."

"Do these thoughts tend towards a common voice, as do the blinking fireflies?" Ram said.

"They do. I stand at the precipice of a cliff and new vistas are beckoning to me. I see deeper and further than ever before. It is like a thick veil lifted off my eyes - a veil I never suspected was there."

"And what of these new vistas?" Ram said. "What are they?"

"When I was young, Yahvah showed me how to dance with my adversities. I embraced them and they could do me no harm. My left danced with their right. My give danced with their take, and we became as None. But now, I see within the Chaos, be it of fireflies or of Chaos unattached and bare, is a yearning which is opposite and complementary to the Dance. The Dance is born of Creation's yearning for a return to the source of its Existence, the Void within Yahvah - the H. But the Wrestle is the yearning within Yahvah to break the vessel of the void into shards of divinities, and for the harmony of Creation within to then flow out. The void yearns for Creation and Creation yearns for the void. The Wrestle creates, and then the dance collapses Creation back towards the void of the H. The dust of Chaos yearns for Creation and then Creation yearns back for the dust."

Ram learned from Abram, as a teacher learns from his student.

"From dust we came and to dust we shall return," Ram said. "But Abram, what your wisdom speaks of is the dust of Chaos from which Creation emanates and not the dust from under your feet."

"That's so beautiful," said Sarai. "I am compelled to render it into a spiritual song, in the tradition of the old Habiru spirituals. If indeed I will be blessed with a son, when he feels vulnerable and alone I will sing this song to him as a sweet lullaby."

Sarai sang her plaintive song and its poignant melody strummed a chord in Abram's soul and he came to know a sadness that he never suspected before. He did not know of what was the sadness. It was a sadness unattached to a source. But it was a sadness holding the promise of its own redemption. It was a sadness born of a yearning for the source of Yahvah, the letter H, Creation's void.

> The void yearns for Creation
> And Creation yearns for the void
> As two primordial lovers
> Their embrace rendered asunder
> During Creation's fire and thunder
> Or as from Dust to Dust
> The circle of life
> But not the dust of the fields
> Nor a circle enclosing a space and time
> But the eternal loop of Creation
> From the the Dust to Creation
> And then back to the Dust
> Each yearning for citizenship
> In another realm

"Bless you Sarai," Ram said, "you have the gift to appease a lost soul longing for its home."

Ram said to Abram and Sarai: "You may think of me as only a trader of silks and other fabrics along the great trading route, but we traders, be it of silks or spices or any other commodity, serve a higher purpose. As I already explained, the commerce between far-flung outposts of humanity compels the creation of the Civilization of Man."

"The Civilization of Man," Abram said, "emanates from the Chaos of humanity as the synchronized blinking of the fireflies emanates from their cacophony of lights."

"Yes Abram, " Ram said, "you have understood this creative self-organization principle deeply. You see that it is ubiquitous within Creation. As traders, we transport far more than just material wealth from place to far-flung place. We also carry the knowledge and wisdom of the many cultures we contact. We cross-fertilize knowledge and wisdom from one corner of the earth to all others. That is the stuff from which the Civilization of Man is built. And by doing so, each culture's insights are reflected off all the others, and they harmonize with each other, as do the fireflies. From this emanates the Civilization of Man. The emergent emanates from the people's seats, not the emperor's box."

"Truly, this would be impossible if not for the commerce along this silk road," Sarai said. "It is a wondrous thing that it has this unplanned side-effect. As if Yahvah's providence is at the helm."

"Yes Sarai," Ram said, "it truly is a silk road. A more apt name I have never heard. I will cherish and keep with me the great wisdom I have learned from you and Abram. I will carry this wisdom to other cultures as the honey bees carry pollen from flower to flower. Their commodity is honey but their legacy is the Civilization of Nature. When I next trade in the lands of India and the Orient, I will teach them about Yahvah. But be humble Abram and Sarai. The insights I have passed on to you are themselves from these lands. During my travels I have encountered thinkers and sages, and I have told them the story of the fireflies and they have enlightened me with the insights I have now passed on to you. When I will teach them about Yahvah, I will be reflecting back their own wisdom which you have infused with yours."

"Civilization is like the stew cooking atop a fire," Sarai said. "Each ingredient flavors the others and receives itself back, flavored by the others."

"I owe these distant lands much gratitude," Abram said. "Their insights about the blinking fireflies have deepened and textured my understanding of Yahvah. I will encapsulate the nature of Yahvah as tersely as I can. During your next travels tell them the seed of Yahvah curves back unto itself, as the mirrors curve back unto themselves, and then it creates and creates - each creation within the other. That is Yahvah's nature."

"I will remember this wisdom," Ram said, "and I will teach it to the sages in India and the Orient. In the distant future your inheritors will encounter the wisdom of these lands and it will resonate with them and they will know within the silence of their soul that they are encountering their own wisdom, flavored by these far-flung lands, and reflected back to them."

Ram gazed into the crimson horizon to the west. The sun was a red ball dipping into the void, past the ends of the earth. He shut his eyes briefly before speaking once more. "But I will not teach the Sodomites this wisdom because they are incapable of digesting this spiritual nourishment, and they will spoil the stew."

Ram's words reminded Abram of his concerns for the fate of the Sodomites, and particularly for Lot's household. He suspected Ram had intended this. His thoughts no longer roamed the idyllic space of ideas and insights, but were instead grounded in the concerns of the here and now.

"Now Ram," Abram said, "forgive me again for my tenacity, but I must take our discussion to where we were before we wrestled with these complex and divine insights. Perhaps I overstep my boundary once again, but I must discuss the dire actions your king will take against Sodom and my nephew Lot, whose household is within its walls."

Sarai snapped out of her reverie and shot Abram a puzzled look. "What dire consequences are you talking about, Abram?" She turned her gaze towards the three men while Abram could only see Ram.

Abram told Sarai of the discussion he and Ram had concerning the danger of the Sodomites to the desert trade route, and the trade routes of the kingdoms beyond. He told her of the military action the kingdom of the East is considering against Sodom, and of the dire danger facing Lot and his household.

"My lords," Sarai said, "be it far for me to exalt Lot. He is far from perfect, he is selfish at times. When Abram gave him first choice of grazing land he picked the choicest land by far, without regard for Abram. But I must protest, he is no thief nor thug and he does not deserve a fate such as this."

"Sarai, I have been negotiating for Lot's fate and the fate of all of the righteous of Sodom," Abram said. "My lord Ram, pay no heed to Lot's imperfections. I am happy for Lot's household to have the choicest land. I am wealthy beyond my wildest expectations as is."

Abram and Sarai exchanged glances of disapproval.

"Why Abram?" Sarai said. "Why do you have such a blind spot for Lot? I have asked you this many times before but you have never granted me an answer to appease my curiosity."

"Forgive us, Ram," Abram said. "Forgive us for airing our grievances in the open. But I have never confided in Sarai about my attachment to Lot, and now is the time for the shadows on the wall to give way to the full, textured light."

"Don't be concerned for me, Abram. I invite you to unlock your heart."

Sarai locked eyes with Abram. "What is this full, textured light?"

"Sarai, since we left Ur I always felt an overwhelming guilt for my harsh depiction of Haran in my composition for the priesthood. I favor Lot as I do because he is Haran's son."

"But I remember," Sarai said, "that Haran was never angry with you. Why, I will never know. I would have been incensed had you attacked my character within those sun-baked tablets, as you did his."

"Haran forgave me for that, but my father never did. My father held me more in contempt for demeaning Haran's character than he did for causing our banishment from Ur. He died a broken and bitter man, and I am the cause of that."

"So why did you attack Haran's character, Abram? Why did you do it? Haran was your only true friend in Ur."

A tear rolled down Abram's cheek. "That he was. I so fondly remember our childhood intimacy. He was my only true confidant. Oh how we loved our philosophical discussions and our almost daily games of Pinot."

"I remember he could eat quantities of food that would choke a large man," Sarai said. "And I remember you said he was a prodigious eater even as a child." Sarai laughed but her eyes were tearing.

"Do you not see it, Sarai? I have told you many times about the composition I wrote. Do you not see who in my composition is truly Haran?"

Sarai locked eyes with Abram again and she reflected with visible intensity on his question. They did not utter a word, and then Sarai cupped her mouth with her left hand and her eyes became like saucers. "My dear Yahvah, why did I not see it before? Haran, he is Khaferu, is he not?"

Abram nodded.

"You were protecting him all this time."

"Of course I was. I could not implicate him in my blasphemy. I could not have the authorities realize he knew about the message of my composition, and that he was even complicit in forming some of its ideas. I had to paint him as a villain. I had to deflect all suspicion away from him."

"Then why did you not enlighten your father about your motives? Surely he would have understood then why you wrote of Haran in your composition as you did."

"I could not do that. How could I have told our dear father that Haran, his first born son that he so loved, was also complicit in our banishment from Ur? He had already lost one son. I did not want him to lose another."

Sarai had never understood Abram's sadness and guilt as she did now. "He suffers from unhealed wounds within his soul," she thought. "And Haran, what did he say of all this?"

"He wanted to reveal the truth to our father. But I forbade him. He begged me to reveal the truth during the trial and the years until our father's passing. But I forbade him."

"And this, my dear Abram, is the reason for the blind spot you have for Lot - your guilt. But you protected his father. Surely you must find solace in that."

Abram's tears now flowed freely, and he made no pretense to hide his anguish. "But I also sullied his character in my composition, and that destroyed our father. I vowed to my father on his deathbed I would always put Haran's safety and interests ahead of mine. And at Haran's deathbed I vowed the same for Lot. Do you understand now, Sarai? I have commanded an army to rescue Lot from the four kings. I would give my life for Lot. I would even wrestle with Yahvah for the sake of Lot's safety."

"Just as you wrestle with me now," Ram said.

Abram turned his focus on Ram. "I apologize my lord. I have forgotten about our discussion. What say you my lord if there be just five fewer than fifty. What if there are forty-five righteous souls within Sodom? Will you still find it in your heart to plead with your king for Lot's safety and the other innocents in Sodom?"

Sarai looked on as Abram brushed aside their discussion. "I will let him forget for now," she thought.

"Yes Abram," Ram said, "even for the sake of just forty-five righteous souls I will plead with our king. But our king is wise far beyond you and me. I cannot assure you of what his judgment shall be."

"If your king sees it in his heart to spare Sodom for the sake of the righteous," Sarai said, "what will become of the endangered silk road? Would it not be wiser to simply have Lot and his household vacate Sodom before your king exacts justice on it?"

"And what of the righteous Sodomites?" Abram said to Sarai. "There is an alternate course of action. The mighty and compassionate king of the East can meet the wicked Sodomites outside of Sodom, in the desert wilderness. The wicked can be cut down while in the act of committing their wickedness. In this way the wise king can exact justice only against the transgressors. But I digress. May the Lord not be angry, but let me speak. What if only thirty can be found there? Will you still plead for the righteous of Sodom to your wise and compassionate king?"

"Yes Abram, for the sake of thirty I shall do the pleading."

"Now that I have been so bold as to speak, what if only twenty can be found there?"

"For the sake of twenty I will ask my king to spare Sodom."

Abram said: "May the king not be angry, but let me speak just once more. What if only ten can be found there?"

Ram said: "For the sake of ten I will recommend to my king he should spare Sodom and seek the alternate plan. But now Abram, I must again plead for your hospitality. May I seek shelter within the four corners of your tent while my left and my right go into Sodom to see for myself the level of its wickedness?"

Abram once more could see the man in the middle, flanked to his right and to his left by the two other men. And Abram, Sarai and the three men departed the garden of the oaks of Mamre, and they followed the redolent, whispering breeze back to their household.

    Abram and Sarai's servants prepared canteens of water and food enough for three days in the desert for two men. That night the two men, one to the right and the other to the left, departed for Sodom, riding on a blazing chariot pulled by Abram's fieriest camels. And then there was One. But the man in the middle, the connector of the other two, did not depart. He entered Abram and Sarai through the four corners of their soul. And then there was None.

The Moon Reflects Our Soul

The moon's crescent hung in the void of the heavens, mid-way to the unseen horizon in the East. The moon threatened to plummet into the desert floor, yet it maintained its oversight above its dominion. When Abram was a child in Ur he often delighted in tracking the snail's pace of the moon's arc across his bedroom window. He would swivel his neck to align the left edge of his window with the moon's leading edge. Gradually, almost imperceptibly, the moon's sliver advanced past the window's edge and widened until it appeared in all its rotund glory as it fell to the other side of the window. When the moon's edge reached the other side, it began shrinking until it was a thin sliver again, and then it disappeared.

The dulcet tones of the moon's milky-white soothed him, but it was not his body. They pierced the ramparts to an unfathomable chamber in the bedrock of his foundation, and he felt a joy not confined to the borders of his flesh. It was a joy emanating from deep within him, and yet it belonged to all. "It is like a tree," he thought, "all the branches suckle from their source - the trunk."

Even as a child, Abram was fascinated by astronomy and he learned of the moon's cycles and its motions across the heavens. But when the moon revealed its subtle dance to his own eyes, he felt an intimacy with the moon no library can offer.

The moon held a life-long mystery for Abram, yet he knew long ago it is not a divinity to be worshiped. The civilization that had banished him into the emptiness of the desert worshiped the moon, but he had rejected such an idolatrous relationship with divinity's creations. On this night, the crescent moon flooded his compound with a pale, milky glow and a mystical silence enveloped the desert's void. On other nights, the silence would, at random times, be broken by a crying baby while her mother sang a lullaby, or by the shriek of an anonymous desert wind briefly racing through the compound as it hurtled across the desert floor to lands beyond horizon's reach. But on that night, the silence was absolute and it felt to Abram like a warming blanket comforting him during the cold desert nights.

It was a time halfway between midnight and dawn. Abram woke earlier due to a troubling dream. Sarai lay sleeping by his side. The dream was blurry to him now, its details he could not remember, but he did remember a shadowy, phantom figure galloping across the desert floor under the crescent moon. He felt a foreboding shudder clutching at his soul, and it would not let go. After a brief, restless time he abandoned all pretense of returning to sleep and he ventured out of the tent into the chilly desert night. "Perhaps a brisk walk around the compound will tire me and clear the cobwebs of my troubling dream," he thought. He passed by Ishmael and Hagar's tent. "They are sleeping soundly," he thought. The compound's perimeter was within a short walk. He felt a pressure within his ears due to desert's deafening silence, and he wondered if he had become deaf. He coughed and the sound comforted him because it confirmed the soundness of his ears. Abram was grateful for the moon's soothing light that paved his path, otherwise he would be as good as blind.

When Abram reached the compound's perimeter he paused, unsure where to go next. Beyond, a short distance away, the moonlight revealed a small sand dune about the height of three men and the width of ten. "I will go there and sit on its top and breath in the desert's cold, dry air," he thought. He climbed on all fours because the sand dune was steep. His foothold and grip faltered on occasion and he slid helplessly while spitting out the gritty sand that had billowed into his mouth. When he reached near the top of the sand dune he heard a rhythmic sound pierce the desert's silence. Previously, the sand dune had shielded his ears. His ears were now unaccustomed to sound as are eyes to light when they emerge from a long darkness into a strong light. Abram could not at first identify the sound but upon reflection he recognized the soulful chanting of a young man. The chant was beautiful, the voice like silk caressing his skin, yet it haunted him because it released a sadness within him he had never recognized before. He lay prone on his stomach, not daring to reveal himself, not daring to interrupt the spectacle below. He craved to see it, whereas until then he had only heard it. But he also craved to explore the sadness that the chanting evoked within him. It was a sadness magnified by his recognizing the magnificent chanter was none other than his son Ishmael. He did not know if he would have felt the haunting sadness had the chanter been a stranger rather than his own.

Ishmael was on his knees and he clasped his hands together under his chin, with his elbows tight against the sides of his chest. He arched his back like a tightly-wound stringed instrument and opened his eyes wide while gazing at the crescent moon. The moon's milky light illuminated his delicate features. His chant was rhythmic, his voice was husky yet at times shrill. It was a plaintive wail that pierced the ramparts to Abram's weeping soul and coaxed the shivers out of his core.

Abram thought: "My heart aches like it has never before. My pain even exceeds the sadness I felt for my father when we were cast out of Ur, and I never imagined I would ever feel a greater sadness than that." But Abram could not tear himself away from his son's supplications that were an ode to the moon. And he listened to the searing, accusatory words emanating from the boy's soul because they demanded to be heard and by none other than the father who bears responsibility for such sorrow and pain.

And the boy's song oozed from the crevices of his hurting soul:

You shall never abandon me.
In you I place my vulnerable trust.
I shall bask in your milky light.
I shall honor your comforting glow.
I shall worship you from crescent to crescent.
And in your fullness in between.
I shall bow in deference to your wisdom.
I shall bow to you in defiance of all others.
And my generations shall be your acolytes.
Never to my father's god.
Never to my father's benefactor.
Because he is not mine.

And then Abram came to know his sadness because it revealed its innermost self to him. Abram reflected on his youth: "When I was a young lad in Ur my father lived vicariously through me. I was his deliverance by proxy. When he believed I would be a priest, it was not I ascending to the priesthood, it was he. I was not overcoming the stigma of being Habiru, it was he. My father blurred the distinction between father and son. But how tragic it is I am now not living vicariously through my beautiful living boy, but instead through an as of yet faceless, unborn son." And then Abram knew a betrayal of a son is so much more grievous than a betrayal of a father, and he became inconsolable in his sadness and despair.

Abram thought: "My beautiful boy's sinking heart is my own now. By a mirrored pain our two hearts become one. The unbearable sadness I now feel is none other than my son's own, and it is a pain I inflicted on him which I now experience as my own. I am now living vicariously through him, but it is not as my father lived it through me. My father experienced my joys and victories as his own, but I only experience my own son's despair and pain."

Ishmael's prostration before the moon was a perverse idolatry that went against the grain of everything Abram believed and taught. He had formed his identity by rejecting the idolatry of Ur. and his outspoken defiance of such things inflicted the wrath of an empire on his household. Under other

The Moon Reflects Our Soul

circumstances he would have been furious and punished Ishmael, but he could not now harbor such antagonism. "Yahvah inflicted me with a troubling dream tonight for a reason," he thought, "and it compelled me to stand here and experience my son's despair as mine."

Deep in the desert, far beyond this spectacle of father and son, he noticed a phantom, shadowy figure galloping across the desert floor. It was the figure of his troubling dream, but it was a fleeting sight and then it was gone. He thought: "Is the moon's milky-white so strong it reveals to me the denizens of the desert's darkness from so far away? And it even reveals the shadowy denizens of my haunted dreams." But through this foreboding sighting, mirroring his ominous dream, he became emboldened to reveal himself to Ishmael. "If such a shadowy figure has revealed itself to me in this darkness," he thought, "then I must reveal myself to my son, for I must not be an unseen, shadowy figure in his life." And then Abram stood up to his full height and walked down the other side of the sand dune towards Ishmael - his suffering and now rebellious son.

The walk down was steep as the crawl up. He governed his steps, fearing the steepness would topple him and he would then tumble towards his son. "It would be unseemly," Abram thought, "for a young son to see his father in such a hapless state." Ishmael's prosecutory wail fell silent when Abram reached the middle of his descent. "He sees me now," Abram thought. Ishmael saw a shadowy, phantom figure approaching him down the sand dune, but its face was hidden in the darkness. He became alarmed and leapt to his feet and then bolted towards the open desert.

"Ishmael, Ishmael, don't flee, it's your father...it's me," Abram shouted. Ishmael abandoned his escape as his fear of immediate danger evaporated. But he now feared his father's wrath for his rebellious idolatry, and he felt his soul exposed and vulnerable for having revealed his anger and angst. He stopped and waited for Abram, who was now at the foot of the sand dune. Ishmael now saw his father's face and he was puzzled he could not detect any anger or ill will, but only pain, sorrow and compassion. "I will let him come to me," Ishmael thought. "Now is the time for a confrontation I will force if I must. I've avoided it in the past because I was intimidated and afraid. I also feared its consequences on my suffering mother."

When Abram reached him, Ishmael saw his tears. Their eyes locked for a long, pregnant moment. Ishmael's large, chocolate eyes with the long and dark, feminine lashes, radiated uncertainty and vulnerability. In that moment Ishmael seemed to Abram like a young deer crossing the path of a menacing lion and frozen with uncertainty, unsure if the lion is hungry or sated.

The Moon Reflects Our Soul

"He's just a young boy of thirteen," Abram thought. "It's an injustice he should shoulder such pain and feelings of abandonment. He deserves to feel he is the first seed of his father's orchard." Their gaze hung in a precarious balance and was broken when Abram threw his arms around his estranged son and sobbed uncontrollably.

When they broke their long embrace Ishmael said: "Papa, you must think I'm an idol worshiping savage. How long have you been hiding on top of that dune?"

"I am primarily concerned for your safety. I'm your concerned father first of all. Why did you come here tonight? Don't you know the desert is a dangerous place at night? Full of brigands and cutthroats. Did your mother permit this?" A rivulet of tears streamed down Abram's cheeks and he wiped his face with his left sleeve.

"No, she has no idea I'm here. I beg you, you must believe me. I snuck out of our tent earlier tonight while she slept. Papa, please don't be angry with her. She loves me and she loves you so much too. I could not hope for a better mother, and you could not hope for a better wife."

Abram was taken aback by Ishmael's pleading on his mother's behalf. He wanted so desperately to broach the subject of Ishmael's feelings of abandonment and disenfranchisement revealed by his ode to the crescent moon, but he could not bear to do so. His heart pounded and his voice quivered. "Why do you feel you must grant the moon your worship? I don't want anger to soil our bond, Ishmael. My question is a sincere one. Please believe that."

"Papa, I didn't want you to see this tonight. Why did you come here?"

"I had a troubling dream. A nightmare of sorts. I could not sleep. But please be honest with me, Ishmael. Have you been coming here to worship at the alter of the moon every night?"

Ishmael hesitated. He appeared stunned when Abram told him of his dream and Abram did not understand why. Ishmael looked down at his feet and then slowly met Abram's gaze. "Not every night. But this isn't my first. I come a few times every moon."

"For how many moons?"

"Only for the last two."

"And your mother has no idea?"

"She has no idea. I told you so."

"Have I failed you as a father, Ishmael? Have I not taught you Yahvah's truth? Since you were crawling on all fours I've shown you Yahvah's love."

"No Papa, you've told me about Yahvah's love, you haven't shown it to me." Ishmael's words stung Abram.

The Moon Reflects Our Soul

"You are courageous to challenge me. You remind me of myself as a lad in Ur when I spoke out against my father's idolatry."

"Thank you Papa. I'm your son. I'm strong willed like you. And I've been toughened by the rugged desert. I'm a citizen of the desert. I want to be proud of being your first-born son."

Abram realized the obvious. The root cause of Ishmael's idolatrous rebellion is not a belief in the divinity of the moon. That is the symptom, not the cause. But Abram's ploy was to attack the symptom and compel Ishmael to shed light on the cause.

"The moon is not a divine principality, Ishmael. It simply reflects the glory of Yahvah."

"Is that how you look at my mother, your wife? Does she just reflect the divine glory of your Sarai?"

Abram was stunned and he could not find the words to respond. "Such stinging words from a fresh-faced boy," he thought.

"I'm no longer a little, oblivious boy," Ishmael said, as if reading Abram's thoughts. "I see your infatuation for Sarai, but you barely tolerate my suffering mother. That's not fair, papa. That's not right. I weep more for her broken heart than for mine. No, I weep for her heart like mine because we share the same heart. My mother and I, we live in your household, yours and Sarai's, but we live separate lives from you. You told me stories of the purebreds in Ur who considered you a second-class citizen, but you and Sarai are the purebreds of Yahvah's empire and my mother and I are the second-class citizens now."

The moonlight glistened off Ishmael's tears, and for the first time Abram saw himself reflected off his son's flooded eyes. Abram maintained his dumbfounded silence. Ishmael was his teacher now.

"I'm sorry papa, I didn't intend to confront you and pour out my angst and my grievances. My meditations under the moon were meant to be locked in a secret chamber inside me, but now that you've discovered this chamber and witnessed my pain I feel I must unlock it."

"Ishmael, why is it the sun's strong light exposes our bodies but the moon's milky-white exposes our soul?"

"Do you see the broken shards of my spirit now, papa? Do you understand my discontent?"

Abram thought: "He speaks with a wisdom far beyond his years. He again reminds me of myself at that age."

"Ishmael...I don't know what to say."

"There is more the moon's milky-white wants to expose of my spirit," Ishmael said. "I will lay my spirit bare tonight to you, here and now, and

The Moon Reflects Our Soul

the crescent moon will be a heavenly witness."

Out yonder, in the murky depths, the phantom, shadowy figure reappeared, galloping across the desert floor. Abram's gaze followed it, as did Ishmael's.

"You see it too Ishmael? But I thought it was only the denizen of my dreams."

"Papa, I too had such a dream on many nights. On each occasion I woke in the middle of the night and I felt a compulsion to come to this spot, under this glorious moon, and pour out my spirit and my pain."

And then Abram understood why Ishmael was shocked when he learned of Abram's dream - they shared the same dream. And he also understood that for Ishmael the moon was a proxy for the kind of father he so desperately craved - not the distant and unapproachable Abram.

"And on each of my outings," Ishmael said, "I've seen this haunting, shadowy figure far out in the desert, racing like a gazelle in full gallop. It's the shadowy figure that appears in my dreams."

"We seem to have been compelled to come to this spot and meet tonight. But this is the first night I have experienced this dream."

"Papa, I must share something else with you."

"Yes, I know. I am listening Ishmael. I am listening to you like I never did before."

"Two moons ago I overheard a conversation Sarai had with my mother."

Abram realized nothing good can come out of such a conversation and he braced himself for the storm.

"It was a few days after that awful heat we had. It was the day after those three silk traders departed."

"What did Sarai tell your mother now?" Abram had an inkling of what Sarai might have said to Hagar.

"She gloated to my dear mother that one of the three men promised her she would bear you a son, an inheritor."

"She said what? Ishmael...no..."

"She laughed in my saintly mother's face and swore to her I would never inherit your household."

"And it was the night you had your first dream, I'm sure."

"Yes, that was the first night."

"Ishmael, there appears to be divine intervention in the synchronicity of our dreams."

"Now that I know you've had the same dream, it appears to be true. But papa, who is this shadowy figure?"

"Listen to me Ishmael. I know Sarai has been less than hospitable to

The Moon Reflects Our Soul

your mother. But I am the head of the household. I will give you your birthright as my first born. I will find a way."

"And one more thing, papa. I overheard Sarai ask my mother to leave and take me with her."

"Leave? Leave what?"

"Your household."

"What? No, I will never permit that Ishmael. Never!"

"Papa, you've told us many times the story of your youth in Ur, that you always felt like a citizen of a different realm. But after these nights of pouring my spirit to the moon, I now know how you must have felt. I feel it too now."

"What Ishmael, what do you feel?"

"I don't feel like a citizen of your household. I don't belong. Sarai is right in her own sordid way. My mother and I belong elsewhere, in a different realm, under the moon, from crescent to crescent and its fullness in between. I think tonight is the last dream, papa, mine and yours. I don't need to come here at night anymore."

Abram wept like never before. His heart ached for his beautiful, innocent boy.

"If you examine your soul you will know I am right. There is no other way. Dear papa, when the dream visited me tonight, the phantom in the shadows revealed to me something wonderful."

Abram reached out and cradled Ishmael's soft, boyish hands in his rough hands that had felt pain and exhilaration, victories and defeats, but had never faltered from his yearning for Yahvah.

"He revealed to me that my destiny and the destiny of my descendants is to be like the majestic and powerful wild donkeys that roam the desert. They are free, papa, free. They are not slaves as my mother is a slave to Sarai. We will be nomadic and free. We will be independent from the shackles of society and we will roam the desert's idyllic space and worship the moon. But papa, the moon will be a reflection of Yahvah for us and we will worship Yahvah from crescent to crescent and his fullness in between. We will know Yahvah in this way."

Abram now knew it is Yahvah speaking to him through his boy. And he sat at Ishmael's feet with legs crossed and head bowed. "I will not challenge you Ishmael. Please enlighten me with the fullness of what Yahvah has revealed to you."

"This time next year Sarai will free my mother from her servitude, but for this freedom Sarai will demand a steep price. She will cast us out into the desert. My half brother will be born by then. Papa, you must not challenge Sarai's will, as cruel as it might seem...as cruel as it is, but it is Yahvah's intent that matters, not Sarai's malice. And you must never tell her of this revelation I received. Not to Sarai and not to my mother above all. I will let Yahvah reveal it to her after Sarai banishes us from your household. He will reveal it to her as he did to me, under the crescent moon. You must let these events unfold as they may and when Sarai banishes us you must happily let me and my mother go. Please be assured we will travel the desert for the rest of our lives under the guidance and protection of Yahvah's reflection off the moon. And the last he revealed to me is a time far off in a future millennia hence. It will be the time of the great convergence in which the thirst of your descendants shall finally be quenched. And during those destined days my half brother's house and mine will become One."

The Breeze of Yahvah: The Desert Beckons At Night

Three moons had passed since the night Yahvah compelled Abram to connect with Ishmael in the open desert under the crescent moon. On the third full moon, Abram could not sleep that night. Sarai lay beside him, sleeping tight. It was the middle of the night, a time as far after sunset as before dawn. The heat of day succumbed to the chill of night, yet he felt his tent's warmth. Abram was drenched in a hot sweat, due more to his restless soul than warmth's embrace. The milky white of the full moon was streaming in like an uninvited yet welcomed guest. He remembered a time long ago and far away. It was a time following the first embrace, when Yahvah thrust his outstretched arm out to him from a place deep within his essence. And then too, the moon's milky-white comforted him after his soul's delight. The moon's light had not stirred this feeling within him since that time, and the oddly familiar sensation he now felt brought shivers up his spine and a sense of impending revelation.

He thought: "Isn't it funny how two events of my life that are far apart in space and time can be connected as one? Is there a symmetry to my life or is the symmetry divine revelation's own? The first revelation immediately preceded the moon's milky-white shining on the shards of my core. Perhaps the last shall now immediately follow the same such light. Yahvah knows the longing of my spirit. Yahvah knows my heart aches for his voice, the most exquisite poetry, the most beautiful melody."

His soul now soared like an angel in full flight. "I am ready Yahvah," he thought, "I am ready for the grand destiny you have surely prepared for me, my household and my times."

Abram quickly stripped of his sweat drenched tunic, wiped his body with a fresh towel and slipped into a clean tunic. He put on his wool boots and slipped into a wool overcoat. A night's desert outing would chill his bones unless he dresses warmly. Before he left the tent he kissed Sarai as she slept.

"I have to go out into the desert my Sarai," he whispered to her silence, "Yahvah is galloping across the desert floor tonight, and all the pretty virgins run away from him in delightful terror; yet he is seeking not their body but their soul. I will match his gallop my Sarai. I will follow him to his desire."

Abram walked briskly across the compound, being careful not to waken any of his household. The chill of the desert wind cut across his cheeks. There was not a sound in the air but the wind's gentle howl. The desert landscape was milky with the full moon's light. The stars could not be seen

The Breeze of Yahvah: The Desert Beckons At Night

due to the moon's upstaging of their light.

He headed towards the camel stables at the far end of the compound. On the way he passed by Hagar's tent and he peeked in. He felt ashamed for doing this, but he felt compelled. Hagar's tent was considerably smaller and less ornate than the tent he shared with his favored Sarai. Hagar shared her tent with their son Ishmael and they were sleeping soundly that night. Abram was mesmerized by the rhythm of their breathing. He felt a great yearning for their embrace at this moment more than ever before, and this contrast saddened him. He longed for an idyllic world devoid of such sadness and heartache. He continued listening to the rhythm of their breaths and he noticed their breaths would periodically but fleetingly converge to become as one and then, after a few breaths in unison, diverge again to become two, like the rhythm of two pendulums synchronizing briefly and then parting once again. When mother and son became one breath he craved they remain as one, as they once did in mother's womb. The moon's light beaming through the opaque flap at tent's top revealed Hagar's oval face and she looked so beautiful in the soft, milky light. Abram became mesmerized by how she was embracing the pillows to her bosom. She was tightly curled around them. This was her lover's embrace and she seemed desperately lonely to Abram. The moon's light revealed to Abram more texture and nuance. Hagar seemed resigned to her loneliness. Abram thought to be resigned to loneliness is so much more tragic than to be lonely yet brimming with optimism and hope for better. Abram knew Hagar deserves so much more than he can offer her. His heart now ached and he silently wept because her heart's aches became his own. Abram again thought, as he did that night under the full moon when he, for the first time, truly came to know his son: "Yahvah, why is it the sun's strong light exposes our body but the moon's gentle milky-white exposes our soul?"

When Abram reached the camel stables he visited his own trusted camel. What an elegant creature he was, tall with long, sinewy legs and lithe muscles rippling and undulating like the elongated waves of a mighty river. The camel was sleeping with his knees tucked under him. When Abram got within arm's reach of him, he woke up and appeared distressed by the unexpected intrusion at that time of night. When he saw Abram his composure relaxed. He was comforted by the sight of his master.

"Wake up my friend," Abram said, "we have a journey ahead of us tonight. Yahvah is expecting us tonight in the depths of the desert, under the milky moon." Abram quickly placed a riding saddle on the camel's back, in between the two humps. The saddle was lined with deep pockets along the bottom on both sides, except for two gaps accommodating the

The Breeze of Yahvah: The Desert Beckons At Night

placement of the rider's legs. He filled each of two pockets, one on each side, with a canteen of fresh drinking water. He also filled two other pockets with a bag of flat-bread that Sarai's servants had baked that day, and a container of pureed, roasted chickpeas blended with olive oil, sesame seeds and spices. He had enough provisions for a full day past that night. But he intended to return just before the break of dawn, before anyone in the compound wakes. But providing for the possibility he would not be back until past the time Sarai wakes, he decided to let Eliezer know of his departure.

Eliezer was surprised to be wakened in the depth of the night. "What is it Abram, are there any dangers tonight?" He remembered long ago being wakened in the depth of the night, not by Abram but by the escaped messenger who told Abram of the kidnapping of Lot, Abram's nephew by his deceased brother Haran. Lot had been kidnapped by the hordes of the marauding kings. Lot and his household had amicably parted ways with Abram's household several years before and had settled in the lush valley by the Jordan River to the east. A few nights later, Abram led over a hundred of his most capable warriors in a daring night raid and freed Lot from his captors.

Abram sensed Eliezer's concern. "Nothing is wrong Eliezer. I'm making my way into the desert tonight. I'll be back before the break of dawn, but if I'm not back by the time Sarai wakes then please inform her of my departure and that I will be shortly returning. I've taken enough water and food to last me past the next night. I don't want her to worry needlessly."

"What business do you have with the desert tonight? Is it wise to be making the trek alone? Perhaps it should wait for daylight or another time? Or perhaps I should accompany you."

"No Eliezer, Yahvah is out there this night. He is galloping across the desert floor tonight and I must seek him alone and negotiate my destiny."

"Is tonight then the night you have been waiting for all these years? How do you know it?"

"It's the voices from within whispering to me."

"Abram, can a mere man negotiate with our lord Yahvah?" Eliezer's green eyes twinkled by the moonlight. Abram noticed how his trimmed, dark beard complimented his chiseled, handsome features rather than obscure them, like a fine silk robe compliments an athletic physique. Abram thought: "Oh to be young again, but I was never handsome as Eliezer."

"Have you not taught your household all these years that we must all be in submission to Yahvah's will? Is it not sheer arrogance for a man to negotiate with Yahvah?"

Abram reflected momentarily on Eliezer's words. "Yes Eliezer, we are all to be in submission, but in submission to what?" Abram paused for Eliezer to reflect on his question. Eliezer seemed puzzled by Abram's question because there did not seem to be any mystery or a knotty complexity to it.

Many times Eliezer had participated in discussions where the men in the compound would sit around a fire, under a moonlit sky, and ruminate on the nature of Yahvah and the ambitious project of which they were all a part. Some nights a hundred men were seated around the fire while on other nights a smaller, more intimate group gathered in deep discussions. They would often build deep cognitive mazes of questions and attempt a path towards new insights into the nature of the divine. They were all members of a revolutionary new sect. They were the first monotheists. They were the first Yahvahists. Where was Yahvahism leading them? You could ask two Yahvahists a question about any theological matter and get three answers. During those magical nights around the fire the men would drink copious quantities of red wine and celebrate Yahvah until the break of dawn. As the levels of wine in their flasks diminished their collective level of merriment and spiritual euphoria heightened and they would dance with abandon in a circle around the crackling fire that was really a proxy for Yahvah. Their joyful laughter boomed as thunder from the heavens. Their arms locked around their neighbors' shoulders, their feet stomped the desert floor ecstatically, rhythmically, and their voices wailed soulful lamentations to Yahvah. For a frozen moment in a timeless eternity they became a collective soul. They became intoxicated by a transcendence knowing not time nor space but only the white-eyed womb of Creation.

Eliezer answered Abram's question, but he knew Abram too well not to suspect the naivety of his answer. "Submission to what? To Yahvah, who else?"

Abram was the spiritual leader and mentor of his household. It was in this capacity he gazed into Eliezer's eyes and answered him. "Eliezer, it is to the Divine Dance we must submit. Two dancers are not in submission to each other nor to any master. They are in submission to the Dance. Yahvah is the primordial Dance."

"So then it's to Yahvah we must submit. After all, you said it's to the Dance we submit and this is no other than Yahvah."

"But Eliezer, when we negotiate with Yahvah, that is the dance, like two primordial lovers swaying to and fro in perfect harmony, in submission to their Dance. All of Creation is such a Dance, the Dance of the ineffable white-eyed H with itself. Do not be in submission to created things, that is idolatry. Be in submission to the divine Dance of Creation."

Abram paused, letting Eliezer digest what he had said. Eliezer was mesmerized and his silence begged to learn more.

"Eliezer, YHVH is not the ineffable god per se, but rather a word which explains the means by which Creation emerges from the ineffable H. That's a very deep distinction I must stress." Abram paused, waiting for the go ahead from Eliezer to continue. He did not want to overwhelm him. Eliezer gently, almost imperceptibly, nodded his head and Abram continued. "YHVH is Creation cocooned within the ineffable H and inseparable from it. Just like the analogy of the mirrors within the outermost mirror I've been teaching since my youth in Ur. YHVH corresponds to the entire complex which is composed of the cocooned mirrors."

"I see," Eliezer said, "YHVH is not Creation outside of the ineffable H but Creation as an intimate and inevitable part of the ineffable H."

"Exactly, Creation is not a choice the ineffable H makes but rather an inevitable emanation from the H. The Dance must be danced. There is no cause to Creation. There cannot exist the ineffable H standing alone, just as there cannot exist a blank mirror. With H must be YHVH. The ineffable H must curve back unto itself and create and create."

"The emergent Y."

"Yes, the emergent Y. Creation is like an infinitely powerful volcanic explosion that cannot be contained by any force. However, this is an explosion in an abstract sense. It's a semantic explosion. From the ineffable void of meaninglessness must inevitably emanate meaningfulness. From Chaos must emanate Creation."

"Wow, just wow," Eliezer, said, "that's such an amazing thought; but I suspect I haven't fully understood it yet, like a fine wine layered with subtle flavors and which cannot be fully appreciated until these flavors complete their dance with your palate and with each other." Eliezer paused and shut his eyes. He was in deep and joyful reflection. "I never imagined there's so much more than what I understood previously. It's like I've been living all my life inside a cave and only seeing the shadows on the wall of a greater reality outside the cave. Or for the first time perceiving the meaning between the lines."

"And Eliezer, is not the meaning between the lines far deeper and richer than the lines themselves? Is not the very purpose of the lines to give birth to the negative space of the meaning between them?"

"Yes Abram, I see more deeply now than ever before. The divine doesn't just exist within the void of meaninglessness, it is the void of meaninglessness. The letter H is unknowable by definition rather than by design. It is the source of meaning, not its recipient."

"You have understood well Eliezer. The H cannot be said to possess Existence because Existence is an emanation from the H. Existence is the Y that emanates when the H reflects upon itself.

"The H is neither this nor that," Eliezer said, "neither good nor bad, neither there nor here. The H is all those things in one yet not one of those things in all."

"I'm elated you've understood so well. Eliezer, you've flavored my words so eloquently. Creation is holy and sacred because it is inseparable from the H. But it's the totality of Creation that is sacred and not any one of its parts taken in isolation. When we offer worship to Yahvah, it is to the totality of Creation we offer it. However, worshiping any one aspect of Creation, be it the sun or the wind or any other, in isolation is sheer idolatry. It's like elevating the status of an inner mirror and disregarding it's an emanation of the outer mirror, and not something with an independent existence."

"I must not keep you any longer. Go out into the desert and negotiate with Yahvah. I will not sleep tonight. I will lie under the moon and the stars and meditate and reflect on what you've taught me tonight. And when you're back I will organize another meeting under the moon and the stars and we shall all rejoice around a bonfire and celebrate this wisdom we've carved out tonight."

"I'll be happy for you to do so, and you're right that I should be leaving very soon or I'll never make it back before dawn. But our discussion isn't complete. There's more weighing on my mind."

"If you have more to teach me about Yahvah then who am I to push you out into the desert? You have my undivided and rapt attention."

"The three traders taught me there are two kinds of submissions: active and passive. When you dance with your partner that is passive submission."

"And what is the active form of submission?"

"Wrestling."

Eliezer scratched his head and squinted. "Wrestling?"

"Bear with me, Eliezer."

"Please continue Abram. I've much to learn tonight."

"I'm learning too. This thing the three traders taught me I am only truly appreciating tonight. In teaching you I have also learned. Now, when I negotiate with YHVH tonight I will not be disrespecting him but I will challenge him. That too is a form of resonance."

"Like two dancers swaying to and fro?"

"Have you seen those wrestling spectacles? No, I suppose you haven't, you were born in Haran. When my brothers and I lived in Ur our father would take us to the wrestling matches every Spring end of week. They were held in the arena by the town square."

"It must have been quite a spectacle. I have only ever seen two men wrestle when they each wanted the other's throat."

"That's not wrestling. That's brawling. Those were spectacles of quite a different sort. There's an art to wrestling and sometimes, when the art is practiced to perfection, a smaller and weaker man can defeat a larger foe."

"That's due to a greater proficiency in wrestling, I suppose."

"Ah yes, but it's the nature of this proficiency that's the crux of the matter here. A weaker man cannot master a stronger foe as a slave owner masters his slaves. Instead he must cease aspiring for control and instead unpretentiously engage in the Divine Dance, or I should say the Divine Wrestle. Wrestling is also a dance of sorts because your weaknesses must resonate with your opponent's strengths. The weaker wrestler doesn't overpower his wrestling partner, he negotiates with him in an abstract sense. When I go out into the depths of the desert tonight I will be a God Wrestler. I will challenge Yahvah, and in so doing I will resonate with him. We are all God Wrestlers, Eliezer. That's the method of our Free Will."

"If dancing and wrestling are two sides of the same coin then what should we call the coin?"

"It's a coin called Resonance."

"So when is it wrestling and when is it dancing?"

"Imagine a great sailing ship cutting its way across a stormy ocean. The ship's expansive sails are made taut by the powerful winds slamming into them. These winds threaten to capsize the great ship or run it aground. But the captain has charted a specific course towards a land beyond the horizon. In order to reach this land the ship's sails must wrestle with the mighty winds and leverage their destructive power."

"And what does a dance with the winds achieve?"

"If there's no specific land to reach. If the sails simply resonate with the winds so that no harm can come to the ship then that's the dance of the sails with the wind. The ship wobbles on the stormy waters, with the ebb and flow of the winds, and the captain achieves inner contentment with any direction the ship takes as long as no harm comes to it."

"So the Dance is closer to unconditional contentment, the kind that freely bubbles from within. The Wrestle is a creative principle focused on a goal."

"Exactly, and they're both forms of resonance. You engage in the Divine Dance when you need to reach inner contentment irrespective of your external conditions. But you become a God Wrestler when you create order out of Chaos in your environment. God Wrestling is creative energy. It is an outward expansion. The Divine Dance is an inner contraction. I call it a tzimtzum. God Wrestling - the birthing of Creation - is the abstract feminine principle. God Dancing - contraction into the H - is the abstract male principle."

"Hmm...so YHVH is the primordial God Wrestling because Creation explodes out, but the return to the state of a naked H is the Divine Dance."

"That's brilliant. Yes Eliezer, the H is also a God Wrestler. It's the H wrestling with itself. And within the H are the inner reflections, the order out of Chaos, and they themselves are also God Wrestlers. You see, to wrestle with god is to wrestle with yourself."

"You said earlier that Creation, the Y, is inevitable, so how can there exist a naked H?"

Abram ruminated on Eliezer's question. He thought: "Truly the student is the teacher. Eliezer's penetrating questions are releasing my creative energy. We are truly wrestling with each other and with ourselves."

Abram had a powerful insight. "Eliezer, imagine you are looking at a painting of a gorgeous sunset in a far away, idyllic land. It evokes powerful emotions in you. You perceive beauty and artistic genius. You feel a longing for that land and a wistful poignancy due to its absence from your life. As you stare at this painting you enter a state of consciousness where you no longer see the beauty or feel these emotions, all you perceive now is a featureless, white-eyed coat of paint. You have peeled away the meaning created by the painting. That is the naked H. The shards of paint that have evoked powerful emotions within you are still there on the canvas, but your consciousness has contracted within itself and does not perceive these emanating emotions, it just perceives the source."

"Abram, I think your ideas have a universal application. They're not restricted just to an intimacy with Yahvah but also can be very effective in surmounting all of life's struggles. You do that by not trying to overpower your adversities and challenges and instead resonate with them either through dancing or wrestling. Dancing grants you immunity from the ill effects of your adversities. Wrestling grants you the power to leverage your adversities and then you create and create."

"Ah yes Eliezer, you are quite correct about that but also very wrong. You are making a false dichotomy. You are compartmentalizing Yahvah. Yahvah is the beauty of a melody. Yahvah is the joy of perfect symmetry, of soul piercing poetry. The Divine Dance of Astronomy. All these are also Yahvah. When you dance towards enlightenment, or wrestle with your life struggles, you are composing the most beautiful melody, the most inspiring poetry. Don't build walls around Yahvah. Yahvah is not confined atop the ziggurat or within the walls of a house of worship. As you dance or wrestle with your struggles, look into their eyes and when you see your struggles as your struggles see themselves reflected off your eyes you will then know you are submitting to Yahvah."

The Navel Of Creation: A Loop In Eternity

The desert is a study of dueling extremes. The day's heat wrestles night's impending chill, yet there is no victor, the pendulum forever swings.

During a summer's midday the desert smolders like the ashes of a freshly extinguished bonfire. The air is thick as honey and the heat envelopes and coddles your soul yet ravages your flesh. Your skin must be completely veiled from the burning sun by a thin layer of porous fabric. Any exposed skin on your face vibrates like the water in a pot just before the boil.

But once the sun sets, the temperature plummets. Soon the chill of night persecutes the heat of day, but for a fleeting moment, as day's dominion gives way to night's control, the two eternal foes become locked in a titanic struggle and neither surrenders. It is during that ephemeral moment, a semantic space pregnant with transition, that the desert is neither hot nor cold, neither this nor that, and yet during that fleeting moment the desert is all those things in one yet not one of those things in all.

Inevitably the chill overpowers desert's heat and the titanic struggle is no more. The heat of day becomes legend's lore but surely will return once more. For now the night chill is unbound and free to roam.

A man not protected from the desert's chill of night can die from extended exposure. The first symptom is a numbing of his extremities. His fingers first and then his nose become insensitive to touch. The mighty desert wind slams against his naked flesh and it soon feels more like the burn of fire than the chill of ice. Such can be the desert at night.

Abram could feel the cold wind on his face. He shut his eyes and braced himself against his camel as an unusually strong gale came howling from between the sand dunes and slammed into him. He was cocooned within his coat and the gale's chill could do no harm. He was heading mostly north and the full moon was high up in the sky a little to his right side. It was almost midnight when he left the compound and he was now a short camel ride into his journey. He wondered how far into the desert night he would have to travel before he could know Yahvah again. It had been thirteen years since the last time Yahvah spoke to him. That was when Ishmael was born.

Abram thought: "before Ishmael was born I yanked my household out of Haran because Yahvah commanded me to go to the land of Canaan. He promised me I will have descendants numerous as the stars under the heavens or the sands as dust on the ocean shores."

The Navel Of Creation: A Loop In Eternity

When Abram was a little past his mid years his household was in the city of Haran. Yahvah appeared to him in a vision one night under the milky full moon and whispered from within the semantic spaces of Abram's soul: "Long ago I have known the affairs of Man and arranged for your household to be banished from the city of Ur - the city of your thoughtless comforts. I have banished your household from Ur as I banished your kind from the white-eyed garden, the womb of Creation. They ate the fruit from the Tree of Knowledge of Good and evil and knew themselves in Creation's mirror and became a new reflection in the mirror as the others. They became an extension within Yahvah, a mirror within a mirror within another."

Yahvah also whispered from within Abram's soul: "Go within yourself and then out of Haran. Leave behind your parents, your siblings and your bond to this land. But take Sarai and your household with you. I will show you the land of Canaan and you will come to know that land and it will reflect all of your generations now and to come. I banished your kind from the white-eyed garden of Creation and then banished you, Abram, from Ur and now from Haran. I promise you Abram I shall never again force you to tear your soul from another land. Not for now or your generations to come. The land of Canaan will forever be inside their hearts even when it is not under their feet."

Abram was venturing deeper into the desert and, as his household receded behind him, he hoped his destiny was approaching. He was in deep reflection and he became oblivious to the chill of the wind.

"Why have I felt such a sense of destiny since my youth, and I'm sure for all my years to come. Why me and not another? Am I really destined for such a mission in life?" The more he thought of it the more it had the feel of the absurd. But not the banal absurdity of the shallowest lie, rather the provocative absurdity of the deepest truth.

He had been riding his camel for a quarter of the night and the full moon was now to his left, to the west, halfway between the heavens above his head and that unreachable fold where heaven dances with land. The moon was tracing a slow arc that would soon take it behind the tall cliffs nearby. The fierce wind was no more and in its place was a gentle breeze. If not for the breeze the desert would have been so perfectly quiet its silence would be loud. The comforting whisper of the breeze flirted with Abram's ears. It seemed to Abram like a benevolent but unseen spirit guiding him to his destiny.

Abram was jolted from his reverie when he had an odd feeling that something had changed in the desert. He had that anguished feeling one gets when trying to remember a word that is on the tip of the tongue. He felt alarmed and he looked to his left, then to his right. He looked behind him and then to the heavens. That is when he realized what had changed. When he looked above he could not see the moon anymore. The desert lost its milky glow and became pitch black. The multitudes of stars now pierced the heavens because their light was no longer upstaged by the moon's milky white. They cascaded across the heavens like ribbons of white silk. At first he did not understand where the moon had disappeared and he felt alarmed at the mystery at hand. He again swiveled his neck above and behind, to his right then his left. He saw the outline of the tall cliffs of sand and rock veiled in the darkness and he realized what had happened. The moon's arc had finally traced a path behind the tall cliffs. The moon's upstaging light was trapped and the stars were now visible in the heavens in full glory.

Abram craned his neck and looked up at the twinkling stars directly above him. The gentle breeze kissed his face and whispered intimately in his ears. The whisper was at his ears and yet it seemed to fill the entire desert void from his ears and out to a distance beyond where the sky, like coal, meets the unseen desert floor. He felt so alive now and all his senses, both of the body, mind and soul, were heightened. He felt the desert's chill etched on his face and he took a deep breath. He felt the strong chill in his nose and just above the roof of his mouth next to his throat. He remembered now, in vivid detail, when he last knew Yahvah. It was a night such as this. He had not felt so deeply connected to that experience for many years. Imagine a man meeting a woman with a beauty so great the mind cannot fathom but only the soul. When the woman is gone only the memory of her beauty remains and it pales. Likewise it is to behold Yahvah and then only for the memories to remain.

Abram reflected: "All these years in Canaan I thought I remembered what it truly was like to know Yahvah but I only retained a shadow of it. A man cannot sustain such epiphany for long lest he release his earthly bond. But I feel it intimately now. I feel the euphoria building in my spirit. The hairs at the back of my neck and of my arms are erect and goose bumps are sizzling my flesh. But most of all I feel my spirit soar with a feeling of the connectedness of all that exists."

It was shortly before he left Haran that he last had a direct encounter with Yahvah. Then too, he gazed up at the multitudes of stars in the heavens and Yahvah whispered from the semantic spaces in Abram's soul: "These multitudes of stars you now see in the heavens are as the multitudes your generations to come shall be. Look below your feet at the desert dust and that too is as the multitudes of your generations to come. I will make a great people from you and whosoever favors them I will greatly bless but whosoever condemns them I will harshly curse and cause to disappear from the Civilization of Man."

The intimacy he now felt with that experience, both in Haran and before that too when just a very young man in Ur, created a tension in his soul that he begged to be released. He craved to know Yahvah again, like a drowning man craves air. He screamed out to Yahvah to appear before him but his screams echoed against the desert cliffs and returned to him flavored by these cliffs and they too were craving for Yahvah to appear. It was like listening to an enthralling tale of adventure and woe and waiting breathlessly for a climactic resolution that always appears to be imminent, yet never comes.

"I know now Yahvah," Abram wailed. "I know of the bliss to come. I can smell it, I can breathe it and I must have it once more."

Abram yanked the reins of the camel and then, once the camel came to a halt, he tapped twice the back of his neck in quick succession. This signaled the camel to drop to the ground and sit. The camel tucked his legs under his body and Abram dismounted and walked a few steps away. He lay on his back on the desert floor. His arms were straight down his body by his sides. He focused on the stars above and counted his breaths. One, two, three, four, five...he did not move a muscle and his breathing deepened. The ribbons of stars in the sky no longer appeared to him as the unknowable denizens of another world. They now seemed to be the denizens of his soul. Abram reflected on his own thoughts, like a snake eating its own tail. His breathing became more relaxed and deliberate. He reflected on the rhythmic expansion and contraction of his chest. Six, seven, eight...he reflected on his altered perceptions. "I am lying here looking at the distant stars above but I am also with them and looking at the desert floor below. But I am not in two places at once, rather two places are at once in me. I can no longer clearly distinguish that which once was from that which will become. I can no longer clearly distinguish my inner world from my outer. My image in the mirror is fading but why should that be?"

Abram wrestled with this question because he wanted desperately to know. "How does the world of my previous perceptions arise from the world towards which I am heading now?" But it was not Abram asking that question, it was an intermediate perception which has one foot in a world woven from the fabric of space and time and another in a world pregnant with space and time.

Abram had an epiphany. "I now understand and it's so simple. The perceptions of my mind are one and the same with space and time. My perceptions are the fabric from which are woven the stars above, the ground below and the totality in between. When I lose the perception of space and time I no longer exist as an individual rooted in the here and now. The soul is not woven from the fabric of space and time; the soul is synonymous with the fabric of space and time. There is but one soul shared by all of humanity. When I strike out against the least of humanity, I am striking out against all of humanity. The most sacred directive is to treat all others as you would have them treat you because they are you."

Abram had not yet finished crossing the bridge between these two worlds and what he had now lost in the understanding of the world of space and time he had gained in the world that contains the world of space and time in its pregnant belly. As he was ruminating on the nature of Existence, he was distracted by a peculiar sound in the distance. It was not a conventional sound, it percolated into his consciousness. He became startled and he jumped to his feet. He attempted to locate the direction of the sound but could not because the sound appeared to originate from all directions.

"What is out there?" He yelled. He waited a few heartbeats for a response but there was none. He awoke from his meditations and shook off the sand embedded in his coat. He left behind his camel and walked north, parallel to the cliffs. That was the same direction from which he came on camel-back. The cliffs were only a few minutes walk away.

"If I can't determine the direction of the sound," he thought, "then I will continue north. Perhaps the sound originates from there." He sprinted across the desert floor. His aged bones and muscles protested. His unrestrained excitement fortified him and the flow of time ceased. The sound no longer appeared to originate from all directions, it now appeared to come from just behind the cliffs, a short distance ahead. But the end of the cliffs was a very long distance away, perhaps a half hour by camel ride. He wondered if he needed to reach the end of the cliffs and walk around their corner, to their other side, and then head back. Or perhaps he should climb the tall, steep cliffs and descend to their other side. He could not muster the strength for such a climb.

A short distance ahead he spotted a gap dividing the cliffs in two. He estimated the the gap to be the length of twenty men. The peculiar sound had a transcendent quality that penetrated and nourished his soul, like hot soup penetrates a hard-working man's bones and nourishes his soul on a cold and drizzly winter's day. The sound compelled Abram, more than ever, to know his destiny and to know Yahvah intimately. The sound appeared to

The Navel Of Creation: A Loop In Eternity

originate from around the corner where the gap between the cliffs began. As he approached the gap, he discerned finer detail in the sound and it strengthened his compulsion to discover its source. It was the sound of a multitude of tiny voices, each whispering in a different language of which he understood none. There was something odd yet familiar about these hushed voices. He was certain he had never heard them before but he sensed a disturbing presence in the cobwebs of his memories. Someone, long ago, had described these voices to him but he could not remember who. Abram stopped walking, shut his eyes, and devoured the Chaotic whispers. He had, at first, wondered if the whisperers were communicating only amongst themselves, or were they calling out to him? He neared the sound's source and it then seemed to him, but he did not know why, that each individual whisperer was communicating only with the others. Each whisperer appeared oblivious of the world beyond. This formed a tight, interrelated web of communications. Each whisperer whispered to all the others and they whispered back to him. But by whispering to the others, each whisperer influenced what they whispered back. Therefore, each whisperer was hearing its own essence being whispered back. Each whisperer heard its Self as he was being heard by the others - like a serpent eating its own tail, like the fireflies in the Malay jungle.

Abram also sensed that even as each whisperer was only communicating with the others, and not with the world beyond, that the whole interrelated web, when perceived as a whole and not as its parts, assumed a cohesive identity that was a new entity behaving not as a multitude of whisperers who only knew each other, but as one unified voice that knew Abram. This unified voice was an entity born from the pregnant web of the whisperers. Its identity was not knowable by each individual whisperers but was knowable by Abram. The emergent entity spoke to Abram and compelled him to approach. Abram wondered what mysteries he would witness once he set foot in that gap - the void between the cliffs. He was not alarmed or concerned for his safety; he was awed by the divinity freely seeping out of his soul. He sensed Yahvah more intimately than ever before.

Abram sprinted again towards the gap between the cliffs. He was panting and huffing and he could barely breathe, but he was oblivious to his distress. In just a few more heartbeats he would arrive at that pregnant gap between the cliffs and he would know the source of the whispers and the beckoning entity emerging from within. His heart pounded, blood barreled through his veins like a legion of battle chariots, not just due to physical exertion but also to a manic anticipation of consummating his relationship with the temptress that enticed him. All his senses were honed on this one thing. All he could focus on was reaching and then plunging himself through that gap. He never felt such focus. He was oblivious to the desert chill. He was oblivious to the crushing pressure in his lungs. They were nearing catastrophic failure.

Abram had been waiting for this moment since his school days in Ur. He knew Yahvah twice before, once in Ur during his childhood, during that unforgettable night in his room when the milky light of the full moon shined on his soul and revealed Yahvah. The second time was in Haran, when he had become too comfortable and attached to a land that did not hold his destiny. Yahvah compelled him to leave his comforts behind. Each of these times, Abram knew his full destiny was yet to be revealed, but now he knew the tension in his soul would be finally released, like the tension in a bow flexed to its limits and pregnant with its release. The stars in the heavens were spellbound by Abram's destiny unfolding in the sprawling desert beneath them. The heavens themselves were spectators to this majestic play that began during times so ancient that legend is blurred into fact. The curtains were now closing on the first act and would soon open again on the second act that would shape the destiny of humanity, for now and the generations to come.

Abram's right foot was the first to pound the ground where the gap began. The rest of his body followed in a blur. He came to a full stop at a distance of three men laid end to end past the beginning of the gap and he turned his body a quarter circle facing west into the gap. He gasped for breath as he bent his knees slightly, hunched his back and braced his arms against his knees in order to support his upper body and regain his breath. When he breathed there was a high pitched, whizzing sound emanating from his lungs. His face was contorted by a grimace of pain – a pain of which he was oblivious until just then. He craned his neck while still hunched over and looked straight ahead. He expected to see far into the depth of the desert where the sky, looking like star studded coal, kissed the desert floor veiled in darkness. However, the gap did not completely cut the cliffs in half; it formed a semi circle with the walls of the cliffs on three sides – west, north and south. The breadth of the gap was equal to its width of twenty men laid end to end. The stars were still dominant in the sky because the moon was veiled behind the cliff wall to the west. The stars above could not illuminate the desert ground sufficiently but Abram could see a patch of dim light emanating from a hole in the desert floor. The hole was a large circle half the area of the gap and exactly at its center.

He could hear the chorus of whisperers very clearly now and the voice of the entity emerging from their collective identity compelled him to approach.

"This is holy ground," Abram thought. He removed his boots as a show of veneration and let them drop to the ground. The cool air soothed his aching feet. He uncapped the water flask dangling by his waist and washed his feet thoroughly, first his right foot starting at his toes and then he washed his left foot in a similar fashion. When he was satisfied, he fastened the cap back on his water flask and put the flask back around his waist.

He took a few cautious steps forward. This was in stark contrast to the fervent gallop that propelled him to this place. His breathing was no longer labored and he was revitalized by the chill in the air. He now felt like a passive observer of a majestic play where only the actors on the stage are tasked with pealing away the layers and nuances of the story. When he was galloping towards this place he was the one charged with the intricacy of the unfolding play.

Abram approached the luminescent hole. He thought he saw a dim figure standing at the edge of the hole at the closest point to him. Abram could not determine if the figure had his back to him or was facing him. It was immobile and as Abram approached he could see it had its back to him. It was a large, naked, marbled figure, like a statue or idol. It was a head taller than the average man and its back was wide and heavily muscled. In the dim light it looked to be an earthy reddish color, like caked and crusty blood. Abram thought he recognized it but he refused to believe his eyes.

"Abram, I've been expecting you tonight," the voice coming from within the hole said. "I have a puzzle for you. I have been waiting for you for many years although I last spoke to you just yesterday afternoon. Abram, can you dig your way out of this cognitive maze?" The marbled statue still had its back to Abram but Abram knew with certainty the voice was of the entity emerging from the hole.

"Who are you?" Abram said. "What is this strange statue I see? Why do you ask me such unfathomable questions? This is the first I hear your voice. Yesterday afternoon I was resting in my household with my beloved Sarai. I did not hear your voice then."

The marbled figure slowly turned around and Abram could now see its face. "You know very well who I am," the figure said, "so quit playing games or I will toss you into this mysterious hole, not on my next desert outing but this very outing tonight."

Abram was startled to learn the voice of the entity was coming out of the mouth of the marbled idol. The marbled idol was the emergent entity. The real shock was when he recognized that face staring back at him. He recognized the rough, ugly features. He recognized the impressive penis as thick as a man's ankle and as long as a cat's tail. It pointed straight towards the stars and there was a thick, ropy vein on its underside. Abram was dumbfounded. He tried to reconcile the impossible sight before him. His mind raced in many directions, trying to find an explanation not based on the absurd. When he realized the futility of his pursuit he finally spoke. Abram raised his voice several notches. He was now standing within almost arm's reach of the marbled figure. "Orofus? Can it be you?"

"I don't understand," Abram said. "What by Yahvah's good graces are you doing here? What's you link to any of this?"

And then, by a flash of inspiration, he connected the dots and the truth struck him like a Sumerian military chariot. The goosebumps, like a bee hive, started on his upper back and splintered into his deepest level. His eyes widened in awe and amazement. The arc of his life broke free from the last shackle of space and time and now freely roamed the unfettered abstract space of the womb of Creation. He could now almost hear the angels performing for Yahvah the most exquisite poetry, the most beautiful melody.

"How has this not occurred to me before?" He thought. "The desert night outing...galloping across the desert...the whisperers each speaking a different language...the whisperers in the hole in the desert floor at night." And then the undertone of his life emerged from its veil and struck him like a tsunami emerging from the calm waters and crashing upon an idyllic shore.

"The strange questions you always asked me and the intricate life lessons you always had the patience to teach me. You...you...have been the voice of Yahvah in my childhood. There was, even from my early childhood, a grand design in my life, wasn't there? Long before I had my moment of enlightenment that night under the moon's milky white, Yahvah was there. Yahvah was guiding me and shaping me."

As Orofus spoke, Abram still marveled that the entity's voice was emanating from the hole but Orofus' lips were synchronized to it. He tried desperately to get accustomed to that odd sight and focus on the meaning of Orofus' words.

"Abram, you have connected the dots admirably but I am not exactly who you think I am. Yahvah is the totality of all reflections in Creation's mirrors. I am a subset of these reflections in Yahvah. You will understand tonight the significance of this. I promise you that. You are now a crusty old man but just earlier today you were a fresh faced young boy unaware of your destiny. I told you then of how I take into the desert at night. Abram,

The Navel Of Creation: A Loop In Eternity

this is my next outing into the desert night I told you of so many years ago. That was decades ago for you but only today for me. We now meet again but this time not in your father's idol shop during the work day but rather in the desert at night, on the other side."

Abram dropped to his knees on the desert floor and looked up at Orofus. Tears were streaming from Abram's eyes. "My beloved Yahvah, you are the love of my life. You have been my everlasting friend since my days in Ur. You have sent me Orofus as a proxy for your voice. Is he one of your angels? I have been compelled towards the solitude of the desert all my life. Now I am beginning to understand the significance of it all."

"Abram, earlier today," Orofus said, "in your father's idol shop I was blowing the winds of transition within you. I was planting within your soul the seeds of wisdom so one day you will reap their fruit handsomely. I promised you that. When I enthralled you with the story of how I gallop across the desert floor at night to this hole, that's when I planted the seed of your compulsion for the desert at night. That is the reason you were compelled to come here this night, across the chasm of the decades, and meet me on the other side."

Abram had forgotten about the whisperers within the hole. He was enthralled by Orofus' revelations about his youth in Ur. He was enthralled with how the dots were now connecting into a cohesive whole. The voice of the entity from within the hole now shifted perspective and seemed to be Orofus' own.

"Isn't it funny," Abram thought, "how again I see a symmetry in my life. I must wonder for the second time tonight if the symmetry is of my life or divine revelation's own."

But Abram's attention was now diverted back to the hole and the whisperers within. "I understand now you are the entity emerging from the myriad of whisperers in this hole. This is the white-eyed womb of your Creation," Abram said. "This explains your compulsion to return to this place but why instill that compulsion in me?"

Orofus extended his right arm towards Abram and unclenched his hand. His palm now faced the stars that were rapt spectators above.

Orofus' throaty voice boomed. "Come closer Abram and take my hand firmly in yours."

Abram hesitated for a few heartbeats. The poignancy of the invitation overwhelmed his sensibilities but he found the strength of character to approach a few steps. He cautiously grasped Orofus' right hand and raised his head sheepishly. Orofus stood to his full height and he loomed so very tall. Abram gazed up into Orofus' haunting deep-set eyes. They were a solid white with no pupils. Orofus' rough and ugly features now softened in a way Abram had never seen before; like an ancient glacier, frozen solid since time immemorial, its jagged corners and deep crevices now cracking and melting under the hot sun of a new age. Orofus radiated a smile more beautiful to Abram than the fairest maiden. Abram felt loved as never before. Even Sarai's love for him paled. But Orofus' love for Abram was not as a love extended to an Other but a love directed inward to none other than oneself. Abram now understood Orofus was not an Other but rather all of humanity as One Self - a collective soul. Abram was not dancing with an Other but rather with himself.

"Abram, you asked me why I have compelled you to this place if it is the white-eyed womb from which I emanate. The reason is that I AM none other than your kind's collective soul. The hole in this desert floor is the white-eyed womb from which your kind crawled out when Yahvah expelled them from the land of their thoughtless comforts and barred their return. And then I was born. Abram, this is the garden of your kind's creation. Welcome home."

"Orofus, I don't understand, " Abram said. "If you are humanity's collective soul why do I perceive my Self to be separate from all others? Why do I perceive my Self to be separate from you?"

"You are my illusion Abram. You are a denizen of my dreams. You are one of a multitude within me, like the multitude of shiny facets of a diamond, each facet believing its Self to be a diamond separate from all the others. But there is just one diamond to which they all belong. Abram, I AM the diamond."

"And what is within that hole?" Abram said. "If I deconstruct your voice, will I hear the chaotic cacophony of the whisperers within this hole instead of hearing you as their emergent soul? When I was seven in my father's idol shop you said they were serpents, each speaking a different language."

Orofus now sat cross-legged on the desert floor. His face was now beautiful beyond words. He was radiating a wisdom beyond the mastery of any one of the diamond's facets. His wisdom was of the diamond as a whole. Abram also sat cross-legged. He was now facing Orofus. He now knew he was seeing himself in the mirror of the collective soul.

Abram stared deeply into the expressionless solid white eyes of Orofus.

He now entered a state of consciousness which knows the collective soul.

Now he knows the diamond rather than any of its facets.

The Navel Of Creation: A Loop In Eternity

He is no longer Abram, just a facet in the diamond, he is the diamond, the collective soul.

He is no longer the fragmented mind of Abram but the collective soul of Orofus.

He is now Orofus observing Abram - one of the denizens of his dreams.
But it is not a switch of perspective.
It is what it is.
The collective soul and the denizens of its dream.
And the process is repeated.
Like the mirror within a mirror within another.
Abram stared deeply into the expressionless solid white eyes of Orofus.
Abram is Abram no more but only the collective soul.
But nothing changes in Eternity.
There never is a change of perspective.
It is what it is.
There still is Abram and Orofus.
The collective soul and the denizens of its dream.

Within the dream Orofus answered Abram. "Abram, I am only one level within Yahvah, there are others preceding me in this hole in the desert floor. Each a collective soul with its own denizens within its dream. Each a world unto its own. The denizens within a dream are the whisperers from which emerges the next level's collective soul. But be not fooled Abram, this hole before you extends far beyond this desert floor. I am sitting here next to you outside the hole in this desert floor but I am nevertheless inside the extended hole where it leads to the next desert floor. And that desert floor beyond is itself inside the hole where it reaches to yet another. And all of that is yet within another. Like the mirror within a mirror within another. As is below so is above. Such is Yahvah, the navel of Creation encompassing all the desert floors. The totality of all collective souls emanating from the ineffable H, the bedrock of Existence, in YHVH. the H is the primordial whisperer at the very bottom of this hole."

Abram thought deeply about Orofus' revelations and he was puzzled. "Orofus, I am again lost in your cognitive mazes. If you are just one of the levels within Yahvah and if you are the collective soul of humanity it follows that humanity is one of the levels within Yahvah. But where do the stars fit within Yahvah? Where do the trees and the bees fit within Yahvah? Where do all of the physical creations that are distinct from humanity fit into Yahvah? Are they also distinct levels within the hierarchy of YHVH? Are they a level within the hole in this desert floor or are they a level beyond?"

Orofus shook his marbled head and momentarily shut his eyes. "Abram, I see you haven't grasped the full extent of the mystery of Existence."

Orofus turned his head towards the opening of the gap in which they sat, surrounded on the three other sides by the cliff walls. He lifted his gaze towards the stars directly above his head. Abram was mesmerized by his strong, jutting marbled profile set against the star-studded sky.

"Abram, look at the stars above." Orofus pointed with his right arm at the stars directly above his head. "Abram, these stars above are far in space and time. I am sitting on this desert floor, in the here and now and yet I am there amongst the stars."

Abram looked up at the stars and squinted his eyes in an attempt to see what he knew he would never see. He could see no sign of Orofus or any proxy of Orofus amongst the stars. "Things haven't changed I see," Abram thought. "As in my childhood, Orofus is answering one riddle by posing another more difficult one."

"Orofus, I don't understand," Abram said. "I am a crusty old man and yet I now feel as I did when I was a fresh-faced child learning from you. How can you be in two places at once? And such places so far apart."

"Abram, I am not in two places at once, rather two places are at once in me. I am not distinct from the stars, the bees and the trees. I do not exist within physical creation as a creature deferring to space and time. I AM physical creation. I AM space and time. The physical realm is one with me."

"Orofus," Abram asked, "are you really stating not only is each member of humanity a denizen of your dreams but so is all that exists within space and time? Can that truly be or am I misinterpreting your words?"

Abram thought about Orofus' words more deeply and came to a startling conclusion. "Orofus, if you are humanity's collective soul then by what you just said, humanity is one with all that exists, be it sentient or not."

"You have understood me now Abram, with one correction I should add. Your statement holds only for the level which is the physical realm. This is the level of space and time. Your mind does not exist within the physical realm. The collective mind IS the physical realm. I AM the collective mind but I AM not the product of disparate minds, rather they are my product. I am the diamond, they are my facets. The collective is the primary existence."

"And what of the other levels of Existence within this hole?" Abram asked. "They are not of space and time?"

"There are other levels of Existence within the hole in this desert floor

The Navel Of Creation: A Loop In Eternity

and the desert floors beyond, each a collective soul unto itself. Each believing it is a concrete reality, the only reality. You are a denizen of my dreams. Your thoughts are my thoughts. There are not a multitude such as you. The physical realm of space and time is only composed of myself and then into the shards of my divinity - the denizens of my dreams."

Abram looked again deeply into Orofus' expressionless white eyes. "Orofus, I need to ask you a question gnawing at me since you revealed your identity to me tonight."

Orofus completed Abram's question. "Why do I expose myself to you as an idol? As an artifact of that which you deny?"

"Yes," Abram said, "that has been puzzling me. It seems profane."

"You angered and alienated the religious establishment in Ur by rejecting their idolatry. It cost your family dearly. You fought like a lion for the truth of Yahvah and yet here I am, a fertility idol."

Orofus paused but Abram saw no need to continue his questioning. He knew Orofus would momentarily reveal the answers he was seeking.

"Abram, do you remember the dream you wrote about in your composition? The one where you framed me with the destruction of the idols in your father's shop?"

Abram nodded cautiously, not knowing what new revelations Orofus would divulge. After all the decades since he left Ur, the composition he wrote as a boy coming of age in Ur was still vivid in his memories. He was breathlessly waiting for Orofus to peal the layers of mystery.

"I didn't know who you were, Orofus. I thought you to be just an idol of stone and marble."

"My point is not to chastise you Abram, far from it. Abram, tonight you will not spare me as you did in your dream. Tonight you must shatter me into shards of divinities and from these shards a new age shall rise. Your generations to come shall compel humanity's chaotic congregation, the Civilization of Man, to seek Yahvah in matters both secular and divine. Your generations to come shall be the yeast that leavens civilization's bread - weak of power yet of great influence. Your generations to come shall never hold the reins of power and yet they shall be prominent in the corridors of influence. There will be a steep price to pay for sowing these seeds. Your generations to come will reap humanity's scorn and they shall be a people subject to expulsion, derision, contempt and rank hatred."

"Why should that be?" Abram said. "Why should humanity hate that which compels it towards Yahvah and its deepest intimacy, the seed of the ineffable H."

"Abram, Yahvah is a great mystery and your generations to come shall embody the mystery of Yahvah and the ineffable mystery of the H within. Humanity will be awed by your generations to come but it will not understand its awe and will instead interpret it as hatred and distrust. Abram, at the bottom of this hole dwells the source of Existence. To know it is to deconstruct all layers of Existence and return to Nothingness, to a state of No Mind. But to accomplish this you must dance with god. Your generations to come will not be God Dancers, they are destined to be God Wrestlers. They are destined to open humanity's eyes to the desert floors beyond. That will compel the Civilization of Man to distrust and fear them. It is the fear of god."

"Is that why you command me to shatter you?"

"You must be strong and do so Abram. Tonight, the covenant between you and me will be sealed. The destruction of Orofus the idol is a symbolic gesture that must be executed. Symbolism is a powerful agent in matters of spirit and mind. You must shatter the final vestige of idolatry remaining in your heart in order for your legacy to bear fruit. And then your unborn son and his generations to come shall become God Wrestlers."

"Before I can summon the courage to do so," Abram said, "I have more questions needing answers. I understand this hole before us is just a subset of the navel of Existence. But does it extend infinitely further and further away from the primordial whisperer at the bottom of the hole or is there an end to it?"

Orofus stood to his full height and he towered over Abram. "Come Abram, I will take you to the edge of Creation. I will take you to the precipice of Existence and I will answer your question."

Orofus led Abram, hand in hand, to the edge of the great circular hole. As Abram approached, his heart raced and he felt the butterflies in his gut and the goosebumps crawling across his flesh and burrowing into his soul. "I truly fear this hole," he thought. "My generations to come will be proxies for this hole. Is this how humanity will fear them? But my fear is not translated into hatred because I understand this. How will a humanity lacking such an understanding see my generations to come? I understand now why they will be hated."

Abram reflected on the composition for the priesthood he had written so long ago. He reflected specifically on the passage describing the overwhelming excitement and awe he experienced as a seven year old child enthralled by tales of this very hole in the desert floor. But he understood nothing then of its significance. He was just a child then and he was far from the third stage of his spiritual development that Orofus explained must be attained before such mysteries can be understood. He would now be able to peer into the well of Existence, the navel of Creation. He would now be able to see the face of Yahvah.

They were now standing at the edge of the hole. Abram was facing the cliff walls to the west. Behind him was the opening of the gap in the cliffs. Ahead of him was the hole. A soft, yellowish glow was emanating from it, like a dozen candles at night inside Abram's tent. The glow offered no warmth. Abram noticed the intensity of the glow did not weaken with distance. The glow was as bright at the edge of the hole as it was when he first saw it some distance back. He thought it absurd it should behave in this manner but he was now accustomed to the absurd. But yet again, it did not seem like the absurdity of the shallowest lie, it was the absurdity of the deepest truth.

"Abram, look down into the navel of Existence," Orofus said, "what do you see?"

"I can't. I can't do it yet," Abram said. "I am too overwhelmed by this. How can I look into the face of Yahvah without preparing myself? I feel too much awe. I feel I am not prepared to witness the mysteries of Existence."

"Abram, look deeply into my eyes."

Abram did as Orofus instructed. "I can look up into your eyes Orofus," Abram said, "but I am afraid to look down into the abyss."

Orofus smiled at Abram. It was a warm and reassuring smile, and again Abram felt loved like no Other can love.

"Abram, how did you feel the first time your father Terah asked you to jump into the swimming hole?"

Abram thought deeply about that experience. It was buried deep in the recesses of his memories but the nuances and flavors of that experience now sprung forth and flooded his consciousness. He experienced again the fear he felt as a young boy at the edge of the swimming hole. It was a fear of the unknown and it occurred to him now that it was a fear remarkably similar to his fear of peering into the hole in the desert floor.

"I was terrified," Abram said. "I had never swam before. I had no experience with swimming and I didn't know what to expect."

"Swimming to you was a foreign concept as sight is to a child born blind at birth."

"Yes, Orofus. And when my father cajoled me to jump into the swimming hole I had only my trust in him as my anchor."

"You had to trust his reassurances more than your own fears. You had to let go and take the plunge. Trust me Abram. Take the plunge now. I am offering you sight of a deeper kind. Trust me that it will be a rewarding gift."

"Yes Orofus, yes. I trust you more than I trust myself. I submit to the Divine Dance. I will take the plunge."

And he did. With eyes shut, Abram craned his neck towards the hole. He quickly yanked his eyes wide open and then he gasped.

Before him, deep in the desert floor, was the cocooned Reality of the mirror within a mirror within another. It was not literally a mirror, it was Existence reflecting upon itself and emanating cocooned levels of itself. He only ever imagined it and speculated about it, but now it was real before him and more perfect than he ever imagined. It was so mesmerizing that he could not breathe. Instead, he could only gasp as his mind tried to orient itself with this unfathomable mystery. Circling each level of Existence were serpents with large solid-white eyes. Each level of Existence contained smaller serpents than the level directly below but also a greater number of serpents. As Abram peered down to the lower levels, the whiteness of the serpents' eyes became more prominent in relation to the size of their bodies. At the very bottom of the hole all he could see was a piercing white glow.

He could no longer hear Orofus. The voice of Orofus was deconstructed and now he heard instead the jumbled and incomprehensible voices of the whisperers. He now realized the whisperers were the serpents circling the uppermost level just below the desert floor. He could not hear the whispers of the serpents in the lower levels. The whispers of the uppermost level serpents were like a white noise vibrating and warming his ears. He could not hear each individual whisperer's voice in sharp detail because there were too many of them.

Abram knew these whisperers were Orofus in their collective and yet he sensed they knew nothing of Orofus. They knew nothing of Abram. They knew nothing of the desert floor above and yet the desert floor emanated from their collective self. He now also realized each level within the hole was a desert floor unto itself. He wondered, in a moment of deep insight, if the scenario unfolding between Orofus and himself on the desert floor on which he stood was repeated for each level down this navel of Existence. Perhaps also, he thought, for the desert floors beyond.

"Am I one of the whisperers who create the desert floor above?" And he thought: "What is below me, so is above. There is a symmetry which is divinity's own. All of Existence is but a reflection of the H at the bottom of the hole in this desert floor. The H truly reflects upon itself and Creation flows. Truly, YHVH is this hole in the desert floor and the desert floors beyond."

The Navel Of Creation: A Loop In Eternity

Abram turned his attention to the serpents again. Each serpent whispered to all the other serpents on the same level as itself and from this interrelated participatory web emanated a sentient entity unknown by the serpents. Each serpent influenced the whispers of all the other serpents on its same level and was in turn influenced back, not just by the others but also by itself reflected off the others and the others reflected off itself. Each serpent only knew another serpent as that other knew itself reflected of the others. Abram focused arbitrarily on three of the serpents and he saw the whisper of the first serpent was influenced by the second serpent which in turn was influenced by the third serpent and yet the third serpent was influenced by the first. Each serpent was, in effect, coiling back on itself and eating its own tail. Each serpent was, through the others, reflecting upon itself.

Abram did not know how long he had been mesmerized by the hole in the desert floor. "Perhaps for a very long time," he thought, "or perhaps for only the fleeting instant of the blinking of an eye." He had lost all sense of future or past and was only in the timeless state of the Now. He longed to hear the voice of Orofus again. He knew that to hear Orofus he would need to turn his back to the hole and only then would he be able to dwell in the world of space and time, the world of the entity emerging from the hole. He knew if he were to keep fixating on the hole he would not be able to tear himself away from its timeless reality. He shut his eyes with great force, grimaced and quickly swiveled a half circle. He kept his eyes closed for a few heartbeats, waiting to orient himself back into the world of the here and now and then he slowly opened his eyes. He saw the looming figure of Orofus standing under the tapestry of a star studded sky. Abram could no longer hear the white noise emanating from the whisperers nor feel its warm vibrations dancing in his ears.

Abram had a startling insight. "I have never both heard Orofus and the whisperers at the same time. When I stare into the abyss of Existence, the navel of an exploding reality, I am lost in a world that knows not of space and time. But it seems to me when I turn my back on the hole my perception collapses the superimposed voices of the whisperers into one coherent voice - the voice of Orofus. Do I truly bring forth the world of space and time with my thoughts? Do my thoughts collapse the cacophony of the whisperers into one coherent voice? How absurd it is."

Upon further reflection, he realized the fact his thoughts yield such power is not surprising. "Orofus is the world of space and time," Abram thought, "and I am merely a denizen of his dreams. My thoughts don't bring forth the world of space and time, my thoughts are the world of space

The Navel Of Creation: A Loop In Eternity

and time. The apparent mystery is just a tautology. The light of day once wondered why it is the darkness of night disappears upon its arrival. How bizarre it is, light of day thought, that with my thoughts I can chase the darkness of night. But darkness of night and the light of day are two sides of the same coin. There is no mystery, just tautology." He snickered at the thought. "It does seem absurd upon a cursory reflection but once again the thought occurs to me it is not the banal absurdity of the shallowest lie, rather it is the provocative absurdity of the deepest truth. It is sheer simplicity shrouded in a fog of complexity."

Abram craned his neck to look up at Orofus. They were standing almost within arm's reach of each other. "Orofus, I have a question. That brilliant white light at the bottom of the hole is the source of all creation. I know that. I know it is the H in YHVH but what exists below it?"

"Abram," Orofus said, "your question is deep and insightful and I will shortly answer it. I must first teach you the white light is not the bottom of the hole in the desert floor. The white light is not the H, it is the first level of Creation emanating out of the H. The H itself is shrouded at the bottom. It is unobservable because the solid brilliance of the white light at the bottom forms a one way, impenetrable barrier allowing Creation to radiate out but allowing nothing in.

Abram was fascinated by the concept of a one-way barrier, which is an irresistible explosion of Existence. "Orofus, what is the nature of the white light? What is it composed of?"

"In the physical world," Orofus answered, "everything is carved out of space and time. There is no physical existence devoid of space and time. But in the world of the white light there is no space and time. The world of the white light is carved out of the abstract concept of polarities. For every good there is an evil. For every up there is a down. For every hot there is a cold. In the physical realm these polarities are attributes of physical entities, but in the world of the white light these polarities are disembodied abstractions. Abram, answer the following puzzle..."

Abram thought: "Here is another of the maddening puzzles Orofus so loves to pose."

"...What do you suppose," asked Orofus, "is the outcome of bringing all the polarities of the world of the white light into intimate contact?"

"Well, if you bring the up and the down into intimate contact then you have not up nor down. If you bring the cold and the hot into intimate contact then you have not cold nor hot. In short, if you do as you suggested to all the different kinds of polarities of the white light, then the net outcome is that you have nothing."

The Navel Of Creation: A Loop In Eternity

"What will happen to the world of the white light then, Abram?"

"I suppose it will cease to exist."

"And where does the world of the white light originally emanate from?" Orofus asked.

"You've thought me it emanates from the H at the bottom of the hole in the desert floor."

"So Abram, if the deconstruction of the world of the white light results in complete nothingness, then what do you suppose is the nature of the H from which it emanates?"

"I see the answer very clearly now," Abram said. "The H, the navel of Creation, is a perfect nothingness. In the physical realm nothingness is always in relation to something, but the H from which all levels of Creation emanate is an absolute nothingness."

"Yes Abram. You have done well. Creation is structured in such a manner that each of its levels deconstructs in this manner to nothingness. At the level of the white light it is a simple concept to grasp because it is easy to understand how the up and the down cancel each other, or how the hot and cold cancel each other, and so on. But the cancellation process exists for all levels of Creation. The H at the bottom of the hole is like a slab of fine Phoenician marble that embodies all possible carvings superimposed on each other. It is at once nothing and everything. It is at once infinite Chaos and infinite order. All the subsequent levels of Creation also exhibit the interplay of polarities because each level inherits this behavior from the previous level. That defines God Dancing and God Wrestling. To dance with the divine is to deconstruct the levels of the hole as you fall towards the H at the bottom. To wrestle with the divine is to create new levels as you head away from the H at the bottom. The former is enlightenment, the latter is a creative process. When you dance with your adversities, you are matching your weaknesses with their strengths, and their strengths with your weaknesses, and the sum total is a void, a nothingness, and they can do you no harm. That is the purpose of the dance of the two primordial lovers - to merge back into the source of Existence, which is the nothingness of the ineffable H."

"So once again there is a tautology," Abram said. "Why is the H ineffable? The answer is a tautology. Nothingness is ineffable because it is in the definition of nothingness to be ineffable. If I could fathom nothingness then it is not nothing, it is something."

"And what of my initial question?" Abram asked. "What lies below the bottom of the hole?"

"The navel of Creation," Orofus said, "is not as it seems to you when

The Navel Of Creation: A Loop In Eternity

you look down this hole. It is a loop in eternity and not a linear hole. The infinite levels of Creation, all the desert floors below and beyond, loop back in eternity and feed into the bottom of this hole. Creation is a series of self-sustaining feedback loops that themselves form a great loop in Eternity. This is not a loop in space and time, which is just this desert floor. This is a loop in Eternity devoid of all attributes. And because it is devoid of all attributes then it must merge back into the ineffable H, at the bottom of this hole, because only the H is devoid of all attributes."

"I understand what you are saying Orofus. I remember when I first constructed the name YHVH. It occurred to me even then that Creation is a self-referential process. This navel of Creation before us is that name I constructed so long ago. You can plainly see the self-referential structure in this name."

"Yes Abram," Orofus said, "the name of the navel of Creation mirrors its structure. But that is not surprising. When you constructed that name it was for the purpose of mirroring the structure."

Abram laughed. "Yes, that's true. I had already forgotten the intellectual boldness of my youth. I was quite a maverick in those days."

Abram closed his eyes and stroked his long, gray beard. He then jerked his eyes open and, with his left index finger, stabbed an invisible foe directly in front of him.

"Orofus, Orofus, I discovered yet another way to explain this."

Abram felt like a child again, pondering the mysteries of Existence with Orofus in his father's idol shop.

"Simply by applying the principle of the Divine Dance of polarities I can reach the exact same conclusion. But not within any particular level of Creation, instead across the levels themselves. You see? If Creation explodes irresistibly out of the H at the bottom of the hole, then it follows that below the H, which is the polar opposite side, the opposite action must happen. Creation must irresistibly implode back into the H. If the bottom of the hole is perfectly white and irresistibly explosive then the other side must be perfectly black and irresistibly implosive. It is the navel of creation: a loop in Eternity."

Abram had a prideful grin on his face, but it was not fueled by his ego, it was fueled by a pride in the beauty and simplicity of Creation.

"Very well reasoned, Abram. All roads lead to the same conclusion. The tapestry of Creation is consistent."

Orofus paused for dramatic effect and then said: "Abram, the time has come to seal the covenant between myself and your generations to come. I have revealed myself to you during the pivotal times in your life. I have whispered to you from within the semantic spaces of your soul. Tonight is like no other night. I have revealed more to you tonight than in all the years past. A man goes through three stages while on this earth. The first is a stage of ignorance. It is a stage of innocence..."

Abram remembered these words vividly. They were the words Orofus spoke to him in his father's idol shop, when he was just a wide-eyed little boy. Abram wrote these words in his composition for entrance to the priesthood.

"...The second is a stage of physical and intellectual maturity. The third is a stage of the spirit, a stage of wisdom. You are now in your third stage, and you are ready to know the mission I have chosen for you and your generations to come."

Abram was silent. He knew this to be the culmination of the saga that began that fateful night under the moon's milky white.

"Abram, I have already revealed to you in decades past that your generations to come shall be numerous as the stars you see sprawled above you tonight, or the desert's grains of sand. I have also revealed to you your generations to come shall form a bond to this land of Canaan that will be sealed in their hearts even when this land is not under their feet. But there shall be much more to your legacy than the sheer number of your descendants, or this land in their hearts. Do you know what you must first do before I reveal more to you?"

Abram answered without hesitation. "Yes Orofus, I know what I must now do. We have already spoken of it tonight, but I also know it because it cries out from the semantic spaces in the soul. I know I must destroy you now."

They were standing close to the edge. Abram was facing Orofus and the hole in the desert floor was to Abram's left and to the right of Orofus.

"Do you also know the reason you must destroy me now?"

"Yes, I think I do. But tell me, will I still hear your voice after it is done, or will I hear the deconstructed voices of the whisperers? By destroying you, am I not returning to the white-eyed womb of the whisperers from which you emanate? Is it not like deconstructing the oneness of the fireflies blinking in unison and returning to their chaotic flashes of light."

"You will hear neither. I AM space and time, but you will not be destroying that. You will be destroying your attachment to it, instead. You will be destroying the remnants of idolatry still infesting your soul. You will be destroying the remaining shards of the previous age that linger in you and which must now defer to the dawn of a new age. My voice will no longer appear as an external reality, as it does now, but will instead seep from primordial Man within the bedrock of your core."

Abram now saw Orofus was clutching a large bronze rod in his right hand. It did not appear large compared to his hulking frame, or hands the size of a fully grown bear's. But it was almost as long as Abram is tall, and in the hands of Abram it would be almost too thick to grasp and too heavy to swing.

"Do you remember your dream where you shattered the idols in your father's shop? Of course you do. You did not shatter me, however. You spared me. Since a very early age you have been outspoken against idolatry, but there is still a remnant of idolatry left in your heart. You are not consciously aware of it, but it lurks within you. I am not faulting you Abram. You have been my faithful servant and I could not ask better from any other."

With both hands, almost ceremoniously, Orofus presented the bronze rod to Abram. He took it from Orofus and immediately felt its metallic coldness biting his hands, and a heaviness feeling like thick tentacles sprouting from the desert floor and pulling the rod down. With great effort he hoisted the rod to his right shoulder. Just before he swung it with all his might, he briefly gazed at Orofus. He knew this would be the last time he would see him.

The rod struck Orofus on the right side of his body, from Abram's perspective, just below the ribcage. Abram was surprised at the force of his blow. Orofus staggered, but remained standing after the first blow. His white-eyed face was expressionless. The entire side of his torso shattered, and shards of marble exploded out of his body and cascaded into the hole. Abram closed his eyes, gritted his teeth, and reached deep into his psyche, desperately looking for a source of rage. He thought of the purebreds in Ur who had banished his family. He swung the rod again and again, smashing Orofus indiscriminately. He felt rewarded because once he found his rage it flowed effortlessly. When his rage subsided he opened his eyes. Orofus was nowhere to be seen. The shards of his broken body were deconstructed into the hole in the desert floor.

"Now what?" Abram thought. "Has my spirit been cleansed of the straggling vestiges of an idolatrous age now officially ended?"

Abram now fell into a deep sleep. He lay on his side, facing the hole. His left arm dangled over the edge. It almost brushed against the oblivious whispering serpents, slithering on the wall of the hole. In his deep sleep he dreamed of a great hole in the desert floor, and a voice spoke to him from within the hole. Abram was aware he was dreaming, yet the dream unfolded.

The Navel Of Creation: A Loop In Eternity

"Abram, Abram," the voice said, "you have been a faithful servant. You have walked with me since your youth and suffered great adversity as a result. I have cast you out from the lands you cherished. I compelled you to banish those lands, not just from under your feet but also, most difficult of all, from your heart. But I now seal this land to your heart, and the hearts of your generations to come. They shall forever long for this land and shall never be compelled to long for another. I will make of them a great people and they shall be a great attractor for the nations. They shall flavor the nations with a longing for this land and for me. From your generations to come shall germinate great ideas of mind and spirit. They will compel the nations to probe the mysteries of soul and mind. Abram, to long for me is not just to long for the artifice of religion. To long for me is to long for the great mysteries of Existence above your head in the heavens, and within your mind and soul. I AM all these things. I AM your soul, your mind, the stars above and the desert floor beneath your feet. To seek me is to seek an understanding of all these things. Your generations to come shall be mavericks, as you have been in your youth in Ur, and they will yield great influence over the hearts, minds and souls of the nations. As is the H at the source of the hole, so shall they be within the source of the Civilization of Man. They shall be at best tolerated and at worst despised amongst the nations. Ever since the dawn of civilization there exists a principality of otherness; yet it is also the yeast upon which civilization is leavened. The yeast must be bread's minutest minion, otherwise the leavening shall be spoiled. The yeast is commissioned for great influence, yet scant power. Ever since the dawn of civilization the Habiru have always felt like citizens of a different realm. Your generations to come will be known as Hebrews, those cross over to new paradigms. They are the legacy of Habiru clans that roamed the earth during times so ancient that legend is blurred into fact. They are like the crashing waves upon a crumbling sandy shore, each wave its predecessor's legacy - a leitmotif. That which is most influential is also the most powerless. So shall be the Hebrews amongst humanity's chaotic congregation. They shall be an attractor shaping civilization's locus towards a communion with me, the I AM."

Abram spoke from within his dream: "But what of Sarai? She is very antagonistic to Hagar and Ishmael. Is Ishmael to be my heir through whom my covenant with you is to be realized? That will drive Sarai away from me. Is she barren and too old to bear me an heir? Or are the words of the three visitors true? Are their words yours?"

"It is as they said, Abram. Their voice was mine. It is not Ishmael who shall be the heir of the covenant between you and me. Ishmael already knows it. I have also revealed myself to him, in the desert, under the crescent moon. But you already know that, Abram."

"Yes, I know it. I have met him one night in the desert, under that crescent moon. We both shared the same dream that compelled us into the desert that night."

Abram was alone, speaking to a disembodied voice. He did not want to peer into the hole for fear the voice will be deconstructed into the chaotic voices of the whisperers. "Then who will be my heir? Sarai will truly be with child?"

"Abram, return tonight to Sarai, and when you enter your tent she will be waiting for you and you shall know her once more. Cleave unto her and she will bear you a son, an heir."

"I've already made this promise to Sarai, but she understandably laughed in my face and in the face of the three visitors. I did not believe it myself, but I so desperately wanted to comfort her with my insincere assurances. When she asks me what is the name of the voice that made this promise to me, what shall I say?"

"Abram, I emanate from the H. I AM inseparable from the H. I AM an inner mirror inseparable from the outer mirror. I AM that which I will become because my inner mirrors reproduce me. Is the tree not the seed from which it emanates? Is the tree not in the seeds it reproduces? The seed is pregnant with that which it will become. When Sarai asks who made the promise of an heir by her, tell her it is the great I AM. Truly, I AM you. I AM her. All which exists in the physical realm, and which I endowed with self-reflection, is a denizen of my dreams. You are under the illusion I AM now the denizen of your dream, but it is you who is the denizen of mine. The dreamer is the dream. You think you are a lucid dreamer this one time, but it is I who is the lucid dreamer since the dawn of time."

"I have complete trust in your promise," Abram said. "I will name my son Laughter because Sarai laughed in disbelief when the three visitors assured her she will bear me an heir."

"Abram, I am marking yours and Sarai's names with the ineffable essence of Existence. No longer shall you be called Abram and Sarai. Your names shall henceforth be AbraHam and SaraH. Your names shall be marked by the white-eyed womb of all Creation because from you shall emerge great nations, and to you shall these nations be drawn when seeking me. This shall mark the covenant between me and your generations to come. You shall circumcise all the male members of your household. Every new born male shall also be circumcised eight days after birth. This will symbolize the seal I have made between your generations to come and the land of Canaan. It will also symbolize the seal I have made between them and myself. Go now, Abraham, and have every male member of your household circumcised: your herdsmen, your shepherds, the keepers of your camels, the most trusted confidants in your inner circle as well as your laborers and the least in your household. They shall all carry the seal of my covenant with you.

Abraham prostrated himself at the edge of the hole. He knew this to be holy ground. He was facing the hole but saw nothing of it because his eyes were shut. He did not want to fragment the voice of I AM back into the chaotic voices of the whisperers. Abraham said: "I will teach my household all you've revealed to me tonight."

"No Abraham, utter a word only to None about the Navel of Creation I have revealed to you this night. Reveal this only to None within your household, not to the living in the Now or in the yet to come. But do reveal it to Sarah because she now carries the mark of the H in her name. Reveal it to None other. Utter not a word of this even when alone, in deep reflection. Not even to the fields where your cattle, sheep and goats roam. The knowledge of this you shall take to your grave. Reveal only the covenant I have sealed between us tonight. And above all, speak no more of the meaning of YHVH that you have discovered in your youth. It shall remain a mystery until a new age dawns, the great convergence, millennia from now. Never again pronounce it Yahvah. That too will be a mystery to your descendants until that new age. In its place they will say My Lord. But in the holy scriptures your descendants will write YHVH, yet its deepest meaning they will not know."

Abraham grimaced with awe. "But I have already revealed this meaning in my youthful composition. You burned, by the sun, into those tablets each day the soul I breathed onto them under the moonlight of the night before. I have inculcated my household with this wisdom since that time."

The Word said: "I promise you that if you never speak it again then your generations to come will not know this teaching. The composition tablets prepared by providence have long ago been smashed by their messenger. On the veneer the smasher is a sprawling empire but underneath it is none other than your own.

Your descendants will wonder about the meaning of YHVH. But only within the unconscious whispers reverberating beneath their veneer will they know. These whispers will compel them to undertake journeys of ambitious discovery and on the way -ports they will uncover many mysteries of Existence, but the source of their compulsion they will not know. It is none other than the urge to know the deepest meaning of

YHVH. It is a meaning they will, throughout their generations, try to understand but it will be just beyond their grasp. Your descendants will wander across the arc of history while wrestling with this compulsion, and it will define their zeitgeist. The relationship your descendants will forge with YHVH will be as much of the intellect as of the soul. YHVH will not to them be an idol disguised as god. And in the great convergence, millennia from now, the world will only then know the meaning of YHVH and it is a deeper truth than even you can now know."

Abraham remained prostrated at the edge of the hole. "Why should you forbid me from revealing to the world the great mysteries I have witnessed tonight and the meaning of YHVH I gathered in my youth?"

"Abraham, a man goes through three stages in life. You have entered your final stage, the stage of wisdom. But the arc of history is now only entering its second stage. Humanity is not yet ready for the knowledge I have revealed to you this night. In the final age that will dawn, during those far off days, the seed of the covenant between myself and your descendants shall bear its final fruit, and humanity will then take its first bite out of this fruit and begin to know the true nature of Creation and its place within.

Those will be the days of the convergence of the promises I have made to you tonight, when the principalities of mind and spirit shall become as one. But those days will not come to pass during your lifetime, or many generations after you are gone. And throughout these generations the meaning of YHVH will dwell just under the veneer of your descendants, in their unknowing white-eyed womb, and they will be compelled to know this thing within them though it will be yet to them unknown.

They will taste an urgency to find a bridge between these two worlds. That veiled compulsion to understand YHVH will define them and enable them to enlighten humanity and to be leaders of revolutions of ideas and thought. That too is the reason they must not know these truths until the close of the age now to start. For if they are to now know it then their way-ports of discovery shall remain unsung. Their kingdoms of power will be short-lived but the realm of their ideas will never die.

Go now Abraham and reveal this covenant to your household. Go now into the world. The curtains on the great stage of history's arc now once more open and the second act is due to start. The Second Age will first dawn and then it will unfold."

***

When Abraham wakened from his lucid dream he was lying at the edge

The Navel Of Creation: A Loop In Eternity

of the hole. He was facing it, as when he first entered his dream state, and his left arm dangled over the edge. He heard the chaotic voices of the whisperers once more. He now had a sense of acute desolation. Orofus was no more. The voice of the I AM was no more. The stolid voices of the whisperers amplified the silence of the desert night. The desert was as the starry panoply above, unchanging, impassive and silent.

"I am now Abraham," he thought. "My wife is now Sarah. We are as babies born into a world of which we know nothing."

Abraham staggered to his feet. His old bones were stiff. He peered into the hole. It looked more like a corkscrew now than a mirror within a mirror within another. He wondered if he was imagining this change of appearance, or if the hole was morphing into another shape. As always, the serpents at each level of the hole were slithering on the circular wall, oblivious to all but the other serpents of their level.

He continued to examine the hole, trying to detect the slightest change of appearance. It reminded him of how he often gazed at the edge of the crimson sun as it almost imperceptibly disappeared into that place where sky meets land. He noticed the white brilliance at the bottom was dimming, and the corkscrew shape was slowly rotating. He soon noticed the edge of the hole was receding from him. Soon, the speed of recession was visibly accelerating, and the hole was quickly shrinking. The interior was now beyond his gaze, and he was compelled to take a few small steps forward in order to keep it in sight. The speed of rotation of the corkscrew was increasing. Soon, he was walking briskly towards the receding edge. When the hole was the width of about five men laid head to toe he could no longer keep pace with its contraction, and then the hole imploded within the time of a blink of an eye, and then it was gone.

Abraham was standing on the spot he reached when the hole disappeared. He replayed, in his head, the events of the night. He reflected on everything he had learned or experienced - both in his dream state and in the world in which he was now. He was trying to dredge any meaning he had not yet gleaned, but he soon realized he was too tired and overwhelmed. He needed time for reflection. He walked towards where he had discarded his boots, and only then felt the sharp chill in the air, and the cold desert sand, biting into his bare feet. He slipped on his boots, composed himself and then made his way out of the gap within the cliffs. The walk back to where he had left his camel would be quick. Before he rounded the cliff wall he looked back momentarily. "I must remember this spot in the desert. It is holy ground, but I must never divulge it to anyone other than Sarah. We will take this knowledge to our graves."

The Navel Of Creation: A Loop In Eternity

When Abraham first heard the haunting chorus of the whisperers he darted towards its source. The desert night through which he ran felt like the current of a mighty river crashing into him headlong, and resisting his every step. But now he meandered back, deep in thought. "Sarah is waiting for me," he thought. "I will give her the good news of her son to be Laughter. I will know her tonight."

The Curtains Open: The Second Act

Abraham could not understand what was pressing against his back, and the back of his head. It felt like a blunt pressure, particularly against the soft spot where the neck meets the back of the head. He was disoriented, and at first he did not realize he was not standing, but instead lying on his back on the desert floor. When he cracked open his eyes he saw a blurry patch composed of the myriad of stars overhead. His awareness was in the twilight zone separating the eternal dream world from the jagged reality of space and time. His earthly senses whooshed towards him, as a genie's animus whooshes out of a bottle which is its primordial home, but is compelled ever towards a locus of flesh and blood.

Abraham's eyes gradually shook off the cobwebs of his sleep and the blurred dollop of light above crystallized into a sprawling tapestry of pinpricks of light. He could not at first understand where he was. He clearly remembered his conversation with Orofus. The next memory he reclaimed was the covenant the I AM sealed with him, and then he was flooded with the memory of the implosive disappearance of the hole. He remembered the last thing he saw of Orofus. "I destroyed Orofus." He shuddered at the memory of that, but he could not yet remember the reason he destroyed Orofus. The reconstitution of his memories was not sequential, it did not follow the sequence of cause and effect. He regained memories of some events while not remembering some others. The last thing he remembered was waking from his lucid dream and walking back to where he now was, lying under the stars and not remembering anything of the walk back - as if it never happened.

When he fully reclaimed his senses he grasped the startling truth. "I've dreamt all this? But...but... it must be real. How can this be?" His heart sunk with the realization. "Orofus was not out there tonight? He did not gallop across the desert floor tonight? And what of the covenant sealed between the I AM and myself and my generations to come? Do I tell my household of the covenant if it's only sealed in my dreams? Do I tell Sarai?"

He then remembered one more thing of his dreams. "My name and Sarai's, I AM changed our names. I am now Abraham and she is Sarah. We carry now in our names the mark of the ineffable H. Is that too only a figment of my dream?"

Abraham reflected: "In my dream I dreamed of experiencing a lucid dream. In this inner dream I spoke to the I AM, and the covenant between him and my generations to come was sealed. When I awoke from the lucid

The Curtains Open: The Second Act

dream within my outer dream, I didn't doubt the truth of what had transpired. Why should I now doubt what has transpired within my outer dream, or the dream within my dream?"

Abraham remembered more of his conversation with Orofus. "Orofus taught me I am his illusion. He taught me we are all denizens of his dream. We are all like the shiny facets of a diamond, each facet believing its Self to be a diamond separate from all the other facets. But we all are just facets of the same diamond, not diamonds unto ourselves. We are all within the dream of the I AM. It's not I who dreamt of the I AM, the I AM dreams of me. The dreamer is the dream. The dream is the dreamer."

And then Abraham felt his concerns and uncertainty evaporate, and he was assured. "Yes, it's all true," he thought. "It's truer than the most indisputable truths of my waking moments. It's absurd, I know, but again I must say it's absurd like the deepest truth, not the shallowest lie. Are my wakeful moments not the dream moments of the I AM? I saw Orofus tonight and I saw Yahvah, the hole in the desert floor, the navel of creation, the loop in eternity. I know all these things to be true because I am a denizen of the dream of the I AM. I speak to the I AM through his dream, and he speaks to me through mine. Like the mirror within a mirror within another. Each desert floor within the loop of Yahvah is like a bubbling stew cooking atop a fire. Each ingredient offers up its flavor to the others and is rewarded with its essence, flavored by the others, mirrored back. Each ingredient perceives its Self only as it is perceived by the others. Each ingredient perceives another only as that other perceives its Self reflected off all the others. And from this self-reflecting, cohesive whole, emanates a new entity which is not knowable by its ingredients, and yet it knows them to be its white-eyed womb of Creation."

When Abraham returned to the compound the sun began its ascent. He had left shortly before midnight that day. He had not ventured alone into the desert night for many years. He reflected: "Soon Sarah will give me an heir, and when he reaches adulthood he will be the steward over all my affairs, and I will fully retire and spend the rest of my days at Yahvah's bosom, looking up towards the desert floors beyond, the desert floors below, and curving the soul out into the loop of Eternity, reaching with the tips of my fingers for the H on the other side of the hole in the desert floor."

"I was once sure," Abraham thought, "that Ishmael will assume control over my household in the next few years. But I know now I must wait longer until my unborn heir reaches maturity. What will he be like? Will he be a man of forceful manner and few words? Will he be a man of poetry and philosophy, able to lead my household not through the force of authority but rather through influence and charisma? How proud I will be when he assumes the stewardship of not just my material household but also the legacy of my covenant with I AM."

Abraham thought of Hagar and Ishmael. "Hagar will be none too pleased when Sarah shows signs of being with child. She will hope it's not a son. I won't tell her of the promise of the I AM. She thought, as Sarah and I did, that Ishmael would be the one to be my inheritor. But Ishmael already knows how the future will unfold. Yahvah has revealed it to him. But little did any of us know the full extent of the riches to be inherited. They are so much more than the material riches of my household, or even of all the land of Canaan. I will pass on the seal of the I AM to Laughter and through him to my generations to come."

Abraham reflected: "My son, the heir of Yahvah's promise to me. Or should I only use the name I AM?". Abraham was now living vicariously through a son not yet conceived. His son to be was not the heir of the covenant, it was he. His son to be was not the one to see the unfolding of the covenant in the next generation, it was he. Do not take this the wrong way; Abraham was not stealing his unborn son's thunder. Abraham just blurred the distinction between father and son. A father beaten up by the vagaries of a life in servitude to a demanding and unpredictable divinity surely has that prerogative.

Abraham led his camel into the stables and then headed towards his tent. Soon everyone would wake, but for now his household was silent. The desert air was crisp and smelled of perfumed dew, but it was mixed with the oddly pleasant pungency of camels. The night's chill began to surrender to day's heat. Soon, the air, thick as honey, would vibrate like a pot of water just before the boil. Abraham slipped out of his heavy coat and slung it over his left shoulder. Perspiration cascaded down his brow and he wiped it with the sleeves of his coat.

He entered his tent and saw Sarah still sleeping. He had grown used to having Sarah pressed tightly against his body every night, and the full night away from her left him yearning for the contentment etched on her face when she sleeps, her beauty that still shone through the veneer of the decades, the feel of her soft lips snuggled against his bearded cheek, and the sensation of her softness snuggled against his body. That made him feel like a man meeting his responsibility to protect and comfort his wife.

When she was a young woman Sarah's beauty was spellbinding and legendary. The pharaoh of Egypt desired her. As she aged her beauty was immortalized by her mesmerizing eyes. With advancing years her skin

The Curtains Open: The Second Act

wrinkled, her sculpted features lost definition, her youthful sheen dulled, her soft and supple flowing hair brittled, but her eyes held on to an eternal beauty immune to the ravages of time. During moments of their intimacy Abraham would gaze at her eyes and he would lose all sense of time. The balls of her eyes were like multi-colored marbles. Shards of greens and blues, browns and yellows radiated from the centers of her eyes and they shimmered and sparkled. But often, when Abraham maintained his meditative gaze into her eyes, he would achieve a state of altered consciousness and he would unsee the rainbow of her eyes. The distinction between each color would fade and then he would experience only a whiteness. But this white-eyed unseeing was no longer confined to her eyes, it reached out and consumed him and they became one soul. It was during such times Abraham knew the meaning of love. It is the dance that undoes the emanation of separateness. "If I could only know such love for all of humanity," he thought, "then I would certainly become the I AM incarnate."

Abraham undressed completely and slipped under the covers. He faced Sarah and rested his head on a pillow. He studied her features that were ripened by age yet sang of the beauty of her youth. Abraham caressed her cheek, knowing that would gently wake her.

Sarah cracked open her eyes and smiled a gentle, content smile. The dawn sunlight streamed into the tent from the open flap near its top. Abraham continued caressing her cheek.

"Good morning Abram. When did you return from your desert outing, just now?"

"How did you know I went into the desert last night?"

"I woke during the night, and when I saw you weren't in bed I went out to look for you. When I couldn't find any sign of you I went to the camel stables and saw your camel was also missing. Abram, did you submit to Yahvah in the desert last night?"

Abraham paused briefly and reflected on Sarah's choice of words. "After you realized my camel was missing, you went to Eliezer's tent, didn't you?"

"Yes Abram. Don't think me too nosy. I was concerned for your safety in the open desert at night. I knew before you left for the desert you would meet with Eliezer and confide in him."

"And what exactly did Eliezer tell you?"

"Don't be upset with Eliezer, Abram. He saw the concern on my face."

"Not at all Sarah. I'm not upset in the least. I actually told Eliezer to let you know of my whereabouts. I didn't want you to worry."

The Curtains Open: The Second Act

"Tell me Abram about your-" Sarah paused. "What did you call me, or did I not hear you properly?"

"You heard me just fine. You are my Sarah now. I am your Abraham. These are our new names by the will of the I AM."

Abraham revealed to Sarah all that happened to him that night. Sarah listened intently, not once interrupting, as he told her of the whisperers, the hole in the desert floor, of his meeting with Orofus, and then with the I AM in his nested dreams and, most startling to Sarah, of the promise she will bear a son. He also instructed her to not reveal to a soul, not even to their unborn son, everything she had learned of his encounter with Yahvah in the desert that night.

"Sarah, you may reveal the seal of the covenant to anyone willing to hear, but say not a word of the mystery of Yahvah. Not even our generations to come may know of it until such time, in millennia to come, that humanity will be ready for this knowledge."

They made love that dawn for the first time in a long while and Abraham cleaved unto Sarah and an heir to the seal was conceived that day. Outside the tent, Abraham's household woke to another day's routine. The camels were washed, the bread was baked, the day's water was drawn from the wells. But inside the matrimonial tent it was dawn's first gleaming of the Second Age. And when they parted the tent's curtains and walked outside it was the curtains opening for the second act of a grand play.

The Third Age: A Quest For En Sof

The First Iteration

My Cell Phone rang, but it was on the mantle piece above the fireplace, being charged. I sat at the other side of the room, next to the kitchen. I scrambled to pick it up before it switched to voice-mail, but I did not reach it in time. The Call Display revealed it was my friend Carl. "It's Carl calling," I told my partner Pam. "I bet he's finished reading the book."

"You didn't tell me he was reading it," Pam said.

Sometimes I don't know what to call Pam. I feel it is not quite correct to call her my girlfriend because we had been living together for six years by the time I published the first iteration of my novel on Amazon. I call her my partner, but I never liked that designation, it feels too utilitarian and like a word used for lack of a more meaningful one.

"Oh yeah, he got it last week when I was on that free five-day book giveaway. I'm anxious, wondering if he likes it."

I called him back. My anxiety jarred the butterflies in my gut. He answered on the first ring.

"Hello?"

"Hey Carl, how's it going? You just called?"

"Yeah right, I just finished reading it," Carl said in his characteristic deep, resonant and soothing voice.

"And? What's the verdict?"

"I'm still processing."

We made arrangements to meet that afternoon at the Bread Garden, close to the sprawling Metrotown mall in the Vancouver suburb of Burnaby. A couple of hours later I walked into the establishment and immediately saw Carl standing by the counter, talking to the cashier.

"Congratulations, you did it," he said while straightening to his full six-foot-four height.

I looked up at him while straightening my own posture in order to mitigate our three-inch height difference.

"You liked it? You really did?"

"Absolutely, it's like you've been writing for ages. It flows so well. It's really impressive, considering this is the first thing you've ever written really, your first novel."

I grinned with relief. Ever since I started writing my novel I felt I had a gift for writing deeply expressive and poetic prose. However, I was writing in isolation, and only one person had ever read my work.

I ordered a large cappuccino with an extra shot. Carl ordered an Apple Crumble pie and an iced cappuccino. We settled at one of the tables next to

The First Iteration

the doorway. It was a hot August afternoon in 2013. I craved the relief of the afternoon breeze.

"I love the way you handled that self-referential aspect of your story. It really works seamlessly. I thought you wouldn't be able to really pull it off, but it really works."

"You mean how the composition Abram is writing is the very story you are reading that depicts how Abram is writing a composition?"

"Yeah, it just works so transparently."

"Well, I should hope so. If that part of the story doesn't quite work that would be bad, seeing as how self-reference is really the central concept behind my ideas."

Carl ran his left hand across the top of his close-cropped and thinning salt-and-pepper hair. "I like the way you describe Orofus'...err...shall we say equipment?" He smirked. His blue eyes twinkled.

"I was trying to emphasize he's a fertility idol. Why? Do you think that's too over-the-top?"

Carl shrugged. "I'm not saying anything. It's up to you."

I took a sip of my cappuccino. The strong bitterness assaulted my palate. It was strong the way I like my coffee. "What else did you like about it?"

"I thought the imagery of dancing with your adversities was very well expressed. It gives your novel an extra dimension as not just a novel of spirituality and philosophy but also a kind of self-help aspect."

Carl took a sip from his iced cappuccino. I scanned the other customers. No one was paying attention to our unconventional discussion. In the years before, Carl And I had, in public places, deep and protracted intellectual discussions that attracted curious stares.

"Yeah, that's a good point," I said, "there are other spiritually based books out on the market that have a self-help aspect, but I think they're mostly non Fiction. For example, the Power Of Now with its emphasis on dwelling in the present."

"That will give your novel an edge to get more sales. People love self-help spirituality."

"Well, that's not really my motivation for writing this book. I just want to express my conviction that humanity is at a precipice of a monumental paradigm shift in its understanding of the nature of god, and how that ties in with the future of physics and our understanding of Creation. I'm not in this to make money. I'm not a novelist per se."

Carl rolled his eyes. I thought it strange his sunny disposition was turning cynical, and I sensed he would soon become confrontational. "But you do want your book to be a best-seller, so money is a primary

The First Iteration

motivation." Carl had a tendency, that I noticed in years past, to offer biting criticism delivered in an oddly soothing, mellifluous vibrato.

"No, you have it wrong," I said. "I want my book to be a best-seller only because I want it to be read by as many people as possible, otherwise it wouldn't have the impact on the human zeitgeist I intend for it. But as far as money is concerned, well... I'll be happy to make a living out of it so I can write the second part of my book full-time without having to make a living as a software developer."

Since childhood I have been a philosopher and a mystic at heart. I never intended my novel to be just one of a string of novels I write. I know myself to be no more a novelist than a mother who frantically hoists a car from atop her child is a weightlifter. Like the mother, I am powered by a compulsion. I am energized by a source, not ordinarily at my disposal, compelling me to free humanity from under the crushing weight of an obsolete world-view. Humanity is now gasping under the heft of a paradigm that will soon defer to a cataclysmic spiritual and intellectual age of enlightenment.

Carl continued his biting criticism. "I find people use that expression 'per se' willy-nilly, without knowing what it means."

"Come on Carl, how long have you known me...since the early nineties? That's north of twenty years. You should know by now I'm too analytical to use expressions willy-nilly, as you say."

"So what does it mean then?"

"To express something per se means to say it without context. As if it's clear unto itself. In this case, I implied I'm a novelist only within a narrow context."

"The context being what?"

I explained to Carl the analogy of the adrenaline fueled mother hoisting a car from atop her child.

"You know, I've never heard anyone explain it clearly like that."

"I have a favor to ask you. Can you write a review for me on Amazon?"

"Why do you need a review? Just let it be and if it's meant to take off then it will."

I chuckled. "That's not the way things work. Good reviews help raise awareness and interest. It's called Social Proof. We're a social species."

Again, Carl rolled his eyes. I felt I was imposing on him.

"OK, fine. I guess I can do that. When do you need it by?"

"The next few days would be fine."

Carl rolled his eyes again. "You do need to invest in a good editor."

My heart sunk. "Really? I thought you said you were pleasantly surprised at how well my writing flowed."

"That's not the point. Do you realize many of the writers we consider great depended heavily on editors? For example, I read that the manuscripts Charlotte Bronte handed to her publisher looked very different from the final published versions."

"I did not know that. What are the weaknesses in my manuscript?"

"There's a lot of repetition. Ideas and expressions that are worked to death."

"But often the repetition is an expression of the theme. The shape cocooned inside the self-similar shapes. So tell me, what else needs editing?"

"Well, how about the contrived plot element of having Abram write out the entire composition on clay tablets. Come on...that's ridiculous. I think that will take most readers out of your story. He actually chiseled pages and pages of composition on clay tablets?" Carl laughed. "And also, the ancient world was an oral society. Most people were illiterate."

I mulled over his objections. I grabbed my half full cup of cappuccino. It was cold. "Carl, you're so wrong on all your objections. While it's true during day-to-day school activities there wasn't much writing, you must remember that Abram was singled out for the priesthood, and in that capacity he was expected to be a very proficient scribe. The priests were the intellectual patricians of their society. Having Abram submit a lengthy composition on clay tablets was a test, and a precursor, of the expectations placed on a priest. Also, the clay tablets were soft and malleable. They were not made of stone that required chiseling."

Carl shrugged.

"But I'll take something positive from this criticism. I'll add a passage describing in detail the way the ancients wrote on clay tablets."

"That will help, maybe make it more relatable."

"Your next point about Sumer being mostly an oral society is...well that's misleading. Did you know the city of Ur had a central library that lent out reading material? Just like modern libraries. Ur was an advanced society with a much higher degree of literacy than most other societies of that era."

"Nissim, I'm just trying to push you to be better. You do need an editor."

"I don't doubt I need an editor. I'm sure I've got typos, misused words, spelling errors and even some plot elements that need to be tightened up or filled-in. But I'll say this about your specific objections, while I don't think they're valid, I do see how other readers can object to the same things. You're prompting me to formulate well reasoned rebuttals. That's a good thing."

"Here's an idea, seeing as how the notion of a self-referencing story is one of your plot devices, why don't you add a section in your novel that discusses the objections I just threw at you?"

I widened my eyes and nodded. "That's a great idea actually. You mean kind of like a discussion such as we're having right now?"

Carl chuckled. "Yeah, kind of like what we're having right now."

"Will do. I'll add that in the second iteration of my novel. Any other constructive criticism you have for me?"

"Yeah, it's about your last chapter."

"What about it?"

"Scrap it or rewrite it. It's your weakest chapter."

I agreed with Carl but I kept my cards close to my chest. "Why do you think so?"

"It's too over the top. You come across in that chapter as someone who thinks they have such an amazing revelation to humanity that will change the course of history. It's just too strong of a viewpoint."

"Carl, we've been discussing these ideas for years. It looks to me like you haven't understood them. Because if you had then you would agree these ideas are the stuff paradigm shifts are made of."

Carl had an annoyed look on his face.

"OK, maybe I'm being a little presumptuous here," I said.

"Yeah, you think?"

"I admit I did put much more thought and care into writing the portion about Abram's childhood."

"Maybe you should just end the story there."

"But Carl, how can you say that when you know the overarching theme? The final portion of the book must be set in modern times."

"Is that non-negotiable?"

I thrust out my right arm while facing my palm upwards and with a slightly bent elbow. It was a gesture of exasperation. "Well of course, that's the crucial part, the climax of the theme I'm weaving. Why did I write about Abram? Why did I pour my heart and soul into the arc of his childhood? I can't explain this unless I jump to modern times, into the arc of my own life. The book must eventually be extended into three parts. The First Age which is set in the times of polytheism, then the Second Age which details the birth of monotheism ushered in by Abraham, and now the Third Age which talks of the dawn of the age of metatheism."

"Well sure, you don't have to recite the chronology. But really, I get what you mean. May I suggest then you just tear out the last chapter and

The First Iteration

rewrite it in a more organic way? You know what they say about great writing: show, don't tell. Show how your world view is the stuff of paradigm shifts, as you put it. Let the reader discover this rather than telling him."

I was in my early thirties when I first envisioned writing a book about the fabric of reality. I was an intellectual and, as is usually the case for intellectuals, an avowed atheist. I had planned on writing a non Fiction treatise that would incorporate the relationship of consciousness to the universe. My position was that consciousness is the fundamental, irreducible building block of Reality. My understanding of the philosophical underpinnings of Quantum Mechanics and the two Relativity theories led me to that conclusion.

"I agree with you. But I'm so eager to get my book out on Amazon. I'm excited like a child unwrapping his birthday gift."

"Well maybe that's a part of your journey."

"What do you mean?"

"I mean that perhaps releasing your book at the wrong time is ironically the right time to release it. Perhaps the bumpy road is the path you must follow."

Words delivered in Carl's soothing, mellifluous voice. Wisdom to feed the soul.

Sometime in my late thirties I experienced an epiphany both exhilarating and frightening. I came to realize the atheistic tradition I had adopted and cherished since my teens, the pantheon of secular scientific ideals - both major and minor - inextricably woven into the fabric of the Age Of Reason, is just a shadow of the textured truth. My new found realization caused me to become drunk with a sudden intellectual and spiritual freedom that need not serve any institution, that bows to no tradition, and is unencumbered with the artificial constraints of a paradigm of rationality constructed to understand Creation but which turns its back on the philosophical and logical implications of its own discoveries. I realized I could heartily drink from this overflowing cup of Truth without following the customs and etiquette of a society steeped in the stinking garbage heap of a paradigm of rationality that has neglected to curve its unbiased rationality upon itself. It is a heap composed of the rotting bodies of a pantheon of prejudices I once cherished as the fundamental, indivisible principle of Creation, but which I now realized could not possibly be at the root of the magnificent beauty and unity of this edifice.

This epiphany was an unexpected visitor, and when it came knocking on my door I greeted it as a lover I had only ever known in the recesses of the

The First Iteration

soul, and who now appeared before my very eyes as flesh and blood. This epiphany was a rose bush whose seed I planted long ago and which now burst the earth after a long and arduous winter in the unknowing, white-eyed womb of Creation. And when I reached for its tempting yet thorny flower I felt a piercing pain shooting through my spirit and I came face-to-face with the awe-full One, the great El-Shaddai, the principle of Creation, the great veiled One, the Truth overflowing my cup. Deep in the soul an unspeaking voice woke from an eternal slumber and I at once came to know that land to which I had always felt a kinship, that realm of which I am a citizen, always will be and always have been.

In my late thirties I encountered the mysteries of Chaos Theory and the mind bending insights of the German logician Kurt Gödel. His two Incompleteness Theorems compelled me to abandon the notion of consciousness as the irreducible building-block of Creation. I now stood on a high summit granting me greater vistas of truth, and I saw that consciousness, as we think of it, is only one level in the hierarchy of a recursive pattern forming the tapestry of Creation. Each level in this tapestry is an emanation from its parent level, like a mirror within a mirror within another. That is when I once again encountered the divine, and my atheism crumbled. But it was not the monotheistic divinity of the Second Age I embraced. In its place, I adopted a radical new concept of divinity I call metatheism. It is a divinity residing in the unfathomable void at the root of Creation, not a supreme principality residing outside of Creation. It is not a Deus Ex Machina; it is a Deus Sive Natura. It is not a god who lives outside a mechanistic universe and animates it as a puppeteer animates a puppet. Instead, it is implicate in the foundations of Existence.

I write of my protagonist's experiences during modern times in the second iteration of my novel. I write about his compulsion to compose a novel that reveals a new understanding of the divine. Early in this section I write about Chaos Theory and Gödel Incompleteness in the manner I already discussed above. I reveal it is these two disciplines that advanced and matured his understanding of the relationship between the divine and Creation. However, I do not, until later in my novel, explain what these two disciplines are and why they transformed my protagonist's world view. I predict the readers of my novel will prefer an immediate explanation, but I stand by the tempo of my writing. In my novel, in the chapter titled Dancing With My Fears, there is a passage speaking to this, and I quote:

"...the art of storytelling and a coherent elucidation of ideas must follow a tempo that cannot be rushed. A beautiful melody when performed at too quickly or too slowly a tempo will lose its charm. Playing it six times faster

The First Iteration

will not afford you the opportunity to compress the same enjoyment into a span six times shorter. All things are to be experienced on their own terms and will only then freely engage you in the dance."

This passage speaks to me and guides the style of writing I have employed in my novel.

I gulped down my cappuccino. Its bitterness now softened by its staleness. "I've gotta get back home soon. Thanks for offering to review me. Before I go, is there anything else I can improve?"

"There's one more glaring weakness," Carl said.

"Oh really? Do tell."

"It's about Abram's friend Khaferu."

I leaned towards Carl.

"Why would Abram endanger Khaferu by basically turning him into an accessory to the crime?"

Carl paused.

"I'm listening. Go on."

"Abram is well aware he'll incur the wrath of the authorities by blaspheming their religion. Would it not occur to him that by including Khaferu in the composition as someone who had foreknowledge of this blasphemy, he is implicating him as a blasphemer by association? And why would Khaferu never raise this point? Not only that, but in the composition you portray him as in full agreement with Abram's heretical views, even after he reads the composition and realizes he's a character in it."

I pursed my lips towards the right side of my face, a gesture of silent acquiescence. "Uhmm...yes, yes... I see your point. This did occur to me, but hearing you bring it up reinforces that it's a valid concern. I was kinda hoping no one else would notice. I'll have to think about how to deal with it. I'll need to introduce more texture into my plot in order to mitigate this plot weakness."

Carl smiled a closed-mouthed, self-congratulatory smile. "I just thought of a way out of this plot hole."

"Yes?"

"Seeing as how your whole novel, except for the last part, is actually the composition itself that Abram writes..." Carl paused and appeared deep in thought.

"I'm listening."

"Does Khaferu need to be a real person? Can't he be someone Abram made up in his composition?"

"Hmmm...yes, I see what you mean. That's not a bad idea actually. I might just go with that. But where should I add that?" I paused, squinted

The First Iteration

and pursed my lips. "I think I'll go back to the chapter called Address To The Examining Reader and mention it there."

"No Nissim, that's too untextured. You have to be more clever about it. Give it some kind of plot twist. It's a great opportunity to show the complexity of Abram's character."

"I'll think about that. Thanks for the great advice. But I've gotta scoot outta here. Thanks for doing the review. I'm looking forward to reading it. Oh, by the way, I forgot to mention, put the review up on Amazon.com, not just the Canadian site. A good review on the U.S. site will attract many more sales than on the Canadian site."

Carl rolled his eyes again. "Sure, sure, got it."

When I left, Carl stayed behind. He was still eating his Apple Crumble pie.

***

That evening, and the following day, I repeatedly checked my novel on Amazon.com to see if Carl's review had come in. In the early afternoon I saw his review posted. It was titled 'An intriguing enigma'. I felt a fleeting sense of literary legitimacy - no longer a writer toiling in obscurity, but instead a reviewed author. My joy was stillborn. I saw the orange stars, but only three of them. Carl had rated it only three stars out of five. Those three lonely orange stars burned a hole in my spirit. I was crushed. I do not know why I expected a good rating. His criticisms had been clear and sharp. Perhaps I thought I countered them convincingly. Clearly I had not.

He used the screen name 'orofus prime'. It was clearly derived from Orofus, the idol who is a character in two of the chapters in the novella. I read his review. It appeared under those three measly orange stars:

I've known the author for many years and we've engaged during those years in the kind of philosophical discussions outlined in this book. Shards of Divinities develops a unique metaphysical framework in the format of an engaging historical novella. It is unique I think in that it uses the structure of the story itself to draw the reader in to the recursive contradictions of existence.

The story is a re-visioning of the birth of monotheism in ancient Sumer as a recurring theme that is being played out now in the inevitable merging of science and spirituality. What a prophet is is re-imagined as a self-emergent phenomenon independent of history - the revelation is always the

The First Iteration

same but only appears to change based on historical context.

The writing needs polish and the last chapter could be expanded but I think this is a solid effort that will be of interest to more than Kabbalah enthusiasts or readers who enjoyed the re–imagining of history in William Burroughs later novels Cities of the Red Night, Place of Dead Roads *etc.*

"That's not a completely bad review," I thought, "despite that little zing about the writing needing polish. And I agreed the last chapter needed reworking. The review sounded to me like a four out of five. Definitely better than I, or any potential reader, would think from the three-star rating.

"But it's the number of stars in the rating that would sway potential readers more than the wording of the review," I thought. The average rating of the book is lowered by a low-rated review, particularly when the number of total reviews is small. I needed to get the sales snowball rolling. I needed the momentum that would be generated by a few great initial reviews.

I consider myself a man of integrity and I would never expect a great review for a piece of bad writing. But I was confident in my writing and felt it deserved a high rating. Just a few weeks earlier, before I published my manuscript, I asked my ex-wife Jenna to read it. She is an intelligent woman with exemplary writing skills and a penchant for all matters spiritual and political.

On July 10 I sent her my request via email:

Hi Jen
...I'm going to be publishing my novella very soon on Kindle and I would like to know if you would be interested in reading my manuscript before I publish it. I have a high regard for your opinion regarding literary and spiritual issues.
Nissim

She replied the same day:

Hey, Nissim:
I would LOVE to read your novella. Thanks for asking. I'm truly flattered and looking forward to it. J.

On July 25 she emailed me her review:

Hey:

The First Iteration

Read your novella. It's really well written! I also loved the historical details.

The only suggestion I'd make is the bit at the end. It almost sounds like an apology for what you've written, so I would either rework it, or ax it altogether. If people can't figure it out, tough shit.

Also, I hate the phrase "but I digress" when used in a fictional context. I think others may feel similarly. It has become hackneyed from overuse. Also, people will understand digression as "filling in the blanks". It's not really "digression" if it serves your narrative! :)

Thanks for letting me read and comment on it. It's great!..........J.

I was elated. She was the first person to have ever read my novella, but I noted she also criticized my last chapter. It was only a novella-length work at that point, clocking in at around thirty thousand words. Much later, when I released the second iteration, it morphed into a long novel of over one hundred and eighty thousand words. Her validation lifted my spirits and strengthened my resolve to pursue my passion for revealing my spiritual and scientific ideas through the medium of a novel.

The day I received Carl's review, Pam and I visited the Pacific National Exhibition, known as the PNE, in Vancouver. It is a two week, yearly end of summer event that combines an amusement park with a plethora of outdoor eating venues, beer gardens and an eclectic mix of indoor and outdoor shows, horse and farm animal spectacles and themed displays. I attend the PNE at least once every year. One of the highlights of the PNE for me are the outdoor night concerts. Each night a different musical group performs. Most are nostalgic Eighties bands. That night the concert was by a Canadian Eighties Pop/Rock band called Lover Boy. I was in a foul mood because of Carl's three-star review and the memory of his biting criticisms the previous day at the Bread Garden. Pam tried to brighten my mood but I was inconsolable. My book was, at that point, the culmination of a passionate dream I kept alive for many years. That day I thought my dream would fade. I felt like an impervious hollow shell not allowing any spark of yearning or hope to penetrate within.

"Are you going to let one negative review affect you like this?" Pam said.

"Maybe I'm kidding myself. Who am I to think I'm some sort of spiritual guru who will change the world? Maybe it's time to give up this crazy dream. I've never been a charismatic person. People never gravitated to me."

My thoughts drifted to a moment in time, ten years earlier, when a work colleague told me he believed in my ideas but I should find someone with charisma to be my front-man when my book is published. "So you're saying I should be a ghost writer?" I said. "I should be like a Cyrano De Bergerac, enlightening the world from the shadows while a more presentable facade is shown to the world?"

"Do you think you have the charisma to pull it off, honestly?"

"I'm not an eloquent speaker, I know," I said to him. "I'm not a charismatic man. However, the message will not be well-served by the thin veneer of meaningless charisma. The Third Age is orchestrating this, not I. The Third Age is at center stage, not I. The leader does not start the movement; the movement chooses its leaders. The movement is a self-organizing phenomenon, a consciousness unto itself."

"So just like that, you're going to give it up?" Pam said.

She pulled me out of the miasma of my inner-world.

"Uh...what?"

"You've been drilling these ideas into my head since I met you. Your feedback loops and your Gödel Incompleteness, and your Chaos and all this wild and crazy stuff," Pam laughed, "and one lousy review is all it takes?"

I did not doubt the Third Age is at hand and that I was on to something big with my spiritual and scientific ideas. But I now doubted I was the one, or perhaps one of others unknown to me, to etch these ideas in the zeitgeist of humanity.

"Has Carl responded to your last email?"

I had been in an email conversation with Carl since Pam and I arrived at the PNE.

"Not yet."

"Do you think he'll pull the review?"

I told Carl his review was not doing me any favors and I asked him to remove it.

"Is this how you treat your friends?" I emailed him.

"I'm just trying to push you into becoming a better writer," he emailed back.

"You keep saying I need to edit but you're not being specific. And don't rehash the points we already discussed yesterday. Apart from the issue with Khaferu, I already pointed out to you that your criticisms were not valid," I emailed.

"Well, for one, remove that ridiculous passage about Orofus' big dick.

The First Iteration

How's that for a start? I couldn't believe you put that in there," he emailed back.

I did not see anything wrong with emphasizing Orofus' phallic proportions. It was organic to the story because he is a fertility idol. Carl was by no means a prude, and his revulsion at that puzzled me.

Pam and I headed to the Westjet concert amphitheater. The road sloped gently uphill. An enticing aroma of sizzling popcorn and deep-fried sweet-dough wafted in the evening breeze. The amusement park portion of the PNE was nearby and the piercing, terrified shrieks of the people on the daredevil rides blended harmoniously with the squeaks and thuds of these rides. The throng of people was mostly heading against us, and as we fought our way through I felt like salmon swimming upstream. When we arrived at the amphitheater I looked downhill at the long road from where we came and was struck by the philosophically pregnant sight of the mass of thousands of people milling downstream shoulder-to-shoulder and looking like an anthill of mindless automatons.

That night's concert was by Lover Boy, a Vancouver Rock band that achieved great success in Canada and the U.S. during the early Eighties. I was only twenty-one when I first listened to their music. They were never in the top tier of my favorite Eighties bands, but I nevertheless looked forward to a show that would alleviate my depressed mood. I harbor a poignant nostalgia for the Eighties, and I was looking forward to this concert particularly for that reason. We took our seats at the back of the amphitheater. The wooden bench seats were hard, and with no backrest.

The concert began at 8 PM and the sun had just set. It had been a very hot day, but with the onset of darkness the heat of day gave way to a pleasant summer night. As the band played through their repertoire of songs I realized I liked their music more than I had previously thought. During almost every song I commented to Pam: "Oh, I forgot about this song. Yeah...it's their song. I haven't heard it in so many years and I really like it."

As the show progressed I developed a respect for their musical artistry and the talent and showmanship of the lead singer. I forgot my depression and was transported to that idyllic space where the Yin dances an intimate dance with the Yang and they become None. Like the trough of a wave aligning perfectly with the crest of another and achieving a state of no-wave, I achieved a state of no-mind by resonating with their music. The crest of my spirit aligned perfectly with the trough of the music and then we became None. I experienced the deepest truth of Yahvah, the innermost mirror and yet also the outermost, the void of the H whispering from within the semantic spaces of the soul.

As I soaked in the music, I contemplated the nature of great art, be it music or literature or any other, and the reason it has the power to enlighten the soul. Great art leverages the intimate dance of Yin and Yang and, via the abstract notion of wave cancellation, consolidates them into None. But the H within Yahvah is that None, the void from which Creation emanates. Therefore, great art is fundamentally a means of connecting intimately with the H within YHVH and becoming that H, that ineffable Ground of Being. Great art is the divine whispering, from a common source, to us all. Great art compels us to become the H, to see the face of god and to then realize it is the soul staring back. That is when our spirits soar like an angel in full flight. That is when YHVH is deconstructed back into perfect nothingness, the H, and we achieve the Zen state of enlightenment, the state of no-mind. That is when Man becomes God.

And then my depression and self-doubt lifted and I regained my passion for writing my book and pouring my heart and soul into it. I craved again to create my art and to speak of that other realm of which I always felt I have been a citizen. I regained the unshakable confidence my book will be an instrument in an orchestra that will mesmerize humanity's soul and trigger a global awakening. It will be a tectonic paradigm shift that will reshape the landscape of our world-view. In the Kabbalah, the Received Wisdom, the name for the ineffable H is En Sof. I call the coming global awakening The Third Age: A Quest For En Sof.

The next day I checked the reviews page for my novella on Amazon. Carl did not remove his review but he bumped its star rating from three stars to four. I again asked him, via email, to remove the review because I did not want to coerce him into increasing the rating. He replied that he had no problem with giving me a four-star review and I should think of it as a four-star rating out of seven. I found his tone to be very condescending, but I chose to not respond. His four-star review was still posted on Amazon when I finished the second iteration of my novel almost three years later. But by then my obsession with securing reviews by my friends and family had evaporated. I removed my novella from Amazon on December of 2013 when I realized I needed to expand it into a full-length novel. When I completed the second iteration I put it back on sale at Amazon and I sought reviews from my Twitter followers, the Goodreads online literary community, and from top Amazon reviewers.

There is a chapter named *The First Iteration* in the second iteration of the novel I wrote. This chapter contains a passage explaining one of my biggest challenges in writing the portion of my novel set in modern times. I quote from that passage:

...The challenge has been in weaving my scientific and spiritual ideas within the context of a plot...

Earlier in the novel, in the portion set in ancient times, I did not have to wrestle with this challenge because I was not explicitly writing about Gödel's theorems, Chaos Theory and other key scientific and mathematical concepts. I only wrote of these ideas obliquely, and only the perceptive reader who is familiar with these ideas would have noticed I was referring to them. But in the second iteration of my novel, in the portion set in modern times, while I still included implicit references to the self-referential aspects of Gödel Incompleteness and Chaos Theory, I could no longer write of these ideas only in that way.

A Leitmotif In The Final Key

I was born in 1963 in the city of Yaffo in modern Israel, just fifteen years after the resurrection of Israel. In those days Israel was not yet the modern and urbane technological powerhouse it has become now days; it was a new country emerging from a difficult formative period.

I was born a Hebrew and in many parts of the world the Hebrews, also known as Jews, are at best tolerated and at worst despised. This has been the case since time immemorial, but in modern times the Hebrews have prospered in Israel and before that time they settled the lands of North America. In those lands they escaped the severe discrimination that plagued them in Europe during the first half of the twentieth century and the centuries before.

My ancestors lived in Spain up to the year 1492. In that fateful year, the year Columbus sailed into the New World, all Hebrews were expelled from Spain by Queen Isabella. My ancestors, to this day known as Sephardic Jews, migrated to the Ottoman empire. On my father's side, they settled in modern-day Bulgaria and on my mother's side they settled in modern-day Turkey. But they never forgot the Spanish language of their homeland. They cherished and coddled their beloved Spanish and they do so to this day. When I was growing up in Israel I heard both sides of my family speaking Ladino, the Spanish language as it was spoken during those distant halcyon days of the Hebrews in Spain.

I trace my ancestry to Spain as far back as the time of the great expulsion and into the golden age of the Sephardics in Spain, but before that time, and into the murky depths of the past, I am not certain of the origin of my ancestors. I suspect the ancestors of my ancestors in Spain were Hellenistic Hebrews who lived in Greece during the time of Jesus and the centuries preceding the Christian era.

The age of Columbus was the last chapter of the golden age of the Hebrews in Spain. It was a harbinger of a seismic shift in the fabric of the Hebrew zeitgeist. In the New World the Hebrews were destined to thrive as they had never thrived before. The New World was destined to be their beloved land, only second to Canaan. And as the Hebrews thrived in the New World then so did the New World ascend to greatness and to great influence amongst the Civilization of Man. The covenant between Abraham and I AM was unfolding.

When Abraham was in the desert that pregnant night under the tapestry of the stars, the I AM promised him: "Look below your feet at the desert dust and that too is as the multitudes of your generations to come. I will make a great people from you and whosoever favors them I will greatly bless but whosoever condemns them I will harshly curse and cause to disappear from the affairs of Man."

The age of the Hebrews in Spain was an age amongst whose luminaries was Maimonides - one of the greatest Jewish philosophers. It also became the center of Kabbalistic writing and thinking, the Received Wisdom of Abraham, at the hands of the Hebrew mystics. Before their expulsion the Hebrews thrived in Spain. They were successful in the arts, in finance and in philosophy and the sciences. They were successful merchants and business owners. As they thrived then so did Spain. And there too Abraham's covenant with I AM unfolded, and Spain ascended to great wealth and influence amongst the affairs of Man.

***

When I was a child my father Shmuel, known by his anglicized name Samuel, would captivate me with tales of his childhood woes. One of the stories he never tired of telling was of his childhood in Bulgaria during the dark days of World War II.

"Let me tell you about those butchers, the Nazis, the scourge of Europe. The Germans conquered much of Europe in those days and they were evil incarnate." He paused for a few seconds, running his hands through his thick, wavy hair. His hair was still mostly dark in those days.

"Yeah abba, you already told me once about the Nazis and how they hated us and killed us."

"Yes I did, but you were younger then and you weren't ready to hear the gruesome details. You are more mature now and you are ready to learn about the evil that spoils humanity's heart."

I was still a child, not much older then ten or eleven, when my father taught me the gruesome barbarism of the Germans during World War II. My sister Linda was only a baby then and would not understand.

"Some say in the years since the war," my father said, "the story I'm about to tell you was invented. Some say it's merely a lie that has been artfully spun by the Hebrews, like golden silk at the hands of a master yarn spinner. But let me tell you here and now that it is nothing of the sort. Every word is as authentic and true as the sun setting in the West. The Germans imprisoned the Jews in places called Concentration Camps, where they either starved to death, died from being worked to death, died from disease or died in horrific medical experiments that would be considered by all decent people too horrific to be performed even on a rat. For the lucky ones who survived, they were sent to the gas chambers. Believe me, it was the unlucky ones who survived and got sent to the gas chambers."

"What's a gas chamber?"

"Well, what the Germans did is this: every day they selected a group of Jews who were already too injured or old to work as slaves in the camps, maybe thirty or forty at a time, sometimes much more, and they herded them into large, airtight rooms. Those rooms could hold up to two thousand people. They then pumped poison gas into the room. Do you know how a person dies in a gas chamber?"

I listened in hypnotic stupor, unable to respond, unable to properly breathe. I soaked in every word of my father's tale. I sat on the couch facing him, my arms slung over my thighs, shoulders and neck slumped forward and mouth gaping in awe.

My father continued: "Their lungs fill with the poison gas until they burn as if gasoline was poured into them and set on fire. They gasp for breath but none is to be had. Their eyes bulge in horrific and confused desperation until their lungs explode and they die with their eyes wide open, staring blankly into space. Sometimes, they would throw garbage bags filled with shrieking Hebrew babies into the gas chambers, as if throwing sacks of old rags, and then gas them. The babies vibrated with agony until their lungs exploded and they suffocated."

My father paused for a few seconds while forming his thoughts. He rubbed the back of his right hand against his left cheek. I studied his face. My father was a little chubby in those days but he was still a handsome man. "That's the only reason I married him," my mother would often chuckle with contempt.

"What happened to you and your family," I asked. "How did you survive?"

"Us Bulgarian Jews were lucky. Unlike what happened in Poland, we were never sent to the camps. King Boris protected us by refusing to cooperate with Hitler."

"So nothing bad happened to Bulgarian Jews?"

"Well, we had to wear a yellow star that marked us as Yehudi. We were ordered to make them ourselves and stitch them on our clothes. I remember your grandmother Victoria making my stars out of old yellow rags. While cutting the stars with an old pair of rusty scissors, she would hum an old Hebrew spiritual song that she often hummed to me when I was much younger than you are now and couldn't sleep because I was afraid of the darkness and stillness of the night. She stitched those Jewish stars on all my shirts and my winter coat and she did the same for herself, your aunt Matty and your grandfather Nissim. If we were spotted in public without the star displayed somewhere prominently on our clothes then we were severely punished. But if we did wear them then we were harassed by the hordes of the marauding fascist thugs who roamed the streets looking for yellow stars to beat up on. We just couldn't win."

My father paused for a few seconds and then spoke with a stern, too dramatic voice: "The most infamous of these death camps was called Auschwitz or Birkennau to be more exact, because that's where the gas chambers were located. It's in Poland. To this day, Auschwitz stands at the outskirts of the city of Oświęcim, in the village of Brzezinka, preserved as a soul-chilling testament of the evil that infests humanity's heart and a reminder to Hebrews about their place in a world that may tolerate them at times but will never consider them as true sons and daughters of the lands they inhabit."

My father paused again for a few seconds and then pointed his right hand index finger straight up and at eye level. "But I do have a soft spot in my heart for Canada and the United States. Us Hebrews have been welcomed here like no place in Europe has ever welcomed us since our golden age in Spain. That's why I always dreamed of living here. And here we are now, living in Canada. This is the golden age of the Hebrews in the New World."

Crossing Over To New Realms

On new year's eve 2002 Jenna and I were at her friend Penny's house. Penny was a nurse and an avid maker of wine at home. Her Ice Wine was heavenly. She was also a foodie and she often hosted lavish meals for us. Jenna and I had recently stopped eating mammals on ethical grounds. This posed a problem for Penny, both ideologically and practically, because she was an avid carnivore.

"Humans have evolved to be able to digest meat, so there's nothing wrong with eating it," she would declare.

"Humans have also evolved," I often replied, "an intelligence and a moral capacity that allows us to transcend our base evolutionary impulses. And, by the way, there's nothing in our ability to digest meat that justifies caging pigs for days without water, in hot conditions, while being transported to the slaughterhouse. That's obscene. That's shameful and disgusting."

She would often tempt Jenna and me with succulent morsels of steak, medium rare the way we used to love it, or with roasted lamb infused with rosemary and spice, its bubbling juices oozing out. Jenna particularly loved prosciutto and pancetta, a taste she acquired during her two years belly dancing in Rome. It was a struggle for her to give these up.

At around 10 PM I was playing with Penny's dog Einstein. He was an acutely gifted Border Collie able to understand numbers and complex commands. For example, he would understand the command to run around a tree six times or that I have placed a gift for him under the sofa.

My cell phone rang. A female voice spoke: "Can I please talk to Mr. Nissim Levy."

"Speaking."

"I'm calling from the Royal Columbian hospital. Your father has been in an accident. Can you please come to the hospital right now?"

I had a flashback to 1996. I had received an identical call then, from the same hospital. "What happened?"

"He was involved in a pedestrian vehicle collision at around six PM today."

"What? Again? The exact same thing happened to him six years ago."

I rushed to the hospital. It is in New Westminster, a suburb of Vancouver, about a forty minute drive from Penny's house.

"Are you his son?" asked his doctor when I entered the area where my father was lying on a bed, hooked up to tubes.

"Is he alright?"

"He's been in a nasty accident. In addition to contusions and general hematoma injuries, he's also sustained a fractured left humerus at the ball of the shoulder joint and a fracture of the right side femoral neck. Fortunately there's no head trauma."

"His neck is fractured? Is he going to be paralyzed?"

The doctor chuckled. "No, no, I apologize for the medical jargon. He's got a broken hip and shoulder."

I was grateful for small mercies. I went to his bedside. He was semi-conscious.

"Nissim?" he said in a low, hoarse voice. His face was lightly bruised.

I was the only link to his family. He was estranged from both my mother Ziva and my ten years younger sister, Linda. He was an idiosyncratic man, unable to understand textured reality and prone to quick fits of anger and to imagined slights inflicted on him. I will never forget the time, I think it was 1997 or 1998, when I was standing with him in line at Starbucks. He ordered a latte.

The young, acne-faced cashier asked him: "Would you like homo milk in your latte?"

When my father heard the word 'homo' his face contorted into a mask of rage and, as he jabbed his right index finger towards the cashier's face, in self-righteous indignation, he yelled: "Do not use that word with me." Spittle flew from the sides of his mouth. The cashier was simultaneously horrified and confused. When my father was out of earshot I apologized to the cashier and muttered something about my father being from the old country and unfamiliar with Canadian customs. Yes, he did harbor homophobic tendencies, but only insofar as he feared the unknown. The word 'homophobia' was appropriate for him because he distrusted homosexuality, but did not hate it. My father was incapable of hate, but he feared humanity's inevitable progression out of its atavistic prejudices and comforts.

He suffered a wanderlust all his life and it is ironic he distrusted unknown cultures and customs, but was irresistibly drawn to them. The fear of the unknown contains the seeds of its own destruction. In the knowing the unknown fades, like a shadow assaulted by light.

He suffered from chronic constipation and heartburn. "Maybe you shouldn't add eight spoons of sugar to your coffee," I often advised him. "All the sugar and sweets you constantly stuff into your face are causing your heartburn." He had an addiction to sweets but an aversion to salt. I never saw him eat a salty snack.

He rebuked my advice. "When I was a boy in Bulgaria during the war it was almost impossible to find any sugar. Sugar is good. It's valuable calories."

I explained that, due to today's overabundance of calories, sugar is not the invaluable commodity it was in war-torn Europe. "This isn't Bulgaria during World War Two, you know?" But my explanation landed on ears impervious to change or modernism.

God forbid I should tell him to eat whole-wheat bread or more fiber, in order to mitigate his ubiquitous constipation. At the very mention of the word 'fiber', or the expression 'whole-wheat', he would go into fits of explosive rage.

"Fiber is not food. Don't listen to those young punks. Those brainwashed dietitians, as if that's even a real job. Telling us what to eat like they know it all. The covering of the wheat kernel is for animals only. We called it Tritza in Bulgaria. People should eat good white bread, like we had in Bulgaria. These young punks have all these crazy politically correct ideas."

And then his face contorted even more and his body shook with a frenetic energy. He flailed his arms. "No, I don't want to hear it."

When I was fourteen I lived in Montreal, under one roof with both my parents and my four-year-old sister, Linda. But my parents' marriage was never a happy one and I often escaped to my room during their bitter and spiteful fights, wishing the walls would swallow me for just long enough so I would not be privy to their vitriols, but not daring to leave my room lest they suspect the trauma I suffered. I do not remember ever feeling love between my parents. I do not blame my mother for this. She was the diametric opposite of my father. She had many friends and everyone gravitated to her. She was generous with me, but he wasn't. She paid for my violin lessons out of her meager earnings. She continued paying for my weekly violin lessons until we immigrated to Montreal Canada when I was almost nine. In Montreal I did not continue the violin lessons because my mother could not afford them. She spoke not a word of English or French and she was dependent on the meager crumbs my father saw fit to dispense. I lost my benefactor.

In Montreal my father was chronically unemployed. Unemployment insurance fed and clothed us. My mother accused him of laziness, but I now know better. He was not a lazy man, he was an afflicted man, and his affliction prevented him from navigating the interpersonal dynamics that are the tapestry of life from cradle to grave. More than anyone in my family I have a window into his deepest nature because I have a part of him in me.

When we lived in Israel my mother's good friend Tamara lived one floor below us. Tamara had a son named Arnon and he became my best friend. My mother would often visit Tamara and her husband and spend the evening with them. But my father never joined her. He chose a solitary existence with his nose buried in a history or political book. Often he spent his after-work hours at the library. He read Marx voraciously, in Russian and English. He was an erudite man and a polyglot. He was fluent in Russian, Bulgarian, English, French and Hebrew and he dabbled in half a dozen other languages. He was a master of Greek and Latin etymologies. When we first made contact with our estranged family in Seattle, in 1972, they noted his English proficiency exceeds that of most native English speakers.

My father regularly argued politics to the point of annoyance, and he alienated many in Israeli society with his Leftist, anti-establishment views. I vividly remember the nights he came home from work and I was mesmerized by his plaintive wails about being passed over for promotions. He was a payroll clerk with the national Israeli airline EL AL. He never identified with Zionism. "I am a Bulgarian first. That's where my heart is," he often told anyone within earshot. There is a congruence between the Hebrews returning in 1948 to the land of their forefathers and their return in 539 BCE, when the Persian king Cyrus freed them from Babylonian captivity. Many held life-long attachments to the Babylonian land of their birth. Upon their return, they felt alienated in the land of their forefathers, the land of Canaan. My father left Bulgaria at eighteen but he pined for the land of his birth until his dying day. He was a Jew in Israel but a Bulgarian at heart.

My father was an avowed atheist, in contrast to the literal religiosity I embraced during my earliest teens. "I lost my belief in god during the war," he once told me. "Where was god when the Germans suffocated our children in their gas chambers?" My father attempted to dissuade others from religion by allusions to Theodicy, but he failed to grasp that a belief in god is not vulnerable to Theodicy's unanswered mystery. Religion is a mirror of a person's character. It is seldom an external commodity vulnerable to the vagaries of life's arc.

One day, in January of 1978, my mother asked me to sit down with her at the kitchen table. She was a young woman then, only thirty-four. She wanted to discuss something important. My father was out and my sister was sleeping. She spoke to me only in Hebrew in those days. Her English was rough.

"You must promise to keep it a secret," she said.

I promised.

She gave me a weak smile. I sensed it was not because she enjoyed what she intended to reveal, but simply as a means to offset its bleakness. "In the Spring I'm leaving Montreal."

I did not digest her words yet. "Where are you going?"

"I'm taking Linda also. We're going to Seattle. I want you to come with us, but it's your choice."

"What about him?"

She sighed. "He's the reason I'm leaving. I can't live with him anymore. I've had enough. We can't live with him anymore." She emphasized the word 'we'.

I did not ask for an explanation. I understood too well and I sympathized. She was a long-suffering wife.

"You can't breathe a word of this to him or to anyone else. Do you hear?"

"Linda?"

"No, she's too young to understand. She might say something."

"So when are you going to tell him?"

She grabbed both my shoulders and gazed into my eyes. "I'm not and you're not. Do you understand? A couple weeks before we leave I'll tell him we're visiting the family in Seattle."

She paused for a few seconds. "So are you coming with us or do you want to stay with your father?"

My heart ached when the words came out of me. "No, no, I'll come with you."

We had family in Seattle. My maternal grandmother Estrellia Alcabes (nee Chiprut) was the youngest of twelve siblings, all born in Turkey. Her oldest brother Behor was born in 1881. He was thirty years older than my grandmother. He left Turkey in 1904, before she was born, for a better life in America, the new world of opportunities. It was only in 1971 she established contact with her brother's heirs in Seattle, but it was only through the mail. She exchanged letters in Ladino with her nieces and nephews - his children. Behor passed away in 1969. My grandmother never met her oldest brother, nor ever communicated with him.

Behor achieved prominence in Seattle's Sephardic Jewish community. I've heard stories of his legendary feats of strength. He would lift, on a dare, three-hundred pound sacks of potatoes with his teeth. Legend has it that once, with the help of a few of his friends, he lifted and repositioned a car parked in front of the synagogue on the Sabbath - the day of rest, when driving is ironically prohibited. I think my natural muscularity and strength is inherited from the Chiprut line. I was a freakishly strong child. I amazed my school mates with my feats of strength. As a child, I was able to hoist weights in the gym that would challenge most men.

I have, in moments of poignant reflection, contemplated what Behor thought, in moments of his own poignant reflections, of the wide gulf he crossed and which forever separated him from his siblings in the old world. Were thoughts of unbearable separation and longing his daily nemesis? If not then were they assimilated into the mosaic of his being or melted into an amorphous thing?

My heart breaks when I contemplate such desolation. It is both my personal and, in general, my people's lot in life to suffer the gut-wrenching pain of exile from the womb of their birth. I come from those that cross over and experience a desolation due to separation from a place or family or ancestry. These are all archetypes of a grand phenotype repeating in the garden eternally. We all eat from the Tree of Knowledge of Good and Evil at our deepest point of origin, and then, through self-reflection, know ourselves and become new branches sprouting from the Tree of Existence - YHVH - a mirror within a mirror withing another. From my perspective: me first, my immediate family then my ancestry, then the Civilization of Man and finally I meet myself again in the eternal garden. But nothing changes in Eternity. There never is a change of perspective in the well of Creation. It is what it is. Each level banished from the previous, as an unprovable theorem banished from its formal system in the kingdom of Gödel.

I kept the secret of our departure festering in me from January until the day we left in May of 1978, and my heart ached every day. As the months passed my ache grew exponentially. I was overcome with guilt for keeping that awful secret from him. I felt I was betraying him. Every meal with him, every car ride, every night watching TV with him and my mother by my side, I knew I was one day closer to the day we would leave him like thieves in the night. I loved my father despite his shortcomings. He was not a bad-hearted man. He was not a liar. I did not know what afflicted him.

The day we left, my father drove us to the Greyhound bus station. We were taking a three-day bus ride to Vancouver, and from there one of the family members from Seattle would meet us. We would try to settle in Seattle. As we boarded the bus my father hugged my sister and me. I turned my eyes away when my father kissed my mother. I cried inside but could not let it out. My four-year-old sister would now grow up not knowing her father. It would be only on his deathbed, thirty-five years later, that she got to know him as a father instead of that distant abstraction our mother reviled.

"Nissim, is that you?" my father whispered.

"Yes, it's me. I'm here. Don't worry, I talked to the doctor and it looks like your injuries aren't as bad as the last accident you had."

He gave me a weak smile. "Where's Linda. Will she be coming this time?"

I was thirty-nine now and Linda was twenty-nine. She has always been my diametric opposite. Like my mother, she has always been outgoing. Everyone gravitates to her. She was a rebellious teenager whereas I stayed in my room with my nose in a book.

My father followed us to Vancouver two years after we left Montreal. That has confirmed for me his love for us, but I did not understand it back then. One Saturday, in May 17 of 1980 when I was sixteen, my mother handed me the phone and when I put it to my ear I heard a voice I had not heard in two years. His voice betrayed the pain of those years and he sobbed. I saw him the next day. I went alone. It was the day Mount St. Helen's exploded.

In Vancouver our relationship was sporadic until his first accident in 1996. Before that accident there were periods of months or even years that I would not see him. It was not due to apathy or discord but for reasons I could not bear to understand. But the passing years have mellowed my hard shell and I am now more reflective of my traumas and scars. It was my pain that distanced me from him as surely as it must have distanced him from me. But how much more severe must the pain have been festering between Linda and him to have created a greater chasm than even mine.

In 1996 I did not yet know about the novel I would one day write. All I strived for in those days was a life of conventional success as well as of thought. It had been years since I last entertained thoughts about the meaning of consciousness. In 1991 I wrote a small essay about it which I kept to myself. Before that time it was in the early to mid 1980s I last thought of these ideas. I read the Tao Of Physics and the Dancing Wu Li Masters. These were books about consciousness dancing with physics and they made an indelible impression that lay dormant within me for the years to come.

In 1996 I did not yet know of the coming age of the convergence of body and soul, intellect and divinity. In me the cocooned destiny still lay dormant. Life can be an enigma. The paradigm shift creates its leader, the leader does not create the paradigm shift. I did not fear then, but my fear has since intensified, that if I shall be an actor of influence on the stage of the Third Age then it is making an uncharacteristic mistake in choosing me. But perhaps it is my self-doubt which is in error. Both Moses and Churchill were stutterers, but their words emanated from the semantic spaces of their listeners' soul. Perhaps the Third Age is not seeking the insincere veneer of generic charisma. Perhaps it is not calling out for an actor to impersonate another, but instead for a cameo role - a person as simply himself.

Our stay in Seattle in the summer of 1978 was short-lived. My mother did not find the welcome for which she had hoped. There came a day when I woke up with a feeling my pain and trauma were soon to dissipate. The family member we had been staying with for the previous two weeks suggested a day's outing to Vancouver BC. But her agenda was hidden. She did not return with us to Seattle. She dumped us at the doorstep of the Jewish Community Center in Vancouver. She assured my mother we would be well taken care of while trying to put back the broken pieces of our lives, and then she abandoned us and drove away. We had no place to stay. The Jewish Community Center suggested we visit the Catholic mission in Vancouver's Downtown East Side. It was located on Powell street. The Catholics took us in and offered us food, companionship and a roof over our heads. We were destitute and my mother contemplated a return to Montreal, her hopes having been crushed in Seattle and with no prospect of employment in sight. Her English was broken and she was now solely responsible for providing for me and my four-year-old sister.

We are all products of our earliest experiences, be they tragedies or triumphs. I will venture to say the greatest amongst us are made more of tragedy than triumph. The greatest amongst us have leveraged the wounds of their formative years. They have wrestled with them as Jacob did and he became Israel - a God Wrestler. I stand before you today as a wounded man. Have I wrestled with my wounds like Israel or have I let them incapacitate me? During the trauma I endured in the summer of my fourteenth year I leaned on my faith in YHVH, but not as I understand YHVH today. I never asked questions of Theodicy. Like a man using his opponent's strength against him, I leveraged my wounds to strengthen my faith. I was a conventional Hebrew worshiping a divinity born of the Second Age. But deep within the semantic spaces of my spirit lay dormant a power that would one day wake.

The Early Years: Why Are All Bachelors Unmarried?

I dropped off Jenna at St. James Anglican church, at the northeast corner of Cordova and Gore streets. It is in the seedy part of Downtown Vancouver, the East Side, the poorest neighborhood in Canada, and is infamously known as the DTE. The stench of overflowing garbage dumpsters from the nearby produce market was like tiny daggers in my nose. The heat of summer was no more. I was grateful for the gentle chill in the October air that mitigated the stench, otherwise it would have been unbearable. The sign posts of Autumn were etched in the air but not on the ground. There were no fallen autumn leaves because the DTE is, with few exceptions, a concrete wasteland, unlike Downtown West which is graced with trees, flowers and other city-hall bestowed beauty.

Jenna had become a regular at St. James shortly after I met her in December of 1998. Now, just ten months later, she had joined several church committees and was contemplating becoming a deacon. The church building is a three-story, Gothic style concrete structure with dark slate steeple roofs. Fifteen years later, when I wrote the chapter named *The Early Years: Why Are All Bachelors Unmarried*, I looked up St. James Anglican Church on Wikipedia and it was described as an architectural hybrid of Art Deco, Byzantine, Gothic and Romanesque Revival. That is quite an eclectic combination, but these varied styles wrestled with each other, and a unique style emanated and became an entity unto itself - an iconic part of the DTE.

I drove Jenna to the church and went in with her for a few minutes. I then returned to my car, parked a block to the north. I tiptoed through a back-alley littered with shards of broken glass, spent hypodermic injection syringes, oozing condoms and Fast Food containers festering with bubbling, rotting food. I reached my car and sat on its still warm hood. I waited for Carl. We had agreed to meet that Sunday morning next to the church. I called and gave him my exact location. He was just a few minutes away on foot. Carl does not drive, he prefers an ascetic lifestyle. The denizens of the DTE were lumbering up and down the street like emaciated, lifeless white-eyed Golems. One approached me, begging for change. He sported the ageless look characteristic of the homeless drug addicts of the DTE. He may have been thirty or sixty, I could not determine. The ravages of addiction muddle the signposts of the linear progression from youth to senescence.

"Hey bud, ya got some change?"

His twisted teeth, the few he still had, were brown like overripe bananas

The Early Years: Why Are All Bachelors Unmarried?

with dark blotches. His face was a gaunt mask of papier-mâché skin, taut over bones like kindlewood, and speckled with both crusted scabs and fresh, oozing self-inflicted wounds. But his dying eyes could not hide a humanity trapped deep within and whimpering to get out. I could no longer smell the rotting garbage in the bins because his layers of stained clothes, reeking of fermented body odor, overpowered it. I struggled to decipher his slurred speech and then pulled out two Loonies from my wallet, knowing he would most likely use this money towards drugs. But does not even a junkie need to eat some time? Yet his body was pleading not for food but for the drugs that sustained his days yet destroyed his years.

"Here ya go my good man, two bucks. That's all the change I've got. What's your name?"

He snatched the coins from my open palm, gave me a vacant stare, and scurried away. I experienced a disturbing, haunting loneliness because I could not see myself reflected off his eyes. I did not exist for him. But it was his loneliness I experienced. I felt the urge to wash my hands and was saddened for feeling that. I brushed my palms against my pants, hoping no one saw me, pretending I did not see it myself. Two minutes later I saw Carl's lanky frame rounding the corner of the block and heading my way. I had not seen him in over a year. He had gained weight and his full head of chestnut hair had grown out into a bouquet of tight curls.

"Hi Nissim, how are you doing?" His mellifluous, deep voice had the usual tranquilizing, almost soporific quality. It took a lot to get Carl excited.

"Good, it's been a while. I've never seen you with such long hair. You always kept it so short. I had no idea your hair is so curly."

"It's been fun growing it out. I'm going to donate it to cancer patients."

"Are you serious? That's awesome. When?"

"In a few weeks. I signed up with an organization that creates natural hair wigs for chemotherapy patients. Believe it or not they're interested in my hair." Carl pursed his lips and twisted his right wrist, palm facing up, as a gesture of mock disbelief.

"You've put on a quite a few pounds. Eating's too good?

"No, I haven't been eating much the last few months. I've been on a mostly beer diet. A twelve-pack a day. Some days a six-pack on top of that."

If I could whistle I would have done so in amazement. "That's crazy. Why? I always thought you were a teetotaler."

"It's just an experiment I'm doing. I'm measuring the effects of an extreme beer diet on my body."

The Early Years: Why Are All Bachelors Unmarried?

"And you're doing that because?"

"Just curious."

"Where shall we go eat? Or should I say drink?" I laughed.

"No, I stopped my beer experiment a couple of weeks ago. I don't drink anymore. Anything you want is fine. Trees is always good."

"That sounds good. Listen, we've got a lot to catch up on. I'm clearer now where I want to go with my book."

It had been seven years since I met Carl. In 1991 I joined an intellectually oriented society. Its members were scattered around the world and I had never met any in person. One day, in 1992, I was reading the publication of this society composed, in part, of articles contributed by its members. At the bottom of each article was listed the name and address of the contributor. I was thrilled and surprised to see a Vancouver address only a few blocks from me. I wrote a short letter introducing myself, folded it into a crisp envelope, and wrote on the envelope: 'To Carl Warden, from Nissim Levy.' My letter explained how I learned of his address and provided my contact phone number. I walked the few blocks and dropped it through his mail-slot. The next day Carl called me and we arranged to meet at my place. The doorbell rang and I bolted down the stairs and opened the door. In front of me stood a tall, clean-shaved, thin man with close-cropped dark hair and deep-blue eyes with thin, dark lines radiating from the centers of the corneas. He appeared to be around my age. I looked up into his eyes and shook his hand. And that's how I met Carl.

"So you're finally going to start writing it?"

"I'm not quite ready yet. I'm still forming my ideas. I'll write it when I'm ready. but I know now I'll write it as a novel."

Carl sneered. "A novel? Isn't that the easy way out?"

"I don't think so. It's really the harder way. I'd need to weave my ideas into a storyline, and not just worry about the scientific or philosophical aspects of my ideas."

"Then why do it that way?"

"Listen," I said, "let's head to Trees for a bite, then we'll talk."

I drove the five minutes to the Downtown core and parked. After feeding the parking meter we headed to Trees Organic coffee shop, a block away on Granville street, between Hastings and Pender streets. That was our favorite spot when meeting Downtown. My mouth watered thinking of the mango cream pie. Santa Claus was, as usual, sitting in the Trees patio area, in a seat closest to the entrance. He was an old, large white man with a full head of thick white hair that brushed his shoulders, and a puffy white beard that cascaded down to his chest. Back in those days he was a constant presence outside Trees. He was a white-bearded sentinel observing the affairs of Man yet interacting with None.

We both ordered cappuccinos and I ordered a wedge of mocha cake. To my chagrin I learned the mango cream pie is only available during summers. Carl ordered a slice of lemon-meringue pie. The narrow interior was packed, but we were fortunate to find a table that had just been vacated. We took our seats against the wall and plopped our coffees and cakes on the small, square wooden table. I inhaled with gusto the rich coffee aromas wafting in the air.

"I've nailed down my argument that consciousness is the fundamental building-block of the universe."

"OK," Carl said in a matter-of-fact way, "I didn't know you were thinking along those lines."

I slurped my cappuccino and devoured a large piece of mocha cake dangling precariously on my fork. "I thought we discussed this previously. Well anyway, there are three areas in physics that strengthen this conclusion. The first is Special Relativity, followed by General Relativity and then Quantum Mechanics."

Carl savored a small bite of his lemon-meringue pie. "I've definitely heard of Quantum Mechanics being said to point in that direction, but also Relativity? Are you sure? How's that?"

"That's the amazing part, even the Relativity theories point in that direction, but you'll never hear the physics establishment say that. They're so good at manipulating the equations but can't, or won't, understand the underlying implications."

"When I was in Tibet, the monks I stayed with taught me the wisdom of the Manjusri Bodhisattva. It's a transcendent wisdom. If what you say is true then these physicists haven't understood their theories in a transcendent way. They haven't seen what lies behind the surface of the intellect."

I nodded. "Yes, they've understood the explicate order but not the implicate order. This sounds to me like the allegory of Plato's cave. The physicists are seeing just a shadow of their theories and not the fundamental truth from which the theories spring forth. I call this fundamental truth the implicate order."

"I love Plato's cave allegory. But did you know Plato detested teaching philosophy in fictional prose format?"

I did not address his last point. "And in Plato's cave allegory, when they see glimpses of the whole truth they reject it. It's too alien to their world-view, and they cling to the shadows."

"What are these shadows?"

The Early Years: Why Are All Bachelors Unmarried?

I looked around. A young, heavily tattooed and pierced couple, sitting at the table closest to us, were giving Carl and me darting, sly looks. I tend to be loud when engrossed in a discussion. My enthusiasm overpowers my discretion. Our arcane topic was drawing too much attention. I hushed my voice. "The shadow they're clinging to is that there's an external, objective Reality existing independently of the observer. They see consciousness as a localized phenomenon that exists within the universe."

"Like a stand-alone computer instead of an interconnected network of computers," Carl said.

"That's a decent enough analogy. But my position is that at the level of the implicate order, consciousness doesn't exist inside Reality, it's Reality observing itself."

"So a universe without anyone observing it is impossible?"

"Yes, and I'll go a step further and say there's only one meta consciousness at the implicate level. We are not creatures occupying the universe, we are the universe resonating with itself."

"You're not the first to say that. As a fan of Tibetan Buddhism, it resonates with me."

"What's the Buddhist view of consciousness?"

"Fundamentally that it's the ground-of-being of all that exists. But to perceive it in this fundamental state one must achieve a vacuum state of consciousness, of no-mind. That's also called a Zen state."

"Would you say that's a primordial consciousness?"

"Yes, that's a good description. It's like a cookie-cutter template from which you create actual cookies."

"As programmers we can relate to that," I said. "It's similar to the idea of Class versus Object in Object Oriented Programming."

"Or better yet, Interface versus concrete implementation," Carl added.

"That's deeper than my take of what consciousness is," I said. "It's the fundamental stuff the universe is made of, but I don't yet have an idea of what that stuff is. Maybe by the time I start my book I'll have my answer."

"I'm curious how you say Relativity agrees with the Buddhist idea of consciousness as the the ground-of-being."

"You can express that a different but equivalent way. Consider the statement that the observer is the ground of being. But first let me tell you a quick story."

I scanned the room. The tattooed couple was engrossed in a conversation. I leaned towards Carl and put my elbows on the table while interlocking the fingers of left and right hands. I spoke in a subdued voice. "There's a man walking in fresh, pristine snow. He walks on a straight path

The Early Years: Why Are All Bachelors Unmarried?

for a few hundred feet, sticks a metal ski pole into the snow at the end of the path, and then retraces his steps back to his starting point. He does this hundreds of times, each time leaving a straight trail of footprints in a new direction. These trails originate from the same point and radiate out to the perimeter of a great circle."

Carl closed his eyes. "Yes, I can picture that. It's like a pie divided into wedges."

"Now, this person suffers from two psychological problems. The first is poor short-term memory. After he completes all the trails of footprints and returns to his starting point at the center of the circle he falls into a deep sleep. When he wakes he's forgotten what he's done."

"And the second psychological problem?"

"I'll get to that soon. So, he sees the metal poles planted into the ground at the end of each line of footprints and he's puzzled."

Carl shrugged his shoulders. "Why?"

"Because there are only poles at the end of footprint trails."

"What's so puzzling about that?"

"He speculates there must exist a law that forbids a pole from being placed anywhere except at the end of a footprint trail. He calls it an exclusion law."

"That's hilarious."

"When he returns to his country he reveals his experimental discovery. His colleagues praise his astute observations. But when he asks why this exclusion law should exist, they ridicule him. 'It's meaningless trying to understand these things,' they say. 'To dig deeper is a meaningless philosophical pursuit. A scientist should uncover how things behave, not why.'"

"Huh? There's no poles where there's no trails because to put a pole anywhere would require him to walk on the snow and put it there, hence the footprint trails. No need for exclusion laws, it's just in the definition of pole planting. Am I missing something here?"

"You're referring to a tautology. Something that's self-evident in a circular way, like saying all bachelors are unmarried."

"Yes, something like that."

"That it's a tautology is obvious to us, but not to him. I'll tell you now what his second psychological problem is. In his way of thinking, and also every member of his society, everything is disconnected. He doesn't understand that the act of planting poles in the snow is what creates the trails of footprints in the first place. He doesn't understand trails of footprints and planted poles are subjective to each other, not objective."

"I can see that poles planted in the snow will never exist without trails, but trails should be able to exist without poles at their end."

"But what if the only reason for those trails is to plant the poles? This underlying Reality, this oneness of pole planting and trails of footprints, is an example of the implicate order."

"So it's what's really causing the observed behavior as opposed to how it appears," Carl said.

"Yes, so his second psychological problem is that he is incapable of seeing the existence of an implicate level."

"It's falling into place," Carl said.

"This relationship between the implicate and the explicate is tautological. The physicist David Bohm coined this term."

"Which term? Tautology or implicate?"

"Implicate, the tautological aspect is my own idea."

"I've heard of him. So the explicate is what we see on the surface and the implicate is the underlying Reality? The truth?"

"Yes, and the explicate often appears in conflict with the implicate. What appears as the greatest absurdity is the deepest truth, not the shallowest lie. That's why Quantum Mechanics seems so absurd to our common sense."

"That's deep."

"In the implicate order there's a oneness to Reality, it's not trails nor poles but a kind of primordial root of these two. Observers see the footprints in the snow and think they are independent and external to the poles. But it's really just a tautology."

"Yeah, I always wondered why all bachelors, without exception, are unmarried." Carl laughed and then brushed his left hand through his curls. The unruly ringlets vibrated like tight springs. "So this allegory is obviously a metaphor for consciousness."

"Bingo."

"So tell me, how is Relativity and Quantum Mechanics like this snow allegory?"

I became distracted and neglected to answer Carl because just then Santa Claus entered the shop. As he crossed the doorway, in that Zeno-like ephemeral slice of time, his bulky frame occluded the light of day streaming through the door and beams of light, like ram's horns, shone from behind him and appeared to radiate from his body. His white, flowing mane and beard shimmered like silk in the noon light. The coffee shop was dusty and within the beams of light a myriad of dust particles vibrated chaotically to a silent melody. If not for the beams of light the dust particles would have vibrated anonymously. He appeared like an anthropomorphic god who is willing light into existence. But the moment faded and the wrestling match of Creation once again merged into the anonymity of Chaos; like a soul-piercing melody fading into a vast and silent night and then repeated with next day's light, forever, eternally.

"What was your question?" I said. "Sorry, but I've never seen him anywhere except on his throne outside." I pointed to Santa Claus.

"Yeah, it's a shock seeing him walking around us mere mortals. I was asking how Relativity and Quantum Mechanics are connected to your snow allegory."

"Let me start with General Relativity. Remember years ago, shortly after I met you? I visited you at that rooming house you lived in."

"Yeah, on East Twelfth. What a dump. That was a tiny room, but it prompted me to build my own retractable wooden bed, remember?"

I laughed. "I remember you showed me the plans for it at first and then you pulled it out from the wall and showed it in action. It was a brilliant design, and you built it from scratch. Another thing I won't forget is that you were contemplating becoming a Tibetan monk at the time."

"Well, that didn't last long. Once you exposed me to programming I became hooked."

"What I remember most about that day is our discussion of the Equivalence principle of General Relativity."

"I remember now," Carl said. "I was blown away by that discussion. We didn't have a discussion of that caliber for a while after that, though."

"Well, I hope you're blown away again today because I'm going to resurrect it, but in a different context."

"I'm listening."

"In case you forgot, I'll explain it again. Imagine a rocket ship far out in space. But the astronaut inside doesn't know if he's in Space or on Earth."

"If he were in Outer Space he'd float around. Wouldn't that be a give-away?"

"I guess you forgot our discussion then. There are no windows for him to look outside, or any other way for him to gather information from outside the ship. The ship is airtight and also information-tight. Unlike him, we know the rocket is actually in Outer Space accelerating at exactly one g. What the astronaut experiences inside the ship is that he's being pinned down to the floor of the ship with an apparent force of one g. That's because of his inertia, a resistance to acceleration. That's why he's not floating around."

"Yes, I remember now. The question is if the astronaut has any way of determining if he's in Outer Space, rocketing at an acceleration of one g and being pinned down to the floor, or if he's stationary on Earth and being weighed down by the force of gravity."

"And the answer is that there's no way for him to know. This led Einstein to a very interesting conclusion. He-"

"You should add there's no way for him to know in principle. It's not just a matter of not having advanced enough information gathering technology."

"Yes, definitely...this limitation is baked into the fundamental fabric of Reality. It's not just a technological limitation. So Einstein's conclusion was that-"

"Sorry to interrupt, but I think I can isolate what's really important here. The challenge the astronaut faces is to determine if he's subject to inertial factors or gravitational force. Does he feel his weight against the floor because he's standing on the ground on Earth, or because he's accelerating through space at one g? However, he's only allowed to determine this by analyzing the phenomenon that's causing him to get pinned down and not by sources of information external to this phenomenon. So if it's inertia causing this then he's effectively asking inertia to reveal itself to him. If it's gravity then the same - not by looking outside through a window."

"Exactly, the question is if the phenomenon the astronaut is experiencing that pins him to the floor has any intrinsic hidden variables that give away this information. Einstein's conclusion was that there are no such hidden variables. He concluded there's no conceivable way to determine if it's inertia or gravity pinning him to the floor, and from this he deduced that the inertia of matter, its resistance to acceleration, is equivalent to its gravitational mass, its capacity for being weighed down by gravity. And he didn't just mean they're equal in magnitude. He meant inertia and gravity are the same physical phenomenon."

"If they can't be distinguished by an observer then they're the same?"

"Yes."

"The Buddha said that for all things the separateness and distinctiveness we perceive is a grand illusion."

"The entire theory of General Relativity," I said, "all its equations, is a consequence of inertia and gravity being the same phenomenon."

I let Carl mull this over for a few seconds.

"So if the universe is out there, existing independently from the observer, then why should the observer's inability to distinguish between inertia and gravity mean they must be the same phenomenon? Why should this have any consequence to the way gravity operates?"

"I still don't see how this affects how gravity operates."

"Because General Relativity is based on this. It's a consequence of the equivalence of inertia and gravity, and this equivalence is based on the observer's inability to distinguish between these two."

"You're saying if inertia is not the same phenomenon as gravity then General Relativity will not be a correct theory?"

"Exactly. But we accept it because it agrees so well with experimental results."

"So you're saying if Reality has no implicate order based on the observer, then the limitations of what the observer can perceive should not have any impact on the laws of physics?"

"That's right. The consciousness of observers would then just be localized to material brains. It would be a biological machine existing within a vast and impersonal universe out there that operates independently of our awareness of it."

Carl was silent while he contemplated this.

"So let me define a principle I call the Epistemological Blind Spot Principle, EBSP for short," I said. "This encapsulates what I've been saying."

"Can you define it in a few words?"

I gulped a chunk of cake while composing my thoughts. This was the first I tried to communicate this idea. "That's very good. You're forcing me to formalize my thoughts about this."

"I hope it doesn't hurt," Carl said in a deadpan way.

I ignored his joke. "It's a gap of information that can never be closed. You can think of it as the visual blind spot in the rear and side view mirrors that a driver experiences. The EBSP is, fundamentally, a distillation of the thinking process that led Einstein to realize the equivalence of inertia and gravity. It states that whenever the observer cannot, in principle, know of something then there are two alternatives: either that unknowable something exists or it doesn't. The EBSP states the correct conclusion in this situation is always that it doesn't exist."

"But what the driver doesn't see in his blind spot nevertheless exists."

"Well, it's not a perfect analogy, but it gets the point across. By the way, have you heard of the Turing Test?"

"I do remember reading about that in a Scientific American article back in 80 or 81, maybe earlier. It was in the form of a dialog between three people."

"Wow, you read it too? I vividly remember reading it in the summer of 82. But it was published a few years before that."

The Early Years: Why Are All Bachelors Unmarried?

"It's a thought experiment, actually," Carl said. "Imagine asking someone a series of questions, but you don't see who or what that someone is. You're told it's either a human being or a computer."

"That's right. And you're supposed to determine if the answers are coming from a human being or a machine, without peeking to see who is doing the answering. You can only make a judgment by analyzing the answers."

"The whole reason for the test is to ask how you can know when a machine truly possesses consciousness, self awareness, or just blindly calculating algorithms."

"And fundamentally," I said, "it's asking what is the nature of our inner world of experience. How can we truly know, beyond a shadow of a doubt, the inner world of others."

"But the Turing Test says the only way to know if a machine is truly conscious is if its answers can't be distinguished from a human being's, or in general from an entity we know is conscious. There's no other possible test of consciousness. Of course, this means the set of questions must be complex and varied enough."

"But do you see how this is just another application of the EBSP?"

"I think so. If the answers can't, in principle, be distinguished from a source we know is conscious then the inner state of the machine is equivalent to a conscious source. It must also be conscious."

"Absolutely. There's no other test possible. It's the EBSP applied to machine and human consciousness instead of inertia and gravity, and the implications are even more important."

"But how do we know the set of questions we're asking are comprehensive enough?" Carl said. "I can ask simple arithmetic questions and the computer will answer me in the same way a human being would. That doesn't mean it's conscious."

"Well, now you're no longer talking theory. You're putting your experimentalist hat on. It's enough that there exists a set of questions that can distinguish between consciousness and non consciousness. I'm not asking you to actually compile that set of questions and do the Turing Test."

"Well, that's kinda sneaky. But it raises the question if there's any possible set of questions that is thorough enough to test for consciousness."

"That's a brilliant question," I said. "But according to the EBSP, if no such set of questions exists then consciousness itself would not exist in others because it would then be unknowable. If you can't measure it, even in principle, then it's meaningless to say it exists."

The Early Years: Why Are All Bachelors Unmarried?

"So would that imply, according to the EBSP, that only your own consciousness exists? That's solipsism."

"I agree. According to the EBSP, if no such set of questions exists then...yes, solipsism. Only your own consciousness would exist. But I didn't say that set of questions doesn't exist."

"Interesting."

"But let's get back to our discussion of the implicate order. My point is that the multiplicity of observers we see at the explicate level are an expression of just one observer at the implicate level. And that one observer is not an entity existing within Reality, it's Reality itself."

"So the multiplicity of observers at the explicate level are just illusory aspects of this one implicate consciousness?"

"Hmm...I like that imagery. The one observer is just observing itself. It's a tautology like the snow allegory. Inertia and gravity can't be said to exist unless they're put in the context of that kind of implicate order."

"So how come it looks like there's multiple consciousnesses? Why are we only aware of an explicate level?"

"Well, imagine a diamond with many facets," I said. "From the vantage point of each facet it looks like it is the entire diamond, and the other facets are separate diamonds. That's the explicate level of appearances. The implicate level is the actual truth that all the facets are a part of the same diamond."

"Nice metaphor."

"Think of the multiplicity of apparent consciousnesses as just one consciousness with multiple, overlapping experiences and each experience unaware of the others."

"That's a real mind bender. So the thoughts in your head are coming from the same source as the thoughts in my head?"

"That will only make sense if you stop thinking in terms of me and you. That's the explicate level. Imagine a person with Multiple Personalities disorder, each unaware of the others. The difference in this example is that for this disorder the personalities are temporal. They don't overlap in time."

"But you still haven't addressed my objections?"

"Which are?"

Carl had an annoyed look on his face. He projected his mellifluous baritone in a slow, deliberate way. "I'll say it again. We are faced with two alternatives. We are trying to decide if the universe is composed of things independent of the observer, or if the observer is the underlying nature of things in an implicate order. But in both these alternatives, if gravity and inertia are the same phenomenon then the astronaut would not be able to

The Early Years: Why Are All Bachelors Unmarried?

tell them apart. So how do you know the correct interpretation is that the universe is built on this implicate order?

"Let's look at it from a different perspective," I said. "Suppose there really is an objective, external Reality where there's no implicate order. Trails and poles are independent in this kind of Reality and there truly is a physical exclusion law. OK, now suppose inertia and gravity are not the same phenomenon. And of course it still stands that it's impossible for the astronaut in the sealed rocket ship to distinguish between these two. That doesn't change. That's what we observe."

"But if they're not the same phenomenon then shouldn't the astronaut be able to distinguish between them?" Carl said.

"Why would you say that? If consciousness is just another epiphenomenon that exists inside an impersonal, remote universe then why must everything be detectable to it. Why can't inertia and gravity be two different phenomena with differences that consciousness can't possibly detect, even in principle?"

"What do you mean by epiphenomenon?"

"Consciousness can be viewed in two diametrically opposed ways: you can say it's just another phenomenon alongside inertia, gravity, electrons, protons and so on, or you can say that it's a primary phenomenon that creates these other things. The first interpretation is the epiphenomenon."

"So, if Reality has an objective existence independent of the observer then consciousness would be an epiphenomenon and the EBSP will not always be correct?"

"It will probably lead to more wrong than right conclusions. In that kind of Reality there should be instances where two phenomena really are different but an observer can't possibly tell them apart."

"That question touches on deep epistemological issues. But I see where you're coming from. If consciousness is just another cog in the machine then why should we expect that it be able to detect everything about the machine?"

"By George, I think he's got it," I laughed. "It's like the snow allegory. The person believes in a Reality where trails of footprints in the snow are completely independent of poles planted in the snow, and therefore it should be possible to find poles where there are no trails."

"Well not so fast. I'm back to thinking my initial objection is correct. If there's an exclusion principle at work, and by that I mean an external influence forbidding poles where there are no trails, then you also wouldn't find poles where there are no trails. Not because of an implicate tautology which plays the role of a primary phenomenon, but because of an exclusion

The Early Years: Why Are All Bachelors Unmarried?

law that exists at the explicate level. That's my whole point. There would be poles only at the end of trails even in an external, independent Reality."

"Let me clarify something," I said. "Perhaps my allegory is misleading on this point. In my trails and poles allegory, each trail is analogous to a different aspect or law of physics."

"What do you mean by that?"

"I mean that one trail represents inertia and gravity. Another represents space and time. A third represents some aspect of Quantum Mechanics like virtual particles, or atomic orbits and so on. It's not just about the equivalence of inertia and gravity. That's just one of the trails. So an exclusion law would be specific to only one of the trails. If there's never an instance of a pole between or beyond any of the hundreds of trails, then we would have a separate exclusion law for each of the trails."

"I see. Each trail represents a different aspect of the universe and would require a distinct exclusion law if there's no underlying implicate order. And your point is?"

"Well, I can accept there's an exclusion law for some of the trails, but it boggles the mind that by some cosmic coincidence there happens to be a separate exclusion law for all the trails such that the universe just conspires to make it look like the limitations of what can be observed line up exactly with the actual laws of physics."

"It reminds me of something Einstein said," Carl said. "He said that god is subtle but not malicious."

"It also reminds me," I said, "of the debate about Evolution between Creationists and Evolutionary scientists. One of the powerful arguments against Creationism is that it's unlikely god would just deceptively make it look like Evolution is the principle behind the diversity of life if it's not."

"That's a good example."

"Come to think of it, wouldn't you say a tautological explanation adheres to Occam's Razor most tightly, that the simplest explanation is the right one?"

Carl reflected on my question momentarily. "Well, if some problem has a set of possible solutions and the tautological solution is one of them, then I suppose that would be the simplest solution."

"I agree, but I'd like to hear your rationale."

"Because it's the solution that doesn't require any additional external factors. The question contains the seeds of its own answer."

"For example?"

"Why are all bachelors unmarried? No need to invoke any external reasons. They're unmarried because it's in the definition."

"Exactly, I call that the Strong Occam's Razor."

"It's extra sharp?" Carl laughed.

I cracked a smile. "No really, it's that for every question the simplest answer is not just the right answer but that it must also be a tautology."

"Hmm...I don't think that's right. There are plenty of questions where the answer is not a tautology."

"Yes and no. The answer does not appear to be a tautology, but if you drill down on the answer you'll find it's a member of an implicate Reality, and at that level it will be a tautology."

"Nissim, you've lost me."

"I'm referring only to deep epistemological questions, not a superficial question like what you had for breakfast."

"I see."

"But back to the multiple exclusion laws hypothesis. It's more reasonable to appeal to one overarching explanation to account for the lack of poles between trails, instead of speculating about separate exclusion laws for each trail."

"That does sound like Occam's Razor. And that overarching principle for the universe of trails and poles is?"

"That it's not due to some mysterious set of separate exclusion laws operating at the explicate level. That it's just a tautology. There are poles only at the end of trails because the act of planting a pole in the snow causes a person to leave a trail of footprints in the snow."

"And by extension to physics," Carl said, "that it's not by coincidence modern physics operates as if what can't be known, in principle, by the observer does not exist."

"You've hit the nail on the head," I said.

"So you're saying the EBSP is a tautological principle?"

"Yes, the EBSP is due to the observer, at an implicate level, being Reality observing itself. If you can't find something in a place where you know where everything is, then it's because it simply isn't there."

"And you're saying it's extremely improbable the EBSP is actually incorrect?"

"So far that's what physics has shown us. And remember what I said previously: if we live in a Reality which is external to and independent of the observer then we'd expect to see some instances where the EBSP is incorrect."

"It looks like you're using an inductive rather than a deductive line of reasoning."

"Yes, it's circumstantial. But that's how science works. You can categorically show something is false by finding just one example where it's false. But you can never show something is true beyond a doubt by showing one or even a million examples where it's true. The next example might be the exception to the rule."

"I see what you're saying. If the EBSP is repeatedly shown to be true then would it not seem reasonable to suspect the observer is not just an epiphenomenon but plays a much more fundamental and organic role in the fabric of Reality? Would it not be reasonable to suspect that there's no set of coincidental and mysterious laws of physics that make it look that way but, just as in the universe of poles and trails, the connection is purely tautological?"

"Meaning the observer doesn't influence the laws of physics. The observer is the laws of physics," I said.

"It blows my mind you've arrived at this conclusion from that kind of reasoning."

"You don't agree?"

"I do agree. I mean it's amazing General Relativity has shown this. I've only ever heard of this conclusion about consciousness and the universe coming out of Quantum Mechanics. But of course, I'm going to ask you to give me those other examples where the EBSP is shown to be correct. After all, that's crucial to your inductive reasoning."

"Of course, that's the crux of my argument."

"Go for it. I'm really curious."

"Great, we're weaving our way down this twisty road with great aplomb. Since the late nineteenth century physicists have encountered many examples where the EBSP can be tested. And guess what?"

Carl had a mischievous grin. "Let me guess. They've never found a pole planted between trails of footprints."

"Couldn't have said it better myself."

"Care to elaborate?"

"Since the first decade of the twentieth century, when Einstein formulated Special Relativity, and even going back to the aether experiments of Michelson and Morley, physicists have encountered many other scenarios where the observer would bump against the limitations of his ability to know something about the physical universe."

"And theories were built on the supposition that those specific things that were undetectable don't exist?" Carl said.

"Yes, but these leaps of intuition were implicit of the EBSP."

"What do you mean by that?"

"The conclusions those scientists made were a consequence of the

EBSP, but they didn't know it."

"Like I said before, these physicists haven't understood their theories in a transcendent way."

"Yes, or you can say they haven't understood the implicate order."

"I've read about the aether. Wasn't it hypothesized to be the cosmic medium through which light waves propagate, like sound propagates through air?"

"That's right. Physicists reasoned that any wave phenomenon must have some physical medium through which it propagates, like water waves through water or sound through air. So they naturally assumed there must be some physical thing permeating space through which light waves propagate."

"Naturally."

"Michelson and Morley set out to experimentally detect its existence. They used an ingenuous device called an Interferometer that leverages the fact the speed of light is expected to differ from different directions if the aether exists. It takes advantage of a supposed aether wind."

"Why would there be an aether wind?"

"Because the earth moves through this supposed aether medium as it orbits the sun. If you stick your hand out the window of a moving car you will feel a wind."

"Oh OK. Gotcha."

"So the idea is that the speed of light would be slower against the wind than with the wind. I think they measured the speed of light in the direction of the wind and at right angles to it. I don't remember exactly how the experiment was setup. But the idea was to prove the aether exists by detecting a difference in the speed of light when beamed in different directions."

"But they didn't find any speed difference in any direction," Carl said.

"That's right. However, they didn't want to give up on their aether prejudice so easily. Physicists of that time formulated theories on what might be responsible for erasing all traces of the aether's existence."

"Weren't the Lorentz contraction equations formulated just for that reason?"

"Yes, Lorentz theorized the reason light was always measured to have the same speed, no matter what direction in the aether it was beamed, is because space itself stretches or contracts just enough so that if light is sped up by the aether wind then the space it has to travel through gets stretched, and vice versa if it's slowed down."

"That quite a convenient coincidence," Carl said.

"Lorentz tried to introduce this ad hoc idea to rescue the idea of the aether."

"So the universe so desperately wants to hide the aether from detection that it bends over backwards in order to conspire that the aether will never be detected?"

"That sounds almost sordid, doesn't it?"

"But again, as Einstein said, god is subtle but not malicious."

"But that's what the esteemed theorists of the late nineteenth century came up with to explain the negative results of the Michelson Morley experiment. They were pretty desperate to cling to the shadows on the wall, eh?"

"OK, I see where you're going with this. If it's impossible, even in principle, for the observer to detect the aether then, according to the EBSP, the aether simply doesn't exist."

I gave a thumbs up. "Enter Einstein. These results led him to that conclusion too."

"His reasoning echoes the EBSP," Carl said.

"Exactly."

"Reminds me of the Emperor's clothes."

I smiled.

"It seems to me Einstein used the EBSP extensively," Carl said.

"Yes, he did for Special And General Relativity, but he never understood it explicitly. He never distilled the EBSP from his thinking processes, and he never understood its full implications."

"The full implications being the implicate order of consciousness?"

"Yes. He was a staunch and stubborn believer in the existence of an external, independent Reality where the observer is just a passive cog in the machine. There's a quotation of his where he proclaims there's a huge world out there which is independent of the observer and which is an eternal riddle. He believed this objective world is only partly accessible through experiments or thought."

"That's ironic," Carl said. "He arrived at insights in the Relativity theories by noticing some things are not observable or knowable even in principle, and then concluding these unobservables or unknowables don't exist."

"He implicitly used the EBSP on some things but not on others."

"Something just occurred to me."

"What?"

"I remember reading something once about Einstein's view about Logical Positivism. It just occurred to me that your EBSP is very similar to

The Early Years: Why Are All Bachelors Unmarried?

that."

"Really? I've heard that term before but I don't know much about it. I'll look it up. I assume Einstein did not agree with it because any person who thinks there's an objective world out there which is unknowable would definitely not accept the EBSP or this Logical Positivism."

"I agree," Carl said. "So it's ironic he scoffed at the ludicrous attempts his predecessors made to hold on to the existence of the aether, but he ultimately succumbed to the same kind of philosophical inertia himself."

I nodded. "Yes. The idea of an external, objective Reality is the modern version of the aether. It's a supposed medium existing in an explicate order through which is transmitted physical Reality. But it wasn't just him. That's a bias held by the physics establishment to this day."

"You're actually drawing the ultimate conclusion," Carl said. "Einstein concluded the aether doesn't exist. Your conclusion is based on the same type of reasoning, but you're denying the existence of an absolute, objective Reality."

I again looked around the coffee shop. The tattooed couple was gone. In its place sat a late-twenties man wearing an expensive looking gray suit. His dark hair was short and slicked back. He wore a large-faced gold watch and his nose was buried in a newspaper. He looked like one of the slick Stock Brokers, or predatory Penny Stock promoters, who clog the arteries of the heart of Downtown Vancouver.

"Special Relativity and Quantum Mechanics are riddled with scenarios where the EBSP comes into play successfully," I said.

"Just to reiterate, by successful you mean that using the EBSP leads to predictions that can be experimentally tested."

"Yes, I mean that drawing the conclusion the undetectable doesn't exist either directly leads to a testable prediction, or a theoretical framework like General Relativity can be built as a consequence of it such that it produces predictions that can be tested."

"Can you list some of the other places where the EBSP comes into play?"

"Well, the speed of light is central to Special Relativity, but do you know why?"

"I suppose because nothing can go faster?"

"It's because light always has the same speed even if you move towards it or away from it. "

"It's not like an escalator where you move slower if you walk in the direction opposite of its motion."

"Yes, light behaves like a strange kind of escalator where no matter if you walk up or down, you would move at the same speed."

"That's so counter intuitive."

"Einstein showed how this strange behavior of light causes Relativistic effects like time dilation and contraction of space. But there's another way to look at it. What's fundamentally important about light speed is that it's the fastest speed at which information can be transmitted. Special Relativity actually permits particles or other phenomena to exceed the speed of light, as long as they can't be used to transmit information. So Special Relativity is fundamentally concerned with a speed limit of information transfer to an observer."

"So we're back to discussing information, or knowability, as the key?"

"Yes, all the Relativistic effects and ideas are a consequence of the fact there's a cosmic speed limit to how fast information can be communicated to an observer. These are physical effects in a supposedly external, objective universe that cares nothing about the observer."

I paused momentarily to let Carl digest what I had said.

"Another example in Special Relativity is the conclusion that simultaneity doesn't exist. The idea that two events happen at the same absolute time is flawed. I'll explain this idea using just one event but viewed by two observers. For two observers at different points in space, the first will detect an event happening at some point in time but the second will detect it later because he is farther from where the event happens. The information of the event reaches the first observer before it reaches the second observer."

"Yeah, but so what?" Carl said. "The fact the two observers detected the event at different times doesn't mean the event happened at different times."

"You're falling into the old bias about an external, objective Reality independent of what we can know about it. In this case you're saying, in effect, that time is absolute and does not depend on the blind spot in our observations of it."

"I disagree. If you fire a gun at exactly 2 PM and person A stands one thousand feet away while person B stands two thousand feet away, then person A will hear the gun go off before person B."

"That's true because the speed of sound is not infinite," I said.

"Well there you go. But the gun was fired at 2 PM. I don't give a damn what time anybody heard it. The speed of light is also not infinite and the same delayed effect exists for it. But the gun does in fact fire at a specific time regardless of when you hear it."

"But you're missing something very central here."

"I don't think so," Carl said. He emphasized the word 'think'.

"What if the gun emits a flash of light when it fires the bullet?"

Carl contemplated my question. "Well, then persons A and B will see the flash of light at the same time but they will hear the sound at different times."

"So the flash of light lets them both know that the shot was fired at 2 PM. The information lag from the sound is immaterial."

"Right, that's my point. Simultaneity exists. It's not subjective."

"But what if at 2 PM you emitted a flash of light into outer space and person A was on the moon and person B was on Mars?"

"Well, then they'll see the flash of light at different times because the moon and Mars are far away enough, even in relation to the speed of light."

"And is there any way," I said, "for them to know that the flash of light was emitted at 2 PM?"

"No, because there's no other means of sending information faster than the speed of light."

"Bingo. That's the difference between the fired-gun example and this example. There's no way, even in principle, to make the two people know about that event at the same time. Therefore, the statement that two events happen at the same time is, at best, a subjective one. Simultaneity of two events does not exist in an external, objective Reality. It's purely a construct of the observer. Two events that are simultaneous for one observer will not be for another."

"Hold on a second," Carl said. "Are you saying there isn't actually an event that happened out there at an objective time of 2 PM?"

"That's exactly right. There's no 'out there.' Remember our old friend the EBSP? If you cannot, in principle, know of something then it doesn't exist. So there isn't an external objective Reality where the event happens at 2 PM. The subjectivity of the event is its deepest level."

"This sounds exactly like Quantum Mechanics, but we're talking about Special Relativity instead. It brings into question the very notion of something happening in an objective Reality. Yeah, I see your point now. This is definitely another example where the EBSP has come into play."

"If there was an external, objective Reality," I said, "you would have to conclude that even though the observer is limited by the information lag, there's nevertheless an actual event that happens at an absolute 2 PM which is, as Einstein put it, independent of the observer and which is in an objective world only partly accessible through experiments or thought."

"But that's not what Relativity says, is it?"

"Isn't it ironic that Einstein believed in a Reality independent of the observer?"

"Give me other examples of the EBSP in action."

"Well, Special Relativity shows there's no absolute motion."

"Explain."

"By using an EBSP way of thinking, you would conclude that absolute, uniform motion doesn't exist because it's impossible for an observer to distinguish between two alternatives: either he's the one moving, or he's at rest and the world is moving past him. So the conclusion is that uniform motion is a subjective thing at the deepest level."

"It's another consequence of the EBSP," Carl said.

"Here's another one. The notion of combining space and time into one indivisible space/time continuum, which is central to Special Relativity and also General Relativity, is a consequence of the EBSP because it's impossible, in principle, to devise any experiment where the observer measures time without also having to measure distance. One always goes with the other. This is again due to the finite speed with which the observer can learn of events."

"Information is the key quantity," Carl said.

"Both Relativity theories, and Quantum Mechanics, even though we haven't discussed it yet, are based on the availability of information to the observer."

"Yes, that alone leads to suspecting the observer is an integral part of the laws of physics."

"It gets me thinking," I said, "of that famous question about why mathematics works so well to explain the universe."

"Einstein wondered about that."

"And many others. Mathematics is something that's deduced within the internal world of the mind. So why is it so powerful in explaining the supposedly outer, independent world?"

"You've used loaded words," Carl said, "so the answer is obvious. There is no outer, independent world. The universe is the implicate level of consciousness. So it's not surprising this strong correspondence exists."

"Everything falls into place when you recognize this tautology. It's the EBSP at work. Actually, the Michelson Morley experiment draws a sharp line in the sand in regards to the era of physics that depends on the EBSP and the era that doesn't. Previously, physics was never concerned with information. It was only concerned with truth. The laws of physics were derived regardless of any consideration for the availability of information to the observer."

"But starting with the physics of the late 19th century it started to look like truth and information availability are tightly related," Carl said.

"Yes, in fact they're equivalent. There can't exist a truth if it's impossible to send the observer any information about it. That's what the EBSP is about."

Carl squinted his eyes as if he had a headache. "Your ideas are so grand, and you've presented them using all these metaphors and analogies, that sometimes I can't keep all that in my head at once. You need to write this down, so when the reader loses one of the threads in your argument then he can go back and reread it and get reoriented."

"That's the idea. That's why I want to write this novel."

"So what are you going to call your novel?"

"God knows. I have no idea. I don't even know what the plot will be about. One idea I've had is to present it as a man hitchhiking across Canada. This man has formulated the ideas we've discussed today, and he intends to travel across Canada on a voyage of self-discovery. The novel could explore his interactions with the people he meets along the way as he enlightens them with his ideas. But I may not write it that way." After a short reflection I said: "I probably won't."

"Apart from these ideas about consciousness, what I find stunning is that you've distilled them from Relativity. I've heard others talk about the role of consciousness in physics, but it's always been in the context of Quantum Mechanics."

"The irony is Einstein himself never understood that his own theories spell the demise of an external, objective Reality."

"The time wasn't ripe back then for this kind of realization."

"And what about Quantum Mechanics?" Carl said. "Surely the EBSP is alive and kicking in the world of Quantum Mechanics."

"Absolutely."

"We can't talk about consciousness and leave out Quantum Mechanics. That would be like talking about fries and leaving out the French." Carl winked.

"That's precisely why I've ignored Quantum Mechanics so far. I wanted to show you how these startling conclusions are derivable from other areas of Physics, even areas outside of physics, like the Turing test."

"Yeah, it seems when it comes to matters relating to consciousness, all I ever hear people discuss is Quantum Mechanics."

"But it's actually ubiquitous in modern physics. Every nook and cranny of Creation reveals it."

"So are you going to show me how the EBSP is manifest within Quantum Mechanics?"

"I'll make it quick. I've got to leave soon. I'll just say that one of the pivotal principles of Quantum Mechanics is a consequence of the EBSP."

"Which is?"

"The Uncertainty Principle. It's the way Heisenberg deduced it that shows it depends on the EBSP."

"Give me the Heisenberg Principle For Dummies version."

"To put it in a nutshell, Heisenberg realized that in order to get information such as momentum and position of a subatomic particle you have to bounce other subatomic particles off it."

"Isn't that how we get information even about non subatomic particles? To see something we need to bounce photons off it."

"Of course, but If I want to see where something is in the dark by shinning a flashlight on it, the photons I bounce off it don't knock it to some other position."

"Well no, it's too heavy."

"But in the subatomic world the particles I want to detect are tiny and they get knocked to other positions and their momentum and position changes when I want to detect them by bouncing other particles off them."

"So the act of detection changes what the observer wants to detect. It's impossible to detect in any other way."

"Heisenberg realized that an observer has no way to both measure the exact position and momentum of a particle at the same time. It's impossible in principle because the act of observation changes what is being observed. The more you know about a particle's momentum, the less you know about its position, and vice versa."

"So what if you can't know both? What does that imply?"

"Well, this fact - this limitation of what the observer can know in the subatomic realm - has huge consequences on how the subatomic world behaves, on the laws of physics themselves. So I'll ask a familiar question: if there's an objective world out there independent of the observer then why should the observer's inability to know about something actually influence the way the universe behaves?"

"What are some of these behaviors?"

"It's huge. The way electronics work is based on this Uncertainty Principle. Did you know that Stephen Hawking concluded that Black Holes evaporate as a consequence of the Uncertainty Principle. Think about it. The behavior of Black Holes is a consequence of the fact there's an information blind spot that you and I have regarding subatomic particles. So clearly the universe cares very deeply about what information we can or can't get. Clearly the universe doesn't seem to act like a remote universe independent of consciousness."

"Yeah, this is the EBSP in action."

"Precisely, the laws of physics are a consequence of the limitations of what consciousness can know."

"But are you actually saying that a particle doesn't have a well defined momentum and position independent of our observation of it? Or are you just saying we can't know both these things at the same time?"

"What do you think I'm saying? What is the EBSP saying?"

"Clearly the former."

"The subatomic world behaves as if a particle doesn't have momentum and position until we observe it. So it's not just that we can't measure it, it's as if that's the way the universe actually behaves. It's like in our discussion of simultaneity, when I explained that according to Special Relativity there isn't an event actually happening at an absolute time of 2 PM in some external world out there, independent of the observer."

"Many professional physicists would disagree with you. I've read their rebuttal to these claims about consciousness. What they say-"

"Yes, I know what they say. They say it's the observation that's important, not consciousness per se. They say an observation can be made by a measuring device instead of a conscious person."

"So what's your rebuttal to this?"

"They're attacking a Straw Man."

"How so?"

"Well, hear me out on this. They're attacking the idea that explicate consciousness controls the laws of physics. But I'm talking about implicate consciousness, which is Reality observing itself. So any observation, whether it's by consciousness of the explicate kind or any measuring device, is the consciousness of the implicate order. Another way of looking at it is to notice that nothing can be said to exist in one part of the universe if there isn't another part of the universe observing it. Observation is the act of extracting information, and information is simply the mirroring of one part of the universe within another. This means that one part of the universe, the observer, contains the other, the observed. So everything is connected in this epistemological sense. This connectivity is the implicate consciousness. The explicate consciousnesses are expressions of this one implicate consciousness. That's what I mean when I say Reality is fundamentally one meta consciousness."

Carl spoke after momentarily reflecting on my rebuttal. "So we're back to tautology. Reality is dependent on consciousness because Reality is consciousness in this implicate sense." He emphasized the word 'is'.

"It's always about tautology. All the weirdness of Quantum Mechanics evaporates once we understand this tautology."

"I'm sure you heard of the idea of entanglement. It says different regions of spacetime are somehow connected in some fundamental way under the hood. What do you make of that?"

"Well, this deep interconnectedness, under the hood as you put it, is none other than the implicate order I'm talking about. It's the fundamental identity of consciousness."

"So where does all this leave us? I mean our entire discussion today. What is the grand lesson?"

"That there's just one consciousness at the implicate level, otherwise the EBSP wouldn't always be correct, and there would be an external, independent Reality where the multiplicity of consciousnesses would just be cogs in the machine. The universe doesn't give a hoot what a cog in the machine knows or doesn't know. But the EBSP has been a driving force in Quantum Mechanics and Relativity. If it's not correct then I'd expect it would be possible to construct experiments that violate both these theories."

"The EBSP says there's no external Reality, but external to what?"

"External to me."

"But I can also draw the same conclusion that there's no external Reality to me."

"But that's my point," I said. "If we want to avoid a contradiction then it follows your awareness is my awareness. You are me. I am you. It's one consciousness with overlapping experiences."

"We are all one. Nice."

"There's another more sophisticated way to reason this out. Care to hear it?"

"Of course I would. You're kidding me?"

"Is there some experiment you can think of that can prove if there's an external Reality or if everything is in your head?"

"This sounds again like solipsism. I think most people would just dismiss your question and say it's obvious it's not all in your head."

"Well then, show me how it's obvious. Maybe it's not so obvious to me. Didn't the Catholic Church refuse to look through Galileo's telescope at the moons orbiting Jupiter? Didn't they say it's obvious everything revolves around the Earth, so there's no need to look through the telescope?"

"Well, I can't think of any experiment that will prove there's a Reality outside my head."

"Because no such experiment exists. That information is unknowable."

"So what does that prove? That everything is in my head?"

"Absolutely not. That conclusion has no conceivable proof either. It goes both ways. Why don't you apply the EBSP to this?"

"Oh, interesting. I suppose the conclusion using the EBSP is that these two alternate explanations are equivalent?"

"You got it. It's shades of inertia and gravity. You can't tell them apart hence they are the same phenomenon."

"So everything being in your head is equivalent to everything being outside? An external Reality is equivalent to an internal one? What does that even mean?"

"What would it mean if there's one correct alternative and it's that everything is in your head?"

Carl shrugged. "It would just mean that. That everything is in my head. Wouldn't it? It would mean I'm imagining the externality of what I can see."

"What would it mean if everything is outside your head?"

"Oh, that's easy. It would mean business as usual. That there's an external, objective Reality like our common sense dictates."

"But if everything is in your head then that would also mean business as usual in the sense that our traditional concept of consciousness would still hold and it would just imagine an external Reality. It would just mean an absence of an external Reality instead of its redefinition."

Carl had the look of a deer caught in headlights. "I'll need to reflect on that. I'm not sure."

"I'll give you perspective. What was the consequence of concluding gravity and inertia are the same phenomenon?"

"It was General Relativity."

"I mean, what did Einstein say gravity really was?"

"The curvature of spacetime."

"Exactly, Einstein showed that in order for inertia and gravity to be equivalent they had to be something other than what we previously thought. They had to be redefined."

"That's right. We thought gravity was a force, but Einstein redefined it to be the curvature of spacetime."

"So in order for an external Reality to be equivalent to an internal Reality we must also do a redefinition, this time it's a redefinition of what consciousness means. We must redefine what Reality means. This isn't solipsism, because in solipsism the notion of consciousness is unchanged. It just posits consciousness is imagining an external Reality."

"Hmm...that's a subtle point."

The Early Years: Why Are All Bachelors Unmarried?

"Sometimes subtlety unearths deeper truths than a jackhammer."

"Yes, Archimedes said 'Give me a lever and I will move the world.'"

"But to put my ideas in a nutshell, the universe appears to be influenced by consciousness not because conscious observers within it are influencing it using some kind of telekinetic powers, but instead because the universe is consciousness itself in the implicate sense. I'll say it again: consciousness is not an epiphenomenon. It's the implicate level of the universe. That's the grand tautology at the root of Existence."

Carl was silent.

"A wise man once pointed to the tapestry of stars above and said: I AM there."

"Beautiful. That sounds like Zen Buddhism," Carl said.

"The illusion of separateness we perceive is the explicate order. It's like the trails of footprints in the snow. This is the interpretation of what Quantum Mechanics really is about. In Quantum Mechanics there's the Schroedinger equation which is said to collapse when an observation is made."

"Yes, I heard of it. It's a mathematical equation that describes subatomic particles as waves."

"Yes, but it's waves of probability of finding a particle at any given location, not something physical like air for sound. "

"I don't know what you mean by waves of probability."

"It's actually very simple. The highest point of the wave is where the particle is most likely to be found. The lowest point is where it's least likely to be found, and likewise for all the points in between. The interesting thing is that in Quantum Mechanics particles are not just found using this probability wave, they are this purely mathematical probability wave. That's their most fundamental state of being."

"So if mathematics is a construct of consciousness then would that not imply matter is a construct of consciousness?"

"Bingo."

"And I learned that a subatomic particle is measured as being localized to a specific point in space, or close to it, when this probability wave is said to collapse. So space and time is created with this collapse?"

"Yes, and it's the observation that triggers this collapse. There's no localized particle that exists out there in an objective type of existence which is independent of its measurement, its observation. The collapse creates the explicate order emanating from an implicate order before the collapse. Consciousness, the one collective consciousness I mean, is the implicate order. It should be very clear to anyone with the open mind of a child that Reality is not a machine where consciousness is a cog within it. The emperor is not wearing any clothes. Reality is a meta consciousness. It's alive in that sense."

"What about the multiverse idea?" Carl said. "It's the idea that at every point in time every possible outcome branches off into a separate universe?"

"No, what you described is called the Many Worlds interpretation. The idea of a multiverse is something different."

"What's the difference? Aren't all these ideas about the existence of multiple parallel universes?"

"Well, not really. The Many Worlds interpretation describes a collection of universes shaped like a tree. Universes branching off lower level universes, like smaller branches branching off larger branches. The multiverse idea is not necessarily about branching universes. It can describe parallel universes that never branch off from a common point. But the main difference is that the multiverse idea is not tied to interpreting what Quantum Mechanics really means. However, the Many Worlds idea has been advanced purely as an attempt to exorcise the role of consciousness out of Quantum Mechanics."

"I didn't know that. How does Many Worlds do that?"

"Instead of admitting the act of observation shapes the outcome of an experiment in Quantum Mechanics, what the Many Worlds interpretation says is every possible outcome of an experiment happens. So the observer doesn't influence anything, he's just a passive passenger along for the ride."

"So each possible outcome branches off into a separate universe?"

"That's the idea. Even the observer branches off into copies of himself in these other universes. There's one universe where you're a serial killer and another where you're the greatest humanitarian. I find it ludicrous the Many Worlds interpretation of Quantum Mechanics is a respected idea within theoretical physics, but the tight connection between consciousness and Reality is considered to be a crackpot idea."

"There's a tinge of mysticism in the idea that consciousness is the prime mover of Reality," Carl said. "I think that's the reason physicists have a visceral reaction to it. There's a bias against what's perceived as mystical in physics, and this bias is rooted in the hard fought struggle between religion and science that culminated in the Age of Reason in the sixteenth century."

"I think you're right. Physicists will bend over backwards like pretzels and invent all kinds of hair-brained speculative frameworks in order to reject the primacy of consciousness. I think the Many Worlds idea is the modern day version of the aether."

The Early Years: Why Are All Bachelors Unmarried?

"It's interesting you should make this analogy," Carl said. "I see where you're going with this. Just as the aether is not detectable by an observer, these other universes are also undetectable. So according to the EBSP they don't exist."

"That's right," I said. "The Many Worlds idea as a means to make sense of Quantum Mechanics is just a desperate attempt to cling to old ideas, just as the aether was. Determining the existence of something physical, I mean something embedded in spacetime, must always be based on the ability to perform an experiment measuring that something."

"Or to be more exact," Carl said, "that there must be some experiment whose outcome distinguishes between the two opposite assertions that something exists or it doesn't."

"Very well said. That's called falsifiability of a theory or assertion."

"So a mathematical argument alone is never enough to conclude something physical actually exists?" Carl said.

"That's right. The EBSP says it must be experimentally observable in principle. Even if current experimental technology is not up to the task, it must nevertheless be possible using some futuristic technology."

"So looks like science is not always an unbiased quest for the truth," Carl said. "Scientists are letting a bias in favor of an external, objective Reality cloud their judgment."

"Science is unbiased," I said, "but scientists aren't always. But it's still light years better than religion. Here's another example of a desperate attempt by scientists to hold on to a bias. Have you heard of Ptolemaic Astronomy?"

"I heard of it. The epicycles, right?"

"That's right. I'll make it quick. I have to get going in a few minutes. It was a desperate attempt to hold on to the geocentric idea that everything rotates around the Earth."

"Wasn't it formulated because observational discrepancies were detected from what the geocentric model predicted?".

"That's right. Looking out at the sky from Earth, the planets exhibit zig zag motions instead of the circular orbits around the Earth predicted by the geocentric model. So instead of rejecting geocentricity, Ptolemy invented a convoluted idea that the planets rotate around the Earth but they also have additional circular motions nested within their primary circular motion around the Earth. He called these the epicycles. And in order to perfectly account for the observations he had to sometimes invent additional inner epicycles within the outer epicycles. What a bloody mess."

"But his model worked. It accounted for the observations, didn't it?"

The Early Years: Why Are All Bachelors Unmarried?

"But it was wrong. It just shows scientific theories should be developed from first principles rather than purely from an attempt to fit observations to a theory. Theories should not only be constructed to fit observations. But observations should always be done to test theories. Ptolemy's theory reminds me of a kludgey piece of software that has layers of badly thought out code just to make the program produce the correct results we are testing for. But what about results we haven't yet thought to test for?"

"I'm afraid I've written a few of those band-aid infested programs. But the most important idea here is biases shouldn't detract from a quest for the truth."

"Exactly. The bias against the consciousness based interpretation of Quantum Mechanics is the modern version of the geocentric bias in medieval times. The simplicity of my tautological model is analogous to the simplicity of the heliocentric idea."

"And you're drawing an analogy between the misguided Ptolemaic system and the Many Worlds idea," Carl said.

"Imagine coming up with all kinds of what I call big-footprint theories to explain why there are only trails where there are poles. And the truth is that it's just a simple tautology. Why are all bachelors unmarried?"

"Let's get back to the conclusion you draw that there is only one consciousness," Carl said. "I think in your novel you should leverage the spiritual aspect of this idea. Dare I say perhaps you can extrapolate to an analysis of god and religion in general?"

"Carl, you know I'm an atheist. I don't think I should stoop to tie all this to some bearded man in the sky."

"God doesn't have to be defined in these terms. Does he?"

"When I first started formulating these ideas I was nineteen. I still remember one day back in eighty-three. I was at the Langara library and I happened upon the Tao Of Physics. Have you heard of it?"

"Yes, definitely. By Fritjoff Capra. I read it right after I returned from Tibet."

"Oh really? So perhaps you'll understand reading that book left me in a daze. I read it from cover to cover that day in the library - hour after hour. It percolated ideas to my surface that had been brewing in me since my childhood. I felt intoxicated with these ideas."

"You read the entire book in one sitting?"

"I couldn't stop. I was siting at a cubicle, and after reading for a couple of hours I would fall asleep, slumped over with my head resting on my elbows flat on the desk. Then after a short nap I would wake up and continue reading. I repeated this cycle until I finished the book."

The Early Years: Why Are All Bachelors Unmarried?

"Well, it didn't effect me to the degree it did you," Carl said, "but it did mesh well with the Buddhism I studied in Tibet. I found the book enlightening. And of course, I learned a lot about Quantum Mechanics from it."

"That was a religious experience for me," I said. "It was an affirmation these notions taking hold of me were shared by some theoretical physicists. I lost my belief in the biblical god when I was fifteen and I don't think I'll ever synthesize my ideas with this Abrahamic god, but the approach Eastern religions have towards the implicate order of Reality appeals to my way of thinking."

"We'd better get going, Nissim. I think it's time for you to pick up Jenna. It's been a great discussion. I'm looking forward to reading your novel. Feel free to mention this discussion in your novel. It was eye-opening."

"Hmm...you know what? It's not a bad idea at all. The novel becomes self-aware. Should I use your real name?"

Carl shrugged. "It's fine with me, or you can change it."

"Let's see...I think I'll change your name to Carmine."

We walked out of Trees Organic into a sunny October afternoon, but there was a chill in the air I hadn't felt before.

"I can feel the change in the air," I said.

"Winter is around the corner," Carl said. "Summer is a receding memory. I'll survive the winter months waiting breathlessly for spring."

"And what will we do then?"

We passed by Santa Claus sitting on his throne, a white-bearded sentinel observing the affairs of Man but interacting with None.

Beyond the Shadows: Existential Whiplash

The greatest ecstasy a mountaineer can experience is to seduce the peak of a majestic mountain, a seduction never consummated before by any suitor, but then once the peak succumbs to advances and impregnated with the flag of conquest, to then see the thick and impenetrable clouds, having been the journey's backdrop all along, part for long enough to reveal this isn't the true peak at all but merely a small bump on the true mountain peak far above all, beckoning the explorer to strive for a greater conquest and loftier vistas.

The ecstasy of such a journey emanates from the explorer's belly as a wave with a trough of despair and a crest of pure joy. Once having discovered the folly of one's assurances that the mountain had been conquered once and for all, despair sets in due to the apparent futility of ever conquering the true peak at all. It seems so foreboding, its rugged contours inhospitable and intractable. But then the explorer discovers a path leading to the true peak after all. It may be straight as an arrow or twisty and convoluted, teasing and fleeting yet conquerable above all. The promise of a renewed flag of greater conquest is thrust into the explorer's soul, and then the explorer thrusts the flag into the true peak now conquered forevermore.

***

"I have some great news, Nissim," Ramesh said, "we have the results of our load-tests from Microsoft."

"You have the metrics for Attendance?"

"Yes, that's the good news. It's performing now more than a thousand percent better. Your rewrite has done wonders." Ramesh gave me two thumbs up.

I had been working as a software developer at Chancellor Software since February of 2000 - over two years. In the summer of 2001 I joined the Chancellor SMS team. It was an initiative to convert the Chancellor school administration system into a web-based platform. I would be learning the new DotNet programming environment.

"It's been a pleasure to work on the Attendance module. Is it mine going forward?"

"You're going to have to let Kevin decide. If it were up to me then you're the man."

Kevin raced by Ramesh's cubicle just at that opportune moment. I excused myself and ran to catch him. "Hey Kevin, I'd like to run something by you."

Kevin stopped and waited for me to catch up. "I don't have much time. I have a meeting with Richard and Roland in ten minutes. What is it?"

Richard was Chancellor's CEO. The Chancellor SMS project was the highest profile project at Chancellor and Richard kept abreast of its progress regularly. Roland was the director of Chancellor SMS and he had appointed Kevin as its development manager.

"I was just now talking to Ramesh and he gave me the good news."

"You're gonna have to give me more than that. I've got a million things up in the air."

"I'm talking about the results of the load-test on Attendance. It's now handling load the way it should."

The first version of the Attendance module was developed by a very senior and respected software developer named Amralino. But when it was released to the school districts it was not able to handle the thousands of users attempting to use it simultaneously. Kevin asked me to fix it for the second release. The irony is that when I was first learning DotNet I was assigned to work on Attendance but Amralino told me, and I do not doubt to others including Kevin, that I was the wrong person for the job.

"Funny you should bring it up now," Kevin said. "My meeting is about the load-test results. Richard is relieved."

"That's awesome. He doesn't have to thank me," I laughed.

"Umm...yeah, well not so fast Nissim. You're not on Richard's radar."

"What do you mean?"

"Amralino is also attending the meeting."

The blood drained out of my face. "Amralino?"

"Richard and Roland want him in the meeting to discuss the improvements in Attendance," Kevin said.

I remained silent. Kevin shrugged.

"Attendance is still Amralino's baby. Richard and Ronald only interface with Amralino when Attendance is concerned. What did you expect?"

"But I'm the one who took his less than stellar rendition of Attendance and made it actually usable."

"Yeah that's because Amralino was diverted to other parts of SMS."

I squinted my eyes and cocked my head forward. "No, I took over because what Amralino did with Attendance just wasn't up to snuff. He wrote it as though only one user at a time would ever use it. A complete disregard for scalability. That's why."

"So what do you want me to do about it?"

Beyond the Shadows: Existential Whiplash

"I want to be in charge of Attendance going forward. I've proven myself."

I've always been relegated to the sidelines. I've always lived in the shadows of those who elicit more respect and confidence for reasons I cannot fathom.

"Look Nissim, I appreciate the good work you've done with Attendance. I'll see what I can do, but you have to realize Amralino is the face of Attendance as far as the higher ups are concerned. Life's a bitch. You haven't learned that yet in your thirty-seven years on this planet?"

Kevin was as much my boss as my friend. He is ten years younger. Chancellor hired us within a couple of weeks of each other. He is the consummate climber of the corporate ladder, an ontological manager. He is my polar opposite, the epitome of that old trope about the person who succeeds in life not due to an intellectual pedigree but due to a social intelligence and ambition emboldened by a lack of the distractions of peripheral vision.

The corporate snub did not bother me to the extent it may seem. It grated on me more for the superficiality of society than for any unfairness directed towards me. I had always suffered a diffidence with daily affairs, the type that most people take to heart and elevate to an importance above all else. Ever since I was a child I always felt like a citizen of a different realm. I was sowing its seeds, but its reaping was still blossoming in an unburst earth within me, frozen over during a winter before its imminent spring.

A year later I was still working on Attendance, Amralino had moved on to other projects - voluntarily I think. However, I was under the oversight of Clayton, a good Christian of the born-again variety, and a devoted family man. He was appointed as my development lead but he did not write any code for Attendance nor have any input into any of its architectural concerns. It was all me. He attended important technical meetings judged too grand for the likes of me. He participated in charting the course for Attendance and what needed to be done was then trickled down onto me.

We sat next to each other, Clayton and I, at desks in an open area devoid of partitions or cubicles. We often sparred over religion, Christianity in particular. He, the good Christian man, proclaiming with unshakable conviction devoid of evidence, or even a glimmer of thought provoking debate, the superiority of Christianity above all else. I, the still reforming ex atheist with an affinity for textured theology and metaphor rather than the simplistic literalism Clayton espoused. He once argued with me that Christianity is superior to Judaism because it attracted far more converts in the Roman empire, and beyond. He claimed that proves Christianity is the truth.

"What about Islam?" I said. "It too had a meteoric rise paralleling Christianity. Is Islam also the truth?"

Clayton was a member of a fundamentalist congregation to which he contributed ten percent of his annual pay. "I take my religion very seriously," I once overheard him say to another colleague after he, the good Christian man, condemned homosexuality as an unforgivable depravity and proposed homosexuals should hide within the dark confines of the closet rather than openly participate in the Civilization of Man.

I intruded into their conversation. "If that's what your religion brings out from within your soul then it's your religion that deserves to scurry into the shame of the closet."

On another occasion I asked him if those who do not accept the divinity of Jesus are hell-bound. "Look Nissim, I am not the one making that pronouncement. Christ himself said that and I have to accept his words."

"Are you a Calvinist?" I said.

"Why would you think that? We've discussed this in my church and I can say with no reservation I'm not a Calvinist."

"Do you reject the doctrine of Unconditional Election?"

"You'll need to enlighten me on that. I'm not knowledgeable about Christian principles like you are." He pressed his tongue against his left cheek and his eyes smiled a mocking smile.

"Do you believe god chooses those who will believe in Christ before they are even born? That they have no free will of their own to believe in Jesus?"

"Of course not. Accepting the Lord is a personal choice open to every person."

"Was it your personal choice?"

"Absolutely. I accepted Jesus in my heart and soul when I was still a child."

"Why is this world so unfair?"

"Listen Nissim, this world is unfair, but the kingdom of god is not of this world. It is in heaven."

"Would you say admission to heaven is fair?"

"Absolutely. There is no one more fair than Christ."

"Then why is it that a much higher percentage of people in North America have accepted Christ than, let's say, people in India?"

I detected a subtle quiver in Clayton's voice. "Listen, I don't know where you're going with this but anyone who accepts Christ into their heart will enter heaven. It's a personal choice open anywhere on Earth."

"But if it's a choice whose parameters are completely intrinsic to the individual making the choice then why are people in India making that choice much less frequently than people in America?"

"No one is tying their hands."

"But the fact stands that the culture into which you are born is a statistically confounding variable that influences your religious inclinations. That is totally out of your control. You do not choose the circumstances of your birth. Do you believe it's god who chooses the circumstances of your birth?"

"Hmmm...well yeah, I suppose. No, of course god chooses it. So what's your point?"

"You're a smart guy Clayton. You have a math degree. You've studied statistics. I think you can see where I'm going with this."

"I stand by my principles. A belief in Christ is a personal choice open to anyone. That's why Christ died on the cross for all of us, be it India, America or the moon."

"I'm not going to let you off easy like this," I said. "You have to be intellectually honest. The fact is the culture you're born into strongly biases your religious choices. That's something out of your control, and so I must conclude a belief in a heaven only for Christians adheres to the Calvinistic ideology of Unconditional Election."

Clayton shook his head and waved his arms. "Oh no. Oh no you don't. Explain to me why there are Christians in India then. That blows you whole Unconditional Election nonsense out of the water."

"Does it? It doesn't have to operate with 100% success. It suffices there's a strong positive correlation between culture and religious choices. We then must logically conclude there are forces outside the individual's control in determining if he or she will become a Christian. This is shades of Calvinism. So either the so-called kingdom of Christ is as unfair as the kingdoms of this world, or the notion only Christians go to heaven is false. Pick your poison."

"Stop right there. Stop. Statistics can be made to say anything you like. I stick to my guns. Anyone can open their hearts to Christ and inherit the kingdom of god. At least we Christians don't believe we are the chosen people." He chuckled a mocking chuckle. I understood his slight.

"At least in Judaism," I said, "there's no belief in eternal torture in a hell reserved for non Jews. We believe the ethical non Jew has a greater place in god's heart than a pious yet corrupt Jew. If you believe all people outside your faith are hell-bound then is that not the epitome of belief in your religion's choseness? The Jewish notion of choseness is more textured and nuanced than you think."

I saw anger in Clayton's eyes. I sensed Clayton's logical side embraced my argument but his emotional investment in his faith created a cognitive dissonance that conveniently swept the logical force of my argument under the rug of his religious allegiance.

"Christianity is not a religion," Clayton said. "It is simply truth. God became a son of man and offered his flesh and his blood to save humanity from its own sin. God, as the man Jesus, took this sin upon himself and absolved humanity, and he died a human death but then rose as god."

"Clayton, I would agree with you but you are taking the Christ story far too literally."

"What do you mean?"

"I mean the story of Jesus the Christ is a parable depicting a leitmotif in the human condition of evil persecuting good but good ultimately rising up from the ashes and prevailing. It's not literal. And if you take it as a parable it doesn't diminish the power of the Christ story, it amplifies it."

"You atheists are very fond of reducing anything to do with god to parables and metaphors."

"But in the metaphor resides the greater truth. In the abstraction resides a more nuanced understanding than in the literal point of view."

"Pure secular gibberish."

"Christhood is an abstraction that has been implemented in concrete terms across history and across cultures. It's not just the domain of a Hebrew carpenter who preached two thousand years ago. And if you open your eyes to this greater truth then the god you worship will become a greater god."

"Thank you, but my god is as great as it can get."

"But if you get what I'm saying you will not worship him, you will feel him at the source of your being and, in an abstract sense which is the greater sense, you will drink his blood and you will eat his flesh and you will then become god born as a man, as much a Christ as that humble Nazarene who played out the leitmotif of evil persecuting good but ultimately rising up from the ashes and prevailing. That's what it means to be born-again."

"I have no need for that Catholic lie of eating the flesh and drinking the blood of my savior. I know what it means to be born-again."

"But much too often I just see hypocrisy instead of new birth. I see the self-proclaimed born-again preaching from a pulpit while yielding the bible as you would yield a sword or a gun - preaching their perverted version of

Christhood while hardening their hearts to the homeless, to the hungry, to the disenfranchised, to the homosexual, to Catholics if they are Protestant or to Protestants if they are Catholic. Petty divisions that mock what it truly means to be born-again."

Clayton wanted no more of our conversation. "And who made you a preacher on your own pulpit?" He then shrugged his shoulders and returned to his work.

One day, after another session of intense sparring about religion, peppered with my scientific perspectives about consciousness as the implicate order, he paused for quick reflection after something I had said about which my memory now fails me. He then said with a smile: "Nissim, do you sometimes feel you are on this earth to fulfill a great destiny?"

While I do not recall what I said to elicit this remark, I do recall being surprised. That is why I deduce I must not have said anything that provoked this remark. This conclusion is further supported by the manner of his expression - it was not mocking nor accusatory but rather philosophical. I wondered if he had meant the question rhetorically or did he expect me to answer it?

"Yes, I do feel that way often," I said. I elected to interpret his question personally because I did feel that way and that is a grand way to feel. To my surprise, Clayton did not respond to my assertion. Perhaps he also felt a sense of great destiny and his question was rhetorical, meant to reflect off me and shed light on him.

That time in my life was wrought with existential confusion and despair, a foamy turbulence of my spirit and intellect. In the intellectual's inner world the spirit is intimately intertwined with the intellect. They are so tightly coupled that for many intellectuals the primary spiritual ontology of Being is eclipsed by the intellect - but the spiritual is still there, vibrating within the seed of Being. For others, the austere world of the intellect plays no role and they use a different paradigm, artistic or intuitive or another, of wrestling with their soul. We are all primarily spiritual beings married to a secondary characteristic which is the signature of our explicate identity. Our spiritual identity, the soul, is none other than the implicate source of Existence. Our explicate identity is a window into the implicate. It is through our explicate quality that our implicate nature is translated into an illusory and fractured world of separation. To aspire for enlightenment in the spiritual sense is to strive to unravel the tight braiding of the deepest spiritual level with our secondary characteristic and to then perceive one's soul, the implicate reality, bare and unadorned. And when we attain that perception then we can no longer distinguish our soul from any other -

there is just ONE.

The spark that triggered my existential despair was struck a few months earlier when my friend Addison, a fellow software developer at Chancellor, recommended I explore Chaos Theory. His father had been a mathematician before he immigrated with his family to Canada, and he nurtured a love for mathematics in his son. I enjoyed many discussions with Addison about my ideas concerning consciousness and he was impressed with my passion for physics and mathematics. I knew nothing about Chaos Theory but I had heard of it because in the movie Jurassic Park the character played by Jeff Goldblum was a Chaos theorist.

"Nissim, have you looked into Chaos Theory yet?" he would always ask whenever I engaged him in a discussion about my ideas of consciousness, Quantum Mechanics and Relativity. I was not at first compelled to follow his advice because he did not enlighten me with how Chaos Theory is relevant to my ideas. I suspected he only implored me to investigate it because he thought it would fascinate me and further ignite my scientific and mathematical passions in whatever unpredictable direction fate takes them.

New ideas and insights often follow a pin ball's unpredictable trajectory when it is struck by the paddle. I remembered the game of Pinot I played as a child on 48th street in the city of Yaffo, Israel. I played this game often after school with my best friend Arnon. I would throw the ball, usually a soccer ball, towards Arnon, aiming for his sidewalk's edge. The ball would sometimes bounce back to me in unpredictable trajectories. The quest for fundamental truth is always unpredictable. In Pinot, if you play against an uneven sidewalk you are hard pressed to predict the ball's trajectory. Fortunately, you can find a paved sidewalk with a straight edge, and the ball's path as it bounces back to you is more predictable. Unfortunately, the great quest for universal truth must always be played against an unpaved sidewalk. The search for a straight edge in the fundamental fabric of Reality is a fool's errand.

There came a day when I did a Google search about Chaos Theory because I fretted once again telling Addison I had not yet investigated it. What I read did not excite me. The explanations were overly pedantic and obscured the essence of Chaos Theory behind the noise of technical pyrotechnics. That is often the tell-tale sign that one does not have a fundamental understanding of the subject matter in question. There is a wide chasm between mere knowledge and deep understanding. Reality is a many layered fruit. One must peal away the layers of effect, masquerading as the cause, in order to eat from the tender and succulent inner flesh of the fruit - the fundamental cause.

The outlines of Chaos Theory I read that day were about systems that are sensitive to initial conditions. One small change at the beginning of the system's evolution will lead to dramatic changes in the later states of the system. That is called the Butterfly Effect, the idea that the beatings of the wings of a butterfly in Australia, representing what appears to be an insignificant early condition, can eventually trigger a mighty storm half way around the world. That idea did not inflame my passions nor inflict me with an existential whiplash. I did not see the relevance to my ideas about consciousness as the implicate order. I did not continue reading beyond the first few entries Google had laid before me.

The next day at work, during lunch time, I went down to the sandwich shop on the main floor. Addison was, as usual, eating his lunch there. I sat with him. He was eating a salami and raw onion sandwich. How he loved his raw onions, and he refused to ever benefit anyone around him by sucking or chewing on a mint - or something a tad more effective like industrial strength bleach. He was, as usual, drinking from an over-sized cup of tea with the tea bag still immersed in the tea and its string dangling over the cup's edge.

"I looked up Chaos Theory last night."

"Nice. Finally. And?"

I shrugged and pursed my lips.

"No shit. Nada?"

I shrugged again.

"You didn't find anything interesting about Chaos Theory?"

"You know, I'm always on the lookout for anything that will take me further with my ideas about consciousness, but I didn't find anything like that."

"I'm kinda disappointed. I thought for sure you would find it provocative at the very least."

"Why?"

"Dude, order from disorder. Why not? You can't find something worthwhile about that?"

"Yeah, I did read something about that, but it was mostly about sensitivity to initial conditions."

"Maybe you read the wrong articles. Focus on order from disorder. You should buy a book about Chaos Theory. Good god, don't become one of those only online learners. Books are cool."

There was something oddly compelling about Addison's earnest appeals. I resolved there and then to continue my investigation of Chaos Theory. I suspected I gave up on it prematurely. That evening, when I got home, I headed straight for the office and googled Chaos Theory, but with the added search string 'order from disorder'. I was committed to understand its fundamental significance - the cause, not the effect. As I read, it dawned on me the Butterfly Effect was a consequence of a more fundamental aspect of Chaos Theory. Why do seemingly insignificant initial deviations eventually propagate exponentially into huge effects? Why would the gentle flapping of a butterfly's wings eventually cause a catastrophic storm? And above all other questions, what does that imply about the implicate level of consciousness and the EBSP? That was forever the fundamental question I needed to address. It was the silent voice within the semantic spaces of the soul that compelled me to seek answers to these questions.

Every Friday, on the way home from work, I bought two bottles of red wine from the liquor store on Commercial Drive - the Bohemian, tree hugger's neighborhood near my home. Friday evenings had an almost religious significance for Jenna and me. It was a sacred time to celebrate the end of another week, and to dwell in an almost Zen-like state of no-mind.

In Judaism, sunset on Fridays has a deep spiritual significance. It marks the border between the six days of Creation and the Sabbath, which symbolizes god's rest from his toil of creating the universe. I had abandoned my traditional religiosity before my sixteenth birthday, and I became an avowed atheist, a man celebrating reason instead of superstition. Around the time I met Jenna I was forming my ideas about the implicate order of consciousness, and these ideas compelled me to re-examine my atheism. But it was not a conventional theism towards which I was drawn. I was forever the man of reason and intellect. I was hurtling towards something new which, at that time, I had not yet clearly understood.

Friday was also our favorite night for television. We watched our shows while drinking a bottle each of red wine, and discussing spiritual, religious and political ideas. I always had loose-leaf paper and a pen on the coffee table during those magical nights, and I would jot down any salient ideas.

I thought: "One of these days, when my inner voice tells me it's time to start writing my novel, I will tap into these little ideas I've jotted down and expand upon them."

Unfortunately, I usually lost track of these loose pieces of paper by the next day. On that night of November 1, 2002 Jenna beckoned me to abandon my Internet surfing for the night and join her in the living room for supper. We were having hard-shelled tacos and Jenna prepared all the components for stuffing the tacos: ground turkey, home made salsa and guacamole and store bought shredded cheese and pickled jalapeños. Earlier that year Jenna and I stopped eating mammals on ethical grounds and we always substituted ground chicken or turkey in any dish requiring ground beef or pork.

"Nissim, food's ready. Come and make your tacos."

I was hungry and the smell of seasoned ground turkey wafted into the office and enticed me. I resolved to continue my study of Chaos Theory the next day. But I had already made some leaps of understanding. I made myself four tacos and joined Jenna in the living room. Our lineup of Friday night shows was about to start. First, it was Leap Years at 8 PM, then Sex In The City at 9 PM, a guilty pleasure of mine, and finally Kink at 10 PM, a documentary following the lives of a group of Vancouverites engaged in the kink and fetish scene. Two years later I joined a Left Wing Jewish congregation and I met one of the cast members of that show. He is David, the burly, bearded, middle-aged, piano playing gay man.

"I have a surprise for you," Jenna said. She handed me a small red shopping bag. Not the type of flimsy bag you put your groceries into, but the smaller, thick-skinned type with a fancy handle that you would get from a department store or a store selling body lotions and aromatic soaps.

"Yeah? What's the occasion?" I said without trying to hide my delight.

I sipped my red wine and peered into the bag. I saw a red, hard-cover, spiral-necked notebook and an expensive looking black and gold pen. I looked up at Jenna.

"Now you don't have to fuss with all that loose paper." She smiled.

"Thanks, that's awesome. I really need to start organizing my thoughts." I leafed through the notebook and then placed it on the coffee table. I then massaged the pen between my fingers. "And this pen is gorgeous."

Jenna sipped her wine and licked her lips. "So tell me, what's gotten you so excited in there?" She pointed to the office.

I ignored her question. "How has your day been, by the way?"

"Oh don't ask. Sandra is driving me up a wall."

Sandra Haffarnon was Jenna's boss and a reverend at an Anglican church in Vancouver's Kitsilano neighborhood. Jenna was the consummate Anglican church lady. She worked at an Anglican church and spent much of her off-time as a member at another.

"Guess what happened today," Jenna said. "I was typing up her paper for the synod and I spotted an error that at first I though was just a typo. She wrote about the Catholic church, but she spelled it with a lower case 'c'. So I corrected it and thought nothing of it. But I kept running into this typo as I continued reading, and I realized it wasn't a typo at all. Can you believe she didn't know the difference? Anyway, so I sent her the edited article with all the changes marked. Later in the day she stomps like an overfed cow up to my desk with a real sour look on her puss, and says she looked over my corrections and she doesn't appreciate my edit to the word Catholic. I explained to her why I made that correction, and she then gives me a look of pure contempt and stomps off with her tail between her legs."

"Did you keep that edit in?"

"Damn right I did. Why shouldn't I? I wanna see her holiness challenge me on that."

Jenna's command of the English language is of the highest caliber. I am no slouch in that department myself, and I understood immediately why Jenna had made that edit.

"Can you believe," Jenna said, "that someone with a PhD in Pastoral Studies would not know that when using a lower case 'c' catholic means universal. Only when the C is capitalized does it refer to the institution of Christ's church on Earth. But her PhD was probably mailed to her by a Nigerian prince. It might as well be in basket weaving. Ha!"

Jenna shares my plight in life of having people almost instinctively underestimate our intellect. Her calling is to be an academic, but her adopted parents did not appreciate her gifts and instead invested in the education of her older brother, a meteorologist. But she also shares in the blame for her non consummated calling. She never had the steely determination to channel her intellectual gifts into an academic setting. I carry the gene for the same flaw.

"But enough about me. I'd rather not talk anymore about it. How's your day been?"

"I had an interesting conversation with Addison today. To make a long story short, last night when you were at church, I looked up something that he has been imploring me to research the last couple of months."

"You never said anything to me about that. What's so interesting?"

"It's something called Chaos Theory. Heard of it? When I looked it up last night I didn't see how it's relevant to my ideas about consciousness, but Addison today convinced me to give it another shot."

"Never heard of it. So did you find anything interesting tonight?"

"I might have. It has a lot to do with order from disorder, from Chaos. But the really fascinating thing is that it's spontaneous order. There's no need for any external agency to intervene into the Chaos and orchestrate the order. It emanates from within."

"From within what?"

"From within the disorder itself. It's spontaneous."

Jenna considered for a few seconds what I had said. "That sounds to me a lot like the debate between the Intelligent Design Creationists and more secular or scientific ideas about the origin of the universe and of life."

"Yes, absolutely. I was thinking the same thing. To me it suggests the question about the nature of god instead of leading me back to atheism."

"That's an interesting thought. What is god really?"

"What is often glossed over in questions about god's existence is what to me is the most obvious question: what does one mean by the word 'god'?"

"There's this vague idea of a supreme being," Jenna said, "but what does that really mean?"

"The conventional view is god as an entity contained within the universe and orchestrating design in nature, like a puppet-master controlling his puppet. It's a god that creates things without the constraints of the laws of physics, or even logic."

"Why can't it be a god that uses the laws of physics to create things?"

"What I mean is that in this view of Reality the laws of physics aren't enough. God is like a puppeteer who needs to intervene because the laws of physics aren't sufficient to animate the puppet."

"That's a good definition of Intelligent Design," Jenna said. "It seems to me Chaos Theory implies there's no need for that kind of god."

"But if such a god doesn't exist then why does it imply there's no god?" I said. "Perhaps god needs to be redefined. Why can't this propensity within Chaos for order to arise be understood as god?"

"Many will say that doesn't fit the definition of the word 'god'."

"So we're back to wrestling with semantics. It's not god in the conventional sense. But the idea of god can transcend convention. I will tell those people that god is too big to fit in their box."

"For sure," Jenna said. "That's already happened before when the idea of divinity shifted from polytheism to monotheism."

"Perhaps the finger of god bursts from the depths of the implicate order, not the explicate order which is apparent to our senses. The conventional view is of a god residing only in the explicate order."

I had explained my ideas of the implicate order to Jenna, but not to the extent I had explained them to Carl. He was the person most privy to my inner world of ideas.

"Perhaps god is not an entity within Creation, but rather the seed out of which Creation explodes," I said. "Perhaps god is the trunk of the tree and not the biggest branch."

"Nissim, as a Liberal Christian I take these ideas to heart and I can't dismiss them. Did Jesus literally rise from the dead or is there greater gravitas in understanding the resurrection metaphorically? I choose the latter."

Jenna was a dedicated church goer, but her passions were more for Liberation Theology and social justice, within a Liberal Christian context, than for a Conservative and literal interpretation of the bible.

"Have you ever read Spinoza?" I said.

"Maybe a few articles here and there. I know he espoused ideas about god remarkably similar to what we've been discussing."

"Yes and no. He lived long before the advent of Chaos Theory, and he never discussed the concept of spontaneous order from disorder. But he did advance a theology where god is not seen as an external entity orchestrating the universe, like a marionette controlled from above by strings, but rather as that from which the universe emanates, and that which contains the universe in his indivisible oneness."

"And what did he mean by that?" Jenna said.

"It means whatever god fundamentally is, the universe is still within that, not outside of it. He rejected Dualism, the belief mind and body are two distinct, irreconcilable aspects of Existence."

"The universe emanates from god but it's still inside god? How can that be?"

"Maybe it's like a slab of marble that contains a superposition of all possible statues inside of it. We can imagine a distinct statue without it having been carved out, or decohered out of, the slab of marble. So in that sense, it's both inside the marble and also distinct from it."

"You know, that kind of makes sense in a 'the sound of one hand clapping' kinda way." Jenna erupted into a hearty laugh.

"I'm now seeing a world of ideas I never thought about before," I said. "I need to find the commonality between these ideas and also between these ideas and my own ideas."

"It's a synthesis. You need to create a system incorporating all these ideas into one self-consistent paradigm. It might turn out to be your life's work."

"When I was a teenager," I said, "I idolized Einstein and I read all I could about him. Einstein always said he believed in Spinoza's god. So I read about Spinoza's ideas. Spinoza said god is not Deus Ex Machina but rather Deus Sive Natura. God is not outside the universe and orchestrating it but rather the essence of the universe. Nature emanates from god, but it's still within god."

"Spinoza didn't accept the old bearded man in the sky idea of god," Jenna said. She tilted her head and took a big bite out of one side of her taco. Guacamole and salsa oozed out from the other side. I remembered my neglected taco and took a large, hungry bite of it. As I ate I made my first entry into the red notebook:

Nov. 1/2002

I suspect that there is a tendency in nature for entitization to happen. This is not a contradiction of the second law of thermodynamics. It is through a tendency towards an increase of entropy that entitization happens. The formation of life is a result of this, as is consciousness, the stock market etc... These are all entities that emerge from Chaos.

When I met Jenna she was in the initial stages of embracing her Christian identity. She precariously balanced her spirituality on a tightrope between literalism and metaphor. During that time I was also negotiating a tightrope between the worlds of the intellectual and mystical. I was transitioning from atheism to something else. I did not yet know to what, but I knew it would be a synthesis of these two worlds rather than a rejection of one in favor of the other.

We poured what was left of our wine into our glasses. Kink was playing on Television. The burly gay man was commenting about the shift in society towards greater compassion for LGBT people and the Other in general. "It's a sudden shift I've noticed lately," he said. "It appears to have recently exploded out of nothing and it's gaining momentum. I'm glad to live in these interesting times."

The next morning I brewed my coffee and resumed my online research. Jenna had left for church again. The previous year she had become consumed by the Church and was working towards becoming a Deacon at Saint James church, an Anglican congregation with a large left-of-center membership.

My investigations quickly revealed the fundamental aspect of Chaotic systems is self-reference, also referred to as feedback loops or self-similarity. A system could not become Chaotic if its components did not self-reference. I learned Chaos, in this technical sense, is not the usual disorder with which people are familiar. It's a disorder from which order can emanate without any external guiding intelligence. I had a cursory familiarity with concepts of self-reference because as a software developer I had often employed a technique called Recursion. A recursive program uses a self-contained piece of code called a function that uses itself in a nested fashion to achieve some calculation or logic. For example, if the task is to compute factorial numbers then the logic of a recursive program would be as follows:

```
//calculates factorial of a number n. For example factorial of
//4 is 1*2*3*4 = 24
//the factorial of 0 is 1
//The function below is pseudo-code
//It is not code that is ready to be executed
Function Factorial(n)
{
    if (n = 0) return 1; else return n * Factorial( n – 1);
}//end of function
```

The non recursive way of achieving this would be:

```
Function Factorial(n)
{
   if n = 0 return 1;
   factorial = 1
   while n > 0
   {
      factorial = n * factorial
      n = n - 1
   }
   return factorial
} //end of function
```

Clearly, the recursive way is much more concise, even for a simple problem like doing a factorial. For very complex problems a recursive solution might only require a few lines of code while the non recursive version might span several pages of knotty and complex code. The recursive solution almost seems like magic due to its terseness and the computation seemingly being computed from nothing. The structure of the recursive code parallels the definition of the problem to be solved. In this case, the recursive code to compute a factorial is simply the definition of what a factorial is. The solution appears from within the definition of the problem rather than from an external guiding intelligence.

I was at my computer that day until the early hours of night. I learned much, and by day's end I felt overwhelmed with the quantity and complexity of ideas. But I also felt joy because I knew the whispering voice within me was leading me to these fertile grounds. I learned of Chaos and of Pseudo Randomness. I learned of Chaotic Pseudo Determinism and of Fractal Geometry with fractional dimensions. I learned of Chaotic Strange Attractors and of the Mandelbrot set. But I could see no path to synthesize these ideas with my own ideas about implicate consciousness and the EBSP. Throughout that day, as I absorbed ever greater reams of knowledge and ideas, I had a growing sense of awe and an unshakable feeling I was at the threshold of a great intellectual and spiritual paradigm shift.

When Jenna got home that evening I told her I had reached a new understanding.

"Tell me more," she said.

"I will over a few beers. Are you game?"

"For good beer and discussion? Always."

We went out to the local pub on Commercial Drive and as we drank Pale Ale and Guinness I told her of my findings, but I did so in an oblique way at first.

"The big picture idea is that there's no god outside the laws of physics. The physical universe is not created and managed from an external vantage. The physical universe is fully a consequence of the laws of physics and logic."

"But you keep invoking god. So how is that in any way a god?"

"Look at it this way: There's no external entity that moves around electrons, protons and so on and organizes them into atoms, molecules and life. This isn't needed. And if it's not needed then Occam's Razor says it doesn't exist. This organization happens intrinsically. It's a self-organizing system. That's what I mean by saying god is Deus Sive Natura. God is implicate in nature, not external to it. God is this self-organizing principle."

"But I'll ask again. Why do you need to name this principle god?"

"Because consciousness is also a self-organizing mechanism. So if all of Creation is due to a self-organizing principle then we can say in that sense Creation is due to a meta-consciousness. This now begins to sound like what most people associate with the idea of god. But it's a god that creates from within the created, not from an external, non organic vantage point."

"I see what you mean. Definitely the meta-consciousness idea is closer to the idea of god. But I think it's also opposed to the traditional idea of Intelligent Design that most people associate with god."

"You're right, but why do you say that?"

"If I understood you, the idea of Intelligent Design is about some controlling external entity that doesn't depend on the laws of physics in order to create."

"That's right, it ignores them. There are no laws of physics by which a car can be spontaneously created. Human intelligence is required. This kind of god is called a Deus Ex Machina. The god outside the machine."

"So according to Intelligent Design," Jenna said, "the laws of physics aren't sufficient to create the order we see in the universe. We need some external entity to step in and create in the way that a human would create a machine like a car."

"Yes, in your example the human being is the creating entity outside the machine. The machine requires Intelligent Design to be built."

"So why do these machines require it but not the universe itself?"

"You see, this is what the ID people just don't get. A machine like a car, a rocket, or what have you, is not a self-organizing system. And by that I mean its construction doesn't use feedback loops, self-referencing components, so the mechanism of spontaneous order from disorder in Chaos Theory doesn't come into play."

"Now you're talking about your findings today?"

"Yes, self-referencing systems can do amazing things without needing an intelligent external designer."

"Give me an example."

"Take the neurons in your head. Through the mechanism of feedback loops between the neurons your consciousness arises."

"So life or the universe as a whole is like that?"

"It absolutely is. And this is the meta consciousness I'm talking about. Intelligent Design is a Deus ex Machina. But god is not that at all. God is a Deus Sive Natura."

"Which brings us back to Spinoza," Jenna said.

"But Spinoza thought the god of the Hebrew bible is a Deus Ex Machina and he rejected it for that reason. He rejected the idea of the Hebrews as leading actors in a divine play. He denied a covenant between Abraham and god. He rejected the idea of a personal god. He was excommunicated from Jewish society in Amsterdam for these ideas."

"Do you agree?"

"With what?"

"With his views about the Hebrew bible."

"I don't know anymore. I used to be such an avowed atheist. Life was simpler then."

"Life is also simpler for the traditionally religious," Jenna said. "There is no doubt, no conflict. All the answers are spoon-fed."

"I think I'm tending now towards accepting a personal god. I know it looks like I'm doing a one-eighty and going back to being conventionally religious as I was in my early teens. But that's not the case at all. I now see the implicate order as the personal god because we are the explicate expression of that order. The implicate order is always within us. It's a personal god in that sense. The creator within the created - the Deus Sive Natura."

"So you're in disagreement with Spinoza then. He didn't believe in a personal god."

"Only because he equated a personal god with an external god."

"So it's a personal god because it speaks from within? Interesting...you've redefined the idea of a personal god."

"My idea of a personal god is considerably more personal than the external kind. There's nothing outside. It's all within. What is within me is the same thing that is within you. There's no me and you. We are one in the implicate order."

***

The next day I gave Jenna a ride to church. She did not have any committee meetings to attend, it was just the regular Sunday service she never missed. It was a chilly and sunny day, a beautiful day for a pleasure drive. I toured Stanley Park, Vancouver's iconic one-thousand acre, densely forested park within walking distance of downtown office buildings. I drove across the Burrard bridge connecting downtown to the Kitsilano neighborhood. I then drove west along West 4th Avenue and then onto the scenic road which offers ocean and mountain views. It is on the way to the University Of British Columbia, known as UBC. Vancouver is a lush, green paradise. Its winters are mild and wet and its summers are hot and dry. Driving my cherry-red, convertible Mustang SVT Cobra was one of my greatest joys during that time in my life. I purchased it brand new in the Spring of 2001. It was pinned-to your-seat fast and nimble, a giddy joy to drive, with a throaty low rumble that sent shivers up my spine. Jenna hated that car because it represented to her raw consumerism and juvenile irresponsibility. She called it the Red Devil, due in part to the numerous speeding tickets I accumulated.

I selected Delirium's Karma from the CD changer. That was the CD I played most often, almost obsessively, during those solitary moments driving my Cobra, alone with my thoughts and tuning in to the silent whispers within the soul. As Karma's haunting melodies and voices pierced my spirit I felt the nimbleness of my car slinging around the curves of Stanley Park, and later the scenic drive on the way to UBC. The car, the road, the music and I became an organic whole. I often experienced a spiritual ecstasy during such times and I was able to peal away the chaff in my life and see my life's purpose, the reason I am on Earth, the cause and not the effects. The textured truth, not the shadows on the wall. During those moments of existential clarity my resolve to write my novel strengthened and any doubts I had for the truth of my vision faded. Was my attraction to my car an expression of pure consumerism or juvenile irresponsibility? Perhaps for many it would have been, but it was certainly not for me.

I decided to put aside my investigations of Chaos Theory for that day. My head was still full of partially digested knowledge from the previous day and I was not yet ready to swim again in the vast ocean of Chaos. I called Addison instead.

"Let's go for a drink," I said.

"Why now? it's only one. I'm at Carla's."

Carla was a work colleague of ours with whom Addison was romantically involved. It was a relationship not immune to the pitfalls of an office romance, and she often leaned on me to get her back in Addison's good graces after each of their heated battles. It was a responsibility becoming too onerous. She had become obsessed and oblivious to other aspects of her life. A few weeks earlier, during one of their estrangements, I spied her car parked outside my apartment building. She had waited for hours because I made the mistake of telling her Addison would be visiting me some time that day.

"Doesn't have to be now," I said, "I can pick you up in a couple of hours."

"What's up," he asked. "I can tell you've got something on your mind."

"I've done more reading on Chaos Theory."

"Nice. You sound like you've done a one-eighty. Sounds good. Pick me up from Carla's at three."

I called Jenna and was relieved to learn she did not need a ride back home because she was staying behind after the Sunday service. She had volunteered for something. I did not always understand why she spent so much time at the church. It had been a while since I spent a full weekend day with her. Not that her activities at the church were without merit. Saint James Church is a steward for the poor and disenfranchised of the Downtown East Side. It is also inclusive of the gay community. I had become very familiar with the priests at St. James Church. The majority were gay. The priesthood, be it Anglican or Catholic or any other, is a refuge for gay men because they are comforted by the celibacy the church imposes on them. And behind the shadows of this celibacy they revel in the light of their god-given nature. It is both their excuse and justification for avoiding heterosexual norms otherwise imposed by a homophobic society.

On the surface it seems ironic the homosexuality vilified by the church is so rampant in its midst. But the divine manifests in mysterious ways. Deep within the belly of the beast resides an undigested divinity, and the beast thrashes with a belly pain that will surely, in the opening days of the Third Age, rip it apart. It is the divinity manifest in the downtrodden, the disenfranchised, the Other. It is a divinity exemplified by the life of a Christ the Church purports to honor. The Christian world has not honored this divinity. The Christian world has worshiped Mammon and the lust for power. The Christian world has not honored the teachings of its foremost son. It is instead on a spiritually vacuous mission to bolster its membership. But the divine breath blows heaven into souls, not souls into heaven.

At three o'clock I waited outside Carla's house. I did not want to intrude. When Addison walked out I saw Carla on the porch and she gave me a look that could kill. I was her annoyance. I was monopolizing her man. We headed to a pub just a few blocks away. I ordered the five-beer sampler and Addison ordered a Bavarian lager called 1516.

"What do you think of Chaos Theory now?" Addison said.

"It's absolutely fascinating."

"What did I tell you? Was I right or was I right?"

"The latter." I laughed.

"So tell me, what fascinates you about it?"

"A couple of things stand out. One is spontaneous order from disorder. Something tells me that's the key to understanding not just specific systems such as the weather or the Stock Market but that it runs much deeper."

"Deeper? What do you mean?"

"The whole universe. The Big Bang itself. Order from Chaos. Complexity from simplicity without the need for a god pulling the strings, or at least a god in the conventional sense. Why doesn't everyone see it?"

"You said there were a couple of things."

"Yeah, the second thing is actually related to the first. It's that spontaneous order from disorder is a consequence of self-reference, feedback loops. I think that's the deepest thing Chaos Theory is telling us. Order comes from Chaos because the Chaos is reaching back into itself and pulling out Order."

"That's an interesting visual image."

"Yes, but I think it's more than that. I think the very act of reaching back into oneself is the mechanism by which Existence emanates."

"Makes sense. When Chaos feeds on itself it applies disorder to disorder...a disordered disorder is order, is it not?"

"That's an interesting way of looking at it."

"But what I really want to know is did you find anything in Chaos Theory that sheds more light into your ideas about consciousness? That was your primary reason for looking into it, right?"

I had explained my ideas to Addison a few months before. It was not to the extent I shared them with Carl, but Addison had a basic understanding of my ideas about consciousness as the implicate order of Reality, of the EBSP, and of my tautological interpretation. We had spent many happy times in pubs and outdoor patios, drinking pints of good beer and ruminating about the nature of Existence. He had urged me to study Chaos Theory because he felt it might propel my ideas forward. When pressed, he could not explain precisely why he thought Chaos Theory could do that for me, but he felt any discipline with the breadth and scope to shed light on such disparate areas as the weather, the stock market, or even the collective behavior of mobs, is something I should look into.

"Yes, there's something that stood out as shedding light on my ideas," I said.

Addison leaned forward and flicked his hair off his eyes.

"Do you remember how I invoked the idea of tautology to explain why the observer influences the laws of physics?"

"Yes, you said the observer is not simply observing the universe. The observer is the universe observing itself. Isn't that your explanation of why observation influences the outcome of experiments in Quantum Mechanics?"

"That's right. The observer is just observing himself. And do you know what else is self-referential?"

Addison stared at me without expression for a few seconds and then I saw the spark of revelation brightening his eyes. "Chaos Theory," he said.

"That's the connecting thread I need to run with. But there's something else leading me to make this connection."

"Nissim, before you continue I need a refill." He pointed to his empty beer and frowned. "Beer and Chaos Theory should be enjoyed together. You too. Next round's on me."

Addison is an avid beer drinker. I once remarked that I lose enjoyment of beer after three or four pints. He expressed incredulity at that. The waitress delivered our refills and Addison raised his beer as a sign we should clink our glasses.

"Nazdrovia." Addison is native Polish. He immigrated to Canada when he was nine. This mirrors my own journey to Canada. I was nine when I emigrated from Israel.

"So where were we before we found ourselves tragically out of beer?"

"I was telling you there's one more connecting thread between consciousness and Chaos Theory."

"Well, don't keep me in suspenders. What is it?"

"Free Will."

"Nice, explain." He raised his beer and we clinked our beer mugs again.

"While it's true self-referential systems tend to produce order out of Chaos, there's a catch. The emerging order is completely unpredictable."

"Huh? Unpredictable order?"

"I know...seems like an oxymoron. The emerging order can't be predicted ahead of time with complete certainty."

"Yes, of course, it's like the weather. But isn't our inability to predict the weather with one hundred percent accuracy just due to technological limitations? Surely, if we could know everything about the weather system to the minutest detail, and if we had the proper mathematical models, then we could predict the weather with complete accuracy up to any time in the future."

"You mean like predicting if it'll rain at any given date in five or ten years? Wrong. It's not like predicting a solar eclipse in three hundred years from now, or the position of Mars at any time in the future."

"Why? What's the difference?"

"It's called Pseudo Determinism."

"Yes, I read about that, but you'll have to refresh my memory. Why pseudo?"

"Ever hear of the expression the sum is greater than the parts?"

"Who hasn't? What's that gotta do with Chaos Theory?"

"It means the behavior coming out of the parts making up the Chaotic system can't be predicted just by looking at those parts. That's why it's pseudo determinism. The behavior is completely a consequence of the parts, so in that sense it's deterministic. However, there isn't enough information in those parts to allow you to predict the behavior of the emerging system."

"I see. Like the weather, for example."

"Yes, the global weather is a Chaotic system. Its parts are the atmosphere, the energy coming from the sun, water evaporating from lakes, oceans and so on."

"So you're saying if we knew everything about the initial conditions of all the parts that influence the weather, and if we had the best possible mathematical models, we still wouldn't be able to predict the weather with complete accuracy?'"

"Bingo. That's what Pseudo Determinism is. Even though the weather is completely determined by these initial conditions, meaning there's no other input that goes into it, it's still impossible to predict, in principle, what kind of weather will emerge out of these initial conditions."

"That's crazy. If you changed any of these initial conditions then the resulting weather would also change correspondingly, right?"

"Yes. That's what's meant by saying the weather is completely determined by these initial conditions."

"So shouldn't it follow that the information required to know the behavior of the weather should be available within these initial conditions?"

"No it doesn't. Welcome to the strange world of Pseudo Deterministic Chaos."

"I can imagine a time in the far future where our technology and mathematics will be so advanced we'll be able to predict if it will rain on any given day in the future."

I shook my head twice while making a sweeping gesture with my right hand. "You're not getting it. It has absolutely nothing to do with technological limitations or limitations of our mathematical sophistication. It's an epistemological limitation baked into Chaotic systems. The behavior that emerges out of the components of the Global Weather System, or any other Chaotic system, acts as a new entity born from its parts, but it assumes an autonomy from its parts. The parts breath Free Will into the emergent entity. It becomes a new, independent, self-determining entity. I like to say that for a Chaotic system, the whole knows its parts but the parts don't know their whole."

"The Chaos is pregnant with Creation," Addison said.

"Nicely said."

"So what makes a system Chaotically Deterministic? How come we can predict an eclipse up to any time in the future? Why isn't that governed by Pseudo Determinism?"

"Two simple words: self reference. It's feedback loops that are the signature of Chaos. That's what distinguishes the Chaos in Chaos Theory from simple random disorder – what I call simple chaos. Simple chaos is inert and dead. It's completely random. But Chaos, with an upper case C, is like a bubbling stew cooking atop a fire. Each ingredient offers up its flavor to the others, and is rewarded with its essence, flavored by the others, and mirrored back. Each ingredient perceives its Self only as it is perceived by the others. Each ingredient perceives another only as that other perceives its Self reflected off all the others."

"Nice. I love that imagery of a bubbling stew. It's alive. It's alive, doctor Frankenstein."

We laughed and clinked our pints.

"You should put it in your book."

"I already have an arsenal of these kinds of sayings in my toolbox. I'll find a place for all of them in my novel when I start writing it, don't you worry."

"But listen, there's still something bothering me. What determines when a system will have these feedback loops? Why doesn't the system that produces an eclipse have them?"

"It's something related to the Three-Body Problem."

"Well, let me tell you, I've participated in a three body situation before and that's the kind of problem I don't mind at all." He winked.

"Funny, but seriously...if you have just two bodies pulling on each other, err...I mean with their gravity, then you can predict with certainty, using the equations of gravity, where each body will be at any point in the future. But as soon as you introduce a third body exerting its gravity on the other two then feedback loops come into play, and voila, Pseudo Determinism. The equations of gravity can no longer provide accurate predictions, or even any kind of prediction."

Addison crossed his eyes as a humorous gesture of utter confusion. "But why? What's special about three bodies?"

"I'm still studying this wild and crazy stuff, remember? I don't know why. But let's get back to what started this discussion leading to Deterministic Chaos."

"What? I already forgot what we were discussing. Waitress, two more pints here. Never mind, just bring us a pitcher."

"Free Will," I said.

"Nice. That's right. I see where you're going with this."

"Tell me where you think I'm going with this."

"Free Will is also an autonomous entity emanating from a lower substrate."

"And what is this substrate?"

"The neurons in your head, I suppose."

"Exactly, Free Will is free because it's an unpredictable type of order, just like the Global Weather System. It's an emergent entity."

"And Consciousness?" Addison said.

"Free Will is consciousness."

Suddenly, Addison's mouth was gaping and his eyes widened. He momentarily covered his mouth with his right hand. "Something just hit me and it's amazing."

"What?"

"Gödel Escher Bach."

"I've heard about that book before, but I don't know what it's about. Something about the correspondence between math, music and art, I think. You read it?"

"I read parts of it," Addison said. He became more serious, no longer wise-cracking and irreverent. "It's a big, complex book. It's not really about the correspondence between art, music and math. Gödel was a logician, Bach was a composer and Escher was an artist. What they have in common is they integrated self-reference into their works. In the book, Hofstadter speculates consciousness is a self-referential phenomenon governed by something called Gödel Incompleteness."

"No mention of Chaos Theory?"

"Not in the parts I read."

"Umm...so this Gödel Incompleteness is also about self-reference? I wonder how Chaos Theory is related to it, since they both are about self-reference."

"Seems to me you've got a lot on your plate. You should read Gödel Escher Bach."

"Addison, why is it every time I confide in you about a new peak of understanding I've scaled, I leave the conversation craning my neck way, way up at yet another peak that looks impossible to climb?"

The waitress plopped the pitcher of beer on our table.

My head was swimming in a sea of confusion. But I have experienced that feeling before. It is the state of undigested knowledge, and venues of thought, that, with the proper effort, get assimilated into one cohesive whole. Software developers often experience this feeling of confusion. The tendrils of disparate algorithms wrestle with each other and vie for supremacy. They are ingredients in a bubbling stew of competing flavors that eventually assimilate into a cohesive whole where before there was only a pantry of solitary ingredients, each knowing nothing of the others and perhaps not even of themselves.

***

The next day, when I got to work, Reza was standing by Clayton's desk. They were having a conversation and I thought Clayton seemed mildly annoyed. Clayton was not the type to lash out in plain, unadorned words when his views or beliefs were assailed. He was always composed, but could sting with words having a benign veneer but meant, under the surface, as an affront or a rebuke. He had a talent to choose his stinging words with surgical precision. They were tailored to the target of his rebuke and understood by no other, like a custom-tailored suit made to perfectly fit only the idiosyncrasies of its wearer. I was often the target of his veiled barbs when we were comparing Christianity to Judaism. He referred to 'the chosen people' in a manner I understood to be derisive but others did not due to their lack of context of our interpersonal dynamic, or of its allusion to previous conversations we shared. Implicit understanding between two people can take the form of an Inside Joke, but also of an Inside Insult. Clayton was fond of the Inside Insult even when there was no one else within earshot. Perhaps he felt uncomfortable with explicit hostility, or perhaps he was crafty and did not want to give the target of his derision undeniable justification for a counter attack.

Reza, on the other hand, was more direct with his rebukes. He delivered his opinions in a mild-mannered yet paradoxically forceful manner. He was a software developer working on other areas of Chancellor SMS. He is a few years younger than me and, at that time, was a recent emigrant from Iran. I took my seat and listened with rapt attention to his conversation with Clayton. Due to Clayton's annoyed, almost detached look, I suspected they were discussing religion. Reza is an atheist and an intellectual. I have had many Muslim friends and acquaintances and I have noticed those from Iran are more secular and free-thinking. Perhaps that is the reason they escaped the theocracy in Iran that had stifled and trampled their identity. For an unbiased intellectual, or a person seeking unrestrained spirituality, the freedom to think without the imposition of society's paradigms is precious like fresh air or clean water.

Reza speaks with the melodic cadence of the Persian accent. When I listen to Persians I often lose focus of the content of their speech and instead get mesmerized by their speech's beguiling musicality. My prose style often mirrors my affinity for musicality or lyricism. I gravitate towards expressing my ideas, fears and aspirations through words that are often as much poetry as prose.

"Genesis is full of things we know are scientifically false," Reza said with a smile.

"Name me one," Clayton said.

I was surprised Clayton left the door wide open to that. A literal interpretation of Genesis is clearly at odds with modern science. It is no

Beyond the Shadows: Existential Whiplash

difficult task for the average person to list scientific inaccuracies in Genesis when understood literally. Clayton has a math degree and he is far from scientifically illiterate.

"Genesis says plants were created before sun. What about photosynthesis? And were all stars created at one time? We see stars created today."

"I'm not going to dwell on irrelevant tangents like these," Clayton said. "Christ tells me what's important is the salvation of my immortal soul. The science of stars or photosynthesis will not wash away my sins and allow my immortal soul to enter the kingdom of god."

"What kingdom? We live in Democracy. That's usual logic from you Christians," Reza said. "We are discussing validity of your religious views and you're using your religion to justify itself?"

"I won't risk an eternity in hell, which is the price for rejecting Christ. That's all I need to know."

"There's no need for god," Reza said. "Creation can come from randomness without help from a god. Scientists are learning that from self-organizing systems. Look at complex structure of snowflake. It forms according to laws of non-linear dynamics."

My ears perked up. I did not know Reza was familiar with these ideas which I had only recently learned. Clayton shook his head without responding. I understood he did not want to continue the conversation.

I intruded into their debate. "Reza, but that's what god is: the tendency of order to emanate from disorder. I agree there's no need for a man in the sky type of god. But why can't you think outside the box when it comes to a redefinition of god?"

"Nissim, for smart guy you sure have soft spot for religion."

"You're being as close-minded as the religious. You've formed an idea of what god is and then you discredit that idea. It's a Straw Man argument. I have a different idea of what god is. So address my idea instead of your preconceived notions."

Clayton rolled his eyes. "Guys, I have a report to write for Roland due in one fricking hour. Can you guys take the conversation somewhere else? Or better yet, can you get to work?"

That day, after work, I approached Reza at his desk across the hall from me. He had his coat on and was ready to leave. "Hey Reza, hold on. Those things you said this morning about self-organizing systems...what do you know about that?"

Reza put down his briefcase. "Oh, I know some. I took couple courses on non-linear dynamic systems and Chaos in university in Iran.

"It's all about self-reference?"

"Yeah, you can say. Because it's non-linear so describes self-referencing systems."

"Self-organization causes self-referencing?"

"Take it other way, if you want self-organizing system then it must have self-referencing components."

"What makes a system self-referencing?"

Reza tilted his head to the right and gazed at the ceiling to his left. He responded after a few seconds. "Each part of system modifies other parts and these other parts modify back the first part. But modification is influenced by how the first part modified them, so really it's first part seeing itself in the other parts, and is modifying itself. It's described mathematically by non-linear differential equations."

"It's like the parts of the system seeing themselves in an infinite nested mirror," I said.

"Yes. Yes. Is good image. Very powerful analogy."

"But why is it called self-organizing? What does self-organization really mean?" I knew the answer but I wanted to hear Reza's answer.

"Because all this internal feedback looping produces some useful ordered state. Imagine randomized deck of cards that puts itself into order so all aces are together and then all twos, threes and so on. All without anything outside the cards giving help."

"So self-reference produces this self-ordering behavior? Is this Chaos Theory?"

"Oh yes. Same thing. Yes."

"Tell me something," I said, "have you heard of Gödel?"

"Yes, yes. Of course, you kidding me? I took courses in Iran university about logic and Gödel Incompleteness. Very fascinating stuff. It's also about self-reference but of logic itself. It's very deep stuff. Why you ask?"

"What is it about? In a few words."

"It says there are statements in mathematics that are undecidable. These statements are theorems, but you can't prove. They are consequence of basic axioms of system. They can be false or true but we can never know for sure. That's not exact description of it but is a good introduction."

I rolled my eyes. "Well give me the more technical description."

"The best is to say in mathematical formal systems like arithmetic, statistics, or other mathematical systems that have enough complexity, there are theorems which are true but is impossible to prove they are true by using the tools inside that system only. That's why we say the formal system is incomplete."

"What do you mean by the tools inside the system?"

"For example, when proving a theorem of geometry, like all angles of a triangle add up to one-eighty, then you're only allowed to prove it using five fundamental axioms of geometry, or other theorems of Geometry that have already been proved from these axioms. Nothing else outside geometry."

"So the system is only allowed to use parts of itself in order to prove any other part of itself?"

"Yes, yes, is very good summary. And these parts are the axioms or other proven theorems that are consequence of axioms. That is very important point."

"But Gödel Incompleteness is itself a theorem. Has it been proven?"

"Of course. It was Kurt Gödel who did it."

"But within what system did he prove it? It's itself subject to its own restrictions, is it not?"

"Of course. But the system that contains Gödel Incompleteness is logic itself which transcends mathematics so it can talk about mathematics. It is called a theorem of meta-mathematics."

"Wow, that's so deep," I said. I actually felt shivers on my skin. "It's mathematics talking about itself. Mathematics is self-aware."

"Yes, yes, is very amazing. Gödel was incredible genius."

"So can you give me an example of a theorem that can't be proved in this way from inside its own system?"

"Nissim, I can't think of a theorem like that now. For example one theorem is that there is infinity of Prime numbers, but is not good example because there is simple proof for that. But imagine its impossible to find proof for something like that."

"What's the connection between Chaos Theory and Gödel Incompleteness?"

Reza gave me a puzzled look. "Such strange question. I never heard that question. They're both based on self-reference but that's all I think. No other connection."

I disagreed with Reza. My gut instincts told me self-reference was a fundamental aspect of Reality and any two fundamental disciplines based on self-reference had deep connections and could be synthesized into one discipline.

"How is Gödel Incompleteness based on self-reference?" I said. "You haven't explained that."

"It's the way an unprovable theorem is constructed. Gödel proved the existence of unprovable theorems by inventing a technique to construct them. The technique uses self-reference type of logic."

"I'm getting confused. It looks like Gödel is making a distinction between something being proved and being true. In other words, it might be impossible to prove some things that are actually true."

"Yes, absolutely. To prove something means to start with one or more axioms and/or one or more already proven theorems and then to make logical deductions in order to derive next theorem. You keep doing these steps until you get to the theorem you want to prove. If you find a path, in this way, to get to it then it's considered proven. But Gödel showed there are true theorems but doesn't exist any set of steps to derive them from fundamental axioms."

"Oh, I see. Very interesting. It's proving a theorem is true by actually constructing it in a rinse and repeat kind of way rather than proving it exists."

"Nissim, that's false distinction. You should study what proof means in logic. You always prove something exists by constructing it. No such thing as this idea you have of 'remote' proof. You must prove a theorem by starting with axioms or theorems already proven and jumping from theorem to theorem, using deduction, until you arrive at theorem you want to prove."

"Like skipping stones," I said. "To jump to the next theorem means you have shown it's a consequence of the previous theorem or theorems."

The difference between a theorem and an axiom is axioms are the ground level statements in a formal system. They cannot, by definition, be proven. The only caveat is that they not contradict each other. If they could be proven then they would not be considered axioms but instead be theorems derivable from lower level axioms. Theorems are consequences of axioms, either directly or through the agency of intermediate theorems. For example, in Geometry Euclid started with five axioms and all the subsequent theorems in Geometry are a consequence of these five axioms. The theorems are deterministically based on the axioms.

"So a mathematical proof is like a ladder? To get to the tenth step you must start at the first and climb your way up."

"Yes, yes, is good analogy. But steps are far apart. You can't skip steps."

"So as you climb the proof ladder," I said, "each step is a theorem which is a consequence of the step below. In effect your proof is really a sequence of derivations."

"Yes, but your ladder analogy has flaws. Often you need to use two or more theorems in order to prove the next theorem in the sequence of proof steps."

Beyond the Shadows: Existential Whiplash

This flaw in the ladder analogy troubled me. Even in those early days I knew I had to devise more powerful analogies and metaphors to make these pivotal ideas more understandable. I favored pedagogy by analogy. A good analogy, like a picture, is worth a thousand words. The novel I planned to compose was a living entity, a demanding master. The prospect of its reader not understanding or appreciating these complex ideas loomed as a failure that would dull its agenda. If I did not clearly explain these ideas, the reader would not grasp their relevance to the overall arc of my novel. As I delved deeper into the intricacies of Gödel Incompleteness and Chaos Theory my world view transitioned, not via a smooth evolutionary curve, but via the sharp, breathtaking leaps that create existential whiplash. They are the fuel of paradigm shifts.

The depth and breadth of my novel's agenda was dawning on me. Its ambitions had now soared to heights I would have never suspected before. I was now aiming for nothing less than a redefinition of divinity based on reason, not superstition and blind faith. I sensed this would trigger seismic ripples through the Civilization of Man, like a tsunami washing away a sandy shore. And a new age would rise based on an understanding of the divine that taps into the bedrock of Existence.

The affairs of Man go through three stages while on this earth. The first is a stage of childlike ignorance and spiritual naivety. It is an age lacking in theological abstraction. It is an age that extrapolates a controlling god or goddess for any natural phenomenon. It is a separate Deus Ex Machina for every phenomenon. Even abstract concepts, such as love or war, are distilled into the domain of tangible, anthropomorphic deities.

The second stage is a stage of more nuanced theological abstractions. All phenomena are considered to cast one common shadow, and in there dwells the one god. It is not necessarily an anthropomorphic god, but always an entitymorphic god. It is an entity external from its creation, a supreme being as master of lesser beings.

The third stage is a stage of the spirit, a stage of wisdom. God is no longer seen as an entity separate from Creation. God is not understood as an entity that exists, but rather that from which all of Existence emanates. From a slab of marble statues emanate, but a slab of marble is not a statue, it is the space of all statues. Likewise, from god Existence emanates, but god does not exist in the conventional sense. In the Third Age, divinity will be synthesized with the rational and scientific. The distinction between divinity and science, the spiritual and the rational, will blur.

After a few seconds of reflection about the flawed ladder analogy I saw a deeper analogy. "Reza, instead of a ladder how about thinking of mathematical proofs as a conglomeration of domino pieces standing on their lengths."

"Yes, I see. Falling dominoes in chain reaction. But why is that better than ladder analogy?"

"For two reasons: the first is that it drives home the point more clearly that each domino is toppled as a consequence of the previous dominoes that toppled. The second is that it improves on the single step in the ladder analogy. Sometimes the previous step involves multiple falling dominoes. This is analogous to having several theorems in the previous proof sequence that are required to prove the next theorem in the proof sequence. The final toppling domino in this chain reaction is analogous to the target theorem that we want to prove."

"Very beautiful I think. You are trying to prove target domino will be knocked over if beginning dominoes are knocked over."

"Yes, this is analogous to trying to prove a theorem by showing it's a consequence of previous theorems or of the axioms themselves."

"And first dominoes is equivalent to axioms in proof sequence. I like that analogy very much. Nissim, please buy Gödel Escher Bach. It has excellent section on these ideas of proof in a formal system. Also many other excellent ideas related to Gödel Incompleteness."

On Friday, after work, I invested in Gödel Escher Bach at the Chapters book store at Metrotown mall. As I laid a stealthy foot in the mystical lands of Gödel and Chaos, I saw sprawled before me two mighty kingdoms up on mount Zion. These kingdoms were far worse than mortal enemies for they were of the same family but separated by a distance born of apathy. They suffered a desolation from each other far worse than the harshest assaults.

One night, as I sat at my home computer contemplating the fabric of Existence, the full moon's milky-white through the window pierced my spirit. It was as an uninvited yet welcomed guest. The kingdom of Gödel sent its swiftest messengers and they spoke to me of the truths that cannot be proved. And when the message pierced the ramparts of my spirit, I shuddered with the revelation I had only seen the shadows all along. And I saw a flaw in my EBSP - an incompleteness. How can the EBSP be true at all if truth exists which, even in principle, cannot be known? Does my cherished EBSP not claim all which cannot be known cannot be true? Yet Gödel proved there exist unknowable truths.

Once I discovered the folly of my conceit that I had conquered the mountain once and for all, despair set in due to the apparent futility of ever conquering the true peak at all. I feared the edifice I had years ago constructed would now collapse, and from its ashes nothing would emerge.

Beyond the Shadows: Existential Whiplash

I thought: "Is the implicate order of Reality indeed woven from consciousness or is that a folly I must now forsake? If truths exist out of reach of the observer then my cherished EBSP is no more, and my textured argument that consciousness is Reality at the implicate level then falls apart and is no more. Are these the times of my destiny's convergence, or for a parting once and for all?"

I trembled that my novel would be swallowed within a collapsing foundation built on falsehood. But there are two kinds of falsehood: one is a falsehood that knows not the path to the truth above all. The unraveling of such a falsehood can teach nothing at all. But the other falsehood is a false peak on the path towards the true peak above all. I wondered which falsehood is mine.

And then I greeted the messengers from the kingdom of Chaos and their indictment now easily penetrated the breached ramparts of my mind and soul. I thought again: "How can the EBSP be true at all if there exists Order from Chaos whose behavior cannot even in principle be predictively known? It is truth existing beyond the knowledge of the observer. It becomes an entity unto its own because it knows its parts but the parts do not know it at all."

And then I realized a profound truth that encapsulates the falsehood of the EBSP: Information and Truth are not synonymous as I had previously thought. Truth can exist beyond information's grasp. But again I thought: "Is the EBSP's falsehood a false peak on the path to the true peak above all? Is consciousness simply a local peak on the path to the peak above all?"

Up on mount Zion were two roads winding down into the valley, one from the kingdom of Chaos and the other from Gödel's. The road from Chaos became progressively more convoluted as it rolled down the mountain, its final destination unpredictable. The other, from Gödel, was likewise twisted and convoluted and its final destination one could never prove beyond a shadow of a doubt. Provability and Predictability are two sides of the same coin. For the latter, it is Pseudo Determinism paving the road to the beyond, while for the former it is an Epistemological Incompleteness - a truth escaping the system and forming a system unto its own.

But the despair that darkened my spirit was a stubborn companion. I could now see a hitherto hidden peak looming above all. But the path to that true peak seemed so foreboding, its rugged contours inhospitable and intractable. My resolve for understanding the fabric of Reality took deeper roots in my spirit.

"If the EBSP lies on the mountain at all then it is a falsehood that will propel me to the true peak far above all," I thought. The silent voice in the semantic spaces of the soul assured me the EBSP was indeed a false peak on the path to the truth, but I did not yet understand how. I resolved to climb the inhospitable path to the true peak and prove it is not intractable after all.

Gödel And Chaos: The Tree Of Creation

I had unsuccessfully danced with the paradox of the EBSP, its feet were not in lockstep with mine, and yet I sensed it is a false peak in the shadow of the highest truth. I went into the forest in a state of Chaotic confusion. It was a cold day, my wispy breath wafted in front of me. It was a sunny day, the sun's explosive light, through the trees bare and bright, exposed my body, my spirit was nigh.

I walked into the forest as far as possible and then completed the journey on the half-way out. I emerged at the precipice above a sea, its shoreline on the other side of a narrow and meandering road. Across the waters were the North Shore mountains. They were snowy and rugged and hoary. The sea was a blue-green marble sparkling by the sun's strong light.

I sat at the precipice. In front of me my feet dangled above a void and behind me the Autumn leaves were dying. I reflected on the EBSP, on what it is truly telling me. I stripped it of all prejudices and banalities. I pealed away its artifices and artifacts. I aimed to see it with a Zen state of mind, deconstructed and bare. How to describe a state of Zen consciousness? Imagine looking at a painting depicting a beautiful sunset. This painting evokes powerful emotions in you - emotions of serenity and your soul's longing for communion with divinity. You have achieved a state of Zen consciousness when upon pondering this evocative painting all you can see is a coat of paint. Zen deconstructs reality and returns you to the white-eyed womb of Creation.

Imagine descending the branches of a tall and sprawling tree, from child to parent branch, and then repeated again and again until you reach the trunk. You are now communing with the Source. When you descend the Tree of Existence, it is for the void, the nothingness, the ineffable H at the core of Existence, that you are yearning.

And when I fell into the Zen within me, I saw a grand tree. But the essence of space and time, the implicate order revealed by the EBSP, was only one branch, not its totality. On each branch I saw a myriad of wrestling angels - the denizens of its dream. They perceived the completeness of their own branch, and all the parent branches below, but could not see the completeness of any child branch emanating from themselves. A litmus test of existence for any portion of their own branch was if by sight they could prove its existence. A blind spot revealed a lack of existence, not a veiled one. But their sight's limitation did not hold such austerity for any other branch. Not seeing the other branches fully revealed did not hold such conclusivity. And then a denizen of a branch's dream soared high above the tree and saw its entirety. How naive it was to think its home branch was the whole tree. How myopic to only aspire to wrestle its home branch instead of yearning to dance with the entire tree. To this wrestler it slowly dawned, freed from prejudices and tethers, first a release of tension due to paradox resolution and then, like a shadow illuminated by the light, the paradox lost its fight.

When I snapped out of my reverie, I witnessed a sunset with a beauty transcending sight's domain, and which can only be parsed as the soul dancing with a divinity reverberating within its innermost grasp - Creation's womb. The sky splintered into crimson shards that pierced the wispy clouds, and then the sun's turgid red ball hung low for an Eternity above the sea's furthest edge, and then sank into the void beyond horizon's ledge.

***

It was the middle of December 2002 when the Chaos of the branches resolved into a tree for me. I needed to discuss it with someone who understood the progression of my ideas. I needed to bounce it off someone who would appreciate the complexities and subtleties of my struggles with the paradox I was finally in lockstep with. I needed to talk to Carl.

The Santa Claus was somber that day. His eyes betrayed his knowing why we were entering there. He sensed I was now yearning to resonate with the angels dancing on the branches of the Tree of Eternal Life, rather than with those wrestling on the Tree of Knowledge of Good and Evil, or maybe I only internalized it. Carl looked gaunt. His cheeks were hollow and his dark hair was close-cropped and dull. He had not shaved for a few days. He wore faded jeans and a military style, faded brown parka winter jacket that looked like he had bought it at a garage sale. But his deep-blue eyes were bright and vibrant. As we entered Trees Organic, we marched past Santa Claus and took no notice. We went through life's formalities of acquiring food and drink and other niceties. I then said to Carl: "I have received an epiphany."

I had not been in contact with Carl since January of that year. It was before I knew of Gödel or Chaos.

"I didn't quite get it right about the EBSP when we first discussed it back in 99. There was an incompleteness in my understanding then, but I now see the EBSP as only a nested shape in a grand tree."

I talked of the equivalence between the unprovable theorems of a formal system and the unpredictable order, the Pseudo Determinism, that emerges from Chaotic systems like the weather, the Stock Market or the Civilization of Man.

"I'm not quite understanding this equivalence," Carl said. "I still can't picture why an unprovable theorem is like the global weather system."

"Do you know how theorems are generated?"

I answered my own question immediately without giving him a chance to reflect. "A formal system starts with axioms which are statements about the system, but they're just assertions you take for granted. There are only two restrictions on these axioms: they shouldn't contradict each other and they should be independent of each other."

"I don't understand the second restriction."

"It means you shouldn't be able to derive an axiom from one or more of the other axioms. For example, in Euclidean geometry there are five axioms from which all the theorems can be deduced. The Pythagorean theorem is not a sixth axiom, it's just a consequence of some subset of the five axioms."

"Gotcha, the axioms are the irreducible statements in the system. But why can the axioms be assumed as true, but yet we have to prove the theorems?"

"Because all what proof means in the mathematical sense is to show that a theorem is a consequence of the system's axioms. By definition axioms cannot be proven, they're the starting points."

"But what if the axioms aren't true?"

"That's the million dollar question. In a formal system, all truth means is that a theorem is a consequence of the system's axioms. If we start with A and B, if C is a consequence of these then C is said to be true. Axioms A and B are their own consequence and not of anything else within the system, so in this sense you can't say an axiom is true or false within its own formal system. There's nothing wrong if you build a foundation made of wood. But if you try to build a skyscraper on it then the skyscraper is a falsehood in relation to the foundation of wood- it won't stand."

Carl crossed his eyes. "So axiom A is a consequence of axiom A? I'll have to chew on that one."

"Look, it's really quite straight forward. The axioms come first and the formal system is built on top of them. Truth is relative to the axioms and simply means membership in the set of theorems, which are the logical consequences, of the axioms of that system."

"But the axioms in geometry are self-evident truths."

"Yes, but what does that really mean? That's the mental box that's hard to break out of. They're self-evident truths to us because we're a part of their system. We exist within a geometrical world. You have the freedom to pick any set of axioms and build a formal system from them, as long as they obey the two restrictions we discussed."

"Yeah, I can see that now. Truth cannot be true with lower case t, it can only be True with a capital T."

I challenged him. "Elaborate."

Carl leaned towards me. "We can't say Truth is true because that would mix levels of abstraction. It's like asking when was the first second of time. The answer is that it happened during the first second of time. The question is its own answer. When Time or Truth are turned back on themselves it doesn't add any additional meaning to the discussion."

"That's what a tautology means."

"Yeah, I think so. What you're saying is only theorems can be true, because truth, by definition, is the proper logical derivation from the axioms. The axioms are not logically derived from anything. They just are." Carl shrugged his shoulders and twisted his palms up.

"You got it. The theorems are like the chain reaction of cascading falling dominoes. A domino which is in the path of the chain reaction and falls over is analogous to a true theorem, but one which never gets knocked down is like a false theorem. It's not a member of the set of dominoes that get hit in this chain reaction. It's not a consequence of the initial set of dominoes that are knocked over."

"That's awesome, Nissim. I love that visual metaphor. Clearly, the first domino can't be said to be true or false in this sense because it's the one that starts the whole chain reaction. I think I can visualize it now."

I had a fascinating thought. "This idea can be applied to god. If everything is created by god then god is the source of Existence. But god can't be said to exist, just as the axioms can't be said to be true."

"Yeah, that's indeed a fascinating thought: god as an axiom. The axiom that all of Existence is a consequence of."

"And if god is the primordial axiom, then I think it follows god can't have any properties or attributes."

"Why? Didn't you say axioms are not consequences of anything. So why can't there be an axiom at the root of Reality that has some properties and attributes? You know...it makes a statement of some sort."

"But that would mean these properties or attributes would be irreducible since they would be the most fundamental aspects of Existence."

"And what's the problem with that?"

"There's plenty problems. Sure, axioms can have properties within the system they create, but they are themselves theorems emanating from another system, a parent system. I don't believe in irreducible complexity."

Gödel And Chaos: The Tree Of Creation

Carl shook his right hand. "Hold on, I see a flaw in this. If the axioms of a formal system are themselves theorems of another formal system, then why can't we just combine these two formal systems into one and have the axioms of the lower level parent system be the only axioms in this coalesced formal system?"

"Aha...you're very clever grasshopper. That's an excellent question. I'll answer it soon. There's a few more things we need to discuss before I get to this."

"Interesting, I can't wait to hear your answer. Here's another question: What kind of axiom has no attribute or nothing at all?"

"You've hit the nail on the head, it's nothingness. If you go all the way down the proverbial rabbit hole, you'll find absolute nothingness. Only nothingness is irreducible."

"Because there's nothing to reduce. No pun intended. Or should I say no tautology intended?"

"Personally, I prefer to call it the serpent hole, as an allusion to the story of the serpent in the garden of Eden. In the first paragraph of Genesis it says the Earth was formless and empty, darkness was over the surface of the deep."

"I don't think there's any such thing as perfect nothingness. What is nothingness in the first place? It can only be defined in relation to something."

"Well, I just gave a definition. It's an axiom devoid of properties or attributes, and there can only be one such axiom. It's not the kind of nothingness inside a hole. That kind of nothingness is relative to the boundaries of the hole. I'm talking about an absolute nothingness."

"But we can't even fathom what that is because as soon as you ponder it then it's no longer nothing. It can't exist."

"But why must it be dependent on what you can fathom?"

"Doesn't your own EBSP say that which can't be known can't exist?"

"And isn't nothingness that which doesn't exist by definition."

"What? Hold on."

"But anyway, as I said, there's a flaw in the EBSP and I'll get to that soon. Nothingness is that which is unfathomable. You can only fathom what emanates from nothingness, not nothingness directly. Your explanation for why it can't be defined can be turned on itself. It's not an 'it'. It's not an entity. It can't exist because it's the source of Existence, not its beneficiary."

"I'll have to think about that, Nissim."

"That's what a Zen state is. You can't think about it. You must unthink it.

Gödel And Chaos: The Tree Of Creation

Zen consciousness is active unthinking, not the passive kind."

"You sound like those monks I bunked with in the Eighties. But let's get back to theorems. How can they be generated from this axiom of absolute nothingness?"

"Another awesome question. But I don't have the answer yet. Gödel shows how unprovable truths emanate from systems that exhibit self-referencing behaviors, so if nothingness produces these kinds of theorems then it must self-reference somehow, but I don't know why yet."

"Nissim, that's the mortal flaw in your system. It's really impossible for nothingness to self-reference because you would need a cause for the self-reference, but by definition there can't be an external influence to kickoff the self-referencing. That would be something rather than nothing."

"What if it's not external? Isn't self-reference, by definition, purely internal?"

"You'd still need a cause."

"What if there's no cause?"

"How is that possible? If you were able to explain that then you'd essentially explain how the serpent hole works. That would be mind-blowing."

"That'd be just insane, wouldn't it? Huh."

Carl nodded with great enthusiasm while furrowing his brow. It looked like his head would snap off.

"What I suspect," I said, "is that the first theorem that emanates from absolute nothingness is of the unprovable variety. This is unlike the other formal systems that contain unprovable theorems - they also have provable theorems."

"What you said about all of Existence emanating from feedback loops within nothingness reminds me of something I read in the Bhagavad Gita."

"Is that some holy book? It sounds like Hindi to me."

"You never heard of it? It is in fact Hindu scripture. It means Song of the Lord. In my opinion, the greatest spiritual truth I ever read. It's such an eye-opening and beautiful piece of writing, that when I read it I can't find the fold between where it ends and I begin."

"Wow Carl. I love, love, love that metaphor. It's so poetic - mind if I use it in my novel?"

"I'd be honored, Nissim."

I jotted it in my notebook.

"I was in India in the mid Eighties when I discovered the Bhagavad Gita. I was fascinated by Hinduism. Still I AM."

I sensed, due to the serenity rippling across Carl's face, that it was the H at the depths of the navel of Creation that was now speaking from within me. For an instant beyond time, I saw the white-eyed look in his eyes. It was the Zen of a deconstructed Reality. I felt goosebumps like ants running down my back, and I shed my outer layers and became the eternal Now.

"There's a passage in it that says exactly what you said. The similarity is quite astounding." Carl breathed deeply from his nose, but it was as if he was being breathed rather than actively breathing.

"Tell me. What does it say?" I held my breath.

Carl shut his eyes and his breath slowed. I was facing the front window and I saw Santa Claus sitting outside. He gave me a fleeting yet knowing look, or maybe I imagined that. There are watershed moments in life when you learn or experience a truth that etches an indelible mark on your soul and mind. I sensed what Carl was about to reveal would create such a mark on me.

"Curving back within myself I create again and again."

The dense column of ants now marched down the spirals of the hole that leads to my innermost home, and at the bottom they danced with the winged angels who yield the fiery, whirling swords. It is the angels who forbid entry into the garden of my innermost chamber and, at its center, to the Tree of Eternal Life. All my life a silent voice has whispered from within me. But it had only been during the last few years that I realized what I thought was a private place within me was shared by all. Later, Gödel and Chaos taught me the serpent hole spiraled far deeper than I had ever suspected before.

The silent whispers now emerged from the white-eyed womb of Existence within me, and I realized Eternity to be not just the absence of time but the absence of all attribute and property. It is the ineffable nullity. The ejection from the white-eyed garden is a fracture within the H and two trees emerge: one adorned by wrestling angels and the other by those that dance. One intended for climbing towards the desert floors beyond, and the other for descending towards the birthing ground beneath it all.

For every up there must be a down. For every action there must be a reaction. And when all is coalesced then only a net nothingness remains. Why is there something instead of nothing? There is not, it is still a net nothing. It is impossible for there to be a net something. The net nothingness, expressed as symmetry at all levels of the Tree of Knowledge of Good and Evil, is the signature the trunk makes on every branch. It is the waters of Eternal life that the branches suckle from the trunk. It is the tell-tale sign of the H within YHVH. The net nothingness is the fingerprint of god on his Creation.

If god exists why is there evil? Because of the emerging polarities, the Yin and Yang reaching out from the fractured H - the Tree of Knowledge of Good and Evil bursting out from the heart of primordial Man. All my life I have looked into my being but could not see beneath this fracture. A hand now reached out from the burst garden within me. It is primal Existence ejected from the white-eyed garden, as is a sobbing baby from its womb.

"It's not a coincidence," I finally said after an Eternal moment walking with the evening breeze in the primordial garden. "The divine also speaks from the Bhagavad Gita."

"Then where do we go from here?"

"We should get back to discussing how theorems are generated."

"Why do I get the feeling all this technical stuff about formal systems is leading towards a discussion about god?"

I looked out the window and I was lost in my thoughts for a few seconds. "Because it is. Everything of substance I've ever said has, in one form or another, been about god. It's only recently dawned on me my life has always been converging on that."

"All roads lead to Rome."

"Or to the Eternal Kingdom."

"When will your convergence happen?"

"When civilization converges on the Third Age."

"In our lifetime?"

"Yes, we are living at its dawn."

"For now let's get back to the theorems, as you were saying."

"OK, here goes. Just like in a dominoes chain reaction, some theorems are direct consequences of the axioms and some come later down the road. They are consequences of already constructed theorems. The analogy is that some dominoes get knocked down by the initial falling dominoes and others get knocked down by later falling dominoes down the cascading chains."

"Remind me again why we're discussing theorems?"

"I'm trying to show you how Gödel Incompleteness is equivalent to the Pseudo Determinism in Chaos Theory."

"Like the global weather system?"

"Yes, Pseudo Determinism is like the stock market, the explicate consciousness that emanates from the network of neurons in your brain, and my contention is the Big Bang itself is also that."

"Ah, yes, yes, now I remember. But didn't we start this discussion today about your new insight into the EBSP? Is all this leading to that? I'm losing sight of the big picture."

"Patience, I'll be getting to that. First is the equivalence between Gödel Incompleteness and Pseudo Determinism in Chaos Theory. So, consider the first set of theorems that are the direct consequence of the axioms. That's the level one theorems. A level two theorem is a consequence of one or more level one theorems and possibly, but not necessarily, one or more of the axioms. Level three is a consequence of at least one level two theorem and possibly one or more level one theorems and axioms. And so on and so on to higher theorem levels. Get it?"

"Yeah, I can picture that. It's like a network of interdependent theorems growing out of the axioms, like a big bushy tree."

"That's a good visual. And that's what logicians call a formal system. Each theorem can be mechanically generated from the lower level substrate by using the rules of inference. There's nothing particularly difficult or mysterious about these ideas. Are you with me so far?"

"What are these rules of inference? That's the first I hear of it."

"That's how you define a formal system. It's got the axioms and rules that tell you how to construct theorems out of these axioms and how to construct theorems out of already existing theorems. In a formal system of logic the rules of inference are the systematic rules of logical deduction. But you can setup a formal system with any kind of rules of your liking. If you want a great read about all this then get yourself a copy of Gödel Escher Bach, or I can lend you mine. Heard of it?"

"Yes, I did actually. But never read any of it. Something about similarities between art, music and mathematics, right?"

I chuckled and shook my head. "Everyone seems to think that. I used to think that. But it's not about that at all. It's really about self-referencing systems. It's got a fantastic chapter early in the book about formal systems: theorems, axioms, rules of inference and all this good stuff we've been discussing."

"Thanks for the tip, Nissim."

"So now let's kick it up a notch, shall we?"

"Wait, I need to fasten my seat belt. OK, go for it."

"The crucial thing to understand is that this process of generating theorems can't help but be self-referencing - feedback loops. Do you see why?"

Carl contemplated my question for a few seconds and then shrugged. "Does each theorem and axiom feedback on itself somehow?"

"Actually yes, but in a sneaky kind of way. Here's an example of how it can happen: Suppose a particular theorem called theorem 3 is generated as a consequence of theorem 2 and theorem 1. But suppose theorem 2 is itself a consequence from theorem 1 and some other theorems or axioms. So, when theorem 1 references theorem 2 in order to generate theorem 3, it is, in effect, seeing itself in theorem 2. This is an indirect or implicit feedback loop. Do you see it?"

"Sorry Nissim, I'm getting lost. Can you give me a concrete example?"

"Yeah, it can become convoluted if it's too abstract." I thought about it for a minute. "OK, consider the following formal system with just two axioms: A1 and A2. A1 says all UFO pilots are green. A2 says all UFO pilots have little bodies and big heads."

I pulled out a notebook and a pencil from my bag. It was not my prized red notebook with the spiral metal spine. I wrote down these two axioms as A1 and A2 with the definition in brackets next to each.

"Now, our first theorem will be a consequence from these two axioms. Call it T1. It concludes all UFO pilots are green and have big heads."

I jotted down this theorem in a similar fashion and drew a single arrow from A1 and A2 to T1.

"Yeah, I see it. It's a logical consequence. So your rules of inference is just logic. You haven't invented your own rules."

"That's right."

"But if I take A1 and A2 I come up with the fact all UFO pilots are green and have small bodies and big heads. You're missing the part about the little body."

"But the theorem I deduce from A1 and A2 doesn't have to be the full consequence. It can just be a partial result, as long as it doesn't violate the rules of inference, in this case the rules of logic."

"I see, fair enough."

"So now let's deduce a second theorem. It will be a consequence of A2 and T1. Call it T2 and it says all UFO pilots are green and have small bodies and big heads."

I added this to my diagram in a similar fashion.

"I see it. It's a simple logical consequence."

"So we created a path that goes from A1 and A2 to T1 and then from T1 and A2 to T2. I call that the proof path for proving T2."

"Yeah, you can just take a pencil and trace that path until you get to T2."

"Now, see what happened. T1 and A2 referenced each other in order to produce T2. But when A2 referenced T1 it saw all UFO pilots are green and have big heads. But the fact all UFO pilots have big heads is already a part of A2, and that's where T1 got it from. So when A2 referenced T1 it saw itself reflected back."

"But this seems so redundant."

"You mean a tautology? This is just a very simple example. It only goes one level deep, so that's why it seems so obvious. It's an obvious tautology, like all bachelors are married. But imagine we do this many levels deep, generating T3, T4 and so on until the tautological aspect is no longer obvious at all. All formal systems are tautological in this way, but we just don't see it for the complex ones."

"Yeah, I see what you mean. It can become a complex network of relationships, and this self-referencing behavior will become veiled, impossible to see."

"Are you familiar with the philosophy of Kant?"

"Can't say I am."

"Kant called these kinds of tautological theorems Analytical statements. He called non tautologies Synthetic statements."

"But it looks like there are only Analytical theorems in a formal system, because they're all tautological with respect to the postulates. What are the Synthetic theorems?"

"Aha, the million dollar question. I'll get to that soon. Now, this is just a super simple example I created, but it gives you an idea of what I mean. A really complex formal system will have theorems that recursively are consequences of hundreds or thousands or even millions and beyond of lower level theorems and axioms. Like a stew atop a fire, where each ingredient flavors all the others, and is then flavored back by its own essence. Do you see now an equivalency of these ideas with the self-similarity that is a signature of Chaotic systems?"

"Hmm...yeah I think so. Formal systems of theorems have a Fractal structure, just like systems described by Chaos Theory."

"And for both, the outcome of all this Fractal self-referencing is the same."

"Which is what?"

"For the system of theorems the outcome is ultimately theorems that can't be proved one way or the other and-"

"What do you mean by one way or the other?"

"I mean they can't be proved to be true or false. They're undecidable. There's no proof path for them."

"But hold on here, if there's no proof path then it's not undecidable, it's just plain false."

"But there isn't a proof path either way, not for proving they're false or for proving they're true."

"Oh yeah, I didn't think of that. Saying something is false is itself a theorem."

"And that's when we enter the kingdom of Gödel. He proved that in any sufficiently powerful formal system there will always be theorems without a proof path either way, but they can nevertheless be true. I say they can be, they're really undecidable."

"But are they true or not? Or is undecidability a non binary state?"

"You mean, can they be reached via a proof path within another system? What I'm saying really is that these undecidable theorems are the axioms of an emergent formal system that explodes out of the parent system."

"But, but how can you have no proof path? I mean, that's how theorems are defined in the first place, as the endpoints of a proof path."

"No need to get into the guts of how Gödel proved it. Basically, he started with a self-negating statement such as 'This sentence is false'. He then asked if that sentence is true or false. But if it's true then it's false and if it's false then it's true. So it's undecidable. He then used a brilliant mathematical technique called Gödel Numbering to show that all formal systems that incorporate multiplication and addition produce statements that are the mathematical version of this kind of self-negating statement."

"So what's the connection of all this to Pseudo Determinism?"

"The undecidability that emerges out of these axiomatic formal systems is isomorphic, or equivalent, to the unpredictability that emerges from Chaotic systems. Will May 19th, 2060 be sunny or cloudy? The global weather is unpredictable. It's undecidable. But it's not unpredictable because we don't yet have the proper technology or mathematical models to predict it. It's unpredictable in principle, no matter what technology we can ever have."

"Provability for one is unpredictability for the other."

"That's right. And for both it's feedback loops, self-referencing, that causes this behavior."

"So for the weather, as an example, axioms are like the initial conditions like temperature, humidity, etc."

"Yes, and the rules of inference are the laws of physics that govern the weather. The predictable aspects of the weather are like the normal theorems with a proof path and-"

"Yes, I see it, " Carl said. "The unpredictable aspects of the weather are like the theorems without a proof path in an axiomatic system. The unpredictable aspects of the weather are completely determined by the initial conditions, and yet the information about the future evolution of the weather does not exist within these initial conditions. I see correspondences to Hinduism."

"I love how you enlighten me with your insights about Eastern mysticism."

"I see myself in you and you see yourself in me, and in so doing you see yourself as I see you reflected off my eyes. And if you go all the way down the serpent hole, as you say, then I shall likewise see the divine in you. In Hindu thought it's called Namaste."

"I'm awed by the insights in Hindu theology."

"Yes, it's the divine speaking," Carl said.

"It says in the bible that god created us in his image. That has been taken literally by the faithful, as if god has a body like us. But what if somehow the writers of Genesis were seeing something much deeper, even if they didn't realize it at a conscious level? Just like the writers of the Bhagavad Gita. What if that image they were talking about is a Fractal self-similarity within the fabric of Reality? What if the Big Bang itself is like a theorem generator, starting from nothingness and creating hierarchies of formal systems via the mechanism of Gödel Incompleteness?"

"Or like a generator of Pseudo Determinism within a Chaotic system. Same thing"

"Yes, exactly."

"So, would you say consciousness is Pseudo Deterministic because it's a consequence of the network of implicit feedback loops created by electro-chemical impulses traveling between neurons?"

"Exactly, that's explicate consciousness," I said, "it's not implicate consciousness. And just by looking at these neurons, it's impossible to predict anything about this emergent consciousness, or to even suspect it will even emerge. The neurons know each other, but they are oblivious to the world of the emergent consciousness that emanates from them."

"You can say each neuron sees itself reflected off the eyes of every other neuron, and what emerges from this network of feedback loops is an independent whole not known by its parts, but it knows them."

"Well said, but it's not just individual neurons seeing themselves in that way. It's also neurons that organize themselves into groups and those groups see themselves reflected off other groups of neurons, or off individual neurons. And-"

"Like the proliferating bushy tree of theorems in an axiomatic system."

"That's right," I said, "then groups of groups and so on and so forth until a level of complexity is reached where something amazing happens, the neurons organize into a network with unpredictable behavior and an autonomous entity emanates.

"Consciousness."

"Yes."

Carl slapped his forehead. "Oh, I get it. The neurons serve the role of axioms of a formal system. And the laws of chemistry and physics are the rules of inference."

I snapped my fingers. "By gosh, give this man the grand prize now." I laughed.

"You mentioned civilization is also like that."

"That'll actually drive a major theme in my novel. Its behavior is unpredictable in the Pseudo Deterministic way. There's no system of mathematical equations or computer programs where you plug in the individual behavior of all the people comprising civilization and the output is the long term behavior of civilization: when wars will start, the name of the president in the year 2100, and so on."

"I see. The pieces are falling in place in your grand synthesis. Principles that apply to Pseudo Determinism in Chaos Theory also apply to formal systems of theorems, and vice-versa."

"Actually, knowing about this equivalence helps us make progress in each of these two areas. If we know of some principle operating in the world of Chaos Theory then we know there must be a congruent principle at work in the world of Gödel Incompleteness, and vice-versa. That's a very powerful realization because whenever we discover two isomorphic systems then we can make discoveries about one by understanding the other. If we didn't know about the isomorphism then we wouldn't have that kind of leverage."

"I'm curious about that major theme in your novel you just mentioned."

"Well, there's a major tipping point coming soon in civilization. All Chaotic systems have these sudden behavior shifts called Chaotic Phase Transitions. That's another word for Pseudo Determinism. These shifts happen relatively abruptly. When they occur in civilization we call them paradigm shifts."

"Like the Renaissance in the 16th and 17th centuries?"

"Exactly."

"But that took over a century, really."

"That's quick in relation to the time span of human civilization. But I can give you another example that really shows an abrupt change. What would you have said, say in the year 1985, if I told you within about five or six years the Soviet Union would suddenly collapse."

Carl didn't answer.

Gödel And Chaos: The Tree Of Creation

"I bet you'd have told me I'm crazy."

"Yeah, probably. So that's an example of a Chaotic Phase Transition?"

"It is, because human civilization is a Chaotic system. And there's another Chaotic Phase Transition of civilization coming soon. It will be a paradigm shift of seismic proportions. The grand daddy of them all, even greater than the Renaissance. I call it the Third Age."

"How do you know this?"

"Because humanity is about to change its perspective on the meaning of god, and whenever there's a paradigm shift about divinity then there's also one about civilization. Since I was a child I felt I was a citizen of a different realm. I've come to realize recently the Third Age is this new realm. It's the messianic age the Hebrew prophets, and other cultures, spoke of so long ago. It will finally happen."

"Ha ha, that's brilliant. The messianic age defined as a Chaotic Phase Transition within the formal system of civilization."

"I call that formal system the Civilization of Man. Science converges with the divine."

"What fascinates me the most about the system of thought you're putting together is it sheds light on phenomena that seem, on the surface, to have nothing to do with each other. It's like a universal skeleton-key to open every door."

I took a sip of my cappuccino and looked around to determine if anyone was listening to our unconventional conversation. I feared I had raised my voice.

"Something seems odd to me," Carl said. "It's the idea behind proof in a formal system and its relationship to unprovable theorems. You made an analogy to a dominoes chain reaction, and you said true theorems are analogous to the dominoes that get knocked over along the paths of the chain reaction."

"Sure, and the notion of provability in this analogy means you can trace a path along the chain reaction and get to the target domino. The proof is in the path, in the doing. No other kind of proof exists."

"And you further said all true theorems are exactly determined by the axioms."

"Yes, a change in the axioms will change which theorems belong to the formal system. A change to the initial dominoes will ultimately determine which dominoes get knocked over. So what's your confusion?"

"Bear with me. So a true yet unprovable theorem in this analogy corresponds to a domino that gets knocked over because of the chain reaction that got started by the initial domino, or dominoes. But, and here's my confusion, no other domino actually reaches it and knocks it over. So why does it fall then?"

"Yeah I know. It sounds crazy, like spooky action at a distance. You can't get there from here type of thing."

"So how do you explain that?"

"Well, like I already said, the domino analogy is not perfect. In the dominoes formal system we don't have any self-referencing dominoes, so we can't end up with Pseudo Determinism or Gödel Incompleteness."

"Another question: what exactly is the significance of this unpredictable behavior? I sense it runs deep."

"It's huge because behavior that can't be predicted even in principle is a new entity. It's independent of the entity it emerges from. You've heard of the expression 'The whole is greater than its parts'?"

"I always wondered what that really means."

"It's everything we've just discussed. If you know the initial state of each neuron within the brain, you will still never be able to predict a consciousness will emerge from that. That information simply doesn't exist at the level of neurons. To use the language of Gödel Incompleteness, you'd say the formal system made up of the neurons is incomplete. It's incomplete because it can't prove a consciousness will emerge from it.

"In general," Carl said, "the incomplete part is those theorems which escape the system and become the axioms of a new formal system?"

I nodded. "That's the significance of Gödel Incompleteness. Without it nothing would be ejected out of the initial nothingness. Adam and Eve would still be in the garden. This ejection out of a formal system is the metaphorical meaning of Original Sin – the whole Adam and Eve story. "

"Wow, that's so deep. I have to wrap my head around that."

"So, to answer your earlier question about how a theorem can be Synthetic, it's these unprovable theorems that spring pseudo-deterministically out of the axioms that are the Synthetic theorems, because they are not tautological with respect to the axioms, they can't be proved."

"So without these Synthetic theorems Existence would be impossible. We would still be in the garden, as you say."

"Incredible, isn't it?" I said. "It's like an organic tree of semantic expression bursting from the Eternal garden of nothingness, and each branch on the tree is ejected from its parent branch. The gap between a system's provable theorems and the unprovable ones is what I often refer to poetically as the semantic spaces within the soul. It's the incompleteness of a formal system."

Carl slapped his forehead again."Oh my god. I see it now."

I flinched in surprise. This frenetic behavior was uncharacteristic of Carl. "For god's sake Carl. Be careful, will you? Before we leave this place you're going to give yourself multiple concussions."

"I have the answer you promised me earlier, remember? About every axiom being a theorem of a previous formal system, and I asked you why the two systems can't just be merged into one?"

"Ah yes, so you figured it out, eh? I'd love to hear your take on it."

"If the axioms of formal system B are the unprovable theorems of formal system A, that means the axioms of system B can't be reached from system A, so we get two independent formal systems that have to keep their own separate sets of axioms. The two systems can't be merged."

"You nailed it. The axioms and theorems of parent system A can't be used to prove the axioms and theorems of child system B, so therefore the two systems must maintain separate sets of axioms, even though the axioms of system B are consequences of system A. Amazing, isn't it? This process of formal systems generated from previous formal systems generates a fractal structure, a tree of formal systems emanating at the lowest level from absolute nothingness. That's how new worlds branch off from each other. Reality is this organic tree. It's the metaverse, it's the Tree of Knowledge of Good and Evil."

"I've heard the term multiverse."

"The metaverse is something much grander than the notion of multiverse that physicists have."

"Well, the multiverse is just speculation."

"The multiverse is imagined by physicists as a collection of different universes, but they're all still physical universes of space/time and matter/energy."

"But they can have different laws of physics."

"Yes, but it's still laws of physics. Meaning space and time, matter and energy. The metaverse is a much more expansive idea. In it a universe is just a formal system that emanates from a previous formal system via Gödel Incompleteness. It's not necessarily a universe of matter and energy. For example, civilization is one such formal system. The Stock Market is another."

"I'm curious, what would be the first level emanating from nothingness?"

"Yin and Yang, the level of polarities. No photons, no electrons, no gravity. Just pure, disembodied, abstract polarities."

"It's ironic," Carl said, "how it seems to us our universe of mass and energy and space and time is the only real thing, and everything else is just an abstraction that only exists in our mind."

"Yes, physicists are still stuck in that box. The irony is that the opposite is true. It's the physical universe which is in our mind, is our mind, in the implicate sense we talked about."

"So the EBSP only applies to the branch on the tree which is our physical universe?"

"Well, it's not that simple. The EBSP applies to each branch of the tree, but it's contained within that branch. It can't make a conclusion about other branches. It can't cross branches."

"But of all the different universes in the metaverse, why is there only one physical universe?"

"You mean our universe?" What does it mean to say a universe is physical? It's just perspective. From inside any universe it would seem to be the only physical universe. Physicality is the appearance that something has a real, objective existence. And by objective I mean something which appears to be external to the observer."

"So how come our universe seems like it's got this hard, objective existence, this concreteness to it, and yet all other formal systems seem like just immaterial abstractions?"

"Do you remember our earlier discussion where you commented on the self-evident truths of the axioms of Euclidean Geometry? What did I say?"

"Oh I see. You said it's because we are a part of the system. So that's why our universe seems to have this self-evident concreteness to it that the other branches don't. Our own universe seems to us more real, more independent of ourselves."

"I'm sure to the Global Weather System its Self seems like the only real thing. It will call itself the physical universe."

"Why? You think there are consciousnesses living inside the weather system?"

"As below so above," I said. "Every formal system having Gödel Incompleteness is a consciousness. That's what consciousness is: the formal systems that pinch off their parent formal system via Gödel Incompleteness. The Tree of Existence is a fractal collection of consciousnesses. It's a meta consciousness."

"So consciousness is not just what we sense in ourselves. It's a more general thing."

"Exactly, Descartes' philosophy was too provincial. It's not just that I think therefore I am. I think therefore the Tree of Existence IS. I am, in the lower case sense, therefore I AM in the upper case sense. The upper case is the implicate oneness. The lower case is the apparent separateness we perceive from what appears to us as the external universe."

"I think this delivers a death blow to solipsism."

"You're right. Knowing I exist necessarily implies the existence of the multiplicity of branches in the metaverse. So I am not the only existence in that sense. I am a part of a Fractal superstructure."

"Fascinating how everything in your thought-system fits like a jigsaw puzzle."

"I'm developing a framework of everything. What explains the weather system can explain the Stock Market, can explain the physical universe and any other formal system governed by Gödel Incompleteness."

"By the way," Carl said, "remember we discussed the question of why mathematics seems to explain the universe so well? Generations of intellectuals marveled at how something which is a product of our mind seems to fit the universe so well. But in light of the implicate nature of consciousness, you concluded it's not so surprising after all. The universe is consciousness at the implicate level."

"But in light of our current discussion," I said, "would mathematics still have this universal character?"

"Actually, no. It should only work so well for us within our branch on the tree. Only that branch is equivalent to our consciousness."

"Beautiful, well said. And in fact, that's why mathematics doesn't work so well for predicting the weather or the Stock Market. These are other branches on the Tree of Existence."

"What about Quantum Mechanics? How do you fit that into your framework of everything?"

"When a branch emanates from its parent branch there's a transitional point - the semantic space. Quantum Mechanics describes this transition between our universe of spacetime and its parent branch. But it's no different than the transition between any two parent-child branches. I predict the Schroedinger Wave Equation, which governs this transition to our physical universe in Quantum Mechanics, can be generalized to deal with the transition between any parent branch to child branch."

"Or you can say the Schroedinger Wave Equation can be explained in terms of the constructs within Gödel Incompleteness."

"Or Pseudo Determinism in Chaos Theory, take your pick," I said. "They're isomorphic. It will be a meta Schroedinger Wave Equation applicable to the metaverse. That's the beauty of finding isomorphic systems. You choose which one is easier to work with for the particular problem you're trying to solve and then apply the result to all the others."

"So about the Schroedinger Wave Equation, what in Chaos Theory is equivalent to it. What about Gödel Incompleteness?"

"Honestly, I don't know. That's the nitty-gritty. My ideas are more like what Copernicus achieved than what Newton did. Copernicus introduced the seed of the paradigm shift. He said everything revolves around the sun. Newton worked out the mathematical details."

"What you said earlier fascinates me. You really think there are conscious entities living inside the Global Weather System, or the Stock Market?"

"Yes, in the implicate/explicate sense. Any branch on the Tree of Existence, the Tree of Knowledge, appears to itself as a multiplicity of consciousnesses. So that's also true for the branch we inhabit that we call the Universe. It appears to us there are multiple consciousnesses, but there is just one and it is spacetime itself."

"Why spacetime?"

"Because that's the fabric out of which anything physical is weaved - I mean physical from our perspective."

"That actually makes sense. Anything we call physical possesses size and duration."

"Exactly, so when the EBSP shows us that the implicate consciousness is the physical universe itself, it's saying that the implicate consciousness IS spacetime. "

"And each branch has its version of spacetime?" Carl made the quote-on-quote sign when he said the word 'spacetime'.

"Yes, each branch has its fundamental fabric out of which it is weaved. This fabric is the implicate consciousness of that branch."

"But I still don't understand why I see you as a consciousness separate from me, what you call the explicate consciousnesses. Why does it appear that way?"

"That's another thing I don't know yet. There must be some mathematical construct within Gödel Incompleteness or Chaos Theory explaining that. I have a poetic way of describing it. I say we are the denizens of the dream of the big I AM, all uppercase."

"What's the lower case?"

"It's the apparent multiplicity of consciousnesses within the big I AM."

"So is the big I AM just one branch of the metaverse, or is it the whole damn tree?"

"You are a small I am. Each of us is a small I am. But at the implicate level of each branch there is just one big I AM. It's the fabric out of which each branch is weaved."

"So each branch is a big I AM?"

Gödel And Chaos: The Tree Of Creation

"Yes, the whole tree is the metaverse. That's what the Tree of Knowledge of Good and Evil is, it's the metaverse. It's a Fractal superstructure where each branch is a big I AM, the implicate consciousness of that branch."

"And this recursively drills down to the trunk of the tree."

"Yes."

"Which is the irreducible big I AM," Carl said, "the H from which emanates YHVH, the metaverse."

"Yes, YHVH is the metaverse - the whole tree."

"So what is the soul? Can you explain it within this framework?"

"Each big I AM is a soul."

"Hold on, what I think you're saying is each small I am doesn't have a distinct soul. Are you saying that you and I share the same soul?"

"Exactly, the soul is a big I AM. The soul is an implicate consciousness. Each branch of the metaverse is a soul."

"Beautiful, everything is falling into place in your system of thought."

"Are you comfortable now with my ideas about the equivalence of Pseudo Determinism and Gödel Incompleteness?"

"I think so."

"Before we continue there's just one caveat I'd like to add. Not all formal systems can produce incompleteness, just as not all systems can produce Pseudo Determinism. For example, Euclidean Geometry doesn't produce unprovable theorems. It doesn't have Incompleteness."

Carl reflected on that briefly. "Why? Can't you create these implicitly self-referencing theorems in geometry?"

"Yes you can but it isn't a sufficient condition. I won't go into the nitty-gritty technical details but suffice it to say the axioms and rules of inference of the system have to be expressive enough to create Gödel Incompleteness. This expressiveness is what allows these unprovable theorems to emanate because it's an expressiveness about the formal system talking about itself."

"Fair enough. I don't want to know the details now. But how can absolute nothingness be expressive enough about itself to create Incompleteness."

"That's another thing I can't explain yet. But let's get to the EBSP. Here's the resolution of the paradox. We've already discussed these ideas but I'll summarize and add more depth."

"I'm all ears."

"I just explained the mechanism that creates the Fractal metaverse. Each branch is a universe unto itself which creates other universes branching off.

Gödel And Chaos: The Tree Of Creation

Now, to put it in a nutshell, the EBSP principle doesn't go across branches, it's only valid within its own branch."

I waited for Carl's reaction.

"Keep going, I'm listening. You've already mentioned that, but I need more explanation."

"I'll tell you a quick story first."

Carl nodded his head and crinkled his forehead. "I suppose it will be an allegory. I know you too well." He smiled a wry smile, but it was meant in jest.

I shrugged my shoulders.

"Never mind. Go for it," Carl said while rolling his eyes.

"Imagine a house with many rooms. You live in one of those rooms and there is someone living in each of the other rooms. Each person knows every nook and cranny of their own room. They can find anything in their own room, even if blindfolded, but they aren't very familiar with the other rooms. Now, your car keys have been placed in one of the rooms, but you don't know which one. You then start looking for your keys. You enter your own room and look for them, but you can't find them. What does that imply?"

"That the keys aren't in your room."

"And what if I looked in someone else's room and couldn't find them?"

"Then it's inconclusive. It may or may not be in that room."

"So why is it conclusive for my own room?"

"Because you know every nook and cranny of your own room. If you can't find your keys in your room then for sure it's not there."

"Do you see I'm really talking about the EBSP?"

"Yes, it does sound like it. I remember our discussions about it. If you can't, in principle, detect something then it doesn't exist. That's because the observer is the observed."

"Good so far. Go on."

"I remember we talked about the Equivalence thought experiment in General Relativity. That you can't, even in principle, distinguish between inertial and gravitational mass, so according to the EBSP they are the same phenomenon. But this allegory you told me diverges from our earlier discussions."

"How's that?"

"It's about the other rooms. Obviously they represent the other universes, the other formal systems in the metaverse. The EBSP doesn't apply to them. Inertial and gravitational mass are the car keys in your own room."

Gödel And Chaos: The Tree Of Creation

"And that's the resolution of the EBSP paradox. It doesn't say the unknowable or undetectable can't exist in general. It says anything in your own branch that's unknowable to you can't exist."

"Meaning the physical universe of space and time?"

"Yes, so the EBSP is valid in this limited sense."

"That doesn't say much. You're basically saying the resolution of the EBSP paradox is that within each formal system only the provable truths can be proven. Well, no kidding."

"Exactly, when you express the EBSP in that way then it becomes one big fat tautology. It's like saying all bachelors are unmarried."

"Not so fast, I see a flaw in your argument. The Global Weather System is unpredictable in principle, which is like saying it's unknowable, so the EBSP would fail if you apply it?"

"Why?"

"Well, since the weather system exists within the physical universe, but can't be predicted within it, then it can't exist. But it clearly exists."

"No, you're missing the point."

"How? I think what I said covered all the bases."

"It didn't. The Global Weather System is a new formal system that branches off the physical universe and it's Pseudo Deterministic. It branches off the physical universe and becomes a new universe unto itself. The EBSP, when applied to our own branch, is only applicable to fundamental physical phenomenon that don't exhibit Pseudo Determinism."

I paused to allow Carl to reflect on what I had said.

"I'm not sure what you mean. Can you give me examples?"

"Sure, it's the fundamental aspects of the physical universe. Things like gravity, inertia, space and time, mass and energy and the laws of physics governing them. The EBSP, as used within the physical universe, only applies to them."

"Hmm...I'll have to wrap my head around that. The Global Weather System is a separate universe? How about if I start my own system that has Pseudo Determinism? Am I like a god that starts a new universe?"

"You mean like writing a computer program that has Pseudo Determinism?

"Yeah, that would be one good way."

"In a way you would be a god, but remember that at the implicate level physical reality is one consciousness. So the system you create is branching off that one consciousness. It's the big I AM, as I explained before. There isn't a you separate from the physical universe. So it's the implicate order, the I AM, which is the god creating that new universe."

Gödel And Chaos: The Tree Of Creation

"Yeah, I guess that flows from your basic system of thought."

"I admit these ideas can seem strange at first."

"It's not just that. Sometimes I lose track of the big picture."

"If I were to write these ideas then you'd be able to reread them and reorient yourself."

"Hurry up and write your novel."

"Patience, when the time is just right I'll start. I still have unanswered questions."

"Here's an interesting question: From which branch does our own universe branch off?"

"You're full of good questions. In the last few weeks I've been trying to tie-in the tree of the metaverse with the Sefirotic Tree in the Kabbalah. Are you familiar with it? If they are equivalent then our universe is three levels up from En Sof."

"I'm familiar with it. The ten Sefirot and En Sof at the root of the Sefirotic tree."

"Of course you are. You're an encyclopedia of mystical knowledge." I laughed.

"Hardly an encyclopedia, but I'm drawn to the mystical outlook in all religions. Are you making an analogy between En Sof and the nothingness you say is the root of Existence?"

"Not just an analogy. I'm contemplating whether the Kabbalistic tree is the metaverse." I accentuated the word 'is'. "But I'm having some misgivings about this idea."

"But if it's the metaverse then it should have many, many levels of branches, but the Kabbalistic tree only has four levels."

"Our perception of it might be limited. Maybe we're limiting it to stop at the level of our branch, but it's really got an infinity of branches beyond."

"You know, that actually makes sense."

"Notice how it's got ten sefirot or nodes. The first level of En Sof is one of them. The second has two nodes, then three, and then the last level has four. I can tie that in to the tree of the metaverse."

"I'm listening."

"The nothingness is the first level. It breaks into two parts and becomes the level of polarities, the Yin and Yang. I'm not sure how to visualize the next level but It would be the level where Quantum Mechanics operates before an observation is made to produce our physical universe. It would be characterized by, or weaved out of, three parameters. The fourth level would be defined by four parameters. These would be the three dimensions of space and one dimension of time."

"It fits, it just fits so beautifully," Carl said. "One plus two plus three plus four is ten, the number of Sefirot, or nodes, in the Kabbalistic tree. And the En Sof is indeed the level of the void, the nothingness. Also, the physical universe is four dimensional."

"So this would imply all of physical reality is fundamentally spacetime. Matter and energy would be somehow constructed out of spacetime, but spacetime itself could not be further reduced and still remain something physical."

"Spacetime could be described as four axioms at the root of physical Reality. But these four axioms would be unprovable theorems emanating out of the previous level."

"You've learned well grasshopper."

"I see a threefold equivalence. Wouldn't the Big Bang be equivalent to the metaverse or the Kabbalistic Tree?"

"Absolutely, the Big Bang is the metaverse."

"So the Big Bang is not just an explosion that creates spacetime and matter and energy."

"No, it's far deeper than that. The physical universe is just one branch on a tree that emanates from the Big Bang."

"Did time originate from the Big Bang or is the Big Bang embedded in time? I'd say that according to your ideas time comes out of the Big Bang."

"That goes without saying. Space and time is the physical universe. It's one of the branches of the metaverse."

"You know the question about what caused the Big Bang? Some people say god kicked it off."

"That's the traditional view of god. As some external entity that acts on things. That idea is diametrically opposed to everything I've said."

"So what caused the Big Bang?"

"God, what I call the H, is nothingness. The Big Bang emanates from nothingness. So god didn't cause the Big Bang. The Big Bang is god looping back on himself."

"And then he creates and creates," Carl said.

"Exactly. God has bootstrapped Existence. The Big Bang is YHVH - the metaverse. It boils down to the question of why nothingness references itself. When I answer that then we'll know why there's a Big Bang. We'll know why there's Existence."

"You said you had misgivings the Kabbalistic tree is the metaverse, why?"

"It just seems to me too coincidental that if the tree of the metaverse has many, many levels, perhaps an infinity, somehow our branch of the tree is in such a privileged position that it's only three levels up from the root level. Don't you think that's unlikely?"

"Yes, I suppose. I didn't think of that. So what are you going to do?"

"What do you mean? I don't have to do anything. The idea about the Kabbalistic tree is interesting and I'll leave it at that for now. I don't have all the answers."

"I see your point in thinking of these ideas as closer to Copernicus than Newton. You've presented a basic framework which is open to being refined and elaborated."

"Yeah, I hope physicists and mathematicians will take these ideas seriously and leverage them."

"They're very materialistic, aren't they? I mean the physicists."

"Yeah, they can't think outside the box, at least most of them. They've taken their understanding back to the billionth or trillionth of a second after the Big Bang started, or maybe even closer, and they're just stuck there. They're basically stuck at the point where the physical universe emanates from its parent system on the metaverse tree."

"So to dig deeper they have to stop looking for physical things."

"Exactly, they have to stop looking for the point of zero time and zero space because they'll never find it. They have to realize there's much more to the Big Bang than just the emergence of spacetime and particles. It's the origin of the entire metaverse tree. It's the origin of YHVH. Spacetime is just a minuscule part of that."

"The tip of the iceberg."

"Not even that. Our universe isn't the endpoint. Like I said, there are other formal systems branching off our universe."

"Oh yes, like the Stock Market and civilization."

"Like any formal system that has Incompleteness. I've made a case for why Gödel Incompleteness and Pseudo Determinism is the key to a theory of everything. It's now up to physicists and mathematicians to take that to the bank."

"But you've also made a strong statement on what god is."

"Yes, I have. In fact my framework is as much about god as about science."

"Actually, I think your framework doesn't make a distinction between these two areas."

"That's what I mean. They're equivalent. That's what the Third Age is about. The convergence of Science and Religion. That's the long anticipated Messianic Age. The age of Aquarius taking over from the Age of the Ram."

"When I hear of the Age of Aquarius I can't help but think of the Hippies of the 1960s and of free love and Woodstock."

"The Hippie movement of the 1960s was just a little tremor that heralds the coming of a cataclysmic earthquake at the bedrock of the Civilization of Man."

"This Third Age you talk about?"

"The covenant between Abraham and the I AM is a grand play on the stage of the Civilization of Man, and the curtains are soon to open on its final act - The Third Age."

I AM Ready

Wednesday, September 29th of 2004 was the first day of the Jewish holiday Sukkot, known as the Feast of Tabernacles. It commemorates the sheltering of the Hebrews in the wilderness of Sinai after they escaped Egypt like thieves in the night. It is one of the most joyful Jewish holidays. Sukkot is also a festival that celebrates the harvest.

It had been almost two months since I was let go from Chancellor Software. On August 8th, 2004 I came in to work at 10 AM and within minutes I received a call to come to the boardroom. I told Clayton about the call and he appeared despondent. As I made my way, I sensed I was a dead man walking. My dedication to the company, often months of seven-days-a-week work, or occasional all nighters, would now be rewarded with a swift kick out the door.

A few days before Sukkot Jenna told me of a social justice oriented Jewish congregation headed by a Rabbi Jacob Flesher. She heard of him from one of the members of St. James Church. His congregation collaborated with St. James and First United Methodist in organizing soup kitchens in the Downtown East Side.

"Would you like to go to his house this coming Wednesday? He's got something called a Sukkah in his backyard. You know what's that?"

I explained to Jenna the meaning of the Sukkot holiday.

The first day of Sukkot was dry and mild. It was late afternoon when we arrived at the Rabbi's house at the Mount Pleasant neighborhood that straddles the border between East Vancouver and the more affluent west part of Vancouver. But even in those days, as the Vancouver real estate boom was gaining steam, the average older house in East Vancouver was selling for well over half a million dollars. We were greeted by the Rabbi's wife, a pleasant faced, thin woman with long, wavy, brown hair. She appeared to be in her mid to late forties. I introduced myself and Jenna.

"Please come in. No need to take off your shoes. We're all in the backyard by the Sukkah."

We followed the Rabbi's wife through the modest yet cozy house and when we arrived at the backyard I saw the Sukkah on the other side of the well kept lawn. It was like a small tree-house but situated on the ground and with a roof made of an assortment of leafy branches, bamboo poles, large dark-green leaves and freshly mowed grass whose redolence I inhaled deeply. Around the top of the Sukkah's perimeter hung strings with various seasonal fruits tied at their ends. The waning early evening light penetrated the Sukkah's porous roof and I saw beams of light radiating into its murky

I AM Ready

innards. The apple trees in the yard rustled by the evening breeze. At one end of the backyard, near the entrance to the house, was a long table covered by a white tablecloth on which lay an assortment of salads, cheeses, nuts, fish, juices and wines.

"Hey hon, I'd like you to meet Theressa. She told me about this get-together. She knows Rabbi Flesher well."

I introduced myself. Theresa was a tall and handsome woman. She looked to be in her late fifties.

"Would you like to meet the rabbi?" Theressa said. "He's one of the most interesting and compassionate people I know."

Theressa pointed towards Rabbi Flesher.

"He's the elegant looking, gray-haired, bearded gentleman over there, sitting cross-legged by the Sukkah."

I looked where she was pointing and I saw a trim, middle-aged man sitting in front of the Sukkah and facing my direction. He had a short, gray beard and short, straight, almost white hair. He was light-skinned and had soft European features, of German origin almost certainly I thought. He was at the center of a small group. They were sitting in a lotus position with eyes closed and appeared to be in deep meditation.

"Would you like me to introduce you?" Theressa said.

"I don't want to interfere, look." I jutted my chin towards the rabbi.

"Oh I see. Well, let's wait a little while then. The night is young." Theressa laughed.

"Hon, let's get a bite to eat first, I'm starvers."

A few minutes later I was eating from a white paper plate and I saw a small girl of around four run up to the Rabbi, who was still sitting in a lotus position. She was shouting: "Abba, abba." Abba is Hebrew for father. He opened his eyes and she jumped on him and embraced him.

"Here's your chance to introduce yourself," Jenna said.

We approached the rabbi and Jenna introduced herself as a member of St. James Church. I immediately noticed the rabbi's sparkling light-blue eyes.

"Theressa has told me a lot about the good work you do at the Downtown East Side, as well as your proposed inter-spiritual center," Jenna said.

"Ah yes, I know Theressa at St. James very well. And Ashem willing, the inter-spiritual center is my greatest ambition. It's to be a center where all faiths can congregate together in harmony for Kol-Adama, the voice of the ground of being."

I detected a subtle American accent I could not localize. I discovered later it was a philly accent. The rabbi eyed me while expecting an introduction that had not come yet.

Jenna noticed his curiosity. "This is my husband. He's an Israeli."

I reached out my hand. "It's a pleasure to meet you rabbi."

He shook my hand while adjusting his large kippah - the round head covering worn by religious Jews. "And your name?"

"So sorry rabbi, I forgot to mention. My name is Nissim."

"That's a very Jewish name, it means miracles. And your last name?"

"Levy."

"Well then, you can't get a more Jewish name than that. What city are you from?"

"Yaffo."

"Beautiful city. I much prefer it to the hustle and bustle of Tel-Aviv," the Rabbi said. "Have you lived in Israel most of your life? By your lack of an Israeli accent I assume you haven't."

"I left Israel when I was nine. I lived in Montreal until the age of fourteen and I've been in Vancouver ever since."

"Nissim has been on a spiritual journey," Jenna said, and then she looked at me. "This congregation might be just what you've been looking for."

"Yes, recently I've been yearning to get more in touch with my Jewish heritage."

"You're certainly welcome to join our little group. We have weekly Shabbos services right here in my modest little house."

"That sounds good," I said, while noticing his Ashkenazic dialect when saying the word Shabbat - meaning Saturday in Hebrew.

"After each Shabbos service we have a potluck lunch, so bring something Kasher. We usually avoid red meat. Fish is fine."

"I don't eat mammals anyway, so that resonates with me."

"Very interesting, what's your motivation?"

"It's on ethical grounds. I don't eat animals I perceive to have higher cognitive and emotional capacity."

The rabbi nodded with approval. "That's a great mitzvah. We should all do that. Do you observe Kashrut as well?"

"That's my Kashrut, Rabbi. It's time to put aside all affectations of tradition. Judaism should now teach dietary laws only based on morality and compassion."

"Ah yes, perhaps one day we will all be there, but when?"

"Soon Rabbi, the world is changing quicker then we think in the age of the Internet."

"How's your Hebrew?"

"I understand everything and can speak it fairly well."

"We need Hebrew readers during the Torah reading."

"My reading is certainly the weakest aspect of my Hebrew, but I'm sure I can be of service with that."

"That's great then. I'm looking forward to seeing you this coming Shabbos, if you can make it. But you'll have to excuse me now. I'm due to give a reading by the Sukkah."

***

I climbed the one flight of stairs up to Original Joe's. It is a restaurant and pub at the southwest corner of Cambie and Broadway in Vancouver. It is just a hop, skip and jump from the Cambie bridge leading to downtown. I was meeting Addison and Rolph, my former manager at Silconefire. I affectionately call Rolph 'the big German'.

When I started working for Chancellor in 2000 I was not an employee. I was a consultant working on contract. Chancellor stationed me at a software development company called Silconefire that it had hired to complete one of its highest profile projects, the K12World home to school web portal. It was a website designed to allow parents to keep track of their children's school progress and activities. Those were the good-old days of the dot-com boom, shortly before the big bust. Chancellor threw money at the K12World project like a tidal wave washing upon a sandy shore.

I entered Original Joe's and looked for Addison. He had not arrived yet. I am very punctual, almost compulsively. Addison is forever compulsively late. We had arranged to meet at seven and I was five minutes early. Addison casually strolled in at a quarter past eight, accompanied by the big German. I had already guzzled two pints of beer while waiting for him and phoned him twice, hoping to light a fire under his tardy ass, yet he seemed oblivious to his lateness.

"Hey Rolph, long time no see. How have you been?"

Rolph is a perpetually jovial sort with an endless appetite for all sausages and sweets. I expect that from a dyed-in-the-wool German, but his appetite for beer fails expectations. He is certainly no teetotaler, but pales in comparison to Addison's bottomless capacity for beer.

"Things are as good as can be hoped, and then I'll die." Rolph pantomimed a noose tightening around his neck and then he burst in laughter. His strong accent was oddly soothing, not at all harsh like the stereotypical German accent. Perhaps it is an illusion due to his jovial personality.

"Addison tells me you're no longer at Siliconefire?"

"Oh no, that gig is down the proverbial toilet. And good riddance. I was starting to feel like an under-appreciated pencil pusher."

"Rolph is working on his own venture now."

"Oh yeah? What is it?"

"I'll tell you but then I'll have to kill you in the most heinous fashion. All I'll say is it feels refreshing to once again be balls deep into bloody code."

Rolph's signature goofy smile rippled across his fleshy face. "I was also getting tired of the big ball of mud my coders were serving me."

"So now you're creating your own ball of mud?" I said with a wink.

"Coding is a young man's game, but old dogs like us...we can always hang on for dear life."

"Speak for yourselves. You guys have ten years on me," Addison said as he flagged down a waitress and ordered a pitcher of 1516 beer. Rolph ordered a large nacho platter with extra cheese. The pitcher was to be shared. I hoped Rolph had the same idea about the nacho platter. A few minutes later we were inhaling beer and devouring fistfuls of cheesy nachos.

"I've filled Rolph in on our discussions of the past few years," Addison said.

"Addison was telling me about your venture into the murky world of Chaos and the book you plan to write. That sounds really crazy but in a good way."

"And Kurt Gödel also, did he mention that?"

"It's pronounced Gurdol. It's a solid name from good Teutonic stock."

"You know, I never knew that. Funny isn't it how I've been reading so much about him and his ideas but I never even suspected I was pronouncing his name totally wrong. But it's been a while since I've discussed any of this with Addison. I've come a long way since then."

"Oh? It's been a couple of years. What have you come up with since?" Addison said.

I explained how I came to question the EBSP in light of what Gödel Incompleteness was teaching me. I told the story of how I endured an existential whiplash, and just as my world view was crumbling on top of me I saw the resolution.

"It was like rising above a giant jigsaw puzzle. As I rose higher the big picture slowly formed below me, and I knew what I saw previously was just a component of a much larger vista."

I told tales of poles at the end of footprints in the snow and of falling dominoes. I painted pictures in the mind's eye of angels, some wrestling and others dancing on the branches of two grand tree bursting out of a white-eyed womb, the garden of Creation. It was a magical night around that table as we drank copious quantities of good beer, ate heaping plates of appetizers and celebrated our joyful discussion until the early morning hours. As the levels of beer in our pitchers diminished our collective level of merriment and spiritual euphoria heightened, and we philosophized and spiritualized and clinked our beer mugs with abandon around the table that vibrated with the energy of food and drink that was really a proxy for each soul's yearning for communion with each other. Our joyful laughter boomed loudly as thunder from the heavens. Our voices boomed ecstatically, rhythmically, and we wailed soulful lamentations to oneness, love, peace. For a frozen moment in a timeless, featureless Eternity we became A collective-soul. We became intoxicated by a transcendence that knows not time nor space but only the white-eyed womb of Creation.

And shortly before the night came to an end I said: "And this is where I am right now in my journey. I need just to know why the nothingness references itself and then I will unlock the secret of the serpent hole."

"Yes, why would nothingness reference itself? That is the maddening question," Rolph said.

And then I saw a look come across Addison's face, like the look of a child who answers a knotty question that has mystified grown men and women. But the child answers the question in the only way a child can, with a Zen-like simplicity, with the layers of confusion peeled away to reveal the answer that had been hiding in plain sight - not an answer to the question, but the question revealed as the answer to itself.

"What does nothing reference?" Addison asked and then he immediately answered:"It references nothing. But it is nothing, so it references itself. It's simple as that"

I was stunned. Tautology's white-eyed face once again peeked at me from under the veil of existential mystery. That magical night, the primordial feedback loop was revealed to not require a reason nor a cause. It does not require an external agent for there is none in the white-eyed womb of Creation, and there need not be. In the beginning was the Word and it shattered into Shards of Divinities, not by fire nor by force but by the ineffable nothingness curving back upon itself and then it creates and creates, forevermore. The Word, the Logos, is this primordial, tautological feedback loop.

I was speechless. I wondered why I had not seen that answer before. I had been rhapsodizing about tautology at the root of it all, but could not make the ultimate leap and be true to this conviction above all. This is the ultimate tautology, the source of Existence. Nothingness self-references because it is in the definition of Nothingness to self-reference. It is not by design, it is by tautology. There need not be a first cause to Creation after all.

In the following days I became convinced I had all the answers required for me to begin writing my novel. But little did I suspect there was one more pregnant question waiting to be answered. It was now October of 2005 and what I next learned strengthened my conviction the Hebrew scriptures contain great metaphorical truths, and the covenant between Abraham and god would soon be completed. The medium through which history arcs would soon be revealed.

***

It was a warm and sunny early Spring morning. I was on the Broadway bus making my way west to the Shabbat service. In my duffel bag was my Talit, a white and blue prayer shawl that, two days before the towers fell, my uncle Sammi gave me as a wedding gift. I also had a bag of assorted nuts. That was my after-service meal contribution. I had become a regular at the Shabbat services, rarely missing a week. I also made a generous monthly financial contribution because I believed then in the message of the congregation. It had been a message of social justice and tolerance. But as I became wiser to the ways of the ideological Left, I had began noticing a few incongruities in that message of tolerance. I looked the other way at first, thinking I was misinterpreting the signs.

The service was well attended that day. Philip was there with his young daughter. We spoke about his favorite topic - Peak Oil. He is a crusader for resources conservation and the imminent dangers of Climate Change. I was not driving my V8 Mustang Cobra in those days, but previously I had always parked it several blocks away from Rabbi Flesher's house, in fear and shame of being identified as an anti-environment ne'er-do-well.

David, the burly and bearded gay man on the Canadian TV show Kink, was also attending. We discussed the nature of god and I revealed my view of divinity as Creation's seed rather than an external providence. I revealed the nothingness from which Creation resurrects in cycles eternal, as does the desert's heat of day forever resonating with its chill of night, sometimes as the harmony of a cheek-to-cheek dance and other times of a wrestling match. David clung to a Second Age view of god, as a watchmaker building a watch. It was a view that in my future novel I would prosecute at trial. It seems odd for a member of a progressive congregation to display an atavistic view of divinity. Perhaps he was a conservative gay man caught between a perpetual tug-of-war; each side fiercely pulling on the Other and then realizing it is pulling on none other than its Self. This is not a dance nor a wrestling match. It is quite the contrary. It is a lack of resonance with the Self.

The congregation initially attracted me, in part, for its acceptance of the Other. Ever since I was a child I always felt like a citizen of a different realm. I craved to see the world through the eyes of the Other. The previous year I assumed the identity of the Other when I marched in Vancouver's annual Pride parade as a representative of the congregation. First the Self becomes the Other but then the Other must, in turn, become that which is the Other from its perspective - the original Self. It is a perpetual toggle like a sentence denying its own truth. Much to my chagrin I learned gradually that the ideological Left has perfected the art of becoming the Other but it is not able to complete the primordial circuit by becoming again the Self, seen through the eyes of the Other.

"Nissim, would you like to be a Torah reader today?" Rabbi Flesher said.

"I'd be honored."

On the first Shabbat of each Jewish new year the congregation would read a few pages at the beginning of Bereshit (Genesis). Each successive Shabbat it would read from the next few pages until completion of the five books of the Torah, known as the Pentateuch, by Jewish year's end. We began the service by chanting the Sh'ma Israel:

Sh'ma Yisrael Adonai Elohenu, Adonai echad

Hear Israel the Lord is our God, the Lord is one

The Sh'ma Israel is from Deuteronomy 6:4 and is the centerpiece of the Shabbat service. It is considered by observant Jews to be the holiest thought that can be contemplated. I also consider it as such. It is a meditative chant. Four thousand years ago a Habiru living in the city of Ur, under the weight of the mighty Sumerian empire, saw a new revelation of divinity. He suffered for this revelation and was forced to cross over into the world beyond the comforts of the city walls. In the desert he met his god and the covenant was sealed. But for that his seed has paid a heavy price. It is to mirror the banishment from the white-eyed garden into a realm beyond. It is to be persecuted and powerless, but yielding great influence, pulling the world towards the revelation like strange attractors, hated yet irresistible. It is written in the great parchment of universal law that the weakest force shall yield the greatest influence and inherit the world beyond. Moses was a stutterer yet he became the greatest communicator of them all.

That Shabbat I read from the Torah scroll and I felt humbled but energized. It was wrapped in white linen cloth and stored in a tall cedar wood cabinet symbolizing the ark of the covenant, where the Hebrews in the Sinai desert placed the tablets of monotheistic law. Philip and I eased the scroll from its home, unwrapped it and then kissed it. We then placed it on a podium and Rabbi Flesher rolled it open and located the passage to be read. I wrapped myself in my Talit and then I read from the passage as Stewart, a local actor and vociferous and uncompromising hater of Zionism, kept my place in the text with an ornamental silver pointer. I had a sense of impending revelation that day and I sensed it would be forever carved into my spirit.

Rabbi Flesher finished each Shabbat service with commentary about that week's passage. That day the topic was the spiritual meaning of the Hebrew letters. He focused on the meanings of the letters in the Tetragrammaton: YHVH.

Every letter in the Hebrew alphabet has a meaning associated to it, a kind of spiritual or religious meaning. At the dawn of the art of writing the letters of the alphabet were just pictures that represented actual objects in nature. So, for example, the letter representing the sound D actually looked like a doorway and the letter for the sound A represented an ox head. As humanity matured it secured dependable food sources through agriculture and the domestication of animals and also was freed from constant fear of predators. This afforded the luxury of time spent in spiritual contemplation. The letters were then also assigned meanings that were abstractions of their simple meanings. For example, the letter D, which originally only represented a door, now also represented the more abstract meaning of a doorway into a spiritual realm. The letter A which originally only represented an ox head now also had the abstract meaning of power or strong leadership. Now days, very few are aware of these intricacies of the origin of written language. They just think of the letters as imparting a particular sound to speech. In today's passage we came across the holiest name of god in the scriptures. It is the Tetragrammaton. I would like to finish today's service by explaining the spiritual meaning of the three distinct letters appearing in it - the Yud, the Vav and the Hey. The Yud represents the initial point of creation. It represents the primordial emergent. The Hey represents the most fundamental and ineffable nature of the divine. In the Kabbalah the idea of the En Sof is equivalent to the Hey. The letter Vav has no meaning of its own, it just serves as a hook or a nail that joins the meaning of two letters - one to its left and the other to its right.

    As Rabbi Flesher spoke I gazed out the window. Every Shabbat service I gazed out that window upon the oak tree by the side of the house. It always mesmerized me from this perspective. But I never fully unraveled its mystery. In the early spring its leaves blossom and it vibrates with the energy of resurrection. The sunlight shimmered off its blossoming leaves like a myriad wrestling angels. During the fall it is the dancing angels that appear on its white-eyed shedding branches. It was YHVH whispering to me that day. It became the Tree of Existence. It became the Tree of Knowledge of Good and Evil.

    When I later arrived home I was fiddling with the keys in my pocket as I took the elevator to my fourth floor apartment. Jenna would not be home. Our marriage was crumbling due to my flaws as much as hers. She had been staying with her friend Penny for the previous few weeks and I had no contact with her. We were scheduled to vacation in Israel in early May and I had come to fear we would not iron out our differences by then. But now my thoughts were elsewhere. I was preoccupied with the Tetragrammaton. Since Rabbi Flesher's lesson about the meaning of its letters I had been unable to focus on anything else. I sensed the meaning of its letters encoded a deep truth, like a forgotten word resting on the tip of the tongue, so close yet beyond reach. But this word was not resting on my tongue, it was resting within the semantic spaces of the soul, and I was craving to hear its whispers.

    I thrust my key into the keyhole and turned it - click. At that pregnant moment the floodgates of the soul were unlocked and I became awash with the mystery of YHVH. I came to know its meaning. It was a secret hidden in the shadow of plain sight. Carl's quotation from the Bhagavad Gita impaled my mind:

Curving back within myself I create again and again.

I replayed Rabbi Flesher's words echoing in my mind's ear:

The Yud is the initial point of Creation. The Hey is the ineffable core of god, the Vav connects the meaning of two letters. The Vav connects the meaning of two letters. The Vav connects the meaning of two letters...

I could not stop echoing this thought: The Vav connects the meaning of two letters. And what if it connects the letter to its own self?
YHVH.
Curving back on itself the H creates again and again.
And then I knew YHVH is the ultimate tautology, the primordial feedback loop. The nothingness that feeds back on itself without needing a first cause, and then it creates and creates, like a mirror within a mirror within another. The jigsaw puzzle was complete. Shivers shot through my body, soul and mind. It was there all along, hidden in plain sight for all to see forevermore.

This epiphany was an unexpected visitor and when it came knocking on my door I greeted it as a lover I had only ever known in the recesses of the soul and who now appeared before my very eyes as flesh and blood. This epiphany was a rose bush whose seed I planted long ago and which now burst the earth after a long and arduous winter in the unknowing, white-eyed womb of Creation. And when I reached for its tempting yet thorny flower I felt a piercing pain shooting through my spirit and I came face to face with the awe-full one, the great El-Shaddai, the principle of creation, the great veiled One, the Truth overflowing my cup. Deep in the soul an unspeaking voice woke from an eternal slumber and I at once came to know that land to which I had always felt a kinship, that realm of which I am a citizen, always will be and always have been.

For thousands of years the greatest riddle of Existence was encoded by the Hebrews as the holiest name of god. But did they realize the innermost meaning of that name? They did not. It percolated from the semantic spaces within their depths, waiting to have its full meaning decoded at a future time for all, when the curtains close on the second act of the Civilization of Man. I could no longer deny the truth of the covenant between YHVH and Abraham. It was time to start composing my novel, my innermost passion, the convergence of my spirit. It was time to open the curtains on the third act of the Civilization of Man once and forevermore.

My Manifesto

Sunday, August 6th of 2006 was the day of Vancouver's Pride Parade. It was a sweltering and clear day as all Pride Parade days have been in Vancouver since I can remember. The parade was scheduled for noon but I arrived at around 10 AM because I was in charge of coordinating the Kol-Adama congregation's parade contingent. This was the second year I marched in the parade instead of being a spectator, and if the spectators assumed I am gay then I felt no shame in that. I had been attending the Pride Parade as a spectator or participant since 2003. I was initially attracted to Kol-Adama, in part, due to its strong support for gay rights and its progressive world view. I was proud to be counted as a member of a synagogue welcoming gay members with love and pride. I was proud to be marching in the Pride Parade and I considered my pride in welcoming the Other to be on equal footing with the pride of the Other.

Jenna had left our marriage two weeks before and I was exiled to my mother's couch. But the previous day she relented. She had agreed to meet me after the parade at her friend's downtown apartment and to hand me the keys to our apartment. She informed me she had vacated most of her belongings and would lodge with her friend Penny until she found other accommodations.

By quarter to noon only three congregants had arrived. I expected more from a congregation priding itself on its passion for gay rights. For me that was yet another chink in the armor of Kol-Adama. My disillusionment with the congregation had piled high and the roof was soon to collapse. While waiting on the congregation's apathy for the Pride Parade, I reflected on a time in 2005 I had lunch with Rabbi Flesher at a Japanese restaurant in downtown Vancouver. Two weeks before that lunch meeting I participated in a heated and angry email exchange with several Kol-Adama members. That was not the first vitriolic exchange, but it was the fiercest and most devoid of decorum. The subject was, as usual, the legitimacy of Israel. I was pitted against those who denied Israel's right to sovereignty and yet they defended the rights of Arab sovereignty.

"Nissim, Israel is a made-up country created by artificial decree."
"So is Jordan. So is Syria," I replied to the email.
"Nissim, I will live to see the day that the indigenous Palestinians will revive their nationhood."
"There never was a Palestinian nation, and most so-called Palestinians are not indigenous to the land of Israel," I replied.

Stewart, a local actor, a denier of Israel's right to exist and a member of the anti-Zionist organization Jews For A Just Peace, replied: *"Nissim, the Palestinians are the indigenous people of the area unjustly occupied by Israel."*

He was referring to all of Israel, not just the territories captured by Israel during the Six Day War.

"Stewart, most so called Palestinians are not indigenous to the land of Israel. They are Arabs from adjoining areas that migrated to the area of current Israel during the late nineteenth century and up to 1948, during the same time that Jews began streaming into the area. And they migrated to the area because Jews developed it and provided better economic opportunities."

"Nissim, so you deny Palestinians the right to their own country? You would only allow Israel that right? Israel occupied Jerusalem, a city holy to three faiths, by force during the 1967 war that Israel started."

"Stewart, stop putting words in my mouth. I resent your accusation that I deny the Palestinians the right to self-determination. But you deny that Jews are entitled to that. The UN partition plan of 1947 defined two adjoining states: one Jewish and one Arab. The Jews accepted the plan. The Arabs did not. It was their choice and they have fallen on their own sword then and many times since. Regarding Jerusalem, the partition plan stipulated that Jerusalem be an international city not controlled by any nation. The Jews agreed to that, the Arabs did not. Also, regarding who started the 67 war, you know very well Egypt was amassing its armies and ready to attack Israel momentarily. Israel launched a preemptive strike but the Arabs are the ones who initiated the war. You know that and I think you are being disingenuous in not mentioning that."

"Nissim, Israel expelled Palestinians with vile brutality during the war of 1948."

"Stewart, the war of 1948 was started by the Arabs. There are one and a half million Arabs living in Israel today. If Jews wanted to expel Arabs there would have been almost none left now."

"Nissim, they couldn't expel them all, that's why."

"Stewart, Israel could have expelled them all if it had the desire. Look at the Arab countries. During the early twentieth century millions of Jews lived there. There are now almost none left."

"The Jews left the Arab counties voluntarily."

"No Stewart, some Jews left voluntarily but most were expelled and their properties seized, and that's a fact. The world never speaks about that. But most Arabs, not all but most, were not expelled. They are the ones

My Manifesto

who left voluntarily during the war of Independence at the behest of the Arab nations that advised them to leave and then come back after they destroy Israel. So they left but Israel won the war and didn't let them come back. But the ones who stayed are still there and are full citizens of Israel, with all the rights of Israeli citizenship."

Israel was declared on May 14, 1948. That is celebrated in Israel as the Day of Independence. The Arabs call it the Day of Nakba, which in Arabic means the day of the catastrophe. Many members of Kol-Adama, including Stewart, adopt the Muslim view of Israel's founding. They refuse to call it a day of independence. They too call it Nakba Day. Stewart refuses to celebrate Israel's day of independence and instead rues that day as a great calamity.

A new Kol-Adama member chimed in: *"I am a proud Socialist and Communist. I came recently from Venezuela and I stand with my Muslim brothers and sisters in Iran, in Syria, in Palestine. The idea a nation shall be identified by a religion in the way Israel calls itself a Jewish state is disgusting and has no place in the 21st century. I hate the Zionist Nazis. You should be ashamed of your hatred towards the Palestinians being slaughtered by those Zionist pigs."*

His hypocrisy drove me almost to tears. *"This is the problem with you hypocritical haters of Israel. You decry with righteous indignation that Israel identifies itself as a Jewish nation but you have no problem with Iran, with Saudi Arabia, with every Muslim country being a Muslim theocracy. Have you no shame for your hypocrisy? The extreme theocracies in Iran, in Saudi Arabia, in other Muslim states, are beheading people they consider infidels. They are suppressing free speech, they ram Sharia law down people's throats. They subjugate women in the name of Allah and yet you criticize Israel that practices the progressive principles that you supposedly should fight for? I'm getting so fed-up with this disgusting hate-fest towards Israel. You are all self-hating Jews and you support violence against Israelis. I won't give names but I've personally heard members of this congregation justify suicide attacks against Israelis."*

"Nissim, " Stewart replied, *"I think you should weigh your words very carefully when you accuse anyone in Kol-Adama of being a self-hating Jew, and especially of justifying suicide attacks against Jews that live in Palestine."*

"Really Stewart? You are going to criticize me for calling a member of this congregation a self-hating Jew who equated Zionism with Nazis? Why don't you speak out against such hatred instead of focusing your self-

My Manifesto

righteous indignation only on me? Where's your moral compass? And I've personally stood next to a member of this congregation as he condoned suicide attacks against Israelis. But I will not say who."

The moderator stopped the email exchange. It was getting out of hand.

From that day until my lunch meeting with Rabbi Flesher, two weeks later, I had not attended a Kol-Adama Shabbat service. I am a firm supporter of the two-state solution, a Palestine existing in peace side-by-side with Israel, and the irony did not escape me that the so-called Jewish progressives, who do not support the right of Israel to exist, were the ones accusing me of not supporting a Palestinian state. It is at once ironic and tragic that enmity towards Israel is endemic in the so-called progressive Jewish community. A community prizing gay rights, women's rights, free speech and respect for secularism should praise Israel for upholding such progressive principles, but instead it delights in demeaning Israel and it coddles the heinous religious fundamentalism of Muslim nations in the Middle East.

I arrived five minutes early and sat by the window of the Japanese restaurant and waited for Rabbi Flesher. I shortly saw him arrive by bicycle. I remembered our conversation a few months earlier about his desire to reduce his carbon footprint. He chained his bicycle and entered the restaurant. Rabbi Flesher had lived in Japan for a few years and he discussed with the restaurant's owner the intricacies of the Japanese decor. We exchanged small-talk and then he got to the point of our lunch meeting. "Let's discuss what happened, shall we?"

"Rabbi, I feel heart-broken about that exchange, but also furious." The rabbi was silent. "I will not remain silent when I'm unjustly accused of hatred towards Palestinians."

"I don't think anyone accused you of that."

"I was accused of denying Palestinians the right to their own state. But rabbi, it is those who accuse me who deny Jews the right to their own state. They are transferring their moral failings unto me."

"You accused the congregation of supporting suicide bombings. I did not participate in the discussion but I read every email."

"And I stand by what I said."

"That's a grievous accusation. Care to elaborate?"

"I will if I have your word this will remain private between us."

"I will certainly respect that."

I hesitated for a few seconds. "It was a few summers ago. I was walking along Commercial Drive with Jenna and as we passed by the park, across

My Manifesto

from Havana restaurant, we saw a group of men handing out pamphlets. It was Jews For A Just Peace. And do you know who was in that group? Stewart."

"Yes, he's an active member. That's not news or shocking to me."

"Wait, there's more. We started discussing the strife between Palestinians and Israelis and the discussion touched on the suicide bombings."

"Wait...you were discussing this with Stewart?"

"We were talking to Stewart and another member of Just Peace. I didn't recognize him. I don't think he's a member of Kol-Adama."

"Ah, I see. Please continue."

"It was Jenna who pointed out the Palestinians are resorting to terrorism against Israelis. You know, suicide bombings and the like. And do you know what his response was?"

"Stewart's response?"

"No, the other man. He said suicide bombings against Israelis is justified."

The Rabbi crinkled his forehead. "Hmm...so it wasn't Stewart who said that."

"No, but Stewart stood idly by and gave his acquiescence through his silence and through his unmistakable facial expressions."

"Look Nissim, I won't comment on Stewart's ideology. That's not for me. But I will say Stewart is much more reactionary against Israel than I am."

"And I thank you Rabbi for taking a more balanced approach to the conflict. But I don't know if I'm a good fit in a congregation that, in my opinion, is overrun by Israel haters, by apologists for Islamic terror, by people who spread historical lies about Israel. I don't think I can remain a member of Kol-Adama and remain true to my conscience."

Rabbi Flesher ran his right hand across his close-cropped, white beard. "You do what you must, Nissim. But the congregation needs your voice in defense of Israel. You provide a balance."

"But I feel I'm a lone voice in the wilderness. I know there are members sympathetic to Israel, but they are silent. They don't have my back."

"Nissim, god promised Abraham he would spare Sodom and Gomorrah if only ten righteous people were found."

I understood his analogy. "Are you one of the righteous, rabbi?"

"If you're asking me if I support the right of Israel to exist, then yes. I am one of the righteous and there are other members like me. But certainly you must agree Israel is not beyond reproach in these hostilities, no? Israel has much to atone for."

"I agree rabbi. I have been known to criticize various actions of Israeli governments." I shrugged my shoulders. "But I can't do that at Kol-Adama because the anti-Israel vitriol is so intense, so outrageous and biased, that I'm compelled to only defend Israel. When the stew is too bitter I must add a pinch of sugar."

"Yes, I can see your point."

"But Rabbi, I will say this, the fault is far more on the Arab side than on the Israeli side. How can you make peace with someone who doesn't accept your right to exist?"

The Rabbi did not address my question.

"Are you a Zionist, rabbi?"

"I am proud to call myself a Zionist. I support Israel and I support a state for the Palestinians side-by-side. That's true Zionism."

"Me too, Rabbi. I can't wait for the day a Palestinian state shares an open border with Israel, but often I feel I'm in no-man's land."

"What do you mean?"

"When I talk to the Left it accuses me of being a member of the extreme Right, and when I talk to the Right it accuses me of speaking for the extreme Left. I can't win."

"Nissim, that's why we need your voice at Kol-Adama. In Buddhism there's the wisdom of the Middle Way. The truth is often there. You are a voice for the Middle Way at Kol-Adama. Please stay."

"Hi Nissim. Are we ready for the parade?"

I snapped out of my reverie when the fourth member of Kol-Adama arrived and greeted me. She was a woman I did not recognize because I had never seen her attend a Shabbat service. But somehow she recognized me. It was almost noon and evident the Kol-Adama representation in Vancouver's 29th Pride Parade would be restricted to the four of us. I thought: "Well, at least 25% of Kol-Adama would be Zionist in this parade." I chuckled but I tasted a bitterness.

I love the pomp and pageantry of the Pride Parades as they snake their way through downtown Vancouver to the cheers of the young and the old, the wild and the tame, the introvert and the extrovert, the straight and the gay. I held the Kol-Adama banner with pride as it proclaimed Jewish support for gay people, for the trans-gendered, for the square pegs who do not fit the round hole, for the disenfranchised and forgotten, for the Other.

The parade's endpoint was under the Burrard Street bridge, across the water from the trendy neighborhood of Kitsilano. The sun's strong light

My Manifesto

sparkled off the Pacific blue waters and its heat penetrated my flesh and uplifted my longing for the transcendent. The pungent ocean aroma transported me to my early childhood in the city of Bat Yam in Israel, when my grandfather Yitzhak Alcabes would take me to the beach and I would wile away my days swimming and snorkeling in the transparent Mediterranean waters, warm and cozy like mother's womb, atavistic like the womb of Creation.

I unfurled the banner and congratulated the other Kol-Adama members who had marched with me. After they departed I saw Rabbi Flesher approach me in the distance, struggling to make his way through the vibrating, viscous-as-honey crowd.

"I'm sorry I didn't manage to march with you. Something come up at the last minute. How'd it go?"

"I absolutely loved it."

We walked down the grassy hill snaking its way along the sea-shore. At the foot of the hill is a large, open grassy area and that day I saw many exhibition tents and food stalls with long lines of hungry people. An eclectic mass of humanity milled about. I saw a small group of young, nubile women wearing string bikinis, their fertility oozing out of their immodest cocoons. I saw a young, shirtless, smooth man meandering about with his turgid genitals sprung out of crotchless leather pants. The rabbi appeared oblivious to these spectacles. An hour later a young woman joined us. She knew the rabbi but I had never met her.

After the introductions and smalltalk she asked me: "Are you gay or straight?"

"I'm straight."

"He's quite pretty," she remarked to the rabbi.

I'm always surprised when I receive compliments on my looks. That is not to say these compliments are frequent. I have large green eyes and full lips that are the sugar cutting down down the strong acid of my otherwise strong, masculine features defined by a jutting, Mediterranean profile and big jaw. I've had a love-hate relationship with my face even before I was a pimply-faced young teen and the hate has had the upper hand by far. My out of control curly hair also aggravated my confidence. I was rarely popular with girls during my vulnerable, formative years when a young man's psyche is formed and ossified. To my dying day I will remember a night in B'nei Brit summer camp, in the Quebec Laurentian mountains, when I was eleven. The boys had taken cover by the veil of darkness and gotten together with the girls from across the lake. They embraced secretively behind bushes and experimented with their budding sexuality.

But I could not find a willing partner. I will never forget the moment when one of the girls spotted me sulking alone in the darkness. "I bet he wants to get some," she said to her paramour and then she burst out in mocking laughter. In the mating game I was a square peg incompatible with the round holes.

Rabbi Flesher's acquaintance left shortly and we then sat halfway up the grassy knoll, feasting on falafel wraps and engaged in conversation.

"Nissim, I hear the round-table discussion you suggested will take place next Wednesday."

In my chronic struggle against Kol-Adama's ubiquitous demonization of Israel I had urged members to meet for a round-table discussion.

"Yes rabbi, I'm looking forward to a constructive discussion. I haven't given up hope for some common ground between me and the rest of Kol-Adama."

"You've been AWOL lately from our Shabbas davenings."

"Well, as you know, I've just split with Jenna a couple of weeks ago and I've been in no mood for social interaction."

"Yes, I've heard. I offer my condolences. I know the marriage was important to you. But perhaps she wasn't the right person for you."

"You could look at it that way if you adopt a philosophical mindset."

"This reminds me of my first marriage. I left the marriage after I realized I'd rather be alone for the rest of my life than spend another minute with this person."

"Perhaps that's the way Jenna felt about our marriage. No, I'm sure it is."

"What are you going to do now?"

"I've started writing my novel a few months ago. I'm hoping to get that going in a big way."

The rabbi peeled back the paper around his falafel wrap, tilted his head and took a sloppy bite. The juices dribbled down his bearded chin. He pulled a handkerchief from his back pocket and wiped his chin. "I didn't know you've started. You've been talking about that book since I met you."

"It's my passion. It's my spirit. It's the soul."

"This god of nothingness you've been talking about?" He chuckled. "Honestly, I still don't understand what that means."

"Perhaps by the time we part today I'll be able to explain it better. We've never had an opportunity to discuss these matters in any depth. I've made some leaps of understanding in the last few months. Actually, for some of my epiphanies I have you personally to thank."

"Really? My pleasure, but how did I accomplish that?"

My Manifesto

"I'll get to that in time. But I'll say this right now: after I finish writing my book the whole world will better understand the nature of god."

The rabbi nodded. "You know, it's interesting you should say that. There's a prophecy in the book of Daniel that when the age of messiach dawns the mystery of god will be revealed and the whole world will come to know his identity and nature."

"I didn't know that. That's exactly the way I see it. And as a part of the revelation of god's nature my book will also explore the most important aspect of Judaism."

"Which is?"

"The covenant between Abraham and god."

"I don't think that's the most important aspect of Judaism. I see the Hebrew scriptures as the history and belief system of the Jewish people. But there are other people with their own scriptures and their own belief systems and the Jewish people do not occupy any privileged or distinct position amongst the others."

"Then, with all due respect rabbi, we have a deep divide in our understanding of Judaism. I don't know what you mean by privileged. But it's certainly distinct."

Rabbi Flesher is a follower of Reconstructionist Judaism which holds that god is impersonal and simply the sum-total of all natural processes. It is an ideology inspired by Spinoza. But what is the sum total? That's a question Reconstructionist Judaism leaves unexamined. I once commented to the rabbi that his take on Judaism appears to me to be atheism dressed up in tradition. He didn't take too kindly to that remark.

"Rabbi, I'm not belittling other peoples. To each belongs a reason for being. I'm saying the covenant of Abraham with god defines a mission unique to the Jews amongst the congregation of humanity, the Civilization of Man. The Jews have not established great empires. The Jews have never yielded great power as did other peoples. But the covenant between Abraham and god has granted the Jews great influence on the stage of history, an influence far, far greater than their meager numbers would suggest, and that alone should lead a thoughtful person into questioning from where such influence originates and how it should be possible. The Jews have shaped history through the influence of ideas, not the imposition of power, not by the sword, not by erecting great structures, not by the legacy of legendary armies and conquests, but by introducing humanity to new landscapes of ideas, to new facets of the divine. And they have sometimes introduced or championed diametrically opposed ideas: capitalism and communism, feminism and biblical traditionalism, monotheism and atheism. The Jews are the Strange Attractor within the system of civilization. They are the yeast that leavens the bread."

"What is a Strange Attractor?" The rabbi laughed.

"It's a mathematical construct in Chaos Theory. Every Chaotic system has at least one Strange Attractor, and because civilization is a Chaotic system then it too must have one. The covenant between Abraham and god is a mathematical construct. God transformed the seed of Abraham through Isaac into the Strange Attractor of civilization."

"But what is a Strange Attractor?"

"In purely mathematical terms it's an equation defining a fractal shape representing a complex shape in a Chaotic system. Nearby points are attracted to and follow the path of that shape."

"Whoa...that's a mouthful."

"Ha ha. I know it is, rabbi. But basically, every Chaotic system has a tendency to have its fundamental elements be attracted towards a common location or locations or a path. A Strange Attractor is a complex path which takes on a Chaotic shape called a Fractal."

"Are you saying the propensity humanity has for understanding the divine is this Chaotic Strange Attractor?"

"Yes, and since the rise of monotheism, which I call the Second Age, the Hebrews have been a Strange Attractor of civilization. They have attracted humanity to the realms of new ideas."

"And there have been no others?"

"A Chaotic system can have more than one Strange Attractor, but the Hebrew Strange Attractor will attract humanity towards the Third Age."

"So what is the behavior of civilization which manifests as a Strange Attractor? You need to explain it to me in concrete terms."

"Yes, of course rabbi. But keep in mind I'm still forming these ideas. If my book will become successful and these ideas trigger the formulation of a new science then it will be like the influence of the ideas of Copernicus that eventually led to the Newtonian revolution. Abraham was the Copernicus of Judaism; Moses was its Newton."

"Moses the law giver."

"Yes, Moses atop Mount Sinai, etching his Principia Hebraica into the tablets and later the other laws."

"The 613 mitzvot."

"But in answer to your question, the Jews have been like lightning rods. They have attracted humanity to the path of understanding the divine. And I don't just mean the traditional quest for divinity which is religion. I mean it in a more general sense. One of the central themes of my book will be that in the Third Age science and religion will be unified. So the path to understanding divinity is not only the province of religion. And starting with the new physics of the 20th century, the distinction between the divine and the scientific has progressively blurred."

"You mean with Quantum Mechanics and its strange behaviors?"

"Yes, precisely. Modern physics has been knocking on heaven's door. The Hebrews have compelled humanity, since the beginning of monotheism, to grapple with the basic questions of our place within the tapestry of Existence. At first the Hebrews were only prominent by their religious influence. After all, Christianity and Islam are offshoots of Judaism. But much later they became influential, far beyond their numbers, in physics, sociology, psychology and other fields, as well as movements such as feminism, communism and capitalism. Wrestling with god comes in a rainbow of flavors and as humanity neared the dawn of the Third Age the Jews played an increasingly decisive role. We are now at the dawn of the Third Age. We are at a time when the darkness of night is locked in a titanic battle with dawn's first light and for a fleeting moment neither surrenders. To most, dawn's first glimmer is not yet apparent, but it will soon persecute the darkness and the struggle will be no more. And then from out of Zion a light brighter than the preceding brightest of days will shine and the Civilization of Man will cross over into the Third Age, the age of the mighty waters that wash away the preceding Second Age, the age of the Ram."

"And before the Ram was the Age of the Bull," the rabbi said. "The symbolism of the bull as an idolatrous thing is strong in the Torah. When Moses came down from Mount Sinai and saw the Israelites worshiping the Golden Bull he smashed the Ten Commandments. But what will be of Judaism when this Third Age is upon us?"

"Judaism, as well as all religions, belongs in the age of the Ram. During the Third Age there will no longer be a need for Judaism. It will have fulfilled its great commission and then will be no more. Religion will be no more, and in its place will be a personal relationship with the Divine Source, the semantic spaces within the soul."

"So humanity will be spiritual, not religious? Why does that sound familiar?" The rabbi smirked.

"Yeah, that's funny. But how much more personal can a relationship with the divine be than when it's not with an external providence but with the common Source within each of us?. It's the relationship of the branches with the trunk."

"Very interesting, your vision is diametrically opposed to Spinoza's vision of god as an impersonal foundation of Creation. In your system of thought god becomes more personal than even the traditional view of god in the Abrahamic religions. What irony. But I have to say your view doesn't jive with Reconstructionist Judaism."

"We can agree to disagree rabbi. But please elaborate on the irony you mentioned."

"Because historically, as science brought us closer to understanding the world, it seemed to have distanced a personal god from us to the point where it was pushed beyond the horizon. But you're saying the true endgame of our understanding of the universe is that god will become much closer to us than ever before."

"Yes, god will be so close he will be found within us, as will all of Creation. But it will not be the god of monotheism. It will be the god of metatheism. The god of Abraham will be redefined."

"Tell me something Nissim, do you really believe Abraham existed?" The rabbi's question was a thinly veiled rebuke.

"It doesn't matter. I don't believe Adam and Eve literally existed, but there is deeper metaphorical truth in the story of the Garden than deep truth in a stack of science books."

"I can agree with you if you look at things that way. But tell me something else. This Third Age age you preach so passionately about, is that the age of messiach prophesied in the Hebrew scriptures?"

"Yes it is. And that has been the only purpose of the covenant between god and Abraham: to usher in the coming age of messiach. That is the ultimate mission of the Jewish people. We have been chosen for that and only that."

"Do you really believe the messiach will come?"

"I do."

"Of all people, I'm surprised a scientifically oriented person like you would say that."

"I'm talking about the Jewish concept of the messiah, not the Christian one. Not a Son of God, but a Son of Man."

"A Ben Adam."

"Yes. The word Messiah has been hijacked by Christianity, but it's a very Jewish idea."

"That's why I say messiach and not messiah."

"The messiach is not a divine being. He is a normal person with a divine calling, a person with a big vision about the coming messianic age. The messiach will simply be a leader of the coming paradigm shift I call the Third Age. Nothing more and nothing less. Just a regular guy who puts his pants on one leg at a time."

"But she might prefer skirts." The rabbi laughed and then abruptly assumed a weighty tone. "But how will this messiach be appointed? By divine decree?"

"Well, when it comes to defining what messiach is I must elaborate a bit about Existentialist philosophy."

"You're getting into deep waters here."

"Yes, but the big fish only swim in deep waters."

The rabbi laughed. "That they do. True enough."

"In Sartre's Being And Nothingness he talks about existence preceding essence versus those things for which essence precedes existence. For example, consider a table. Something is a table only if it possesses certain attributes. It must be flat and level so objects on it don't slide off. It must have at least one leg and so on and so forth. So for a table its essence must precede its existence. It cannot exist apart from its functional description. A table is a concrete object produced from a template which defines the attributes that must be possessed by all types of tables."

"I've read a bit of Sartre. I get what you're saying. Sartre was saying a human being's existence precedes her essence because a human being transcends a collection of attributes."

"It's not so much that a human being transcends a collection of attributes. A human being possesses Free Will and the attributes that define a human being are emanations from this Free Will; they're not deterministic properties. Unlike animals whose behaviors and social structures and constructs are deterministic. A Polar Bear will never transcend the vagaries of its arctic origins, but human beings have escaped the earth's tentacles. Evolution has shaped each species to survive in the environment in which it evolved. Humans are the only species able to transcend the environment in which it evolved."

The rabbi nodded in appreciation. "That's a very impressive analysis. I'll need to meditate on that."

"It was Sartre's atheism compelling him to arrive at the conclusion humanity's existence precedes essence. If there's no god to create a template of what is the essence of a human being then a human being can be anything he or she wants. In Dostoevsky's Brothers Karamazov one of the Brothers, I think it's Ivan, says that without god everything is permitted. A human being exists first and then assumes a set of attributes later."

"What do you think Dostoevsky meant by that?"

"The part about everything being permitted?"

"Yes."

"Well, on the surface it seems to be referring simply to morality. That without god there's no absolute morality but only moral relativism. But if you dig under the surface, if you look at it more abstractly, then you see shades of Existentialism. It means humanity's existence precedes its essence, and therefore what defines a human being is open-ended. It's actually a commentary on Free Will."

"But Existentialism came after the publication of Brothers Karamazov, did it not?"

"Sartre came after. Existentialism began earlier. Dostoevsky was a brilliant and inspired man. I think he had an inkling of the idea of existence before essence. Einstein said Dostoevsky had given him more than any scientist. More than Gauss."

"Gauss?"

"He's called the Prince of Mathematics. Without a doubt, the greatest mathematician who ever lived."

"That's quite a compliment coming from Einstein. So now, I'm curious as to how you extend these ideas to the idea of messiach."

"I'll quote the wisdom of one of our greatest modern philosophers, 'Stupid is as stupid does'."

"Forrest Gump? That's your great modern philosopher?" The rabbi laughed.

"I'm being a little tongue-in-cheek of course, but not by much. I'll paraphrase Forest Gump's penetrating wisdom. Messiah is as messiah does."

"Hmm...interesting. I think I see where you're going with this."

"The messiach is not a divinely appointed being who then fulfills his messianic existence. A person is the messiach only insofar as he carries out the duties of the messiach. Properties or attributes come first, not messianic identity or existence. So for the messiach, essence precedes existence."

"It's quite breathtaking you've echoed what is a central tenet of the Jewish idea of messiach, which is that in every generation there's a person born with the potential to be the messiach, but if the times are not ready for the age of messiach then that person will not become the messiach. I think this mirrors very closely your idea that the messiach's essence precedes existence."

I nodded, pursed my lips and widened my eyes. For a second Clayton's question to me, three years earlier, echoed in my head:

"Nissim, do you sometimes feel you are on this earth to fulfill a great destiny?"

But it then occurred to me that for any destiny realized, essence must

My Manifesto

precede existence. The destiny is looking for the person to fulfill it. The movement creates the leader, not the other way around.

"Rabbi, I did not know that. I often discover my way of thinking unknowingly mirrors the Hebrew zeitgeist. I think I'm ontologically a Hebrew. But on to our discussion...that brings me to the new paradigm of what god is."

"I suspect this is where your idea about nothingness comes in?"

"Yes."

"And in light of our conversation, you'll tie in the existentialist idea of existence before essence?"

"Rabbi, you're already ahead of me. My proposition is that Creation emanates from an absolute nothingness which is completely devoid of any attributes or properties. And I will show this mirrors the idea of existence before essence. Indeed, it's the epitome of such a philosophy."

"But nothingness cannot exist. Wouldn't you agree?"

"You are obviously correct, rabbi. Nothingness cannot exist otherwise it would be something. Nothingness is non-existence."

"And non-existence cannot, by definition, exist."

"Rabbi, you are like a Euclidean geometer who reduces geometry into its bare essence, its orthogonal postulates."

The rabbi chuckled. "What is this ploy you're using to agree with me? By your own admission nothingness doesn't exist, so nothing can be created from it since it doesn't exist. Am I missing something?"

"Rabbi, we are creatures of time and space. We can't fathom nothingness. It's like asking what came before the Big Bang or what came before the creation of time itself, or what exists beyond the end of space."

"It's like trying to visualize one hand clapping. But be that as it may, I still say nothing can come out of non-existence."

"Why? That's a bias."

"Because it doesn't exist, that's why." The rabbi shrugged and rotated his palms up as a gesture he had stated the obvious.

"That's a logical fallacy called Begging the Question. You're saying existence cannot come out of non-existence because non-existence is non-existence. So you're using your conclusion to support your conclusion."

"But it's obvious."

"Now you're no longer a pure geometer." I laughed.

"Then please explain to me how existence can come out of non-existence."

"Creation emanates from nothingness not despite its non-existence but because of its non-existence."

"I'm afraid that's a bit much for my poor brain." The rabbi chuckled.
"Have you heard of Gödel Incompleteness?"

"No I haven't."

"This statement is a lie."

"I didn't lie. I never heard of this Gödel Incompleteness."

"No, no," I laughed, "I wasn't calling you a liar. I made an unrelated statement. Is what I said true or false?"

"But what did you say? Amarta Klum - you said nothing."

"This statement is a lie. If my preceding sentence is true then it must be false. If it's false then it must be true. Agree?"

After a short reflection the rabbi understood. "I see. The statement is about itself and it negates itself but then the negation negates the negation and so forth indefinitely. But what is the significance of all this? It seems like a cute little exercise, but nothing more. Ze rak shtuyot - it's just silly nonsense."

"Rabbi, what has the appearance of the greatest absurdity is not the shallowest of lies but the deepest of truths."

"Hmm...I like that. That's very deep. It's got hohma - wisdom. So tell me, where is the deep truth in all of this?"

"This kind of infinitely nested, vibrational, self-negating statement has a very deep implication to the nature of mathematical truth, and truth in general, because everything is fundamentally mathematical under the hood. I won't go into detail, but starting with this self-negating statement the German logician Kurt Gödel proved that given any sufficiently powerful mathematical system there are truths which are the consequence of the fundamental postulates of that system but which cannot be proven by the tools available within that system. In other words, these truths originate from the system but then transcend the system. They emanate out of the system and form a new, independent system. You are only able to see their truth once you step out of their parent system."

"I suppose you'll, hashem willing, enlighten me about what all this mathematical hocus-pocus has to do with god as nothingness?"

"If you really think about the idea of existence preceding essence you'll see this implies essence must emanate from non-essence."

"Care to elaborate?"

"What I'm saying is that everything that exists is itself the essence of some other existence, and if you take this regression all the way down the serpent hole, existence itself is the essence of that which is non-existence."

"Don't you mean the rabbit hole?"

"This past spring I wrote a chapter in my novel where I re-imagine the rabbit hole by using the metaphor of the serpent instead. It's a whimsical chapter about a conversation between Abraham when he was a child talking to an idol in his father's idol shop."

"Oh nice, you've written a midrash. It's interesting how you've used the existence-precedes-essence idea and flipped it around. Now, existence is the essence and non-existence is the antecedent. But I ask again, how can existence emanate from non-existence? How can something come from nothing?"

"In the same way action comes from nothing via Free Will. In the same way systems emanate from other systems via Gödel Incompleteness. It's all done through the tautology of the Gödel self-negating statement."

"What do you mean by tautology?"

"The statement that says all bachelors are unmarried is a good example of tautology. Its truth is self-reflecting. It doesn't depend on anything external to validate its truth."

"And the statement: this statement is false?"

"Its a form of tautology, but it's a self-negating tautology. It's a super tautology because unlike the bachelors tautology, this tautology reaches in and changes its own meaning. It bootstraps itself. It's a statement wrestling with its own truth. That's the kind of tautology required for new systems to emanate spontaneously from their parent systems, as in order from disorder in Chaos Theory, or the truths that transcend their parent systems in Gödel Incompleteness. Chaos Theory and Gödel Incompleteness are saying the same thing in different ways."

"So I'm still waiting to hear how the self-negating tautology gives rise to something from nothing."

"Non-existence doesn't exist. Or the statement: I don't exist. If non-existence doesn't exist then it exists and if it exists then it doesn't exist."

"Or if I don't exist then I couldn't have said I don't exist hence I must exist, and if I exist...well you get the point."

"Actually, I can just say 'non-existence' and the 'doesn't exist' part is implied immediately. So this is the tightest kind of self-negating statement. Its self-negation is itself tautological and doesn't need to be explicitly added to the sentence. The Big Bang is simply the one word sentence: Nothingness."

"Whoa... I need to wrap my head around that. But even so, how does that create something from nothing?"

"Rabbi, how can you say that? If non-existence doesn't exist then it exists. There you go. Something exists from non-existence."

"But that's just a word game. It couldn't possibly mean anything relevant. Are you saying electrons and protons and energy came out of the Big Bang because of this silly word game?"

"You must wean yourself out of the habit of assuming physical existence must, at the most fundamental level, originate from something also physical. Remember that existence precedes essence and the very idea of Existence must then itself become the essence. But the essence in this case is Existence, hence it must follow from non-Existence."

"I still don't buy it."

"Rabbi, the foundation of mathematical logic as we know it today is a consequence of the self-negating statement. Something which according to you is just a silly word game."

"But that's mathematics. It's not electrons and protons and cars and rabbis and philosophers."

"Yes, but we are physical creatures conditioned to believe, through the circumstances of our physicality, that the physical is the only reality and everything else is a phantasmagoria. But that's just a bias. Physical reality is not the fundamental reality; It's an emanation of something deeper and non-physical and ultimately it comes out of nothingness via the self-reflecting, self-negating sentence. The sentence that says non-existence doesn't exist has as much legitimacy and consequence as the sentence that denies its own truth. If the latter is the foundation of modern mathematical logic then the former cannot be dismissed as mere inconsequential word play. The Big Bang is nothing more than the tautological statement that non-existence doesn't exist."

"You're saying the Big Bang is a word game?"

"In the beginning was the Word and the Word became Flesh."

"You're not talking about the Christian idea of Jesus as son of god. Are you?"

"No, I'm talking about the Gödel self-reflecting, self-negating statement producing emanations that are banished from their parent systems. Think of it as nested mirrors. The Flesh emanating out of the Word is the Tree of Existence emanating out of Adama - the Ground of Being. The Tree of Knowledge Of Good and Evil in the primordial garden is none other than YHVH itself, the Tree of Existence."

"In a way I see what you mean. It's Evil denying Good and Good denying Evil. It's like the self-negating sentence. It's the serpent eating its own tale."

"I like that. Thank you rabbi. Adam and Eve consumed YHVH and then they became like YHVH, a mirror within a mirror within another. But this new mirror is just another mirror within the preceding mirrors, just another

My Manifesto

nested reflection within the existing reflections. In this way we are made in the image of YHVH. We are a Gödel truth banished from our parent system."

"You are what you eat." The rabbi winked. "In the book of Genesis god creates Adam out of Adama - out of the ground."

"Yes, that's a metaphor. It refers to the Word becoming Flesh. It doesn't mean god created Adam from literal mud. It's Adam out of Adama."

"It's no coincidence the word for man is Adam and the word for ground is Adama," the rabbi said.

"The relationship of the two words, and I agree it's an intended relationship, implies humanity is a reflection of god, in the image of god, in the same way the inner mirror is in the image of the outer mirrors. The inner mirror is not external to the outer mirrors, it is within them. Humanity is not external to god, it is within god and god is within us. We are the Word becoming Flesh, all of us."

"And the word for blood is dam. Another member of the related family of words. The life essence," the rabbi said.

"Good point."

"They ate from the Tree of the Knowledge of Good and Evil and then they knew they were naked. I see the theme of self-knowledge, self-reflection, self-reference."

"Yes, another good point, rabbi. Like a mirror emanating within a mirror, like Adam emanating within Adama. The mechanism giving rise to our consciousness is the very same mechanism giving rise to the physical universe as it hurtles out of the semantic spaces of the Big Bang. The Torah contains one other instance alluding to this idea of Creation emanating as a copy, I say self-reflecting copy, out of its parent system. When Moses is talking to the burning bush on Mount Sinai, he asks god what his name is."

"And god says I AM."

"So here again we have a similar idea to Adam out of Adama."

"How so?"

"We are the little I am embedded in the big I AM. It's a Fractal shape, the copy embedded within the original but becoming an independent system unto itself - Free Will."

"Nissim. Have you ever heard of Tat Tvam Asi?"

"Hmm...sounds like Hebrew but I can't make out the meaning."

"It's not Hebrew, it's Sanskrit. It means something like you are that or that which you are. It's a pronouncement in Vedantic Sanatana Dharma. I think it mirrors what you've been saying. It means the original pure form of the self, the primordial form, is also the ground of being of all phenomena.

Pretty much what you've been saying. Tat would be equivalent to the H you speak of or the Adama and Tvam is the Self, Adam emanating from Adama."

"You know rabbi, I'm always amazed when my ideas have such parallels in the divine revelations of other cultures. But I shouldn't be. These cultures have also received the wisdom of the I AM."

"Nissim, the divine speaks to all cultures."

"I'm in awe of the divinely inspired wisdom of the Eastern religions. If I believed in reincarnation I'd say I was a Hindu in a previous life."

"Oh really? I want to hear more."

"There's a stunning pronouncement in the Bhagavad Gita. It's also a Sanskrit word. It means Song Of the Lord."

"Yes, yes, I'm a little familiar with it."

"The pronouncement goes something like this:

I curve back on myself and then I create and create."

I explained to the rabbi how that parallels my interpretation of YHVH.

"I heard of that passage before but I certainly didn't understand it in the way you've just explained it. But can we legitimately attribute to the writers of the Torah and the Bhagavad Gita, and all the other holy books, this kind of insight? They knew nothing of Gödel or Fractals or any modern scientific concepts."

"Well, this suggests the question of what is divine inspiration? Is the Torah divinely inspired? I say it is but clearly not by the traditional idea of a divine entity literally reciting the contents of the Torah to its writers in the sense a human being would to another. There is no place for such a divine being in my system of thought."

"I see where you're going. Divine inspiration is the flow of insight from the big I AM to the little I am, from the outer mirror to the inner mirrors. It's not an external flow of information."

"Rabbi, I must be doing something right in explaining my ideas because that's exactly what I mean by divine inspiration. In a Fractal shape, as you drill down to smaller scales you see the shape keeps getting repeated. So how does that happen? How do the smaller scales know the shape of the scales above from which they originate? There's no external being, some controlling entity, orchestrating this repeating process."

"So you're saying the writers of the Torah were divinely inspired in this new way of understanding divine inspiration? They are the little I am within the big I AM? The little shape within the big shape?"

"Yes. They didn't consciously know about the ideas of Gödel and Fractals, but there was what I call a whisper emanating out of the semantic spaces within their core."

"The core being the big I AM?"

"Yes. The semantic spaces from which meaning emanates as do the unprovable truths emanate from a parent system via Gödel Incompleteness, as does order emanate out of disorder in Chaos Theory."

"A whisper emanating from the big I AM to the small I am within."

"And that, rabbi, is what divine inspiration or revelation really is."

"You mentioned you don't accept Reincarnation. I'm curious about your reasons."

"What do the Hebrew scriptures say about Reincarnation?"

"That's a complicated issue. It's not straight forward as it is in Buddhism or Hinduism. It's actually never mentioned in the Torah, but it's mentioned in the Zohar."

"That's Kabbalah, right?"

"Yes. The Zohar calls it Gilgul, which means recycling in Hebrew."

"Galgal means wheel in Hebrew," I said. "So it makes sense as a circling back of the soul back into the body."

"So there you have it. As with most things in Judaism there's no black or white answer. So what are your reasons for not accepting Reincarnation?"

"It stems from my position of an implicate Reality that defines what the soul is. In my framework we all share the same soul. We are One."

"How does that view negate a belief in Reincarnation?"

"Because Reincarnation holds that after death we maintain the individuality of our soul and this unique soul is then pumped back into another body. Reincarnation says there are a multitude of souls."

"Interesting, so you're saying the idea of Oneness contradicts Reincarnation."

"Yes. I like to say I AM not someone who used to live. I AM everyone who have ever lived, live and will live."

"That's a fascinating way to look at it."

"According to Reincarnation each flesh and blood body is a link belonging to a continuous chain of bodies into the past that have shared the same soul. So this view says humanity is composed of many of these chains that never intersect. But in my view every body who has ever lived or lives now or will live is the same soul."

"So there is only one chain."

"I don't like the chain analogy for this Oneness idea. I use the diamond analogy. We are all the same multi-faceted diamond, but each facet looks i at this diamond and believes it is the whole diamond unto itself and each other facet is a different diamond."

"That's a powerful imagery."

"But regarding Reincarnation, look at it this way: believers in Reincarnation accept a soul can be shared. But they're stuck in a temporal way of thinking. They believe, perhaps subconsciously, that this soul sharing can only be done across time but not simultaneously. They believe implicitly in the primacy, the irreducibility, of time and so their version of soul sharing can only be done in series, like a chain, not in parallel, like a diamond. But I take the idea of soul sharing to the ultimate conclusion. There's only one soul being shared both across the ages and across all humanity living in the Now."

"So you're saying it doesn't then make sense to single out only specific individuals in the past who are you. Everyone has the same soul. But what is the soul?"

"It's consciousness at the implicate level of the physical universe. That's the level where the Oneness reverberates."

"It's curious you stress the physical."

"There are other levels in the Tree of Existence. Each level is an implicate consciousness - a soul. By the way, I keep going back to Reincarnation, the fact the human population is growing shows that for Reincarnation to be true there will always be people born who are brand new souls, a one-link chain, while others belong to a multiple-link chain and are old souls."

"That doesn't sound impossible."

"It denies the soul is eternal. But that's not my reason for my rejecting Reincarnation. I've already given you my reasons. Basically, Reincarnation is an attempt to hold on to the ego. It says the ego persists after death."

"What do you mean by ego?"

"It's the instinctive sense we all have that we are separate from anyone and anything else. It's the belief we each have a separate soul. But this is just an illusion. Any ideology built on top of this illusion will crumble like as house of cards."

"Like Reincarnation?"

"Yes. Reincarnation says the fundamental bedrock of Existence is an irreducible plurality of souls. But I say we are all the same soul. An I AM within an I AM within another, all the way down to the void of the H - the primordial I AM, the Adam Kadmon."

"Like the branches progressively proliferating out of this Tree of Existence."

My Manifesto

"Yes. When you look out at the world through your eyes it is everyone who has ever lived, lives or will live looking out through your eyes. When you close your eyes and ponder your inner world it is everyone who has ever lived, lives or will live looking inward through your mind's eye. You are everyone. Everyone is you. And if you again take that to the ultimate conclusion you will know that when you look out of your eyes, or inward through your mind's eye, it is the Source of the Tree of Existence doing the looking. It is god doing the looking through your eyes."

The rabbi scrunched his forehead and widened his eyes. "What an awe inspiring concept. Nissim, you should write your book. It's a mitzvah. I think it's needed in this world."

"I've come to recognize when a person looks at me with god's eyes. I gaze into their eyes and I can see down that spiraling navel that reaches into the ineffable depth. I see unconditional love. I see pure compassion. It's the highest pinnacle of enlightenment. But I can't teach how to recognize it and I can't teach how to look through god's eyes. All I can teach is that it is there. The rest must emanate from your depths."

"Do you look at the world with god's eyes?"

"Sometimes I can manage it. I try my best but I still have a lot to aspire to. I'm very far from perfect, trust me. I still feel anger and sometimes even hate towards those who've wronged me in my past. But I know I must defeat that beast within me. I want to be able to forgive the unforgiving, but it's so hard."

"Listen, I don't mean to jump so abruptly to a different question, but you said earlier you have me to thank for helping you advance your ideas. How's that?"

I told the rabbi the story of how I came to realize the meaning of YHVH after he gave the lesson about the meaning of the Hebrew letters. He listened with rapt attention until my last word.

"That's certainly an original interpretation of the Tetragrammaton. I will need to give it more thought. But it definitely fits well with your overall ideas. So are you saying the letter H is this nothingness you call god, or is YHVH god?"

"The H is the ineffable god - the Source. HVH is the self-reflecting, self-negating sentence. Y represents the first system emanating out of the H. Again, a good analogy are the nested mirrors. Their cocooning is also due to self-reference, a feedback loop. YHVH is the entire nested complex of all the mirrors. It's the Tree of Knowledge of Good and Evil at the center of the primordial garden."

"So these three things are actually the same thing?"

"Which three?"

"The Tree of Existence, the Tree of Knowledge and YHVH."

"Absolutely. They are one and the same."

"So when Adam and Eve ate from the fruit of the Tree of Knowledge they were actually eating YHVH?"

"Yes. It's a form of cannibalism because the H is within them. And then they became another branch in YHVH, another branch on the Tree of Knowledge, with the power to give birth to child branches."

"Like another mirror within the nested mirrors with the ability to contain more nested mirrors. It's the same shape again repeated."

"Yes, in that way we have eaten the Fruit, and we became like god."

But tell me, what is ineffability? What does it mean to say the H is ineffable?"

"Well, as with most things in my system, tautology is the driving mechanism. Nothingness is ineffable because it is nothingness."

"Again with tautologies that seem like a silly word game."

"But I'll explain. Something is ineffable if it can't be conceived of or expressed in some language. Now, that can be understood as a complete lack of attributes and properties. If something is definable by at least one attribute or property then we can say it's understandable or expressible."

"That is its language - these properties."

"Exactly. So it follows that true ineffability can only be absolute nothingness because the truly ineffable must be without properties or attributes, otherwise it would be understandable, if not in practice then at least in principle. Nothingness, or non-existence, doesn't just happen to be ineffable, it is ineffable by its very definition. It is tautologically ineffable. True ineffability must be tautological."

"Nissim, are you going to include these ideas in your novel?"

"Well, of course rabbi. How can I not? I hope you can understand now what I mean when I say god is nothingness?"

"You've given me a lot to process and to meditate on."

"I'll cap off our discussion with yet another way to understand how Creation emanates from nothingness."

"Another tautology, I suppose."

"Why Rabbi, you've come to know me very well today."

"I'm actually quite eager to hear it."

"I hope I've impressed on you today the self-referencing nature of Gödel statements and how it's this self-referencing aspect which is responsible for why Creation is built from the bottom up. I like to say Ontology is Tautology. In the branch of mathematics called Chaos Theory we have order spontaneously emanating from disorder in systems exhibiting self-referencing behavior. These are also known as positive feedback loop systems. The idea of feedback loops is equivalent to tautology. The former is usually associated with physical systems, the latter with logic."

"Gödel's ideas are the foundation from which you construct a new vision of god."

"Indeed they are. Here's something which is most fascinating, and I'm convinced is not a coincidence."

"You've piqued my curiosity."

"As you know, in Hebrew the word for god is 'el'."

"Of course."

"So do you notice what's so fascinating about the name Gödel?"

The rabbi contemplated my question and within seconds his eyes widened in wonder. "Why, yes I do. The name Gödel is a doubling up of the word god, starting with the English word and ending with the Hebrew word for god, god then el, most curious."

"It's a stunning realization that the name of the person whose ideas will be the foundation of a new vision of god has this property to his name, is it not?"

"I must agree that it seems not coincidental, as if the hand of god is at work here. But Nissim, before my synapses shut down, you said you have an alternate way of understanding why Creation emanates from nothingness."

"Oh yes, here is the question: What does nothingness reference?"

"You mean what does nothingness speak of or point to?"

"Yes."

"Well I suppose nothingness, being nothing, references nothing."

"There you go."

"There I go? There you go. Where do I go?"

"You just said it. Nothingness references nothing."

"So?"

"Nothingness references itself."

A momentary lapse and then a look of understanding rippled across the rabbi's face. "Nice." The rabbi laughed. "Very nice and so very sneaky. A beautiful tautology."

"There you go. That's the primordial positive feedback loop. There is no cause to the Big Bang. There is no need to ask what happened before the Big Bang or what caused the Big Bang. It's all one big, beautiful tautology. And anyone who is not blown away by how this answers, once and for all, how Existence came to be, hasn't really grasped the enormity of what I'm

My Manifesto

saying."

"And it answers one of the big theological questions."

"Which is?"

"Did god have to create the universe or was it his choice? According to what you said, god had no choice. Or more succinctly, it's in the tautological definition of non-Existence that it must bring forth Existence."

"Well said, rabbi. The creation of Existence is the passion of the H, and true passion is irresistible because it is the tautological ontology of its bearer." And then I hesitated because there was more I wanted to say, but it would come from the depths of my spirit and I questioned if I should expose my spirit naked and vulnerable. The rabbi sensed my hesitation.

"Is there anything else on your mind?"

"Yes. Before I go rabbi there's one more thing I want to say."

"Judging by our conversation today, I'm sure it will be eye-opening."

"Our discussion today has touched on an array of deep questions. I've leveraged my ideas about Gödel Incompleteness, Existentialism, tautology, and so on, to shed light on the Big Bang, on primordial cause-and-effect, on Free Will, on the fundamental nature of the divine and divine inspiration and revelation. My intent is to enlighten the intellect. But at least on equal footing is the impact these ideas can have...no, should have, on our spirituality, on our soul's yearning for communion with the divine and on our urge for the transcendent."

"The transcendent is the land we've left long ago. Our urge for it is really a homesickness."

"Yes, rabbi, it is. But if the ideas we've discussed today have only raised your intellectual awareness but you don't feel goose bumps crawling on your skin, like an army of ants, and if you don't feel the ramparts to your core breached and your being's hidden chamber fully revealed, then you have not truly understood. You have seen it with your two eyes but not with your third."

"Yes, but it might take time for these ideas to sink in and to percolate into the soul."

"Certainly, and when I use the word 'you' I'm using it in the general sense, not you in particular."

"No offense taken. I understood that."

"These ideas are revelations that have emanated from within the deepest level of my being. They are from the big I AM whispering to my little I am which is within the big I AM - from the soul to my spirit. God is not outside. We all are reflections of god, within god. Ever since I was a child I've listened to these whispers reverberating within me and I've submitted

My Manifesto

to these whispers during timeless moments of my life, and I became a citizen of the Eternal Realm, the kingdom of the ineffable H. And during my forays in the Eternal Kingdom I saw a new age soon to dawn upon humanity. It is the age prophesied so long ago by the Hebrew prophets. And I saw Jerusalem, the shining city of Zion atop a hill, but in the Eternal Kingdom it is not a city of brick and mortar, it is a city of the spirit's yearning and of effervescent light. And the whispers lingered within me and they proclaimed with the final trumpeting of a ram's horn the coming Third Age, when all of the Earth will become the city of Zion, a Jerusalem spread from pole to pole and around the great circles of our world. But before the Third Age can dawn, Jerusalem, that shining city of Zion atop a hill, must be gifted to the world so that no one people shall exercise dominion over it. Before the messianic age dawns the third temple must be rebuilt, but all of Jerusalem is that third temple, and the rebuilding is its gifting to the world. In the Eternal Kingdom it is not a temple of brick and mortar - that is just its shadow on the cave's wall. And once that comes to pass then the Third Age will emanate in all directions from out of Jerusalem, ground zero, and it will ripple across the lands and the waters and it will reach every kingdom and every nation and the Third Age will then dawn. The Hebrews will gift Jerusalem to the world, not because they don't have a birthright to the city of Zion but because they do. Only the Hebrews can gift it to the world because it is theirs to gift. And when Jerusalem is gifted to the world then the world will be gifted to Jerusalem, and they will become one within the other. And there will no longer be a need for Judaism, it will have completed its mission and the covenant will be consummated. All religion as we know it today will begin to collapse like a house of cards."

"I like your idea about Jerusalem becoming an international city. But are you saying in the age of messiach Jews should stop being Jews?"

"I'm saying that will happen and it should happen. Take the dietary laws for example. To this day observant Jews can't even have a meal in the home of gentiles. This kind of segregation, of self-inflicted ghettoization, has been effective historically in creating the Jewish zeitgeist which has had such out of proportion influence on humanity. It has been the agent of the covenant. But the time for that is now past. The only dietary laws of consequence now are based on the ethical treatment of animals, not on religious traditions. There is nothing godly about the mistreatment and killing of animals that possess feelings and a good level of awareness."

"Well, I can't give up my Judaism so easily, if you don't mind. But I do minimize my intake of meat."

My Manifesto

"But in the age of messiach there's no sense in holding on to labels that group people by religious affiliation. An understanding of divinity will no longer be in the religious domain. In the age of messiach the whole world will understand the meaning of YHVH in the rational, mathematical way that I explain through the ideas of Gödel - god-el. So you won't need to call yourself a Jew if you want to be a Yahavist, because Yahavism will then be defined within a broader domain transcending religion. So in a sense the whole world will become Jewish. But the whole world will also become Buddhist and Hindu and Muslim and so on, because each religion contains some wisdom which will be synthesized within a broader rational, scientific perspective. So holding on to a particular religion will not make sense in the age of messiach because they are each just shadows on the wall of a cave. At the beginning of the age of messiach humanity will take its first baby steps out of the cave and embrace the light, and there will be no Jew, no Buddhist, no Hindu, no Christian, no Muslim...only the one soul as a branch on the Tree of Existence. Do you understand what I'm saying, rabbi?"

"Yes, I do understand. Your words are noble and inspiring. But I don't think this can be done so easily."

"I don't expect it to happen overnight. The current generation must pass before humanity plants both feet squarely on the promised land. But what I've been saying the last few minutes is what the whispers emanating from within me have revealed. That's the purpose of my book, in all its facets. When I will write about what is the Big Bang or about Gödel and the worlds within worlds, it will be with the overarching intent of planting a seed within its readers that will trigger the dawn of the Third Age. When I will wax poetic about wrestling angels and dancing angels, it is with the overarching intent of planting this seed. That's my manifesto of the coming Third Age."

"I've come to know you better today than in all the previous few years I've known you. You said you've been hearing these whispers since you were a child?"

"These are not whispers of sound."

"Of course not. I understand."

"The first time was during the summer of 73. I was at the B'nei Brit Jewish summer camp in the Laurentian mountains in the province of Quebec. I lived in Montreal in those days. I remember one hot afternoon, I was exploring the woods surrounding our camp grounds. I wasn't far off and for the first time I heard a song that would captivate and mesmerize me for the rest of my life."

My Manifesto

The rabbi waited for me to continue, but I paused for dramatic effect. "Which song is that?"

"One of the camp counselors was playing Stairway to Heaven. It was quite loud and I heard it clearly."

"Yes, I remember that song very well. Brings back memories of my young self in the early Seventies. It's an amazing song."

"For the duration of that song I stood on that spot, within the breathing, self-aware forest, motionless and mesmerized, unable to breathe but not needing to breathe because the forest's breath was my own. I heard the lyrics but I didn't understand them. The song bypassed my mind and dug its hooks deep into my spirit. It fused with my spirit's DNA and I changed that day. I experienced an unshakable and even disturbing feeling the song was meant for me. And then I could no longer experience the fold between the place where the music ends and I begin. And I became the forest that day because the forest's breath became the song captivating me. Throughout the three weeks of summer camp that year I made many solitary forays into the forest and I heard that song each time to the same effect. It never occurred to me to question why that song should permeate the forest on each of my outings, but only now it occurs to me how strange that is. Were my counselors playing it on their record players each of these times, or was it reverberating in the forest, like a ghostly melody, only for me to hear? As the years went by I understood more of the lyrics, the ones that would be meaningful to all and the ones that have personal meaning for me."

"You mean seemingly written for you? I'd love to hear an example."

I closed my eyes and recited the passage I had committed to memory long before:

Your head is humming and it won't go, in case you don't know
The piper's calling you to join him
Dear lady, can you hear the wind blow and did you know
Your stairway lies on the whispering wind?

"And what does that mean to you?"

"When I was a teenager I dreamed of becoming a theoretical physicist and contributing to humanity's understanding of the universe. Yes, I know, I always dreamed big, it's in my spiritual DNA. Einstein was my idol. But this passage spoke to me and it troubled me during those years when I still hoped for scientific greatness. This passage was telling me my head is humming with the potential to become a great physicist, but it's not the way my life would unfold. As I grew older these words resonated progressively with me and I understood my destiny is to write about the Third Age, the messianic age, and to uplift humanity's yearning for such an age."

"So when did you finally let go of your desire for scientific greatness?"

"By my early twenties, around 1986 or 87. But let me tell you of the overarching meaning of the song, the part that should be meaningful to all. It's about the Third Age. Every word of it, every comma, every period, every syllable is about the coming messianic age."

It was now almost 4 PM and the heat of day was still sweltering. Once we left the protective shade in which we were sitting I was assaulted by the sun's savagery. We walked up the grassy knoll.

"Just one more thing, rabbi."

"Yes?"

"Do you give me permission to mention you in my novel when I start writing about the modern age?"

"By all means. I'll be honored."

"I won't use your real name. I'll call you...let's see, what should I call you? I got it. I'll call you rabbi Fromeatsky."

"Nice name," the rabbi laughed. "I get its connection to my actual name. But you're welcome to my real name."

I bid the rabbi a good day and headed north on Pacific Avenue to pick up the keys to the next chapter of my life.

***

Two weeks after the Pride Parade I disembarked the Skytrain at Main Street station and headed three blocks east along Terminal Avenue. It was a warm and clear day during the last few weeks of the summer of 2006. A comforting, redolent westerly breeze caressed my face as it raced the passing Skytrains on the tracks above which were parallel to my path. I climbed the three flights of stairs and entered the room where Kol-Adama members would discuss Israel, the Palestinian conflict and the fundamental question of the right of Israel to exist - as if that should be in question at all. I had grown weary of the email discussions amounting to nothing more than rancor and discord. When people lose the intimacy of face-to-face interaction they become more sociopathic. They forget the humanity of others. They forget the humanity of the Other. At Kol-Adama it was not the homosexuals who were the Other. I, and others like me, had assumed that mantle.

Half a dozen members had indicated they would attend and Stewart was in that group. Rabbi Flesher would not be attending. In those days he never

My Manifesto

showed a bias in favor of any ideology or opinion that had polarized the members into adversarial groups. A congregation's spiritual leader should be above such squabbles. He kept his sights high on the two pillars of Kol-Adama's agenda: acceptance and nurturing, within a religious Jewish fold, of society's outcasts, and the bringing together of communities of disparate religions and, in particular, healing the rift between Muslims and Jews. I fell in love with his magnanimity in those days.

Stewart and two other members had arrived before me. He was stroking his dark, close-cropped, gray-speckled beard and perused notes he had scrawled in a pocket notebook. He greeted me with a quick smile, but his eyes were not smiling. I helped myself to hot coffee and chocolate-chip cookies provided for the meeting. I sat by the windows with a view of the Skytrains gliding on the elevated tracks, now at eye level with me. It was quarter past six, the meeting was scheduled for half-past. At the designated meeting time I counted seven members including myself, four male and three female, ranging in age from the early thirties to the late sixties.

"I will now call this meeting to order," Stewart said. "Let's start by having each person take turns describing why they chose to participate in this meeting. I will go first and we'll proceed in a clockwise fashion. So, about me: the Israeli-Palestinian conflict tears my heart and I've devoted much time and energy to understand its causes and its possible solutions, and to be an activist working towards justice for the Palestinians who have been uprooted and cast aside due to this conflict. As some of you might know, I'm a card-carrying member of Jews For A Just Peace and in that capacity I've been fortunate to travel to Palestine and to observe the injustice, the horrific oppression, the apartheid under which Palestinians must carry out their tragic lives. I witnessed the hardships the Palestinians endure at the hands of a brutalizing Zionist regime. I witnessed the completely and absolutely unprovoked aggression the Zionists have committed against these innocent, beautiful and peaceful people who desperately want to be allowed to live their lives like human beings alongside their Jewish neighbors who have stolen their ancestral lands. I remind you all the ancient Hebrew prophets preached incessantly for social justice and were strong and resolute in their condemnation of Hebrew society when it trampled the weak, the disenfranchised."

Stewart glanced at his notes. "In Amos 5:24 it says let justice roll down like waters. Isiah presents a god denouncing the elders and princes of his people for mistreating the poor. The Hebrew prophets present a vision of a just society where tyrants are no more and the evil are cut off. The prophets taught us a nation will be judged by how it treats the least amongst itself, the weak and the helpless. I take what the prophets said to heart, as I believe every Jew must, and that's why I speak out untiringly for the plight of the Palestinians at the hands of imperialism, religious extremism, military oppression, Zionist lust for land at the cost of the lives of children. So that's my story and I'm sticking with it." Stewart smirked and winked and slammed his notebook shut.

Two others spoke. Their positions were similar. Their narrative was milder than Stewart's but they also accused Israel of oppression and of being solely responsible for the conflict. And then it was my turn on the soap-box.

"Thank you all who have spoken so far. I've listened to your positions and I'd like to present my position on this important issue and address some of the points you've brought up. Stewart, I agree the voice of the prophets regarding social justice is powerful and should be mirrored in our lives, but I disagree with your position that Israelis are guilty of the oppression you've stated. You've basically presented a Straw Man argument. You state as an irrefutable fact that Israelis oppress the Palestinians and then you argue the obvious, that oppression is never justified. There is no denying what the prophets have said regarding social justice is beyond reproach. But the question is if the Israelis have committed such sins against the Palestinians in the one-sided manner you claim, or you seem to claim due to your lack of any finger-pointing towards the Palestinians and the Arabs in general. The causes of the current conflict are far more complex than you would have us believe. You present the Israelis as sociopathic monsters who are solely responsible for the plight of the Palestinians. In doing so you do a great disservice to the quest for the truth. And the truth is this conflict is not the one dimensional, black and white struggle between good and evil, innocent and guilty. Stewart, you say you visited Palestine recently, and by that I think you mean Gaza, maybe the Westbank. But did you bother visiting Israel? Did you bother mixing with the rainbow of Israeli society, or did you just confine your outreach to those who, like you, believe Israel is the only devil in this conflict? You only speak of justice for Palestinians. But what of Israelis? Do you think only Palestinians suffer in this conflict? Do you think Arabs have committed no wrong-doing against Israelis? Your complete lack of effort in discussing the well-being of Israelis leaves a deep hole of omission in your narrative. Twenty percent of Israelis are Arab citizens who enjoy the full rights of citizenship. So your accusation of apartheid against Israel holds no water. You didn't make the accusation of apartheid today, but I know you've said it before. Israel vacated Gaza last year. The Israeli army forcibly removed the Jewish settlers and Israel left behind all the infrastructure intact to be enjoyed by the Arabs living in Gaza. So let's see where that takes us. Let's see if Gaza residents decide to live in peace with Israel now. And I assure you if this experiment pays dividends then Israel will sooner than later do the same in the Westbank and pull out all the Jewish settlers. But I also assure you if the Arabs in Gaza waste this opportunity for peace and they bite the hand that offers them an olive branch and autonomy then their fortunes will take a turn for the worse. And Stewart, you will then lose your credibility if you accuse Israel of violating the tenets of social justice spoken by the ancient Hebrew prophets. You will lose all credibility in declaring Palestinian ill fortunes are not at all self-inflicted."

Stewart did not immediately address my rebuttal to his accusations against Israel. He waited for all to state their position. I was, by far, the most sympathetic to Israel. The others who were sympathetic to Israel in the Kol-Adama community were not in attendance that day. They were silent. During the Holocaust years, when my father suffered the yellow star like a cut that would not heal, there was a martyr named Dietrich Bonhoeffer who listened to the voice within and he proclaimed it only takes the silence of the good for evil to triumph. But Stewart is far from evil, he is a good man in all ways except his demonization of Israel. Most members of Kol-Adama are good people who support rights for homosexuals, for full equality of women, for the rights to medical care regardless of economic status and for free-speech and freedom from theocracy. They speak out with passion whenever such rights are trampled by Christian traditionalists in the Western world, but they are silent when far greater injustices are committed by Muslims in the Middle East. And in the Muslim Middle East such injustices are ubiquitous and epidemic. They are silent when the Muslim world enshrines such injustices within their social manifestos and governments. Their disease, hatred for Israel, is immune to the medicine of truth. Israel is the only state in the Middle East that champions Liberal ideals, but that has no bearing on their hatred and they disregard the inconvenient truth that the Muslim states in the Middle East assail the dignity of the soul.

The Civilization of Man kicks and screams against the pull of its great Strange Attractor, but it cannot prevail. Yahvah will bless those who resonate with the Strange Attractor. The sailor who resonates with the ocean's winds will voyage to lands of mystery and discovery and will bless all the families of the Earth. But the sailor who rebels by turning his gaze away and refuses the siren's song of the winds shall be cursed and will crash against the rocky shores and will be destroyed.

My Manifesto

After all introductory speeches were completed, I addressed Stewart: "Hatred of Israel is a new kind of antisemitism that has reared its ugly head since the creation of the state of Israel. In today's world there's still the traditional antisemitism of those who openly admit their hate for Jews. But there's a new kind of disingenuous antisemitism. It projects its hatred of Jews unto Israel, which is their undeclared proxy for the Jewish people. This new kind of antisemitism is far more sinister because it hides in the shadows. It hides behind insincere declarations of love for the Jewish people. But I see through its facade."

"Nissim," Stewart said, "criticizing Israel is not antisemitism."

"That is a very disingenuous statement," I said. "When I criticize various policies of the Canadian government, as an example, I'm not denying the right of Canada to exist. But the criticism I see coming from the Left against Israel is to deny its right to exist. That is antisemitism. The Left denies Israel's right to exist only because of Israel's Jewish character. I make no distinction between the right of Israel to exist and the right of the Jewish people to exist. That's where I stand. There is much hatred for Jews in the world."

"Well, and why do you suppose that is?" Stewart smirked and then he pressed his tongue against his left cheek.

I was stunned. For a few seconds I studied his face hoping for a sign that I was wrong in my initial appraisal, but I found none. His question was clearly meant rhetorically. He was making a veiled statement, not asking a sincere question. At that moment I wanted to lunge towards Stewart and slap that smirk off his face, but I restrained myself.

"Stewart, what do you mean by that question?"

Stewart smirked again. "I simply asked you a question. Nothing more."

"Don't you think I know what you meant by that?"

I glanced at the others. The tension in the room was like an unsprung crossbow. That was proof to me they had also understood Stewart's intent.

"Why don't you tell me what you think I meant by that?"

"I think you insinuated Jews deserve this hatred."

"Nissim, I'd be very careful in the accusations and assumptions you make."

June, the email moderator who was also in attendance at the meeting, stepped in because the discussion threatened to get out of hand. I thought it wise to abandon my line of questioning. But at that point I resolved to quit my membership in Kol-Adama. I could no longer stomach its rabid hatred of Israel. I could no longer tolerate the self-hating Jew. The next week I instructed the congregation's treasurer to stop my monthly contribution of eighty dollars automatically withdrawn from my bank account. I resolved to be a voice against Kol-Adama, and since that day I have never attended another Kol-Adama function and I, a Liberal, have completely distanced myself from the Left.

The Dancer And The Wrestler

It was a mostly sunny early November day in 2012. It had rained earlier, but the clouds had now parted and let through the invigorating rays of the sun. Pamela parked the car and we walked across the outdoor visitor's parking lot to the entrance of the building that had been my father's home since the early Nineties. As I walked, I shut my eyes and pivoted my face towards the sun. I savored the comforting heat as the skin of my face vibrated. In the previous week, after much wrangling, I had convinced my father to purchase an electric scooter. He had been wheelchair bound for almost a year due to the car accidents and falls he had sustained over the years. A year earlier he had careened down a hill after disembarking from a bus while on his wheelchair. He suffered severe head trauma.

"Your father is seriously hurt and you should come and see him ASAP," his nurse at Burnaby General Hospital advised me over the phone.

In the following days he was transferred to the Royal Columbian Hospital, his home away from home, and he was put in the Intensive Care Unit. But he recuperated within the next few weeks and released back home. Since 1996 he had sustained half a dozen accidents for which he was hospitalized, sometimes for months at a time, but he maintained a steely determination to be self-sufficient. I helped him to the best of my abilities, or so I convinced myself, but he often refused my offers of help.

"Do you want me to do some food shopping for you?"

"Oh no. I don't need it. I will go to the mall and do my own shopping."

"Are you sure? You're in a wheelchair."

"Yes. Oh yes. I'll take the bus. It's only one bus to Metrotown."

"Why don't you arrange for the HandiDart bus to pick you up?"

"Absolutely not. It's too expensive. I have a free bus pass. Why should I pay those corporate HandiDart crooks?"

"It's a government service, not a public corporation," I reminded him.

His face contorted into a mask of rage and he shook his head with ferocious indignation and flailed his arms. He yelled: "Listen, I don't want to hear it. They're crooks. All of them."

His two greatest self-appointed nemesis were, in his words, the corporate crooks and the politically correct, young punks.

"The dietitians telling us what to eat, the fashion Nazis brainwashing us, the politically correct young punk Lefties polluting our universities." That was his mantra, his manifesto. But he did share with those Leftist young punks a hatred for big corporations.

He lived in a tiny, rent-controlled bachelor apartment in one of

Burnaby's social housing buildings. His ex girlfriend once told me it was a huge improvement over the rat-infested rooms he rented previously, during the years that I could not bear to see him because the pain I felt was unbearable and I ran away from it.

Pamela and I took him to a medical equipment store just a fifteen minute drive away. The electric scooters on display were shiny and tempting, but very expensive.

"I will not pay these exorbitant, outrageous sums," he said.

"You have over $120,000 in the bank just from your ICBC settlement," I reminded him. That was the money he received from the automobile insurance corporation due to his accident on new year's eve 2002. But he had never spent a cent of it. He also saved hundreds of dollars each month from his meager $1200 a month government pension. When you buy bread from the day-old bin, and you buy produce so old its rotting parts must be surgically carved out, then even a meager pension goes a long way. I knew he would die having never enjoyed his money. His money was a comforting blanket reserved for a cold night that would never come. His money was expensive china to be served only to special guests that would never visit. His only luxuries, his passionate wanderlust, were twice a year, months long trips to Thailand and Europe, during which he stayed in ten dollar a day shared-room hostels and broke bread with the native plebeians. But he had not indulged his wanderlust for several years because his health and strength had deteriorated. His spirit was broken and numbed.

"You need this. Don't you want a better quality of life?" I tried to reason with him. "What is your money doing for you in the bank? Do you think you'll live forever?"

"Can you look into buying a second-hand scooter?" He asked. "I don't need any bells and whistles." And then he wheeled himself up to the nearest salesman. The manual wheelchair he borrowed from the Red Cross squeaked. His scrawny arms worked beyond their apparent capacity. "Do you have any used scooters under $200," he asked the salesman.

I had a flashback of those arms scooping me up and playfully tossing me into the pool at the Y in Montreal when I was ten years old. They were strong arms then. I remembered his youthful, handsome face and wavy, dark hair. He was now gaunt and frail. His hair was now snow-white yet still thick and full. I decided to buy him a new scooter and tell him it is a used one. I would make the difference in the cost. I knew my sister and I would inherit his wasted money. I laughed at the tragic irony. Sometimes money is wasted by not spending it. I then had another flashback. It was of my mother asking me, just a year before, why I was not buying myself a car. I had been taking the bus since 2009. I seldom bought myself clothes. I lived well below my means.

"You used to spend so much. Are you becoming cheap like your father? You make enough money for a family of five to live off comfortably."

But I had a plan. I was saving for the time I knew would soon come when I would be jobless and writing my novel, my passion and spiritlust, full-time. That trumped any material comfort or luxury.

After leaving the store we saw a breathtaking double rainbow in the east sky. Raindrops falling from a sun-drenched sky bounced off my face. We stood there, Pamela and I, transfixed for those moments the inner rainbow melted back into the sky. And then the outer rainbow was fading but we turned our backs to it and headed for the car. We ate at McDonald's afterwards. It was across the street from my father's building. I bought him a chicken burger but he could not eat it because he had trouble swallowing that day and for the few days before. But it had now worsened. Upon finishing our meal we dropped him off at his third floor apartment and bid him a good night.

The next day I received a call from the Royal Columbian Hospital. My father was readmitted but he had not fallen or suffered another car accident. He simply could not swallow. At the hospital I learned the head trauma he sustained the year before had damaged the area in his brain that controls swallowing. I saw him being fed through an IV tube.

"He will probably never be able to eat on his own," the doctor informed me. "But we'll have to perform tests to be sure of that."

I visited him at his hospital bedside every evening, but then he took a turn for the worse. I received a call one night from the hospital informing me he had been transferred to the ICU. "Why would he need to be at the ICU for a swallowing issue?" I said.

"He's not here for that," the doctor said when I arrived at the ICU. "He's had a Pulmonary Edema attack."

"I don't know exactly what that is. Sounds to me like a breathing problem. It's caused by the swallowing issue?"

"No, it's not related to that. We think he's contracted some kind of super bug that has compromised his lungs. We're also seeing some kidney impairment. These bugs are common in hospitals. It's probably C. Difficile, but we'll need to perform tests."

I called my sister Linda that night. "I think you should come see your father. It might be your last chance." I knew my father would not die within the next few days, but I wanted to afford my sister enough time to form a relationship with him. That would require at least several weeks. I feared this would be her last chance to have him in her life for that length of time. She had only seen him once during the previous nine years. That was also at the Royal Columbian hospital, in 2003, when she visited him once, after his car accident. He was well recuperated at that point and she clipped his toe nails. Before that night she had no contact with him since 1986, when my mother needed his signature on travel documents that would permit her to travel with my sister to Israel. Linda was only 12 years old then. I took my sister to Kaplan's Jewish Delicatessen in Vancouver where she was introduced to a father she could not remember. She was a month away from her fifth birthday when she had last seen him before that time. It was at the Greyhound bus station in Montreal the day my mother escaped her life with him and took us with her towards an uncertain future. But it was due to a desperation that only cares for escape and does not calculate its consequences, like a woman jumping out of a burning building into the jaws of death.

I craved for Linda to come to know her father during what my inner voice told me were his last weeks. I had always felt intimidated to broach this subject with her but I could not afford now to let my intimidation cheat her out of this final opportunity. I feared she would forever feel a void in her soul and a maddening regret if he dies as a stranger to her. I feared she would forever resent me for having formed a relationship with him, but to never have cared enough to leverage this position by bringing her closer to him.

After his first accident in 1996 he told me of a day, a few years before, when he was at Metrotown mall with a friend and he saw a group of young women walking by.

"One of the girls caught my attention. I told my friend I think the pretty brunette girl in the middle is my daughter, but I wasn't sure."

Due to the vagaries of life he could not be certain if she was his daughter. My heart ached for him and for my sister, and I had to hold back my tears.

It was a rainy, November evening when Linda, her husband Avi and I visited him at the ICU in the Royal Columbian hospital. He was unconscious and we stood at his bedside. Around him, and at the back of his bed, were numerous pieces of monitoring devices beeping and humming and he was hooked to numerous life sustaining tubes for feeding, hydration and breathing. He could not breathe on his own and a tube was lodged deep down his throat.

To pass time I discussed the novella I would soon publish on Amazon. There was a white-board and markers on one of the walls and I wrote the

Tetragrammaton in large letters: YHVH. I explained the meaning of these letters and the message encoded within. I drew curved arrows. The first arrow was on top and it pointed from the first H to the second while the second arrow was on the underside and it pointed from the second H to the first. These arrows represented the tautological feedback loop of the ineffable H. Linda and Avi listened with rapt attention.

"How did you ever think of that?" Avi said.

"I've been thinking about these ideas for many years. I formed these ideas because I've read about Chaos Theory and Gödel Incompleteness."

"I want to read your book."

"This will just be the initial installment. I will later release the full novel and it will go into much more detail about the scientific aspects of my ideas."

The next evening I visited the ICU alone. Linda and Avi could not come because they were preoccupied at Linda's furniture boutique L'Atelier, located at the border of Downtown and the Gastown district. My father was awake. The doctor indicated he would soon be able to breathe on his own, but his inability to eat on his own had not improved. When my father saw me, the dullness in his eyes brightened but he could not speak due to the paraphernalia lodged down his throat.

"Don't try to speak. You gave us all quite a scare, but the doctors said you're improving and you'll soon be able to breathe on your own. They said you have a fantastic will to live."

He nodded as a sign he understood. His eyes showed fear.

I leaned and whispered into his ear: "Do you know who visited you last night?"

He shook his head.

"Linda."

He furrowed his brow and gazed into my eyes. He looked shocked and helpless.

"She couldn't be here tonight, but we'll all be here again tomorrow night. Linda is married now, you know? Her husband is a young Israeli called Avi." He grunted and nodded. I sensed he was happy I shared this with him.

My father was released from the ICU a few days later. He could now breathe on his own. But he still could not eat on his own and most likely would be hooked to feeding tubes for the rest of his uncertain life. I lied to him, I told him he would soon be eating his favorite foods. He talked hungrily of good lamb kebabs and beef stew with those delicious caramelized baby onions he so adored. He rhapsodized of traveling to

The Dancer And The Wrestler

Thailand and Europe upon his release from the hospital. He talked of visiting his soul's delight, his love above all, his cherished Bulgaria, and above all, Sofia, the city of his birth and of his unquenched yearning. I listened to his hopes and dreams but I knew they would never be realized. He yearned to return to his modest apartment that was a king's palace to him, and to live the solitary life that he had known since that day, so many years ago, when we left him like thieves in the night. But it was out of despair that my mother did so. I never doubted the magnanimity of her soul.

Linda and I visited him at the hospital every evening. Avi always accompanied her. At first I had to be there with Linda on her every visit because she did not yet feel comfortable to spend time with him alone. It was a blessing that my father came to know her during his last weeks, not as that distant intellectual abstraction named 'daughter' but instead as a loving and nurturing woman. She tended to his needs and they became accustomed to each other. We then split our visits on alternate days because she was able to be alone with him and caress his pain away.

He was in and out of the ICU those last weeks of his life because the super bugs ravaged his body. There came a night when I visited him alone and he whispered to me that he wanted to die. I had never before heard him give up on life - not during his years living in rat-infested rooming houses and not during his numerous accidents that left him close to death. He always was driven by a compulsion to live. But he knew now he would never eat the beef stew with the delicious baby onions, or the mouth-watering lamb kebabs. He knew now he would never set foot on his beloved Bulgarian soil again. He knew now he would never return to the independence of his tiny apartment. I remembered then a time when I visited him at his apartment a week before he was first rushed to the ICU. He told me then of a dream he had the previous night. His mother Victoria was whispering to him from the beyond. She asked him what he was doing alone in life. She told him it is time for her little boy to return home.

He asked me: "What do you think this dream means?"

I shook my head but I sensed he already understood the verdict of his dream.

Linda offered to rent him a TV during his hospital stay, but he refused. "It's far too expensive," he said. We then lied to him that the hospital provides free rentals for seniors. The last movie he ever saw was the Sound of Music. He was transfixed. This was a movie reminding him of his youth. Later that night he reached out to me and I put my ear to his mouth. I expected him to open his soul to me. I expected him to say he loved my sister and me. I expected him to reflect on the mistakes he had made. I expected him to speak the words of wisdom often revealed to the dying.

His voice was weak and hoarse. He motioned for me to come closer and he spoke into my ear: "Nissim....is my money safe in the bank?"

I don't know why I expected from him an outpouring of fatherly love or deep insights about life and death. He was an afflicted man and he would coddle his affliction into his grave.

His health deteriorated soon after, during his last week he was moaning in pain. I could hear his wails in the hallway as I approached his room. Linda sat by his side for hours and stroked his clammy forehead. His cries of agony were too hard to bear. Linda was in tears. My mother visited him one night but he was delirious. The next day he drifted in and out of consciousness and during fleeting moments of his lucidity Linda told him of our mother's visit. His eyes revealed indescribable fear. He knew his estranged ex wife's visit was an ominous sign. He knew only his imminent death would soften her hardened heart towards him.

During his last two living days he was back at the ICU, but he was administered drugs that would render him unconscious. That was the only way to eliminate his agony. His doctor showed us x-rays confirming his kidneys and lungs were shutting down. He was on life support and Linda and I agreed to pull the plug the next day. On Saturday, January 12, 2013 my mother, Linda, Avi, Pamela and I were outside the ICU. Darnell, Jenna's long time friend, was also there. He had known my father during my years with Jenna and he enjoyed my father's quirkiness and manic energy interspersed with moments of deep wisdom and erudition. Linda entered the ICU first. This was her last time to see him and share her soul with him in her own private way. And then it was my turn. He looked so vibrant. He looked so good. His skin was rosy. His hair was neatly combed. He looked so peaceful. The angel of death was kind to him. I kissed his forehead.

"I tried to be a good son to you abba, but I know I've failed you on many occasions. I wish now I had taken you up on your offer to visit Bulgaria with you. Your body will soon be resting in Vancouver, but your soul that had been so tortured during life will now be at peace in death, and I'm sure it will find its way to your beloved Sofia and be rewarded with eternal peace. Your family is finally back with you. We abandoned you like thieves in the night at that Greyhound bus station so many years ago, but our lives have a funny way of looping back."

I remembered again that day when he told me of his dream about his mother whispering to him from the beyond. Do the dying dream in their

The Dancer And The Wrestler

last moments? Was my grandmother Victoria now whispering to him again during his last moments of life? Was she reaching her hand to him out from that eternal hole in the desert floor, the navel of Creation, and pulling him back in?

I kissed my father's forehead and bid my farewell. The shadow he had cast on this branch of the Tree Of Knowledge Of Good And Evil would now fade away.

My sister and I buried our father in Schara Tzedeck cemetery in New Westminster, a suburb of Vancouver. The cemetery's name is Hebrew for gate of justice. A week after the service I contacted the office for Social Housing and gave notice my father had passed away. I requested to keep his apartment until the end of February. I had to remove his belongings, but I could not bear to enter his apartment and do so yet. The memories were too poignant and searing.

"Of course we can do it for you," Avi said, "but I know you want to be in his apartment when you're ready. We won't leave you out of this, don't worry."

In early February I was ready to enter my father's apartment. The passage of time would temper the trauma, but I realized the experience would be draining. Before I left home for his apartment I cleared the miasma in my spirit by listening to music. As the magic of Pink Floyd seeped out of my computer speakers I sipped from a glass of red wine. Within half an hour I was mellowed and prepared to face the echoes in my father's apartment. But before departing I checked for new emails. I saw an email from Kol-Adama.

When I cut my ties with Kol-Adama in the summer of 2006 I had requested to be removed from the email list, but to no avail. I continued to receive email discussions and announcements. I made repeated requests but I had long ago given up hope of being removed from the email list. My requests were either ignored or the email list administrator did not know how to delete ex members from the list. It is through these emails, and my Google searches, that I learned, with a heavy heart, of rabbi Flesher's downward spiral from a social justice oriented Zionism into rabid hatred of Israel.

I reflected on a time during late 2008 when I received another unsolicited email from Kol-Adama which compelled me to participate in yet another toxic email discussion. It was regarding the Israeli historian and social activist Ilan Pappé. He is a far-Left extremist, a vociferous demonizer of Israel. He had written a book named *The Ethnic Cleansing of Palestine* in which he claims Zionists committed horrific and unprovoked aggression against Palestinians during the War of Independence in 1948 and the years before. He claims Israel is a Nazi-like society. He was to visit Vancouver the next week, March 29th 2008, and to give a talk at the main branch of the public library in downtown Vancouver. As to be expected, Jews For A Just Peace rolled out the red carpet for him. Stewart had formed a strong bond with him and sang his virtues to the Kol-Adama community.

I replied: *"I've done my research on Ilan Pappé and here's what I learned. He is opposed to Israel based on his preconceived agenda instead of any actual hard-nosed scholarship. He has actually stated that precision about the facts is irrelevant. This should raise some very bright red flags about his academic scholarship. He portrays himself as the victim of blacklisting but it is he who attempts to blacklist those who disagree with him about Israel."*

Stewart wrote: *"Nissim, where did you read this?"*

I wrote: *"I've researched various sources and they all corroborate this. One source that comes to mind is Alan Dershowitz."*

Stewart emailed back: *"Nissim, please pay no attention to what Dershowitz claims. He is a Right Wing fanatic."*

I wrote: *"Stewart, I make no claims about Dershowitz. I haven't researched his credibility. But, as I said, multiple sources corroborate his claims regarding Ilan Pappé. So you would have me instead take seriously the claims of Ilan Pappé who is a Left Wing fanatic? Is that who you would substitute for a Right Wing fanatic? It seems to me you also have an ulterior agenda."*

Rabbi Flesher contributed to the discussion but he did not address me directly. He had never addressed me explicitly in these email discussions. *"I've read The Ethnic Cleansing Of Palestine and I find it well researched and argued and I find its scholarship to be beyond reproach. I had no idea the founders of Israel where such murderous psychopaths. It is with a heavy heart that I must accept this truth."*

I replied, also not addressing the rabbi explicitly: *"I don't think any person who supports Ilan Pappe's shoddy scholarship and demonization of Israel can call themselves a Zionist. I would say they are anti-Zionists."*

Towards the end of the email discussion rabbi flesher wrote the following: *"I think all those today who called me an anti-Zionist owe me an apology."*

I was the only one that day who implicitly called him an anti-Zionist. I did not offer him an apology. My silence offered him my contempt.

In 2011 rabbi Flesher posted a Youtube video in which he condoned the Hamas rocket bombardment on the civilians of the Israeli town Sderot.

These were unprovoked rocket attacks on civilians, they were not in response to Israeli military aggression. I remembered then what I had said in that Kol-Adama meeting five years before, during the summer of 2006:

Israel vacated Gaza last year. The Israeli army forcibly removed the Jewish settlers and Israel left behind all the infrastructure intact to be enjoyed by the Arabs living in Gaza. So let's see where that takes us. Let's see if Gaza residents decide to live in peace with Israel now. And I assure you that if this experiment pays dividends then Israel will sooner than later do the same in the Westbank and pull out all the Jewish settlers. But I also assure you that if the Arabs in Gaza waste this opportunity for peace and they bite the hand that offers them an olive branch and autonomy then their fortunes will take a turn for the worse. And Stewart, you will then lose your credibility if you accuse Israel of violating the tenets of social justice spoken by the ancient Hebrew prophets. You will lose all credibility in declaring that Palestinian ill fortunes are not at all self-inflicted.

Rabbi Flesher was condoning unprovoked attacks by Hamas against Israeli civilians. "What's next?" I thought. "Would he condone suicide attacks against Israeli civilians?"

Pink Floyd's song Learning To Fly was playing when I snapped out of my reverie. I opened the Kol-Adama email I received that day. It was from rabbi Flesher and it was addressed to the entire email list. The rabbi was lamenting another failed peace negotiation and he made a startling pronouncement. *"I am no longer a supporter of the idea of the state of Israel. I no longer believe that the existence of Israel is a viable proposition. The opposition to Israel's existence by the surrounding community of nations is unbreakable and as long as Israel continues to exist then only sorrow and death will be the outcome. I can no longer be supportive of the idea of Israel. I repudiate the idea of Zionism as it is known today and I look forward to a time that the dissolution of Israel will bring forth a multi-cultural and pluralistic society within the borders of what is today known as Israel and including Gaza and the Occupied Territories."*

"So it is done," I thought. "His downward spiral into the abyss of anti-Zionism is complete and I'm vindicated. I said he was an anti-Zionist back in 2008 and he has proclaimed himself explicitly as such today. His charade is no more."

I did not feel a need to reply to his statements. I had moved on from concerning myself with this man's anti-Israel ramblings.

The Dancer And The Wrestler

Pamela came into the office. "How much longer are you going to be just sitting there listening to music? You need to get going soon."

Pamela offered to accompany me to my father's apartment. "I want to support you. I know this is still difficult for you."

"I appreciate your support. But when we get there can you give me half an hour to be alone with him in the apartment. Avi and Linda will be there around six."

"Sure, I can go to the Starbucks across the street."

Indeed, I was still traumatized. During the last days of my father's life Avi videotaped him in the hospital. I was in the room during the taping. My father was delirious in his last few days of consciousness. "Nissim, what's happening with me? I'm so confused. I don't understand."

After his funeral, Avi offered to show me the video but I declined. I could not bear to see my father in that hapless state. I wanted to internalize and control my memories of him. I refused to allow an impersonal, external medium to choreograph my dance with his death.

Avi and Linda arrived an hour later. I had my opportunity to sit in silent reflection on the makeshift sofa on which I sat during the years when I visited him. The "sofa" was an old, discarded car seat my father implored me to help him salvage. This was in 1997, a year after his first accident. The previous day he had spotted the car seat two blocks from his building, next to a hardware store garbage bin. It was a light blue bench style car seat common in early Seventies cars. He was still mobile and strong in those days and he was able to help me carry it for the two blocks to his building and up to his third floor apartment via the elevator. It was tiring work and puzzled bystanders on the street glared at us. But, unlike me, he was oblivious to them. That became his sofa to the end.

"Let's get to work," Avi said.

"This place is a disaster," Linda said.

This was her first time in his apartment. She confided to me later that she was overcome with disgust and pity at his living conditions. It was only then she came to know his world.

"As small as this place is we'll never get everything done today," I said.

"Let's start with packing all his stuff in boxes," Linda said.

We rummaged through his drawers and closets and we found photo albums and stacks of photographs wrapped in grocery plastic bags. I knew these must be old pictures because he stopped collecting grocery plastic bags years before that time, when stores started charging five cents per bag. We looked through the pictures and I felt as if I was invading a privacy he had kept under lock and key. I entered a world he had kept to himself during the living years, and I was introduced to a father I did not recognize.

Avi exploded in laughter. "Look at this one," he passed me the picture. It was of my father at the beach with the right side of his face pressed against the large, turgid, naked breasts with blossoming nipples of a young, attractive woman who I did not recognize. He sported a devilish grin and two thumbs up. I had never seen him so content, and for a second I felt a strange sense of jealousy because he had never shown such joy around me. But then I felt a resentment both for allowing this picture to influence me this way and towards him for never having experienced the fatherly joy and contentment a son craves from his father. The picture was taken in Vancouver's famous clothing-optional Wreck Beach. He appeared to be in his mid fifties and beaming with joy and peace. Both my father and his nubile friend where only visible form the torso and up, but I knew they were both completely nude.

When my father followed me and my sister to Vancouver, two years after I abandoned him at the Greyhound bus station in Montreal, he could not secure employment and he quickly settled into a life of collecting welfare and rummaging for bottles and cans. Those were the years when I mostly avoided him because his plight was too painful for me and I did not have the material resources to help him. He was an afflicted man and could not navigate the web of interpersonal relationships that form the tapestry of most people's sojourn from cradle to grave. I learned during the years of our estrangement that he was frequenting Wreck Beach and living his Summer days there, before the unavoidable Fall. He sold beer, collected bottles and cans and dropped off the face of the Civilization of Man. And my heart so ached for him and I could not bear to see him or think of him in those days because the pain that shot through my spirit was too intense and I would have rather suffered the superficial pain of my flesh than a pain emanating from my aching depths. The agony of the body is soon forgotten after it subsides, but agony of the soul can never be forgotten - only accepted in the same way impending death is accepted but never forgotten.

I devoured his photographs that day because they revealed to me my father's joy for life during those dark years that my spirit ached because of his supposed plight. Photograph after photograph revealed to me how tightly integrated he became within a community of like-minded souls. His joy for life was forged in a manner I could not have appreciated nor understood during those distant years, but that I now understood were his halcyon times. With each additional photograph, as the piles of discovery outgrew the piles of mystery, I began to understand how he wove the tapestry of his interpersonal relationships on that seashore cherished by society's castaways. And it was in my father's apartment, shortly after his death, that Yahvah revealed to me my father's soul and I came to know that he was a God Dancer, not a God Wrestler. It was by Yahvah's whispers oozing out of the primordial ground deep in my being that I came to understand the distinction between God Wrestling and God Dancing.

The inner whispers, like an ethereal gossamer spider's web, reached out to me: "Nissim, your father did forge a relationship with me. But I did not appear to him as the god of Church, Synagogue or Mosque. I did not appear to him as a god of convention or tradition nor as a god of pomp and circumstance. I did not appear to him as the god of Abraham, Isaac and Jacob. Nissim, I danced with your father and he danced with me all his life. To those with whom I dance I appear as exquisite poetry, as the most beautiful melody or as the wind caressing a flowery meadow and rustling through the branches of a mighty oak. To your father I appeared as wanderlust. His heart burst with giddy anticipation for the faraway lands of his desire and discovery. It is in those faraway shores that I danced with him. And I also danced with him on that Vancouver seashore. I was the collector of cans and bottles looking for his next meal. I was the bohemian Hippie shedding my clothes as proxies for society's conventions and artifices. And they each dance to the rhythm of their own soul and then they dance the dance of dances amongst each other. There are those who crave to wrestle with me and there are those, like your father and his soul mates on that castaway seashore, who crave to dance with me."

I now understood that my father was an ontological Hippie, though he would have been loath to admit during the living years what he was now admitting to me in death. And I understood what it is to be a Hippie - it is a dance with god. God Wrestling is a creative process, it bursts out of the white-eyed womb. It is soul-piercing music emanating from unthinking musical notes. God Wrestling is humanity's banishment from the garden. It is an unprovable theorem bursting out of the confinement of the system of its birth. It is Creation exploding out of the broken shards of ineffable divinity and into the world of space and time and then beyond. It is the Tree of Knowledge bursting out of the core of Primordial Man - Adam Kadmon. But when you dance with god you mend the broken shards of divinities and you return to the white-eyed womb of Creation. The Dance and the Wrestle co-exist. The Wrestler creates the painting and he that gazes upon it then falls into the Dance. The Wrestler creates the soul-piercing novel formed by an interrelated network out of unthinking words, each word flavoring all other words and being flavored back in turn, and she that reads the novel then begins the Dance. And god reaches out from within the novel's hidden chamber, a chamber common to us all, and whispers to you and invites you to join your outstretched finger with his. You cannot dance with that which was not created by a Wrestler. You cannot wrestle with that which can never allow for the Dance.

God Wrestling is a thinking process. God Dancing is an unthinking. God Wrestling is climbing out of the hole in the desert floor. God Dancing is leaping head-first back in. God Dancing is Zen. It is peeling off the artichoke layers and drawing spiritual nourishment from the innermost heart. My father achieved Zen on that castaway seashore and at the faraway lands of his wanderlust. My father was a God Dancer - he refused to eat the fruit from the Tree of the Knowledge Good and Evil. My father never felt at home with Judaism because it is a wrestling relationship with the divine. And that is why the Third Age will emanate from the Strange Attractor of the Hebrews, because the emergent emanates from God-Wrestling as it does from the self-negating Gödel sentence. The Eastern religions are God Dancing religions, and I suspect my father would have felt a kinship had he explored them.

I understood then that my calling is to bring together those that Wrestle and those that Dance. I understood then what the legacy of my novel must become. My father was a citizen of a different realm but it was a realm deep inside the hole in the desert floor, yet I was seeking a desert floor beyond. I was a Wrestler but he was a Dancer. But then I knew I must become a Wrestler who wrestles with the Dance and dances with the Wrestle. I must become a Meta Wrestler. I must become a Meta Dancer. I must become a Meta Theist.

A year after his death, in accordance with Jewish custom, we installed our father's tombstone. It was during that day in my father's apartment, shortly after his death, that my eyes were opened to his mystery, his zeitgeist, and when, months later, Linda asked me what his epitaph should be I knew the answer without a doubt. If you visit Schara Tzedeck cemetery in New Westminster and walk to his grave-site near the southwestern corner, you will see the epitaph inscribed on his tombstone. It says:

In Loving Memory Of
Shmuel (Samuel) Levy
Son Of Nissim And Victoria Levy
He Was A Citizen Of A Different Realm
And Is Forever In Our Hearts

The Story Unfolds

By October of 2013 I realized I had to pull my novella from Amazon. I had two reasons for doing so: it was selling abysmally and it was not communicating my expansive vision. The handful of reviews I received made that clear. This failure was not due to poor writing but instead to brevity of writing. My literary and spiritual program was ambitious, but my nuanced and layered writing begged for the wide-open spaces of a larger literary work. Only then would it be able to spread its wings and soar into the heart, mind and soul of the reader. Only then would the pieces that had all fallen into place in my mind be likewise mirrored in the reader's mind. Only then would readers peer deep into the navel of my soul and see themselves gazing back up and they would understand that my soul is also theirs.

Hardly a soul knew about my novella, and those that did, be they friend or stranger, did not understand my vision and agenda. My novella revealed the meaning of YHVH but it went unheeded. My novella heralded a momentous event in the Civilization of Man, the Third Age, but no one paused for thought or understood the scope of my message.

My meager marketing plan consisted only of what I called Piggy Backing. I would promote my novella by responding to reviews of other spiritually themed eBooks or physical books on Amazon. I would ask reviewers of such books as The Alchemist, Jonathan Livingston Seagull and The Celestine Prophecy to buy my novella. Some did buy it. It was priced at only ninety-nine cents, but even on the best of days I only sold a handful of copies. However, I only received one review from these purchasers. Did they even read it?

I occasionally suffered the wrath of a reviewer or commenter bemoaning my hijacking of the review thread for my own promotion. On occasion Amazon deleted my purchase requests. Was I wrong to leverage reviews of other books for the promotion of my own? Certainly. Why did I do it? Desperation. It was not sustainable.

On September 29th, 2013 I was looking through my book page on Amazon when I spotted a review not there the day before. It rated my novel a four out of five stars. My heart raced with joy, more for the rarity of a review than for the favorable rating. I read the review under those glowing four stars. It was written by a Jennie Sorrel:

The author asked me to read this novella. He has a masterful command of the English language and his concepts are complex and evolved. The book is written in a story form but the subject is for conversation among deep thinking persons for a late night discussion on the evolution of spiritual beliefs. The story is the vehicle the author uses to convey the message but almost detracts from the complex thinking. I will read it again and only rate it this way because I am still thinking about the message.

That was my third review and the only one from a stranger. But it was nevertheless a review I had solicited. I was still waiting for my first unsolicited review.

When I finally made the decision to remove my novella from Amazon, it was with hope, not despair. It was with excitement, not helpless resignation. It was with unbridled enthusiasm for what is to follow. I was brimming with joy because I knew I had to expand my novella into a more mature work that better conveys my spiritual and scientific vision. I was excited to resume the art of weaving words into a tapestry of ideas and poetic musings that would uplift not just my spirit, as their writer, but also the spirit of the reader. And when I imagined the reader in my mind's eye, overwhelmed by the sheer beauty of ideas and poetry, I was overcome with a cathartic frisson that further intensified my spirit's uplifting.

I remembered the waves of joy cascading over me when I wrote the first four chapters, particularly the indelibly imprinted feelings of catharsis triggered by the writing of passages such as the following passage in the chapter named Maturity:

This epiphany was an unexpected visitor and when it came knocking on my door I greeted it as a lover I had only ever known in the recesses of the soul and who now appeared before my very eyes as flesh and blood. This epiphany was a rose bush whose seed I planted long ago and which now burst the earth after a long and arduous winter in the unknowing, white-eyed womb of Creation. And when I reached for its tempting yet thorny flower I felt a piercing pain shooting through my spirit and I came face to face with the awe-full one, the great El-Shaddai, the principle of creation, the great veiled One, the Truth overflowing my cup. Deep in the soul an unspeaking voice woke from an eternal slumber and I at once came to know that land to which I had always felt a kinship, that realm of which I am a citizen, always will be and always have been.

Years before, when I first conceived of writing a novel, I intended to release my work as one book. Then in late 2012 I learned of the ease of publishing an eBook on Amazon, and I became impatient and wanted to release my work sooner than later. By that time I only had the first four chapters, which I wrote in early 2006. These chapters were about the childhood of Abraham, then known as Abram, in the city of Ur. I set out to complete this story and to then write a short final chapter, set in modern times, which cocoons all previous chapters like nested dolls, or a mirror within a mirror within another. This final chapter was to introduce the notion of the Third Age - paradigm shifting as a leitmotif of the Civilization of Man. What emerged was a novella of about thirty-one thousand words - almost a hundred pages. I had decided to partition my novel into novella sized chunks of which this would be the first.

I had always wanted to sing because that would expose my spirit to others. However, I do not have the voice for it. But through my writing I could do that. I could expose the nooks and crannies of my spirit, and when the reader saw it bare and vulnerable she would know we share a soul, we all share the same soul, and she would wonder, for a brief moment of spiritual clarity, why she never saw that before. That is the meaning of art - the dispelling of the illusion of the separation of souls. Great art exposes the world for the way it really is. For those who have hardened their souls to great art, it appears as a chimera of Reality because they are only accustomed to the shadows on the cave's wall.

It was Saturday on a bright and hot early September. Pam and I were sitting on the his-and-hers couches in the family room. I was sipping my obligatory morning coffee - strong with a hint of cream and no sugar. Pam does not drink coffee in the morning, but she craves it at night. My then fourteen year old cat Ginger was perched on my lap. Her Rocky Road ice cream fur was warm due to the sun's strong light streaming through the large windows.

"I forgot to tell you," I said, "I have a three o'clock meeting with Andrew on Friday."

"Who?"

"You know, Andrew at AquaFlow, about buying out my contract from Banichex."

"Oh, OK. Finally," Pam said. "And tell him to be firm."

I had been a self-employed consultant at AquaFlow since March of 2011. I developed water engineering related software. Banichex was the headhunter firm that connected me with AquaFlow, and it collected a percentage off my hourly rate. I had long ago become dissatisfied with this arrangement. I longed for the opportunity to sever ties with Banichex and collect one hundred percent of the hourly rate paid by AquaFlow for my

The Story Unfolds

services. But that required paying Banichex a buyout fee.

"It will all boil down to how much Banichex wants for the buyout."

"How much are you willing to pay?"

"Well, they're taking seventeen bucks per hour off the top."

"Wow, that's a big chunk, and they've been collecting this for the last three years."

"Yeah, almost three years. Next march will be three years. Well, the first year I was getting fifty-five per hour and they were getting seventy-five from AquaFlow."

"When will this status change take place?"

"It's early September now, so I think reasonably by November 1st."

"AquaFlow will then pay you directly seventy-seven per hour?"

"That's my plan. I hope so."

"You didn't answer. How much are you willing to pay for the buyout?"

"well, a seventeen per hour differential is like making about, hmm...let's see..." I pulled out my phone from my pocket and punched in the numbers into the calculator. "Conservatively, working only forty-five weeks per year at forty hours per week it amounts to an extra $30,600 per year. Now, I know I'll have to pay tax off that but it's still a sizable chunk of extra income. I can pay half of that and feel good about it."

"You're going to cut Banichex a cheque for fifteen grand?"

"I'll try to go under that, but even that's worth it to get them off my back. Don't you think? And I'll still be considerably ahead financially. But there's something else I'm thinking about."

"What's up?"

"It's my book. I'm going to deactivate it from Amazon."

"What? You worked so hard on it. All that grief and sweat. And what does that have to do with Banichex?"

"Oh no, I haven't given up on it. Quite the contrary."

"I don't understand."

"It's not selling," I said.

"I thought you're doing great with the Piggy Backing."

"No, that's peanuts. I've come to the conclusion my idea about releasing a bit at a time isn't working the way I planned. As the book stands now, it's not enough to get the snowball rolling. The few people who've read it just aren't getting it. And it's not their fault. A hundred pages isn't gonna cut it."

"You're going to write a full novel before releasing it again?"

"Not the whole thing. Maybe half. I'll be shooting for a couple hundred pages. It lets me flesh out more of my ideas and more convincingly set the stage for the second half."

The Story Unfolds

One of my dissatisfactions was with the abrupt way I capped the story of Abraham's childhood. The last chapter pertaining to his childhood is called 'Address To The Examining Reader' and its intent is to create the self-referential aspect of the story - a story talking about itself, like a set of nested mirrors. It achieves this goal well enough, but I suspected then that the readers felt cheated because I had not revealed the consequences of young Abram's actions in defying the religious establishment of Ur. An ex colleague who had reviewed my novel on Amazon remarked that it left the consequences to the reader's imagination. He wasn't satisfied with that.

"So how long are you going to keep it deactivated?" Pam said.

"Ideally I'd like more time to write. Working full-time makes that difficult. It's too difficult writing after a full day of pushing my brain to the limit creating software."

"You've done OK so far. Haven't you?"

"I'd still like more time to focus on my writing. Weekends aren't enough. I'm going to try to reduce my hours. I'll talk to Andrew about it. That, by the way, is what Banichex has to do with this. I figure that even if I just work at sixty percent capacity, I can still make more than enough at seventy-seven per hour. How would you feel about that?"

Pam flicked her long and thick wavy black hair off her shoulders. She has wavier hair than the typical Chinese woman. "That's fine. It's up to you. Your mom might not like it though."

"Never mind. My mom doesn't understand this is my passion. When I'm on my deathbed I don't want to look back on my life and regret I didn't pursue writing my book."

"Your mom is just worried about you."

"Yeah, I know. I shouldn't be too hard on her." I got up slowly, letting Ginger jump off my lap. "Let's go for a walk up to Enchanted Forest. I need to burn off calories after last night's huge meal with your parents."

Enchanted Forest is a term I coined for the forest on top of Capitol Hill. Pam and I live in a two-level house at the foot of the hill. The twenty minute steep walk up to the summit is a challenge we often crave, and as we make our way up the verdant neighborhoods that speckle the side of the hill we are rewarded with breathtaking, lofty views sprawling at our feet. They are views of the downtown Vancouver skyline, Stanley Park, the Lions Gate bridge, the North Shore and other adjacent suburbs.

***

It was three PM on Friday when I climbed the stairs to Andrew's second floor office. He was sitting at his desk. His right shoulder pinned the phone to his ear as he entered numbers into a Spread Sheet. He motioned for me to take a seat while he informed the person at the other end of the line that he would be calling them back in half an hour.

"How's your day so far?" Andrew said.

"Very busy. This is a nice break from the grind."

"What are you working on?"

"I'm creating a new formula for the Calculation Engine."

"Jaxon has you working hard, I see."

"No complaints," I said.

"So we're here to discuss your relationship with Banichex. Before we get into that...well as you know we've reduced our projects going forward. You know we haven't extended Bryan's contract?"

"Yes, he told me last week. What does that mean for me?" I was worried they were going to terminate my contract.

"I'll get to the point. We don't have enough work to keep you full-time."

"How much work do you have?"

"It's hard to say. We have five-hundred hours of development budget that we can commit to right now for 2014."

"That's about a quarter of full-time. But there could be more, right?"

"Sure, that's always a good possibility. We just can't guarantee you more than that."

I thought: "This is pure serendipity. This is exactly my wish and it has landed in my lap. Could this be a sign the time is ripe for my book? Is this the beginning of the convergence of my destiny?"

"I'm amenable to working part-time," I said. "This is a good turn of events for me. I'm writing a book and I could use the extra time for my writing."

Andrew adjusted his black-rimmed glasses and then ran his bony, slender fingers through his short, dark hair. "A book, really? What are you writing?"

"It's a spiritually themed novel. The overarching theme is the convergence of science and religion."

"Really? That's a fascinating topic. I have somewhat of an interest in these things. Where are you with it?"

"It's on Amazon right now as an eBook. It's only at around a hundred pages, but I'll be deactivating it and expanding it soon."

"I'd love to discuss your book and learn more about your ideas, but unfortunately I'm too busy today."

"Perhaps some other time."

"What's your book called?"

I told him.

Andrew nodded. "That's a great name. If you're fine with working part-time then that could work out well for both of us. We'd like to keep you. You do good work."

"And this brings us to Banichex," I said. "If I only work part-time I'd like to keep more of what you're paying for me."

"Naturally," Andrew said.

"I don't know how the logistics will work with Banichex. What's the buyout percentage right now?"

"We're at eight percent now. It won't go down anymore."

"But If I don't even know how many hours I'll be working then how can we even calculate the buyout?"

"That's an excellent question. I'll be calling them tomorrow to discuss the logistics."

We drilled down into the details and compiled a short list of questions to ask Banichex.

"I'll let you know when I learn more from them," Andrew said.

"OK, I'll be getting back to work then."

I got up and shook Andrew's hand.

"And good luck with your book."

On Friday, November 1st my part-time tenure at AquaFlow started. I did not have a set weekly schedule. My work was project based. I would work full-time when AquaFlow had projects for me.

I worked full-time the first week but I was able to devote the following week to my novel. My first task was too deactivate my novella from Amazon, and then I began the long trek towards completing my expanded novella. I envisaged adding an extra fifty or sixty pages. I thought at that length the novella would be commercially viable and allow me to include just enough of my ideas of the convergence of science and divinity to compel the reader to anticipate its sequel. I planned on a late February or early March re-release on Amazon. I did not imagine that by the time I finished, it would be another two and a half years and I would have a novel of over a hundred and eighty thousand words.

The first task on my agenda was to add more dialog to the first chapter. In late August of 2013, a week after I initially released my novella on Amazon, I participated in Amazon's online writer's community. I sought feedback on my novella, but also a general sense of camaraderie with fellow self-published writers. I wanted to sharpen my writing skills and learn more about marketing a self-published novel. My experiences were mixed. I had the pleasure of communicating with a small number of helpful writers who provided constructive criticism. Unfortunately, I encountered far too many mean-spirited people who reveled in offering biting criticism devoid of any constructive content, and who rejoiced in predicting the failure of my novella and accusing me of a complete lack of writing skills. Others offered simplistic recommendations. I received an opinion about the cover:

I really think you need more ziggurats. I mean, ziggurats is showing up a lot when I scan the look inside. You should definitely have that as a keyword.

Only the first paragraph mentioned a ziggurat and the book blurb said nothing about ziggurats. There was no reasonable basis for any reader to surmise my book is about ziggurats.

Others accused me of writing my own reviews because they claimed all my reviewers used 'big words'. When I replied, perhaps facetiously in kind, that my novella is attracting a more literate reader, I was rebuked with 'I highly doubt it'.

I was asked what the premise of my book was. I replied the overarching message is that god is a self-referencing Reality. I was ridiculed instead of being asked to elaborate:

A what? This forum is becoming an intensive care unit for premature books.

I did not understand that comment in the context of my book's overarching premise, but it clearly was not meant in the spirit of constructive criticism. I came to realize the Amazon writer's community is not a nurturing place for me. This was not only due to the proliferation of mean-spirited people but also to the subject matter and agenda of my book. I did not write about vampire romances. I did not write about sex. I wrote a philosophical novella that diverged from the often formulaic, purely plot driven character of the bulk of eBook Fiction sold on Amazon, or at the very least of those writers responding to me in the online community.

Within a couple of weeks after I began my odyssey in the online community I decided to never return. Perhaps I was too sensitive to the harshness of others. Perhaps that is the pill one must swallow when grasping for success in any field under the public spotlight. But everyone is

The Story Unfolds

a product of their life experiences and mine were defined by opportunistic psychological bullying in my childhood, teens and early twenties, that I suffered from my peers. The Amazon community forced my face into the toilet bowl of those painful years in the school yard, the halls of high school, the Canadian military reserves, and numerous other bumps along my life's path. I felt as if a menacing, opportunistic colony of Army ants had engulfed me and was tearing, without a shred of mercy, the flesh from my bones. I wanted out.

I did benefit from more nurturing souls who offered constructive criticism. I learned how to properly punctuate dialog and I was receptive to the criticism that my book cover did not reflect its spiritual tone. The cover was of a pair of hands holding a Kindle Reader. Within this Kindle Reader appeared another pair of hands also holding a Kindle Reader. The inner image was an exact copy of the outer image, and this nesting continued for several iterations. The book cover mirrored the message of the book that divinity is a self-referencing phenomenon. It mirrored the meaning of YHVH, which is a central theme of my book. It also alluded to the self-referencing nature of Abram's composition within my book; the composition that contains itself as its own subject. The message is the medium. The final chapter was set in modern times, and it was aware of itself and the context of the previous chapters because it nested them all within itself. The reader was invited to imagine his or her own hands grasping their own Kindle showing the nested Kindles. In this way the book reached into the real world and became an entity not within a fictional world but within the reader's own world. The book confused the barrier between Fiction and Reality, like a pop-up book exploding from a fantasy world into a child's world, like the universe exploding from the Big Bang, like Adam and Eve ejected from the white-eyed womb of Eden into the harsh world of space and time.

I acquiesced to criticism that my first chapter is a narrative used as an information dump. I did not agree it contained no other redeeming qualities, but I did see how it could benefit from dialog and storytelling that add more expressive and evocative brush strokes to the legend and atmosphere I painted. The next day I added dialog between Abram, his siblings and his father. I painted with words an evocative picture of military chariots engulfing their enemies like Army ants engulfing their prey.

I left my home office and walked into the family room. A cooking competition was on TV. "Pam, I just finished my enhancement to the first chapter. Can you give me your opinion?"

The Story Unfolds

Pam was curled on the couch. Ginger was standing on her lap. Pam was brushing Ginger's fur in continuous strokes from top of head to base of tail and also from the sides of her face and along the sides of her body. Ginger craned her neck upwards trying to lick Pam's face and her purrs sounded like a sports card strumming along the spokes of a child's bicycle barreling downhill.

"Can you print it out?" Pam said.

Pam always wanted a printout when I asked her to read passages from my novella. I was prepared this time. I handed her a twelve page printout. The remainder of the first chapter was unchanged since her previous reading. She read it silently while I made myself a grilled-cheese sandwich.

When I took the first bite of the grilled-cheese Pam said: "Yeah, I see where you went with this, I love the part about the Army ants. It's such an intense metaphor. I really like your changes. It makes me want to read more."

"What about the dialog?"

"It's good I think, but there's one place where I don't like your word choice."

I plopped next to Pam. Ginger stopped purring and gave me a stare that would freeze fire. "Where?"

"When Haran and Abram speak to their father they use the word 'dad'. That sounds too modern."

"That's exactly what people told me on the Amazon online community."

Pam was silent.

"So I guess I'd better change it," I said. "My thinking was that using the word 'father' sounds too formal. No child would talk like that. Someone suggested 'pa' instead. Does that sound more like how children of the ancient world would speak?"

"That's much better. Someone else already read this?"

"A few days ago, before I finished these changes, I had people in the Amazon writer forums read it. I already had that part written by then."

"When are you starting to add new chapters?"

"Next week. Before that I'll be doing one more small enhancement to one of the other chapters."

"But what will your first new chapter be about?"

"It will be about Abram's old age."

"Oh cool, he's a kid and then he becomes an old man. That's an interesting transition."

"And I also need to rewrite, or maybe even just throw out the last chapter and start from scratch."

"Why? You told me Avi liked it. Don't let Carl intimidate you."

My brother-in-law Avi read my novella shortly after I published it on Amazon. Both Carl and my ex-wife Jenna remarked the last chapter was the weakest, but Avi did not share that opinion. Carl was explicit in his condemnation. He objected to the message of that chapter. The message being that the ideas I would teach in the sequel to my novella would change the world.

"No, it's not just him," I said. "I've had doubts about that chapter since I wrote it. Not for the same reason Carl pointed out. I do believe these ideas will change the world. I just think the chapter is too rushed and anti-climactic."

The last chapter told of a coming age of enlightenment I call the Third Age. I explained it will be the culmination of the covenant between Abraham and the I AM that I describe in the, at that point yet unwritten, chapter of my novella called 'The Navel Of Creation: A Loop In Eternity'. The following is an excerpt pertaining to the Third Age from the last chapter of my novella as it was then:

My iterations will crash upon humanity's shore as do the crashing ocean waves upon a crumbling sandy shore. I AM the Third Age. I AM the long awaited Messianic Age. I AM the promise on the lips of the Hebrew prophets. In me humanity will come to a deep understanding of what God is. In me Humanity will come to a deep understanding of what it is. Humanity will shed its puerile notions of divinity and come to a deeper and more sophisticated understanding.

The iterations referred to the yet unwritten sequels of the novella. I did not distinguish between these sequels and the intellectual and spiritual paradigm shift which is the Third Age. I described the narrator as the Third Age itself. Did I believe that my novella and its sequels would change the world? About that I had troubling doubts, but never about the foundational ideas. I questioned my sanity in believing I could light a bonfire of passion in others and subscribe them to my lofty agenda. My grasp faltered and I lost resonance with my demons of self-doubt.

I am not a charismatic man in the traditional sense. I do not possess the thin veneer of all-purpose charisma. I cannot sell ice to Eskimos nor sand to Bedouins. I cannot compel others to accept a message I have not passionately accepted myself, otherwise the attraction would be to the person and not the message. The attraction would be an idolatrous relationship with the leader of the paradigm shift. But I felt a certainty the ideas I espoused would change the world. These ideas were not my own. They gushed from the implicate order - the collective soul. Since my childhood a voice had whispered from the semantic spaces at my core. It was always there, in the background behind the shadows on the wall. I had tapped into a well and its waters quenched and invigorated me, but the well was there for all.

The paradigm shift creates the leader. The leader does not create the paradigm shift. The leaf is the reason for the tree. The leader of a paradigm shift has but to push the opportune stone atop a mountain and the ensuing chain reaction will cascade mighty boulders and the mountain will be forever changed. But the instability has to pre-exist. No person can carry these boulders down the mountain. When the Civilization of Man is pregnant with a paradigm shift then the time is ripe for an agent of change to induce the birth. But no one person does the impregnation, it is the collective whole.

If the Civilization of Man would take no heed of my words then another would take the mantle of leadership and proclaim these same words. If the words I proclaim were to echo into an empty desert then I would welcome the desert as my home and instead honor these words coming from the mouth and pen of another. Perhaps the Third Age will favor a more enticing public speaker, a velvety voiced serpentine. Or perhaps it will favor the transparent simplicity which is mine. Is there another out yonder, voicing the same thoughts, convictions and the same fears, but it is I who will steal his or her thunder? Are there others offering their bounty to the whisperer within their soul but it is my offering which will be favored above all? It matters not who the leader will be. Only the coming paradigm shift is of import. The convergence of science and divinity as one voice. The Third Age - that is the good news for all.

In mid November, 2013 I bought a laptop. I intended to expand my writing venues to libraries, coffee shops and, during the warm months, to outdoor patios, beaches, parks and mountain tops. I fancied myself the sophisticated urbanite, composing his literary masterpiece in the style of Hemingway drawing inspiration from the buzz of humanity around the coffee shops of Paris, or of finding my own Walden's Pond as did Thoreau.

It was a late November early afternoon. Pam and I were hiking through the densely forested trails of Burnaby Mountain. It is just a ten minute drive from Capitol Hill. At the top sits Simon Fraser University, as a king does on his throne.

"I'm thinking about joining a writer's group?"

The Story Unfolds

"Yeah, go for it. Is it an online group?"

"I'm thinking of joining a brick and mortar group, but now that you mention it, I should try an online group too."

I was craving contact with the literati. I wanted to immerse myself in the literary experience and to parse it, but also to perceive it as an undivided whole. I longed to be a reader seeing the writer as the writer sees himself reflected off the reader's eyes. I longed to be a writer seeing the reader as the reader sees herself reflected off the writer's eyes.

"Have you researched which groups are out there?"

"You know that place on Main Street we went with Kian a couple of years ago?"

Kian was a high school friend with whom I had lost touch in 1991. In October of 2011 I attended my thirty-year high school reunion, the first reunion I had ever attended, and I connected with him again. For the few months prior to the reunion I subscribed to its website but had no intention of attending. When I learned through the website that Kian would be attending I committed to attending myself and rekindling our friendship.

"Yeah, vaguely. I don't even remember where it was. What was it called?" Pam said.

"Cottage Bistro at 29th and Main."

"Right, now I remember. Have you heard from Kian since that time?"

"I haven't contacted him and he hasn't contact me."

After the reunion I had grave doubts about reviving my friendship with Kian. Around him I felt engulfed in the miasma of a time long ago - my awkward days in high school and the following decade. I was again that pimply, frizzy-haired social outcast because he tended, perhaps without malice, to remind me of that in both words and actions. Throughout my adulthood I struggled to only look to the future as a drowning man only looks up towards air and never towards the murky depths of his despair. I could ill afford to be thwarted by a jetsam of my past.

"Cottage Bistro seems to be one of the literary hot-spots in Vancouver. They have Open Mike nights. I'll be able to read passages from my novella to an audience."

"Can you do it? You won't get nervous?"

"If I want to be a successful writer and spread the word about my vision of the Third Age then I have to suck it up and read in front of an audience, don't you think?" I laughed. "There's also another group that meets at Cottage Bistro called The Writer's Studio. They don't have Open Mikes. I'll have to make a request to do a reading and hope to be selected, but I can always attend the readings."

The Story Unfolds

We crossed an area of the trail with unobstructed views of the Burrard Inlet waters far below and of the rugged North Shore mountains far beyond, their desolate peaks entombed in snow. Across the waters was the district of Deep Cove, like a sparkling emerald gemstone. In the distance I spotted the cliff at the top of the trail I hiked a few years before. After the hike I sat on that cliff and I felt frightened because the waters seemed so far below. But from my current perspective it looked like a pygmy amongst giants and I could not fathom how previously it appeared to me so tall. The breathtaking beauty of the view overwhelmed me. The wide open spaces appeared more remote than the stars at night. We leaned against the fence separating us from a mortal tumble down the steep, tree-covered cliff, and I gazed at the majesty before us, soaking it in and trying to no avail to grasp its grandeur.

I turned my gaze to Pam when I could no longer probe any deeper into the spiritual layers of meaning this panoply had for me. "I'm not going to look into these literary groups just yet. I need to write some more. I need to follow this literary arc and see where it takes me."

"Don't wait too long. You don't have to finish the book first, do you? This will be good for you. You've been writing in isolation for far too long."

"I know and I won't wait for long. I just need another few weeks of solid writing. I've been granted an opportunity to devote more of my time to write, to immerse myself in the book without distractions. For the next few weeks I need to see where that takes me."

I paused and noticed the dwindling daylight. "The days are getting too short. Just in the past hour it's gotten a lot darker. Let's head back before we have to walk through the woods in complete darkness."

On a drizzly, late November afternoon I slid my new laptop into the laptop bag Pam's mother bought me for my birthday the month before. It had three zippered compartments and within two of the compartments were nested compartments for holding notepads, cellphones, pens and the like. I filled these compartments. I felt a satisfaction from cocooning within my elegantly stitched bag the instruments of my literary and spiritual aspirations. My agenda for the evening was to begin a new story arc in my novella - the story of Abram's later years as an old man still on his life's trajectory to know his god and close the loop of his life's arc.

My evening's destination was Cafe Divano, a coffee shop in the south side of Hastings street, just a fifteen minute walk from my house. I slung the laptop bag over my right shoulder and braved the evening drizzle. It

The Story Unfolds

was only five PM and already it was dark. Is Daylight Standard Time not an insult to the injury of days already too short?

When I entered the coffee shop it was humming with the sounds of laughter, of hushed conversations and of not so hushed and far too brazen public exchanges between those oblivious or apathetic to their milieu. I ordered a large cappuccino and, for a taste of something sweet, the specialty of this coffee shop, the warm, buttery croustadas baked with tart rhubarb and assorted berries. The cappuccino was poured before my eyes into a large white porcelain cup with an over-sized handle. The barrista poured the coffee in subtle gyrations and a delicate impression of a leaf emerged. It occurred to me the driving force forming the leaf was not localized to the barrista's gyrations, as it would be to a chisel in a sculptor's hands. The leaf's blueprint was not hidden within the gyrations nor within the cappuccino, it resided within the wrestling match between gyrations and cappuccino - an epigenetic marvel spread across an implicate space.

I sat by the window and booted up the laptop. I opened my novella document and positioned my cursor between the beginning of the last chapter and the end of the penultimate chapter named Address To The Examining Reader. I was set to begin a new chapter. But it was not to be just any new chapter, it would be the first chapter unfolding the story of Abram as an old man. I started typing:

The old man climbed the steep, rocky terrain. He had made this climb countless times in years past but with advancing age his limbs protested and ached. The scorching sun felt like arrows impaling his flesh during a fierce battle as he climbed up the terrain, step by step, slowly but surely gaining ground against the onslaught of an invisible enemy.

"That's a good opening," I thought. "I'll refer to him as the old man at first without giving away his identity as Abram, the precocious child, now an old man grizzled by time. What should I call this chapter?" I could not think of a title that would capture the soul of this chapter. I searched for a title that once I discovered it my heart would skip a beat and my search for another would be no more. I resigned myself to a temporary utilitarian title conveying the basic message of the chapter. I intended it to be the penultimate chapter but it would later be a chapter with many to follow. I typed a title:

The Covenant

It lacked subtlety and lyrical grace. Often a difficult or deep idea is best understood, in all its layered complexity, not by blunt inclusion but instead through poetic allusion. The sun's strong light exposes our bodies but the moon's milky-white exposes our soul.

The covenant referred to the agreement between Abraham and the I AM, the collective soul. It was the convergence of Abraham's legend into a destiny ripening since his nascent inkling, in the city of Ur, of a coming age of spiritual enlightenment - the Second Age: A Quest For The One. In the chapters following *The Covenant,* which I later renamed *The Semantic Spaces Within The Soul,* I further broadcast the voices of the whisperers within the soul - the same whisperers for any other because we all same the same soul.

On March 30, 2014 I emailed my manuscript to a man named Paul Hamersky. I had been communicating with him on Twitter for the previous few weeks. He is an orthodontist in Colorado. Paul had recently purchased from Amazon the first iteration of my novel, the story of Abraham's childhood and teenage years, and he enjoyed it. When I informed him that I had written more chapters, continuing the story of Abraham, he requested to read them. At that time I had completed four of the six chapters I would eventually write about the life of Abraham's later years. I had not yet written the chapter about the visit of the three traders nor the chapter about Abraham and Ishmael's meeting in the desert under the crescent moon.

On April 3 he emailed me. The subject of his email was:

Finished Reading Shards II

Nissan: You nailed it. Loved the additions. Were you hiding those chapters for only those that are insane enough to see the sanity in them? :-)

Perhaps its because I am assuming (based on what you have told me) these chapters written at a more recent time than the original version of Shards, so perhaps my view was prejudiced from the beginning. But, I have to say...the author has grown in his skills. Quite frankly...I would hope so...we are not the same person we were but yesterday. These new chapters were written by a "different" author.

It does need an editor...I am a big picture reader and will "fill-in" most punctuation, missing letters and improper spell check substitutions...I caught a few which means there are likely many more :-) Totally expected and don't ask me for any "point-outs"...I went right over them.

The Story Unfolds

Couple of spots had some very fast verbal foldbacks and circular acceleration that I hit escape velocity and shot out of orbit...had to re-read to get the message. I was able to resolve the verbiage and reestablish a stable orbit.

One thing I went back and forth on (still kind of am) is this line: "Idolatry is the belief in this irreducible complexity". My struggle was should that be "reducible complexity"? I can resolve it both ways...but the strongest is that the complexity is reducible to a simpler answer yet we still believe it all the complexity which is the Idolatry???? Whatever...small point.

Beyond that...I have to say.... I AGREE ....with it ALL.

What I loved about it all is you got to the same conclusions I have using different analogies, metaphors and stories. But that's the best we can do is "Point at IT". I tend to "see" it in stories of "vertical" time. Creation and existence itself as our ability to access point of reference through our memory. But the bottom line is the negation of the polarities of all separation and what's left is God (YHVH).

Lastly...I definitely think should should consider something different for the last Chapter. I have some thoughts about that and a couple of other things...but see below.

BTW: Maybe you noticed my last name...ironically you attracted a... H AM. Not Jewish, Czech by heritage. Catholic by up bring somewhat rural eastern Nebraska.

OK...where do we go from here? I honor your creation...I do not want to offer any unsolicited suggestions. There is nothing, in my opinion, wrong about the content ...in fact I 100% agree with your message, premise, conclusions etc, etc. The Story is yours and there is nothing wrong with it.

Anyway...enough for now.

Here's to our reflections

Paul

The Story Unfolds

I was walking on air the rest of the day. His remarks about my nailing the new chapters and growing as a writer emboldened me to continue writing. Throughout the ensuing months and years, whenever I felt discouraged about my prospects as a writer and spiritual communicator, whenever I doubted my ability to inspire others, whenever the old voices of my tormentors intruded into my head and mocked me, I reread that email and I regained my confidence. I was then able to shake off that musty old baggage and keep my eyes focused on the pot of gold at the end of the rainbow - a book that will trigger a change in the world, the Third Age.

Paul and I continued our correspondence until the end of 2014 and then we lost touch.

In September of 2014 I added another chapter to my novel. I named it *The Early Years: Why Are All Bachelors Unmarried?* It is set in 1999 and it synthesizes many conversations I had with my friend Carmine, named Carl in my novel, around that time in my life. In it I reason consciousness must be the implicate order out of which all of Existence is built. But during that drizzly November evening in the coffee shop, when I first wrote of Abram's old age, that chapter was still months in the future.

By 2003 my world-view had matured and I realized the collective consciousness which is synonymous with the physical world of space and time, is only one of the hierarchical emanations from YHVH and not Existence in its totality. I realized the consciousness of space and time is an emanation of a meta consciousness - a pregnant template - the trunk of the Tree of Existence. That is when I first conceived of Gödel Incompleteness as the mechanism by which the branches of the Tree of Existence emanate.

The Tree of Existence is a meta tree. Each branch is an implicate order emanating from lower level branches, themselves implicate orders, and down to the trunk of this meta tree. In 2003, before I knew of this tree, I thought I had already escaped from the cave of the shadows on the wall. I imagined what I was then seeing was the full textured truth. But I then suffered yet another existential whiplash and I came to know the textured truth I had seen up until then was but a shadow on the wall of a deeper cave - like a mirror within a mirror within another. And then my eyes were opened and I recognized the identity of the trunk of the Tree of Existence - the innermost cave and yet also the outermost - like a loop in Eternity.

I AM Writing Gödel And Chaos: The Tree Of Creation

It was Monday October 13, 2014. Another week lay before me without an income, but it was by choice. I did not pursue new software development opportunities because I resolved to write my novel full-time. I was at once exhilarated and terrified. But I tried to assure myself I could find another contract, or a full-time position, if I were so inclined. I had options. I was, nevertheless, terrified to disengage so thoroughly from a software career spanning twenty-one years. But I was at the home stretch, or so I thought. I had written over 89,000 words. Far more than I imagined when I deactivated my novella from Amazon during November of 2013.

Since early August of 2014 I had no work at AquaFlow. On October 1st, I logged into the AquaFlow web application from home and discovered my access had been deactivated. I was puzzled why AquaFlow chose to not notify me of this beforehand. I imagined there was a sinister reason why I was not getting any work. A seemingly crazy suspicion tugged at me. In early July I attended a barbecue on the terrace at work and I entered into a discussion regarding Islamic terrorism. I criticized the rampant religious fundamentalism in the Islamic world and the silence within the Left regarding the global threat. I also commented on the suffocating theocracies of many Islamic nations. Perhaps, I conjectured, I had offended someone and they had reported me. I dismissed my suspicions upon further thought. They seemed to me too paranoid and conspiratorial.

I am fiscally and socially left-of-center. I am, in my opinion, more of a true Liberal than those on the extreme Left. They succumb to Political Correctness that often cherishes the veneer of Liberalism more than its honest practice. The Political Correctness of the Left is equivalent to the book burning of the Right. The goal of both is to suppress inconvenient truths. I do not subscribe to the Left's apologism for the rampant and murderous homophobia, misogyny and theocracy endemic to Islamic societies. I have been mired in numerous arguments on Twitter regarding this issue, and I have had self-described 'spiritual' Liberals unfollow me because I criticized the global threat of Islamic fundamentalism. But these hypocrites have lauded me when I criticized Christian fundamentalism in the Western world.

"Christianity also practiced such evil in the past," was their paint-by-the-numbers rebuttal. "You can't condemn only Islam."

"I'm not criticizing Islam per se," I responded. "I'm criticizing the Muslim world's current relationship with its religion. I'm criticizing the Muslim world for allowing a fundamentalist brand of Islam to silence all others and to spread like a cancer. Any religion can be used for evil. Yesterday is one religion's time to be center-stage in this respect and today is yet another's."

During the Dark Ages the Catholic church choked the intellectual and spiritual life from Christendom, but the forces of reason rose against it and the Age Of Reason then flourished. But it is a tragedy Islamic fundamentalism has succeeded in extinguishing the Islamic golden age of science, mathematics, art and philosophy. Such is the evil of fundamentalist religion. The covert danger of religious fundamentalism is that its acolytes only obey the devil but believe it is god. This will be no more in the Third Age. That is the purpose of the covenant between I AM and the Hebrews, to usher in this great age of enlightenment and then to be retired to the annals of history.

The difference between Liberals and Conservatives is the former will mostly direct their criticism inward while the latter will mostly direct their criticism outward. Conservatives are less likely to empathize with the Other, while Liberals are less likely to empathize with the Self. Liberal Jews are the epitome of this phenomenon. From this originates the expression: self-hating Jew. That is a consequence of the Hebrew prophetic heritage. The disproportionate intellectual and social achievements of the Hebrews, and their transformational influence on the Civilization of Man, is a consequence of their heightened propensity for self-reflection. This harks to Gödel Incompleteness which is a logical consequence of the sentence 'I am a liar'. It is self-invalidation. It is the donning of sackcloth and ashes and the prostration of the Self.

In the coming Third Age, religion as we know it will fade as will the materialistic dogma of science. From polytheism to monotheism and now we are at the dawn of metatheism. Humanity will undergo a paradigm shift of its understanding of divinity and then be awed it is the same shift shattering the biases of science. I will quote an excerpt from a chapter I am currently writing in my unfinished novel (this is a quotation from that chapter):

To ascend through the navel of eternity
one must wrestle with divinity.
Two trees are in the white-eyed garden.
The first, a tree on which angels wrestle,
and the second a tree on which they dance.
The first grants knowledge of good and evil,
alternating like a self-professed lie.

I AM Writing Gödel And Chaos: The Tree Of Creation

But reaching for its tempting fruit forces our fall
through the gate of the burning sword,
and to the unknowable shells beyond.
The second offers a fruit granting life eternal.
But eternity is the garden devoid of time,
not its infinity beyond and for all time.

Humanity will mature into its Third Age and put away childish things. I will criticize religious bigotry and evil wherever I see it. If I see evil ten times in one place and only once in another then I will criticize the former ten times and the latter once. I will not allow pseudo Liberalism to sacrifice my outspokenness on the alter of Political Correctness. I will not allow pseudo Rationalism to sacrifice my scientific and philosophical outspokenness on the alter of Atheistic Correctness. But above all, I will not allow Conservative two-faced followers of pseudo Divinity, which is crass idolatry, to sacrifice the voice of the soul's semantic spaces on the alter of evil masquerading as good. I will never tire of speaking against the homophobia, misogyny, plutocracy and theocracy of those who hide behind their religious hypocrisy. These are affectations of an age soon to be washed away by a monumental tsunami. And in its place will rise the promised land - the Third Age.

I have recently debated on Twitter with an atheist who has taken great offense to my use of the word 'divinity'. He calls me a liar and a deluded, backwards thinking simpleton. I tell him I promote a redefinition of divinity but he is uninterested in understanding my textured meaning. He argues against a Straw Man, not against me. He is an atheistic fundamentalist, a form of fundamentalism no less insidious and unreasoning than the religious variety.

Not since my early Thirties have I been without income. My concerns are mitigated by the generous sum I was able to save during my time with AquaFlow. I also shared with my family my father's modest inheritance, the bulk of which consisted of his legal award for an accident he suffered on new year's eve 2002. There is a chapter in my novel where I unfold the events of this accident. I can live comfortably without income for a few years. I have the luxury of immersing myself in composing my novel.

I am aiming to complete my novel by end of 2014, but I have missed my self-imposed deadlines before. My novel is now almost 110,000 words. I have written almost 80,000 words since I deactivated it on Amazon and began writing about Abraham's old age. I now have a novel length work, no longer a novella aspiring to sit at the literary adult's table. I wonder how many words I will write before I satiate my spirit.

Months ago, when I began writing the portion of the novel set in modern times, I thought I would be reactivating my novel within a few weeks. My intent then was only to rewrite the last chapter. Carmine and my ex-wife Jeline (there is a character named Jenna in my novel who is fashioned after her) had criticized it as my weakest chapter. I have refrained, apart from my family, from naming characters in my novel with the real names of the people after whom they are fashioned. But I use the real names of venues such as coffee shops and restaurants.

Carmine's criticism was blunt: "The claims you make in your last chapter are too strong. You say your ideas can change the world but there's nothing in what you say that can do that."

Jeline was more diplomatic in her criticism, but I sensed she agreed with Carmine. "Don't tell your reader, let your reader discover it for themselves. Change the last chapter or ax it altogether."

Carmine's affront was not without merit. I have always been a better writer than speaker. My charisma flows and bubbles freely only from within my writing. Will I find my speaking voice after my novel is released? I must admit I never properly explained my ideas to Carmine. When communicating a complex framework, the connections between its parts must be laid out in sharp contrast. It is like a picture with a positive and negative space. The observer's perspective can toggle between these mutually enforced spaces. Such a two-tiered picture wields greater meaning when its toggled spaces are not isolated, they reference each other because the meaning of one incorporates a commentary about the other. Within each part resides the essence of the other. From their marriage emerges meaning which is absent from any one part in isolation. The fabric of Reality is such a dynamic, but I failed to make it clear for Jeline and Carmine. I hope my novel does not suffer that shortcoming. When I wrote the chapter introducing the EBSP I embellished my conversation with Carmine. Perhaps if I had distilled my ideas for him with the same clarity the protagonist of my novel distills it for Carl then he would have been less prone to belittle their paradigm shifting potential. Or perhaps even then he would not have grasped my vision. Our friendship has faltered since a day, in the summer of 2013, when we met at The Bread Garden near Metrotown mall. It is no longer called The Bread Garden, its new name is BG Urban Cafe. Carmine had read the first iteration of my novel at that time. Is our friendship beyond resurrection? My novel's protagonist has a similar experience and I explain the reason for the dissolution of his friendship with Carl. It's a subplot in my novel but I will not go into detail here.

I AM Writing Gödel And Chaos: The Tree Of Creation

When I deactivated my then novella from Amazon its last chapter was the only one set in modern times. Its agenda was modest. I meant it to whet the reader's appetite for the sequel, not to divulge all my ideas. My ideas can be grouped threefold: the EBSP, the imminent paradigm shift I call the Third Age, and the leveraging of Gödel Incompleteness and Chaos Theory to redefine god and to explain the EBSP as a limiting case – a principle operating at the scope of individual branches within the Tree of Creation, also known as the Tree of Knowledge of Good and Evil. I planned to have all the pieces fall in place only in the sequel and to then have the reader see the world, momentarily or for a life changed, through my eyes. But as the months passed the scope of my novel exploded. I pushed my projected release dates successively further. At first I intended for a February 2014 release and then end of Spring. I then promised my Twitter followers I would be finished by end of Summer and then I projected an end of December 2014 release. Some time around mid-summer of 2014 I realized I would not split my novel in two separately released parts. I knew I had to write the full novel in one piece. If I separated the pieces then the positive space would not marry the negative and my novel would fail to emanate from the semantic spaces of the reader's core. That is my novel's mission, not words on a flat page but textured meaning leaping out from within the depths of the reader's soul.

On November 11th, 2014 I started writing a chapter opening with the two sentences:

It was Monday October 13, 2014. Another week lay before me without an income, but it was by choice.

Einstein showed Newton's physics is a special case within the grander framework of Relativity. In the aforementioned chapter I aim to show the EBSP, as I explain it earlier in my novel, is also a special case within a more comprehensive framework built by appealing to Gödel Incompleteness and Chaos Theory. My previous ideas were consequences of the EBSP and they are not wrong in the sense of having no bearing on the truth. A shadow is a consequence of a more textured Reality. It is a falsehood pointing to a great truth. The Relativity theories do not completely invalidate Newton's physics. They reveal his equations are a mere shadow, but of a great truth. Imagine sailing a vast and melancholy ocean far beyond land. All around vibrates the existential despair of a perfect flatness that appears to swallow all who seek escape. But you struggle against these primal tethers and then they shatter and you rise and witness greater vistas and soon realize the flatness compares to the curve's truth as walls of cold bricks compare to the warmth of the home within.

The parts know not the whole but the whole knows its parts. The greater truth is sprawled beneath you, its curve hides swaths of the truth behind its arc. The illusion of the flatness assured you all of knowledge lay within your sight. But now the curve's truth reveals the folly of thinking the flatness could ever capture its completeness.

I have written a chapter in my novel recounting the events and ideas leading me to rethink the EBSP. That chapter begins with a poetic prose passage drawing an analogy between peaks on a mountain and peaks of knowledge successively revealed through paradigm shifts. At first I thought of using a mosaic of shapes as an analogy to this. I imagined standing on a sprawling surface made of a mosaic of interlocked shapes, unable to see the big picture these shapes produce. But as I zoom out above the mosaic, I gradually see an image taking shape below. The small-scale shapes do not know the truth of the emergent picture but they are its building blocks. The emergent image is as a truth unprovable within the myopic world of its constituent shapes. Truly the whole is greater than its parts. From the white-eyed, unknowing building blocks emanates a new system which cannot be known by its parts.

I started that chapter with the sentence:

The greatest ecstasy a mountaineer can experience is to seduce the peak of a majestic mountain.

It was early afternoon when I began writing that chapter, but first I savored a glass of red wine and reveled in the beauty of music moving me to heights of such ecstasy that my spirit soared with pure abandon and joy. My spirit swayed, cheek-to-cheek, with the ethereal music of Enya, Pink Floyd, Enigma, Delirium, Vivaldi, Mozart, Bach, Led Zeppelin and others. It is music breaching the ramparts to my source. That has been, so far, my ritual each day I compose my novel, since that dark and drizzly November evening in 2013 when I sat in the coffee shop on Hastings street in Burnaby and typed the first words of the saga of Abraham's later years, after he was banished to the desert. These were my cherished days of wine, music, poetry and prose.

From the first word I have written in the third part of my novel I have aimed to share with the reader the mind and soul of its protagonist. I yearn to reveal his strengths and weaknesses, his insecurities and his passions. He is an encapsulation of parts of me. I do not reveal everything about myself,

I AM Writing Gödel And Chaos: The Tree Of Creation

just a subset of the mosaic of my explicate self. But I aim to reveal the fullness of my implicate self, and to then have the reader sense it is none other than theirs. I suspect I will not succeeded fully in that regard. But I pray I, at the very least, will reveal the shadow of the truth. The rest must come from within the reader's deepest level. And when the reader breaches the ramparts to her innermost temple she will discover it is not isolated from any other. It is the same inner space she shares with me and with every other.

My goal for that chapter is to gently introduce the reader to the ideas of Gödel Incompleteness and Chaos Theory. These two are the pillars upon which rests my framework, my redefinition of divinity, the emergence and nature of Reality and the connections between. In the novel I'm writing, I gently introduce my reader to these ideas. I employ as much poetry as logic. Each serves the truth in equal parts.

I remember seeing the movie The Karate Kid back in the Eighties. I was fascinated with the way Mr. Miyagi was prodding Daniel LaRusso (Ralph Macchio) to repetitively wax his car, much to Daniel's annoyance. Daniel questioned what this has to do with learning Karate. We learn, eventually, Mr. Miyagi was instilling in Daniel a manner of thinking and moving necessary to effectively master Karate. Daniel learned not how to do Karate but how to become Karate. Daniel learned Karate as a resonance between himself and his opponent. I am employing the same learning philosophy in the novel I am writing. My protagonist, in the guise of an ancient and then a modern, is guiding my reader to become, as much as learn, the ideas of Gödel and Chaos Theory. Through poetry, allusion, reasoning and the higher meaning of my plot structure, I am hoping the assiduous reader will learn to resonate with Gödel and Chaos. This is the divine resonance - be it dancing or wrestling with divinity.

In the TV series of the late Seventies The Paper Chase professor Kingsfield tells his first year law class:

You come in here with a skull full of mush and you leave thinking like a lawyer.

My hope is the reader of my novel will start reading with possibly a skull full of mush but finish the novel thinking like a citizen of a different realm - the Third Age.

Starting with the story of Abraham's old age, I have stored copies of each writing day's story in progress. This is how I can retrace the incremental progress of my novel for any day. It was during November 9th and 10th of 2014 that I wrote of the existential whiplash my protagonist suffers during late November of 2002 when he realizes the EBSP is not

I AM Writing Gödel And Chaos: The Tree Of Creation

valid in the way he initially thought. This happened to me exactly as it did to my protagonist. I can pinpoint the approximate date by referencing the red notebook that I had faithfully inscribed with my thoughts since Friday, November 1st, 2002, when my ex-wife Jeline gifted it to me. The entries I wrote during late November of 2002 indicate that is when I first realized the EBSP, as I understood it, was flawed. I still have that red notebook and I will keep it until the day I die.

The events I chronicle in the third part of my novel are all based on real events in my life, but I embellish them to various degrees only to give my reader a more fluid reading experience and for a fuller exposition of my ideas. Not all chapters are embellished; some genuinely reflect my life's minutiae. An example of an embellished chapter is the one where I first reveal the EBSP through a lengthy dialog between the character in my novel named Carl and the protagonist. That dialog is a mosaic of many conversations I have had with Carmine over the years, some of which I chronicle in my novel. There is a coffee shop named Trees Organic exactly as I describe it in my novel. The Santa Claus is real.

In the chapter I am currently writing in my novel there is a paragraph of exactly one hundred and forty three words in which I reveal its protagonist's concerns with dialogs that are too long. My protagonist is writing a novel. That is central to the plot in my own novel. The protagonist is concerned that a particular dialog he has written between two of his main characters is far too long and its ideas too intense for his readers. It is a lengthy dialog where the two characters meet in a coffee shop called Trees Organic and discuss a pivotal heuristic named EBSP which had been at the foundation of my protagonist's world view. After much soul searching my protagonist decides to keep the lengthy dialog intact. For the reader's reference, the number of letters in the paragraph's last word is four.

I once told Pam: "The unconventional self-referencing structure of my novel must straddle the worlds of Fiction, non Fiction and Memoir, and show how these are three worlds in one. It is what it is." She retorted I am a master of the feedback loop when it concerns the ideas of which I write in my novel, but I do not extend that proclivity to cleaning up after myself.

"Please use a feedback loop," she would often quip after I would leave dirty dishes in the sink or well spent empty bottles of red wine on my computer's desk.

Three protagonists inhabit my novel. One protagonist is Abraham, the breath of the Second Age. Another is the writer of the novel I often refer to within myself. They are a leitmotif, like a recurring musical passage differing only by pitch. But the main protagonist of my novel is the novel that contains itself. The names of the two secondary protagonists are unaltered. However, I never name my main protagonist within the formal system of itself. I only mention its name in the world of its readers. I am not a fool to believe my reader does not know the name of my main protagonist. The mystery is not in not-knowing, it is in not-telling. The reader can only know the main protagonist's name by emanating out from the formal system of my inner novel and into the outer shell. That, in a nutshell, is Gödel's Incompleteness Theorem. That, in a nutshell, is YHVH, the worlds emanating from the ineffable H now speaking to you like an eternal burning bush. That is the voice of divinity, its poignant whispers now crying out to you from the semantic spaces between the words on my page. A new age is dawning upon us all, an age of messiah and humanity within the womb of divinity. Like a new age I come to you and speak of the people who are a Strange Attractor within the Chaos from whence emanates all. They are those that cross over to worlds from the womb and to the beyond. They are the Habiru expelled from the Civilization of Man. Two non local realities commingled - a space and its negative, eternally toggled like a self-professed lie. In one key of the leitmotif it is those expelled from the Civilization of Man and in another key it is that which is expelled from the shards of the fractured H at the source of it all.

***

In my novel I include a dialog between a character named Reza and one of my three protagonists. This dialog never happened to me personally, although I did have a Persian coworker named Farshid after whom I fashioned the character of Reza. I changed his name to protect his privacy. My own exploration of Gödel Incompleteness was a solitary pursuit.

I also include a conversation between Reza and another coworker at Chancellor Software named Clayton (real name Clinton but also changed to protect privacy) where I describe coming into work and seeing Reza standing by Clayton's desk and engaged in a theological debate. This is based on a conversation in 2003 or 2004, I don't remember exactly, where Farshid explained to Clinton why god is not necessary because order can spontaneously arise from disorder in self-organizing systems. I intruded into their conversation and commented this is precisely what god is, the tendency in Chaos for order to arise out of disorder via self-referencing loops. Clinton just rolled his eyes. He did not deliver the sanctimonious lecture about the soul redeeming message of Jesus Christ that I mention in the embellished conversation in my novel. I do not know if Clinton's eye-rolling was directed more towards my comment or Farshid's.

The reason I present Farshid (aka Reza) as the person who introduced my novel's protagonist to Gödel Incompleteness is because of Farshid's remark to Clinton regarding self-organizing systems. I will never forget that remark, nor that day.

The following are the actual events: The falsehood of the EBSP dawned on me one day at work in late November of 2002 (I surmise from my red notebook). I was mulling the implications of what I had learned about Gödel Incompleteness and I then had an epiphany. I realized if truths exist whose proof is not accessible to the observer then the EBSP cannot stand. In the novel I'm writing there's a chapter named *The Early Years: Why Are All Bachelors Unmarried*. In this chapter I explain the Equivalence thought experiment of General Relativity which shows the indistinguishably of inertia and gravity. But if the EBSP is invalid then indistinguishably should not imply equivalency. Their distinctiveness may very well be an unknowable truth. And what of the other conclusions I list in that chapter which also depend on the EBSP? Does absolute uniform motion actually exist? Is consciousness not the implicate order of Reality after all? I abhorred abandoning these cherished notions, but I could not dismiss the implication of Gödel's unprovable truths, nor of Chaos Theory's unpredictable behaviors.

I did not want to forsake the EBSP, nor ignore Gödel Incompleteness. But the latter seemed to contradict the former. The EBSP appears to apply to physics without exception and yet, according to Gödel Incompleteness, it is false. This paradox occupied me for a few weeks without a resolution. The EBSP works so well for the world of space/time and mass/energy that I sensed its falsehood is a shadow of a textured truth. I sensed its falsehood is a false peak in the shadow of the true peak above all.

I am currently writing, on and off, a chapter in my novel titled *Gödel And Chaos: The Tree Of Creation. M*y intent is to reveal in this chapter the resolution to the EBSP paradox. I intend to show under which circumstances the EBSP is valid.

Each day, as I write this chapter, my cat Ginger purrs on my lap and I devour soul-uplifting music while sipping red wine. I always sip red wine when I write my novel and I resonate with the music which is my spirit's delight, and I then cannot find the fold between fiction and reality, between the place where the music ends and I begin, between my novel and the soul.

Composing my novel is my joy, my muse, my compulsion, and as the years progress it tightens its grip on me and it will not let go. It has become an unforgiving master whom I have to serve, but I do not want to become a free man. It has orchestrated my life even before it was conceived. During those chaotic years it spoke to me in my dreams and in my waking moments. But I was never truly awake; I only listened to the whispering wind blowing from within my depths and it compelled me to follow the Piper towards that other realm.

There came a day when Pam and I visited my mother and she inquired when I would go back to work.
"My book is my work now."
"Nissim, stop this nonsense. It can be a good hobby but a good paying job should come first."
"I need to write this book. You don't understand me. I'll never be happy if I don't finish it, but I can't just work on it on weekends and evenings. I need to fully immerse myself in the experience of writing it."
"You are becoming like your father was. He never wanted to work. Yeah, you're going to become a big shot writer. Stop your fantasies."
"Look, I don't need to hear this. Enough! Come on Pam. I can't listen to this anymore."
I grabbed my coat and stormed out of the apartment. Pam followed me a few seconds later.
A few days after that incident Pam spoke to my mother on the phone.
"What did she tell you?" I asked later.
"She's upset you stormed off."
"But she demeaned the novel, the message. She demeaned my passion."
"She doesn't believe in your book."
"Is that what she said? No one believes in my book. But I believe in it. I have a vision that no one sees."
"Take it easy on your mom. She's concerned for you. She doesn't understand this obsession you have with your novel."

***

In my first part there appears a protagonist writing a composition whose true agenda is admission to the Second Age, and in my third part there appears a protagonist who is writing a novel for admission to the Third. For both protagonists, as above so below. In the novel my protagonist is writing there also appears a protagonist writing a novel. Like a mirror within a mirror within another, into Eternity. Ultimately, the innermost mirror reflects the outermost. It is a Navel of Creation: a Loop in Eternity.

I AM Writing Gödel And Chaos: The Tree Of Creation

The three protagonists of my novel are Abraham, my nested identity, and the novel that knows itself. On October 17th of 2014 I began writing the chapter describing my resolution of the EBSP paradox. This chapter is set in late December 2002, that's actually when I discovered the resolution. I explain this resolution through a discussion at Trees Organic between the character named Carl and the protagonist who is my nested identity. Did this discussion ever take place? Yes and no, it is stitched together from various conversations I have had with Carmine, the friend on whom I base the character of Carl. I must also confess I have never explained my EBSP paradox resolution to Carmine as thoroughly as my protagonist explains it to Carl.

I began that chapter with the following paragraph:

It was the end of the two weeks following the events I describe in the chapter I currently name Story Of 2013. During these weeks I had unsuccessfully danced with the paradox of the EBSP, its feet were not in lockstep with mine, and yet I sensed it is a false peak in the shadow of the highest truth.

I AM Not An Island

During autumn of 2013 I began to yearn for contact with other writers. I craved to learn from them and to gage their reactions to my writing. I satiated my yearning in two ways: by joining, in late December of 2013, a writer's critique group, and by attending a monthly gathering of writers and poets at a pub on Main street named Cottage Bistro. This pub is a literary hot-spot; it hosts gatherings of literary groups of various stripes.

On each bi-weekly meeting of the critique group, two members, who had volunteered the previous meeting, read an excerpt from their works in progress and were critiqued by the others. It was never a large group during the best of times, no more than ten members for a rare, fully attended meeting, and often only four or five. Sometimes a meeting would be canceled due to poor attendance. No member had achieved literary success. None were professional writers. But we all clung to hopes of literary recognition some day.

The monthly gatherings at Cottage Bistro had a different character. They were not opportunities for critique. They were meant to spotlight featured writers who had achieved a modicum of success. The only expected audience response was applause. These writers each read from their works for about fifteen minutes. Some of the greater luminaries, like Evelyn Lau, were afforded much longer readings. During these literary nights, unknown and unaccomplished writers, or perhaps some were semi-accomplished, were offered open-mikes - five minutes, standing on a dimly lit and tiny stage, to read to a packed room of people sipping from their drinks, eating from their plates, whispering in each others' ears, some focused on the spectacle on the stage of those reading their hearts out, others apathetic to these unknowns with allusions to success and illusions of grandeur. It was a dance between the beggars and the choosers.

"Are you sure you'll be able to do this?" Pam said.
"Absolutely, I'm so excited."
"How many minutes?"
"Five, on the dot. They're strict."
"Where is it on Main?"
"Main and 29th, you remember? That's where you met Kian a couple of years ago. We discussed it a few weeks ago. You forgot?"
"Oh, is that where it is?"

It was a rainy, moonless November night. We arrived at Cottage Bistro at seven, half an hour before the first reading would start. The place was already packed, but we found two side-by-side seats at a long table near the front of the pub - close to the tiny stage on which I planned to deliver my first reading. The long table was composed of several small tables culled together as one. After we sat, I asked a bearded, middle-aged man sitting across from me, how to request an open-mike opportunity. He pointed to a table towards the back of the room and advised me to inquire there. I located the event organizer and filled out a one paragraph biography. I was one of three open-mike readers. But first the evening's featured writers were to deliver their readings.

At half past nine it was my turn. "Our next open-mike reader is Nissim Levy," announced the MC. "I hope I pronounced that correctly, yes? Where are you Nissim?"

I raised my arm and gave the thumbs-up sign.

"Nissim is a software developer and he's currently writing a spiritually and philosophically oriented novel titled Shards Of Divinities. So will you all welcome Nissim on to the stage with a round of hearty applause?"

I grabbed my two printed pages and took my place on the stage. I adjusted the microphone stand up towards my lips and looked out at an audience veiled within the dim light. During the two hours that I waited for my five minutes of fame, my nervousness had progressed from a mild unease to a kaleidoscope of butterflies fluttering against the walls of my gut. But my stage-fright had evaporated when I began reading and I felt a high-frequency wave of confidence ripple through me, and there was no other place I wished to be at that moment.

That night I read a passage from my novel about the ethereal dance between the desert's heat of day and chill of night. I had written that chapter almost a year earlier. It is a passage set during Abram's old age, as he ventures into the desert night to find Yahvah and negotiate for the convergence of his destiny. This passage opens a chapter titled *The Navel Of Creation: A Loop In Eternity*.

I began to read from it:

The desert is a study of dueling extremes. The day's heat wrestles night's impending chill, yet there is no victor, the pendulum forever swings.

During a summer's midday the desert smolders like the ashes of a freshly extinguished bonfire. The air is thick as honey and the heat envelopes and coddles your soul yet ravages your flesh. Your skin must be completely veiled from the burning sun by a thin layer of porous fabric. Any exposed skin on your face vibrates like the water in a pot

I AM Not An Island

just before the boil...

Five minutes later I finished my reading with the following:

...I promise you Abram I shall never again force you to tear your soul from another land. Not for now or your generations to come. The land of Canaan will forever be inside their hearts even when it is not under their feet.

I thanked the audience and walked back to my seat while acknowledging the applause.

"Thank you Nissim for a beautiful reading," said the MC. "That was wonderful."

The MC introduced the next open-mike reader. The pub erupted again with applause and, as I sat, the bearded man sitting across the table leaned towards me and spoke over the noise. "I really enjoyed that, by the way. Very well done." He then turned his focus to the stage where the next beggar started performing for the choosers.

***

The next week, on a Wednesday as usual, I attended another bi-weekly writers critique meeting. I was one of two readers. I had, by then, already served as a reader three previous times. My enthusiasm for this group had waned on each of these readings. I contemplated quitting.

Six members had previously indicated, via email, they would attend the meeting. I prepared seven copies, one for myself, of the passage I selected to read. It was a chapter titled *The Four Corners* in the second part of my novel. That chapter tells the story of Abram and Sarai's meeting with the three visitors who announce the good news of Sarai's impending pregnancy and the dire news of the city of Sodom's impending destruction. I wrote that chapter six months earlier, after I had already started writing the third part of my novel, in order to give my novel's saga of Abram more nuance and texture. I revisited the story of Abram and filled in more detail right up to the last few weeks of completing my novel.

Pam dropped me off at a nearby library. I was fifteen minutes early and the first one to arrive when I entered a room at the back reserved for the meeting. Five minutes later Ray arrived, and by 7:30 PM I was sitting around the table with six other members. I was the first reader and I handed to each a printout of my chapter.

"I will be reading an entire chapter that continues the saga of Abram, the old man seeking his god in the desert. A few weeks ago I read an excerpt

I AM Not An Island

about his childhood in Ur. Before that I read a complete chapter that begins the story of his old age in the desert, and before that I read another excerpt about his childhood in Ur. Sorry for skipping around like that. Today's reading tells the story of Abram's meeting with three strangers who visit his household in the desert. Who are these strangers? You, as the reader, decide. This chapter builds on a story told in the book of Genesis."

I began reading:

The desert is freedom and the freedom is pregnant with potential.

The desert is the white-eyed womb of humanity's chaotic congregation.

The desert is a blank mirror, pregnant with its reflections.
Great civilizations and empires are the fruits of Habiru clans that roamed the desert during times so ancient that legend is blurred into fact....

I finished my reading with the chapter's ending:

...Abram and Sarai's servants prepared canteens of water and food enough for three days in the desert for two men. That night the two men, one to the right and the other to the left, departed for Sodom, riding on a chariot pulled by Abram's fieriest camels. And then there was One. But the man in the middle, the connector of the other two, did not depart. He entered Abram and Sarai through the four corners of their soul. And then there was None.

Following each reading were ten minutes of silence during which the other members annotated their copy with corrections, criticisms and, hopefully, praise. On completion, each member offered a few minutes of commentary. The first was Ellan, a mid-twenties man of average height, slim build and straight dark hair that perpetually threatened to fall over his eyes. He wrote mostly paranormal-detective short-stories. He sat directly across from me.

"First of all, let me make it completely clear I am not in your target audience. I'm not into Judeo-Christian myths. I'm more of a free-thinker and I'll never read this kind of novel."

"Ellan, each time I've done a reading you've made that crystal-clear, so I got it by now." I chuckled as a way to mask my dismay at his repeated rebuffs.

I AM Not An Island

I found his redundant proclamations that he is not in my target audience to be revealing. Ordinarily, a person who offers a literary critique in the setting of a group meeting will not be so adamant to proclaim his dislike for the genre of the excerpt being critiqued. Doing so hints his world-view has been threatened or he has been offended. I sensed it was the former.

"Also, your attempt at a lyrical or poetic prose style, I must say, falls flat. I've noticed from your previous readings you often attempt this style, but you can't manage it or you haven't yet learned how to manage it. I recommend you read some Cormack McCarthy, particularly Blood Meridian, to see how sentences in the lyrical style should be constructed and why your constructions are falling far short."

Ellan continued to lambaste my prose. I attempted to find the pearl within the oyster of his criticisms. When he finished his critique he passed me his marked-up copy of the chapter I had read. It was hemorrhaging red ink.

"Thank you Ellan for your review," I said. "Stella, you're next around the table. I think we're going clockwise, yes? Are you ready?"

Stella was in her late thirties or early forties, with an average build and soft, light-brown curls cascading down to her shoulders. She wore glasses with thin, black frames that were rectangular and much wider than they were tall. She would have appeared to be a prim and proper librarian type if not for her casual attire - purple t-shirt, faded jeans and red sneakers.

She cleared her throat. "I must say, I find the message and tone of this chapter very disturbing. These three men, who I'm sure represent angels or god in your story, are threatening to destroy a city full of human beings, children and innocent people. And all this in the name of their king, who I'm sure is your metaphor for the Hebrew god. Reminds me of a similar situation happening in the world right now."

Stella gazed at her copy throughout her critique. She avoided eye contact with me. I knew her last comment was an allusion to the then raging Israeli military operation against Hamas in Gaza. She knew I was an Israeli Jew. I bit my lip.

"I also find it very disheartening that Abram and the three men are more concerned with the loss of commercial trading along the Silk Road than with the impending loss of life of innocent children."

"Sorry to interject," I said, "I know I'm going against protocol to comment before you've finished your critique, but I must say this: did you miss the part where Abram pleads with the three strangers to rethink their attack on Sodom because he wants to save innocent lives?"

Stella maintained her gaze at her papers. "I did not miss that, but I don't buy it. Abram didn't convince me he is concerned for the lives of these people. He comes across more as a religious fanatic who would rationalize brutality for the sake of his god delusions. If you intended to humanize Abram by giving him some empathy then I'm afraid it doesn't shine through your prose. So it might be more a failing of your skills as a writer due to inexperience or what have you."

"Stella, forgive me for interjecting again and I promise I'll give your critique uninterrupted attention, but did you also not notice the allusion to the modern information highway, the Internet, that I discuss in the context of the exchange of information along the Silk Road? Did you not understand I present the trading route as far more than just the exchange of commerce and material wealth?"

"Hmm...perhaps you did in your own way, I don't know, but in the grand order of things it doesn't elevate your themes or prose style to a level I'd like to see of a work ready to be published, and one more thing-"

"Please forgive me Stella for another interruption but I must say, what if there are just three or four themes woven through my prose demonstrating why I've written this chapter as I did, and which are of a noble character, would you then spare my chapter from these criticisms? Would you then recognize the merit of my literary, spiritual and philosophical agenda?"

"For three or four well constructed and noble themes I would spare this chapter."

"Then I think you should reread this chapter and let its themes and ideas enter the four corners of your soul." I emphasized the word 'your'.

"Listen Nissim, to be honest I can't sympathize with any religious tradition that would demean women by subscribing to this ridiculous notion that the first woman emerged, like some sort of pustule, from the rib of the first man."

"But you misunderstand the story of the Garden in Genesis. You are being far too literal. You see, this story depicts the feminine and the masculine as abstractions. Adam and Eve are not flesh and blood humans until they're ejected from the Garden, which itself is not a literal garden, and-"

Stella smirked. "I don't know if I want to enter into a theological debate now."

"Please just hear me out for one minute. In the Garden, Adam and Eve represent the abstract male and female polar principles that operate within all the levels of Existence. It is the Yin and Yang in the Eastern spiritual traditions. There is an eternal tension between these. In physics it's the tension between the creative spark of Energy - light, Lucifer - and Gravity, which pulls everything inward and attempts to extinguish the Created. The female abstract principle, the Forms Plato talked about, represents Creation. The male abstract principle represents the Source of Creation. That's why the story in Genesis depicts Eve emerging from the rib of Adam. It's Creation emerging from the Source. And that's why it's the female abstract principle - Eve - that has first contact with the snake, who represents the creative spark of Light, Lucifer, and it's Eve who goads Adam into eating from the Tree of Knowledge, because it is this eating that represents the emergence from the white-eyed womb of the Garden. It's Creation - abstract female - from the Source - abstract male."

Stella hesitated a few seconds. The others did not interrupt. "Well, I've given you my opinion. Take it with a grain of salt or what have you. I am done."

Stella slid her copy towards me from across the table. I reached to grab it. The pages felt cold between my index finger and thumb. I did not see any corrections, but when I flipped over the last page I saw two long paragraphs of commentary. She shot me a tight-lipped, expressionless stare.

"Thank you Stella for your time."

"I'm next, Nissim."

"Thanks Ray, I always look forward to your commentary." I emphasized the word 'your'.

Ray was in his mid-fifties, of average height and build, with short salt-and-pepper hair, thinning on top, and a matching bushy mustache. Since my first reading, almost a year earlier, he had always offered me encouragement and even praise. I had never detected a mean bone in his body, nor any evidence of heightened ego. He was a talented novelist and I suspected he would achieve literary success some day.

"No, I actually think your poetic language is really, really well done. And your themes are deep and engaging. Your lyrical style put me in the perfect mood to absorb and appreciate your spiritual and philosophical ideas. My only criticism is about the beginning of the chapter, where you discuss the desert. It's too rambling and repetitive. Definitely leave that part in, but trim it and it'll be great."

"Thank you Ray, much appreciated. I always learn from your critiques."

"I did catch on to your allusion to the Internet when you were discussing the trading route as an information route that shapes nations and empires. I thought it was actually very thought-provoking and clever you would make that analogy and propose that this kind of mechanism shaped ancient civilizations. I do have a few questions though."

"I'd love to answer them."

I AM Not An Island

"Well, the way you end the chapter. What did you mean by saying..."

Ray quoted from his copy. *"But the man in the middle, the connector of the other two, did not depart. He entered Abram and Sarai through the four corners of their soul. And then there was None."*

"Good question. I'm alluding to the divine experience as emanating from within. These three strangers are just regular men. They're not angels in the literal sense. But the experience they trigger within Abram is what is the divine. It's the whispers reverberating deep within him. They allow Abram to recognize the divine."

"So anyone can be an angel?"

"Precisely. And someone who is an angel for you is not an angel for everyone."

"And why was there then None?"

"It's another allusion, to the fundamental nature of the divine, which is absolute nothingness. I explain that later in the novel."

"Whoa, this is not beach reading, is it?" The speaker was Mica, a late-thirties man who always attended the meetings in a suit and tie because he came straight from work as an insurance underwriter.

"Ray, are you done? If you are then Mica can take it from here."

"Yeah, I'm done. I like this chapter. It's made me see things in ways I didn't before. Mica, take the wheel."

Ray handed me his copy. I saw comments written in a spidery blue ink. They reminded me of blood cursing through my veins.

"I think overall it's very well written," Mica said. "A bit of a tough slog in places though. There's too much of everything. Too many themes, too many ideas, too many sub-plots. My two cents worth is that perhaps you can lighten up a bit on the complicated metaphors and, as you say, allusions. I do have one question though. Do you think there's a big enough market for this kind of novel?"

"Well, my main motivation for writing this novel is not money. It's a work of passion for me. It's something I must write or I'll feel I've wasted my life when I'm on my deathbed."

Mica smiled. "Umm... nice."

"But having said that," I continued, "I do think there's a big market for metaphysical and spiritual novels. Just look at the best-seller lists of the last twenty or thirty years."

"I don't think your novel can succeed."

The speaker was Lili, a thin, late-fifties grandmother with straight, ash-blond hair that hung past her shoulders.

"I learned long ago to ignore comments of my impending literary doom." I laughed an insincere laugh. Lili did not elaborate. Mica completed his critique. It was fair, I thought. I did not detect the tinge of undeserved hostility I sensed in some of the previous critiques.

The last person to critique my chapter was Keisson, a gruff and, to some, humorless man. His critiques could be blunt, without a false facade of politeness. The previous meeting Mica was a reader and he was on the receiving end of Keisson's literary wrath.

"This is not my idea of good writing. You struck out this time, Mica." And then Keisson tossed his copy at Mica's end of the table, to the shock of the other members. He appeared disgusted. But I understood Keisson and I liked him. Keisson does not tolerate fools. He does not tolerate insincerity. He does not tolerate superficiality. The difference between myself and Keisson is he only takes people into his confidence after they prove themselves but I, on the other hand, trust freely and give people the benefit of a doubt. But once a person disappoints me and I see through their veneer of insincerity, or their miasma of banality, then I withdraw my trust and friendship.

"So here's what I think," Keisson said. "I also think it's well written. But I'll echo what others have said. Try to ease up on some of the intense philosophical or metaphorical elements. By the way, what the hell is a chariot pulled by Abram's fieriest camels?" He laughed.

"It's an allusion to a recurring imagery in the Hebrew scriptures of fiery chariots carrying prophets and angels to the Kingdom of God. I'm hinting the earthly kingdom from where these three men come is a metaphor in my novel for the Kingdom of God. I'm using a bit of an exegetical approach here. I'm allowing the astute reader to analyze or shed light on one part of my novel by using another part. The reader, in this way, can draw meaning out of my novel."

Ellan rolled his eyes. In the corner of my left eye I saw Lili shrug at Stella and then, across the table from me to Ellan's right, I saw Stella smirk in response.

"Good god," Keisson said, "this is heavy stuff."

"I'm not writing Paranormal Detective, you know?" I laughed. I meant this as a retaliatory jab against Ellan, and I am sure he knew it.

When I left the meeting that night I felt more sure I would quit the group. But I did not want to commit myself to that decision yet. I had two weeks to reflect until the next meeting. When Pam picked me up I recounted the meeting's events.

"Just quit," she said. "They don't get your kind of novel. And some of them are pretty rude."

"But in a civilized kind of way," I said.

It was on the Tuesday of the following week I decided to quit. I emailed my decision to all the members.

I have learned much the last year from attending this group and I wish you all much success with your literary ambitions. I've decided that a writer's group is not effective for my circumstances. I will instead be seeking a spiritually oriented group in which I can discuss my ideas and receive feedback on these ideas instead of a literary group whose feedback is only on the quality of the writing irrespective of the ideas it communicates.

Sincerely,

Nissim Levy

The next day I received a reply from Ray addressed to all on the email list.

Thank you Nissim for letting us know. I'm sad that I'll never get to hear your great readings again. Take care and best wishes.

Ray

Ray's reply to my resignation was the only one I ever received. My departure from the group was otherwise met with an apathetic silence. But this was a silence louder than their cruelest words.

I AM Writing My Manifesto

Socrates taught that a life unexamined is not worth living. But what is the benefit gained from a life examined? It is the revelation of what is your passion. To know your passion is to eat the fruit from the Tree of Knowledge of Good and Evil, and your eyes are then opened and you see your soul as if reflected off a mirror, and you see its nakedness and you are compelled to pursue your passion. You are then forever banished from the land of your comforts and are compelled to venture out on a path towards fulfilling your passion. But a life examined, once it consummates its passion, offers the pinnacle of ecstasy a soul can experience. It is the soul consummating its ontology. It is the painter painting. It is the writer writing. It is the lover loving. It is the creator creating. I've eaten from the fruit of the Tree of Knowledge of Good and Evil and I'm only truly ecstatic when I write my novel and when I dream of one day soon sharing it with the Civilization of Man.

To live in a world that does not allow you, through the fault of circumstance or the imposition of force, to consummate your passion is to live in a world that does not allow you to be you. It is like the Black man born into a racist White society. It is like the Jew born into antisemitic bigotry. It is felt by anyone who has ever yearned to live in a different realm.

On October 26, 2015 I was rereading a chapter named *Story Of Montreal* in my unfinished novel. I wrote that chapter during November 24, 25 and 26 of 2014. This was a temporary placeholder title. I prefer my chapter titles to convey the philosophy of their chapters and to evoke feelings of transcendence in my readers. My novel is the story of a man, in the guise of an ancient and a modern, who has a new vision of the divine and of a new age of enlightenment and justice. He develops a compulsion to write a manifesto of his vision in the form of a novel of passion. I named my modern protagonist after me because we are similar in so many ways, but there are key differences. I am not as magnanimous as he. I have treated others unfairly at times. I have let selfishness dictate my actions on occasion. *Story Of Montreal* details the traumatic time in my protagonist's life when, at the age of fourteen, he was compelled, due to the vagaries of life, to uproot himself from his life in Montreal. The chapter also touches on the life of the protagonist's grandmother's thirty years older brother, and how during the first decade of the twentieth century, before said grandmother was born, he uprooted himself from his life in Turkey and left behind his parents, his siblings and his bond to that land. He crossed over the Atlantic and, via Ellis Island, embarked on a new life in America. It dawned on me the overarching theme of that chapter mirrors the life of Abraham and, in general, the leitmotif of the Hebrew people. The leitmotif is of forcible banishment, be it self-imposed or external, and a crossing-over from the lands of comfort and into new realms of passion. I further realized the crossing-over of the Hebrews is not limited to unfamiliar geographical realms but also to abstract realms of new ideas and paradigm shifts. The Hebrew people's name translated into Hebrew is Ivrim and it means 'those that cross over'. Four thousand years ago, under the tapestry of a desert's starry sky, the I AM made a covenant with Abraham and thereafter Abraham's seed spawned generations that compel humanity to cross over into new realms of ideas and passions. I then had an epiphany and I renamed the chapter to *Crossing Over To New Realms*.

The first sentence of my novel is its leitmotif. It is played in multiple keys throughout. In one key I reveal my novel's protagonist, in the guise of an ancient and then a modern, has always felt like a citizen of a different realm. In another key I rhapsodize about the Civilization of Man having always yearned for a realm it inscribed in its holy books - the Messianic Age. But in the primordial key I write of Gödel and Chaos and of new worlds hurtling out of their white-eyed wombs - the banishment from the Eternal Garden where at the center are rooted two trees: the Tree of Eternal Life with the dancing angels and the Tree of Knowledge of Good and Evil with its wrestling angels. It is via the latter that the banishment from the eternal garden is effected.

During the years I composed my novel I often experienced epiphanies when I understood, in an unanticipated way, a passage or chapter I had previously written. To my novel's readers it may appear I had engineered or pre-planned such meanings within my chapters, but I scarcely played the role of watchmaker or external providence. I deferred to a greater authorship - the Civilization of Man. In the brain, the neurons do not create paradigm shifts within consciousness; it is consciousness that selects and grooms the neurons by which it shifts itself. Likewise, the leaders do not create paradigm shifts within the Civilization of Man, it is the Civilization of Man that selects and grooms these leaders.

An example in my novel where I feel my writing is inspired by the Civilization of Man is the chapter titled *Childhood Musings* where I write of a giant hole in the desert floor with hierarchical layers of whispering serpents. The abstract meaning of this serpent hole did not occur to me until much later. I am confident the dedicated reader will have long ago understood the significance of this hole in the desert floor. In that chapter I whimsically describe the giant naked idol Orofus galloping nightly across the desert floor to that serpent hole. It was not until I wrote the chapter *The Navel Of Creation: A Loop In eternity* that I connected young Abram's conversations with Orofus and the elder Abram's compulsive quest for his god, and it became an eternal loop between Abram's childhood and his later years, and then also a grand loop in the fabric of Existence. I was no longer writing my novel, the emanation known as the Civilization of Man was writing it through me, and revealing a monumental and tectonic shift within itself that would soon give rise to the Third Age. My novel has become Deus Sive Natura, not Deus Ex Machina. It has become a self-organizing novel transcending its writer. It has become a novel whose existence precedes its essence.

During the early evening of October 27, 2015 I was lying in bed with Pam. In the early stages of our relationship we often lay in bed and reflected on our lives, our aspirations, fears, joys and passions. We often delighted in playing games of Twenty Questions but often the questions exceeded twenty by far, and yet an unanswered question forever reverberated between us. Most matured relationships lose the easy intimacy, like breathing air, of their early years and ours was no exception. After eight years of highs and lows, joys and moments of despair, we had reached a point of no longer indulging in those evenings of joyful abandon and soulful intimacy. But the essence of love is when people connect and then the greatest truth is effortlessly revealed, like breathing air: we all share the same soul.

I mostly blame myself for the hiccups in my relationship with Pamela and to a lesser, yet not small, extent also for my failed marriage to Jelene. My life traumas have planted a festering anger and self-doubt within me. When I wrote Crossing Over To New Realms the previous year, my intention was to pour my heart out by revealing the traumatic manner by which I left behind my father in Montreal. But my traumas are not limited to that event. I craved to further reveal my inner demons in the chapters yet unwritten, but I feared I lacked the courage to reveal the injured underbelly of my psyche.

Pam and I lay a foot apart on the King bed while gazing at the ceiling. The light from a shaded lamp filled the room with a fuzzy and comforting orange glow. Between us, by our navels, our geriatric cat Ginger, colored like Rocky Road ice-cream, was curled and she purred softly that night. Pam and I turned to face each other.

"Do you remember earlier today," I whispered, "I told you I had a special story to tell you?"

"Yes, now's a good time. I'm listening." Her eyes were closed and the sides of her content smile reached for the beauty of the curves of her cheekbone.

Pam also had a life examined, and her passion was to become a mother and nurture a child.

"It's the story of Sarah, Abraham's wife, and how she was barren but she was desperate to have a baby boy."

"Sounds exactly like me. But a daughter would be equally great."

Due to medical complications, when Pamela was much younger she became barren.

"And she wasn't just infertile; she was already an old woman and believed it was too late for her to have children."

"Sounds like a reasonable conclusion to me." Pamela opened her eyes and shrugged her upper shoulder.

"You know how I wrote about the life of Abraham in the first part of my book? Well, I wrote a chapter last year called *The Four Corners*. It's about a very hot day when three men visit Abram and Sarai in their household in the desert."

"Is that really a story from the bible?"

"Yes, I transformed it into a midrashic story. Do you remember I explained what a midrashic story is?"

"Yes, yes. That was years ago."

"In the book of Genesis three angels, disguised as men, visit Abraham and Sarah for two reasons. The first is to warn them the cities of Sodom and Gomorrah are so corrupt they'll be destroyed soon. You see, his nephew Lot and his family lived there. The second was to inform them Sarah will bear a son the next year."

"But in the real world miracles like that don't happen. I suppose Sarai thanked them for the good news?"

"Actually, Sarai was thinking pretty much like you. You see, she also believed miracles don't happen in the real world."

"Ha...sensible girl. So what did she do?"

"She laughed in their faces."

"She knew they're angels and she still laughed?"

"In the bible she knew they're angels, but in my midrashic story they're just three regular men. They're fabric traders from a far-off kingdom. That kingdom is my proxy for the kingdom of god. But what is an angel really? If god is within us then an angel is a regular person who channels in our lives that internal divinity. An angel to me will not be an angel to someone else. An angel is as an angel does."

"So what did the three angels do when she laughed at them?"

"They told her that because she laughed then she must name her son Itzhak. The anglicized name is Isaac. It's a Hebrew word which means Will Laugh. In my novel I don't use that name. I say his name will be Laughter."

"But I don't believe a miracle like that will happen to me." Pam sighed.

"The moral of my story is that you too should not give up hope. You won't get pregnant of course, but we will adopt a child."

"No, I'm too old now. Birth mothers will not select us."

"Are you going to laugh if I tell you that in a few years we will have an adopted child?" I emphasized the word 'will'.

"And where are my three angels?"

"They're right here between us."

"Oh yes. Is Gingie our angel?" Pam laughed. "Oh no, I'll have to name the child Itzhak now."

On Wednesday, November 11th, 2015 I began writing the chapter I eventually named *My Manifesto*. I gave it the placeholder name *Story Of 2006*. When I sat at my desk that day to write, I played Enya's haunting masterpiece *Storms In Africa* and I became an angel in full flight, soaring towards the divine within me. Its poignant melodies seemed to emanate from beyond the horizon of space and time, yet were synonymous with the soul. I yearned for a place that is the Jerusalem of my innermost chamber. I have always prepared myself for a day of writing by drinking two glasses of red wine and meditating to music that dances with my spirit. My writing days always begin with the dance and only then I can wrestle. I must first go within myself and find the eternal place, and only then can I loop back on this place and then create and create.

That night I returned to my home-office desk and scoured the Internet for an image to be my new book cover. The previous image did not convey the visionary and divine vibe I knew my cover must project. I had spent many hours the previous couple of months in this pursuit, but nothing struck a cord within me. I needed to discover an image that once found I would know, without a doubt, my search is over. I was willing to pay an artist for the rights to use his or her art.

Since October 6th I was again not working. In April of that year I took another position as a software engineer, but my inclination to be an ombudsman, a voice speaking out for the denizens of a broken system, put me at odds with a manager and his sidekick who did not tolerate voices of conscience. I had not been happy at that company since the first month and I welcomed the opportunity to free myself from its shackles and again have the opportunity to compose my novel, unfettered from the imposition of a full-time job.

On the morning of Monday, October 5th I received an email from the sidekick instructing me to meet him at the boardroom at two PM. I knew I would be dismissed. The previous Friday I again raised my concerns about flaws in the manner by which time was allotted to developers for their projects. I knew from previous experiences that my manager did not tolerate dissent, but I have never been a Yes Man. As I walked through the boardroom door I saw the sidekick sitting with Daisy, the Human Resources manager. I heard a voice immediately behind me, squeaking like the white rabbit of Alice In Wonderland. "Let me in, let me in." And then the voice cackled. It was my manager saying those words in a whimsical way as he squeezed past me and shuffled with exaggerated little steps. I saw a big grin on his face. He then sat at the edge of the table, to my immediate right. I remember thinking his flippant attitude towards my dismissal betrayed his motive of revenge on me for having voiced my dissent. His glee at taking vengeance against me exposed his banality. The sidekick had a dead, emotionless look in his eyes, like a Golem. When I looked into those eyes I could not see myself reflected back. My humanity did not exist in his world.

Immediately after my dismissal I was commiserating outside the company building with two colleagues. Daisy approached me and asked if I would like to have a chat. We entered her office and she closed the door.

"They didn't want me to talk to you, but I want to treat you like a fellow human being. I don't know if you've checked your separation documents yet, but I insisted that your separation not be classified as a dismissal."

We had a rewarding chat that afternoon and I thanked her for her humanity.

"This is the opportunity you were hoping for to finish your novel," Pamela said later that day and then she lowered her gaze and whispered: "I'm happy you can pursue your passion."

I could smell her resignation to a lot in life she believed would never satisfy her passion. She seemed to me like a queen without her throne, like a lover in a world devoid of her beloved, like a great warrior living in the cradle of peace. She was an ontological mother without a child. She heaped her love, tenderness and nurturing on me but also on our cat Ginger and on the numerous dogs and cats she took care of for friends and family on vacation or otherwise indisposed. "I am the dog whisperer," she once told me. Animals have always flocked to her. They sense her love and tenderness, and when I too sense it I feel a bleak and dismal emptiness because she has not consummated her passion to nurture a child. During such times I imagine the H unable to reflect within itself and create the tree of Existence - an H without YHVH.

"I just might be able to finally finish the novel by the end of the year." I felt joy at the opportunity to again immerse myself in days of wine and music and soulful writing.

The first chapter I wrote after my dismissal was *The Moon Reflects Our Soul*. I intended that chapter to bring down Ishmael from the distant pedestal of a father of nations and to humanize him by exposing his vulnerabilities, fears and yearnings. He would no longer be the abstract father of the Arab people. He would simply be a normal boy experiencing all the vulnerabilities, insecurities and heartbreak of a boy living through such regretful circumstances. I would only allude to his legacy.

I needed to reap the fruit of the seeds I had sown in my novel. The seeds had grown into unripened fruit up to that point. My novel's subplots were the unripened fruit. The story of Ishmael was such a subplot, another was the story of the layered and painful relationship my sister and I had with our father, hers far more hurting and dysfunctional than mine. I bared my spirit in the next chapter I wrote which I named *The Wrestler And The Dancer*. It was the climax of our relationship with our father. It was like the relationship of a planet with its parent star, forever yearning for its parent and falling towards it in a grand orbit's arc, but never reaching it. I understood my father that day in his apartment, after his death, but only from a distance, he never invited us into the atmosphere of his innermost chamber. We were his unprovable consequence. He never connected with Linda and me, as a system's axioms never connect with their unprovable theorems. We emanated from him but inhabited a different realm. Writing that chapter was an experience so cathartic I vowed I would finish my novel's last few paragraphs while sitting cross-legged at the cemetery, in front of my father's gravestone, like a mirror reflecting my spirit.

My protagonist's interaction with the Kol-Adama community and its rabbi was another subplot remaining unripened at that point. I had long wanted to write a chapter that would put the exclamation mark on this ultimately soured relationship. It was through this dynamic I intended to explore the tumultuous relationship Israel has had with the world, both as a nation since 1948, and more in the abstract as the spawn of a covenant that has shaped the spiritual and intellectual arc of the Civilization of Man. I also intended to proclaim my manifesto about a revolutionary new vision of the divine and the coming Third Age triggered by Israel's gifting of Jerusalem to the world. A few weeks after I completed *My Manifesto*, as I was writing a chapter in my novel titled *I AM Writing My Manifesto,* I realized I had not completed the story arc of my protagonist's spoiled relationship with the Kol-Adama congregation. I would have to season previously written chapters in my novel with references to the adversarial email exchanges my protagonist had with the Kol-Adama congregation throughout the years. It was from these emails I learned the rabbi had eventually abandoned all pretense of Zionism, though such pretense had become progressively tenuous during the years he still clung to the Zionist label. He had morphed into an obsessive and biased critic of Israel and its right to exist.

I opened *My Manifesto* with the events of Sunday, August 6th, 2006. It is the day of Vancouver's 29th Pride Parade, where my protagonist is representing the Kol-Adama congregation (real name of this congregation is Beit-Tzedek, meaning house of justice). I really did march in that parade as a representative of my congregation. Another parallel is the vociferous email exchanges I outlined in that chapter. These exchanges were with the large anti-Zionist contingent of my own congregation. It is in my nature to speak out against an injustice or a wrong, and this propensity has brought me, throughout my life, much grief and animosity. But I will not be silenced.

In *My Manifesto* I intended to write a short dialog between my protagonist and rabbi Flesher (real name is Saul Fromeatsky) in which they discuss and refine many of the pivotal ideas my protagonist had previously included in his novel. His life reflects my own. He too is writing a novel heralding a new vision of the divine and a new age for humanity. As I wrote the dialog, it took a life of its own and became much longer and more intricate than I intended. My novel, as an agent of the Third Age, guided me and breathed new ideas and insights into me. These were ideas and insights of which I was not yet in possession during that sweltering day of Vancouver's 29th Pride Parade, when I had the real world dialog with rabbi Fromeatsky while sitting on that grassy knoll next to the Burrard Bridge and the sparkling blue sea. We did briefly discuss the identity of god as the Nothingness, and the rabbi did remark that in the Hebrew bible there is a passage proclaiming the whole world will come to know the nature of the divine during the messianic age. I don't remember to which book of the Hebrew bible he referred. In *My Manifesto* I have rabbi Flesher say it is written in the book of Daniel.

Most of the dialog on that grassy knoll never transpired. For example, I never discussed Sartre's idea of existence preceding essence. It was only as I was writing *My Manifesto*, during November of 2015, that I saw the relevance of that idea to my notion of the nature of the divine, and particularly its relevance to the concept of Nothingness as the source of Existence. I put those words anachronistically in my protagonist's mouth. I was not yet familiar with Sartre's ideas during 2006.

I discussed this anachronism with Pamela and she remarked: "It's only anachronistic if you see the protagonist as being exactly you. If you see him as an independent character in your novel then you don't need to worry about synchronizing the events in your life with his."

"You know, I never thought of it that way. I always felt like I was cheating when I embellished my protagonist's dialogs. But I do need to keep a reasonably strong affinity between myself and my protagonist. But come to think of it, my protagonist in my novel thinks the same way when it comes with the similarity between his own life and that of his own protagonist."

"I'm getting confused."

I explained to Pam how the protagonist in my novel is doing pretty much what I'm doing in real life - writing a novel about a protagonist who is writing a novel about the coming Third Age.

"The major events that occur to my protagonist also occurred to me. I haven't fictionalized anything in that respect. Every character in my novel is mirrored by a character in my own life. Every dialog corresponds to a real dialog in my own world."

"Well, not in the first part of your novel about Abraham and Sarah."

"Obviously not, but the young Abram does write a composition where he's the protagonist and it's about him writing the composition. So I use the same self-referential literary device there also."

"Oh OK. I didn't read that part. I read that weird chapter about that big ugly statue guy with the big dick, ha ha. I was shocked at first but after you explained this represents him as a fertility idol then I agreed it belongs."

"That was a part of the self-referential composition the young Abram writes. It's all the chapters from the first until the chapter named *Address To The Examining Reader*."

"I should read the whole thing."

"But in the part of my novel set in the modern world, every discussion or event has really happened to me, though it may be embellished to some degree. And it happened to me in the same venues I write about in the novel."

I AM Writing My Manifesto

"Well I think it's got to be that way," Pam said, "otherwise you wouldn't be able to create that kind of cocooning in your novel. But tell me something." Pam paused.

"Tell you what?"

"In your novel the protagonist knows he is writing the story of his protagonist and all the way down the rabbit hole, but-"

"I call it the serpent hole. Do you remember I mentioned that in the big dick chapter?" I laughed.

"Oh yes...I forgot. But here's an interesting question: Does each protagonist know he or she is a character in someone's novel? Or does each protagonist think he's at the top of the serpent hole?"

I nodded and crinkled my forehead. "That's a brilliant question, actually. But let me ask you a question in the same vein." I paused for effect.

"Yeah?"

"Is this conversation also embellished?"

My motivation for writing the chapter *My Manifesto* was two-fold: I wanted to discuss the idea of Nothingness, and in particular the idea of creation ex-nihilo, in more depth because I felt the mystery of Nothingness, when properly elucidated, would captivate my reader with a sense of wonder and enlightenment transcending the mind and touching the soul. I also aimed to discuss the role of Israel and the Hebrews as agents of the coming Third Age. These two points of exploration are the heart of my manifesto, and they're discussed in *My Manifesto*. They are the passion compelling me to compose my novel.

One of the primary lessons of the novel I'm writing is that Existence is hierarchical (fractal) and the mechanism by which the hierarchies emanate is Gödel Incompleteness and its related mathematical discipline Chaos Theory. Gödel Incompleteness is a more fundamental aspect of Existence. The behaviors emanating out of Chaos are its consequences. All aspects of Existence can be mapped to some aspect of Gödel Incompleteness/Chaos Theory. In *My Manifesto* my protagonist explains the Abrahamic covenant as a particular mathematical mechanism within Chaos Theory called Strange Attractor. He indicates the Hebrews are that mathematical mechanism within the Chaotic system of the Civilization of Man. In reality, I am not certain of that. It might be a different aspect of Chaotic systems which maps to the Hebrew covenant. But regardless, the monumental realization within my novel is the Abrahamic covenant as a feature of Chaotic systems and that every Chaotic system has its version of an Abrahamic type of covenant.

"Give me examples of other Chaotic systems," Pamela asked when I explained these ideas to her.

"The global weather system. A boiling pot of water."

"So you're actually saying there's something in boiling water which corresponds to Jews in civilization?" Pam laughed.

"I prefer the word Hebrews - those that cross over to new realms."

During December 15, 16, 17 and 18 I composed the chapter in which I describe the writing of the chapter named *My Manifesto*. I gave it the straightforward name *I Am Writing My Manifesto*. The previous Sunday I met for brunch an ex-colleague named André with whom I worked from March 2005 until early 2008. I woke up from a nightmare at 6:30 AM that morning. An over-sized tiger was stalking me in the forest and I woke up just before he had the satisfaction of making a meal out of me. I could not return to sleep and I logged into my Facebook account. I responded to a comment André had made and Lo and behold, at around 8:30 he responded.

The following is a word-for-word transcript, including all typos and out of order responses, of the last part of our Facebook conversation that morning:

Nissim: Why are you already up? Don't you need your beauty sleep?

André: Well, this is late for me...only on my first coffee LOL Yesterday I was up at 4

André: What you up to?

Nissim: Why so early?

André: Wish I knew

Nissim: I woke up at 6:30 because i had a nightmare of being attacked by a huge tiger

André: Interesting...well I was also having weird dreams night before....might be the weather then LOL Hmmmm...a tiger eh? Symbolic of anything going on in life for you right now?

Nissim: I am almost finished writing my novel

André: Hang on... I thought you were done?

Nissim: It was only a novella at that point i pulled it from amazon a while back. It's a 400+ page novel now

André: Holy smokes! Okay...you're going big...do you have a publisher? Or still going self-publish route?

André: Hey, wanna do brunch? I haven't seen you in ages

Nissim: No publisher. It will be an eBook

Nissim: Sure. Let's do that

I AM Writing My Manifesto

***André**: Cool...check your messenger inbox*

We arranged to meet at 10:30 AM at a French bistro called Oui Paris Cafe Couture located at Hastings and Gilmore in Burnaby.

The above exchange with André occurred while I was still writing *I AM Writing My Manifesto*. I am quoting below the last part of that chapter where my protagonist is having a similar experience with a character also named André. I actually asked André for permission to use his real name in my novel and he agreed. I will not italicize it due to consideration for my readers. I would myself not want to read a very long passage in italics. So without further ado, here it is:

The conversation I had with André at Oui Paris that morning was enlightening and it forced me to address his objections and confusions in ways that had not occurred to me before. This often happens during such conversations and my head feels hot and its juices start bubbling and humming and I then hear the whispers emanating from the semantic spaces within the soul. Initially, before I included the above exchange in *I AM Writing My Manifesto*, I intended instead to weave its salient points into the chapter titled *My Manifesto*. It was on that grassy knoll overlooking the sparkling Pacific blue waters, during Vancouver's 29th Pride parade, that I intended to put these ideas into the mouths of my protagonist and his rabbi. But upon further reflection, I grew tired of putting words into the mouths of my characters that were not spoken by their real life counterparts at that point in time. I wanted to outline the conversation as it happened in the real world. I also intended to keep the dialog short. After I wrote *My Manifesto* I did not want to write yet another lengthy and intricate philosophical and scientific dialog. I have peppered a number of such lengthy dialogs throughout my novel and I feared my readers would grow weary of these.

"I will find out in the reviews if they became bored of the lengthy dialogs," I thought.

While writing *I AM Writing My Manifesto* I was determined that any part of my novel that I had not yet written would only contain short dialogs. Of course, some chapters that are placed after *I Am Writing My Manifesto* contain long dialogs but they had already been written by then.

I gave André the obligatory introduction to my ideas which, I admit, can be overwhelming when done in one sitting. I explained the tautological feedback loop by which nothingness references itself."

"But how can something come out of nothing?"

"Existence is a Zero Sum Game. For everything there's its polar opposite and everything cancels out. To answer your question, there's still nothing."

"But I see something."

"Did you know that when a bomb explodes it has zero momentum?"

"How can that be? Tell that to the people it killed. They sure got an ass-full of momentum." He laughed.

"But you have shrapnel flying in all directions. A car heading west at sixty miles per hour has momentum. Another car with the same weight heading east at sixty miles per hour has the same momentum but in the opposite direction. The system of these two cars has zero momentum. They cancel out."

"I see."

"In physics we have all these conservation laws of momentum, energy and so on. You can have an explosion where all the parts fly out in many directions. Each part has momentum but the system taken as a whole still has zero momentum in relation to its frame of reference. All these conservation laws and also symmetry laws in modern physics, they're all consequences of one overarching conservation law: the conservation of Nothingness. There can't be a net something if everything originally emanates from nothing. And that's what god is, the nothingness which is forever conserved and is the signature, the stamp, of the divine on all of Creation."

"I'm a fan of the Kabbalah. How does all this relate to the ten nodes of the Kabbalah tree? Is there a connection?"

"Oh yes, the Kabbalah. The Kabbalistic tree is the Big Bang itself."

"Whoa...what?"

"My Nothingness corresponds to the En Sof which is the source of all the other nodes on the tree. The Big Bang is much more than just the emanation of the physical universe of space and time. That's just one branch of the tree."

"I've never read that about the tree."

"That's my interpretation I should stress."

"Gotcha. So what on the tree is space and time as you say? Is it two of the nodes?"

"Notice how the ten nodes of the tree are $1 + 2 + 3 + 4$."

"OK"

"The first level is the level of nothingness - the En Sof. The second level is the level of polarities - the Yin and Yang. The third level is the level in Quantum Mechanics before an observation is made. I'm not sure how to categorize its three nodes. But the fourth level is the physical universe. It is the level characterized by four nodes."

"What are they? I thought it was two nodes, space and time."

"The three dimensions of space and one of time."

"Oh yeah, I didn't think of it that way. You're saying three of the nodes on the tree are space and one is time?"

"Yes."

"Phew...that's a lot of stuff to think about."

"In my novel I try not to dump on the reader such deep ideas so quickly, like I've done to you today."

"That's good. It's a lot of heavy stuff."

"I use the Karate Kid approach in my novel."

"Hang on...what?"

"In the Karate Kid, Daniel Larusso wants to learn Karate and so he enlists the help of Miyagi. But to Daniel's frustration, the first thing Miyagi does is-"

"Wax on, wax off." André chuckled.

"That's right. Miyagi's intent is to make Daniel get acclimatized to a Karate way of thinking and moving. A great teacher of Karate helps his pupil not learn Karate but become Karate."

"Hmmm...very profound. But let's get back to your idea of Nothingness. I'm having problems when you say this nothingness is the source of Existence. What is Nothingness?"

"It's the absence of all attributes and properties. I use the word 'it' because of the inability of language to speak of Nothingness."

"But when you define it that way then you are giving it an attribute, aren't you? The definition is the attribute."

"Not really. We are now entering the domain of paradox in the style of Russel's paradox. The set of all sets which aren't members of themselves."

"Russel what?"

"Never mind. I'll explain some other time."

"The way I see it," André said, "all of Reality emanates from the unfathomable. But I don't necessarily agree the unfathomable is Nothingness. It's something but unfathomable."

"What do you mean by unfathomable?"

"We can't understand it."

"Who's we?"

"Us...we humans."

"What about aliens on another planet with a higher intelligence? Can they fathom it?"

"No one can fathom it. Not earthlings, not aliens, not intelligent machines of any kind."

"So it's unfathomable in principle," I said, " and not just because we aren't intelligent enough."

"Yes, it can't be fathomed by any conceivable intelligence."

"Careful, you're using the word 'conceivable'. That's circular reasoning. Better to say it can't be fathomed without invoking the conceivable part."

André scratched his scalp and squinted. "I'll have to think about that."

"But anyway, the formal way of saying what you're saying is that no form of symbolic language can be isomorphic to it - can describe it. In that case I'll show you this unfathomable quote-on-quote 'thing' you talk about is the Nothingness I talk about."

"Really? How?"

I noticed a young man sitting in an adjoining table, intently listening to us. I wondered what he is thinking of our esoteric conversation.

"Anything with properties and attributes can be described by some language. In Gödel Incompleteness unprovable theorems emanate from any sufficiently descriptive mathematical system, but these unprovable theorems are only unprovable within the system from which they emanate."

"Hang on...you're equating provability with fathomability?"

"Bingo!"

"Hmmm...interesting."

"They become provable if we go out of their parent system and view them from a higher perspective. So anything with attributes and properties is fathomable from some perspective. Only that which has no properties and attributes is absolutely unfathomable. I like to use the word ineffable."

"Holy smokes! OK...you're going deep...it's a lot to think about."

"Think of properties and attributes as hooks that can be latched into and exploited for our understanding, or any intelligence advanced enough to hook into them. But only Nothingness is too slippery. It offers nothing to latch into, no pun intended, or maybe it is intended...ha ha."

"Yeah, I see what you mean."

"It's a real mind fuck, isn't it?"

The listener at the adjoining table smirked at that.

"My point is that the unfathomability of Nothingness is baked right into its definition and only nothingness is baked that way, and therefore only nothingness can be unfathomable in principle. This is a tautology. Nothingness is tautologically unfathomable and furthermore, only that which is tautologically unfathomable can be unfathomable in principle."

"What do you mean by tautology?"

"In my novel I've written a chapter asking why all bachelors are

I AM Writing My Manifesto

unmarried."

"Isn't that the definition of what a bachelor is?"

"Bingo! It's baked into the definition. Likewise, the ineffability of nothingness is baked into its definition."

"I see. It's a clever way to loop back on the definition."

"And do you also see we are actually in agreement? If, as you say, the source of all Existence is unfathomable, and I've just shown you the absolutely unfathomable must be Nothingness, then we are in agreement that Existence emanates from Nothingness."

The man at the adjoining table smirked again. His efforts to conceal his interest in our discussion had the opposite effect, they betrayed his interest.

"So to summarize what we've been discussing, all of Existence is due to the tautological inclination of Nothingness to self-reference. That's the primordial tautological feedback loop from which Existence emanates. There is no initial cause required."

"It just is."

"Exactly, but more specifically because of tautology. Existence is one big, fricking white-eyed tautology. That's why I'm fond of saying ontology is tautology. Being and Nothingness."

"Holy smokes! But what do you mean by white-eyed."

"It's a very evocative image. It brings to mind the idea of no-mind in Buddhism. And of course, the H in YHVH is exactly this ultimate notion of no-mind, absolute Nothingness."

"Yeah, I can see that. Tautology is like this self-referencing emptiness."

"It's the tautology of Nothingness and that's the innermost aspect of the divine. We all come from the chaotic white-eyed dust of Nothingness, and to that we shall return. It is the navel of Creation: a Loop in Eternity."

Above is the end of the quotation from my novel.

On Friday, December 18 I was putting the finishing touches on *I AM Writing My Manifesto*. I was making last minute changes to the conversation André and I had at Oui Cafe Couture when I remembered I had recently learned the Bhagavad Gita rejects nothingness as the source of all Existence. Instead, it posits matter has always existed, at least in some primordial form. This troubled me because in *My Manifesto*, as well as other chapters, my protagonist draws an equivalence between YHVH and the eternal feedback loop, described in the Bhagavad Gita, that creates and creates. I considered injecting into my discussion with André my rebuttal against the position that matter has an a priori existence, but when I reread

I AM Writing My Manifesto

that discussion I remembered I had never discussed the Bhagavad Gita with André. I then opted to weave my rebuttal into my protagonist's discussion with his rabbi, during the day of the 29th Vancouver Pride Parade in 2006. I injected that rebuttal much later, on January 9th, 2016. This is because I had spent the previous two weeks editing my manuscript from its first sentence to its last and then back again to its first. I wonder how many typos I did not notice and are still there.

On Wednesday, November 30th I completed the chapter *My Manifesto*. In the last section of that chapter I describe a meeting attended by my protagonist and a handful of other members of Kol-Adama. As usual, this mirrors an actual meeting I had attended with my own congregation. It was a meeting I had suggested as a means to diffuse the tensions and hostilities, within the Beit-Tzedek congregation, regarding the issue of Israel and the Palestinians. Before my protagonist severed ties with Kol-Adama he was the most outspoken critic of its enmity towards Israel and Zionism in general. I write that his outspokenness infuriates a good number of the other members. He is a lone voice in the wilderness.

This meeting has the opposite effect than my protagonist had hoped. Instead of healing his wounds, it aggravates them. The exchange between my protagonist and Stewart is the straw that breaks the camel's back. My protagonist remarks in the meeting that much of the world hates Jews. Stewart's one sentence response to that convinces him of the self-hating character of anti-Zionist Jews. His response is, and I quote:

"Well, and why do suppose that is?"

I write that when Stewart makes this remark he smirks and then he presses his tongue against his left cheek. This alludes to his snarky and veiled intent. That happened to me exactly as I describe it. But I did embellish the exchange that ensues. I write that my protagonist calls out Stewart on that remark. I quote:

"Don't you think I know what you meant by that?"

He now smells the stench of self-hatred permeating Kol-Adama and he wants out. This is indeed the straw that broke my own camel's back. The member of my congregation who is the inspiration for the character of Stewart (his real name is Stanley, but I changed his name in my novel to protect his privacy) really made that remark but I did not call him out on it. To this day I regret I did not. I am living vicariously through my protagonist.

That evening I sat at my home office desk and scoured the Internet for an image I would use as my new book cover. The previous image did not convey the visionary and mystical vibe I knew my cover must project. I had spent many hours the previous couple of months in this pursuit, but nothing struck a chord with me. I needed to find an image that once found I would know without a doubt my search is over. I was willing to pay an artist for the rights to use his or her art.

I AM Done

After my separation from Jelene in July of 2006 I stopped writing. At that point I had completed about half the story of my protagonist as a child living in ancient Ur. I had lost my passion to write, to think and to meditate on the I AM, and I instead became consumed for the next year in living a shallow lifestyle in pursuit of casual relationships with women. I am not proud of that year. For that one year I lost sight of my citizenship in that other realm. It was only when I met Pam during the last day of July 2007 that I gave up these pursuits, but I was still not ready to resume my writing.

Five years later, during September of 2012, I learned of Amazon's Kindle eBooks and that rekindled (or should I say it Kindled?) my passion to again write. I saw an opportunity to publish without needing to complete the entire novel - a task that seemed unachievable to me at that point. I resolved to split my intended novel into novella sized chunks and to publish each in its own time as a Kindle eBook.

I intended to upload my first novella to Amazon by year's end, but my father's illness and death sidetracked these plans. It seemed to me that whenever I start writing there comes along a life trauma to derail me - first the separation from Jelene and then my father's death. I again stopped writing, but this time the compulsion did not recede into a deep hibernation, it slept close beneath my surface and it awoke from its slumber by the middle of spring. I was working full-time at AquaFlow during that time and I wrote mostly on weekends. I released the first iteration of my novel during mid-August of 2013.

***

It was a sunny and chilly afternoon on January 9th, 2016. Pam and I were walking up the steep hill known as Cardiac Hill. It is a forty-five minute hiking path beginning with a gentle incline at an entrance off Gaglardi Way in Burnaby. The path becomes progressively steeper. Its last ten minutes are up an incline that would require climbing gear if it were any more severe. Cardiac Hill ends at a road just a five minute walk from the Simon Fraser University campus. The path begins as a wide dirt road that cuts into a dense Rain Forest, but becomes a narrow path half way up.

The previous week I started a contract of indefinite length at AquaFlow, the company for which I had already worked before. But it had now been bought by a company called Carlyle Informatics Processing. Pam and I reached the midpoint of the hike, after which the dirt road narrows into the

I AM Done

thick Rain Forest and morphs into an unforgiving incline. We had Misty with us, an eight year old Golden Retriever with a sweet disposition. We were taking care of her, on a long term basis, for a friend. Misty had been with us since October 31st. She got along well with our geriatric cat Ginger. I once remarked to Pam: "Whenever I see these two dawdling side by side into the TV room I can't help but be reminded of the comic characters Mutt and Jeff. One is a tall man and the other is very short, and they're inseparable friends."

"Let's stop here before we tackle the steep part," I said. "I need to rest. My cardio isn't as good as the last time we came here." It had been a couple of years since we hiked Cardiac Hill.

"Misty wants to run," Pam said. "I'll run up the hill with her just for a couple of minutes and we'll come back to get you."

Pam's cardiovascular fitness has always been better than mine. While I waited for Pam I checked my emails on my phone. I was waiting for an email from one of my followers on Twitter. Her name is Karen Smith from the city of Rifle Colorado. She had been patiently waiting for several months for my novel to be published on Amazon. Earlier in the day I tweeted the following to all my followers:

"Who wants to read a deeply philosophical novel?"

Karen replied: *"Me please. Is it ready?"*

I informed her the manuscript is not yet finished. I felt guilty for having tantalized her with a novel that never seems to be ready. I offered to email her my unfinished manuscript.

Before we left the house that day I messaged her on Twitter: *"Send me an email and I'll reply with an attachment of my manuscript."*

I now received her email. The subject line was: *"Here I am."*

I replied I am out of the house and will send her my manuscript when I get home.

Over the next week Karen sent me nightly reports about her impressions of my novel. On January 11th she sent me the following email:

Wonderment

Oh my. This is huge. Brilliant.

She inserted a quotation from my novel:

"I also live during an age that is ripe for spiritual change. These times

are reaching out for a person who will shatter idols and from these shards of divinities will rise but one god. A new zeitgeist will form and change the world."

This is what you are doing. You are revealing yet another new zeitgeist!

I am sitting here chuckling at myself, remembering when I first met you on Twitter, that you tweeted: I was born a Habiru and the Habiru are at best tolerated and at worst despised. And I thought, Awww.... I have to cheer this guy up. So I replied: Embrace your heritage and do the work to heal what you came here to heal. Know that in the big picture you are loved and precious". Oh my! I had no idea who I was talking to...

And another time I replied to one of your tweets with, "If helping people is your aim, just reading your tweets raises a person's vibrations." Boy oh boy, did I have that right!

I feel so privileged to be reading your book. Wow. Thank you.

I showed Pam this email. "Wow, she really likes it," Pam said.

I continued receiving Karen's effusive with praise emails nightly as she progressed through my novel, from chapter to chapter, until she reached the end of my novel's second part that details the life of my protagonist's later years when he receives the covenant from the I AM.

I do not remember if I have already made this clear, my novel is structured into three parts. The first part is called *The First Age: A Quest For Divinities* and it details the early life of its protagonist living in the city of Ur as he struggles with a vision of a new divine consciousness at odds with his society's polytheistic idolatry. The second part is called *The Second Age: A Quest For The One* and it details my protagonist's later years when he seeks the convergence of his destiny and ultimately meets his god in the desert, under a canopy of stars, and seals the covenant. The third part is called *The Third Age: A Quest For En Sof* and it details the saga of my protagonist, now played in the higher pitch of a modern man, as he yet again redefines the divine and announces the good news of the coming paradigm shift - the Third Age.

When Karen completed reading the last chapter of the second part she again sent me an email expressing effusive praise. But I knew what is awaiting her in my novel's third part.

I emailed her:

I AM Done

"I hope you will like the third part of my novel. It's very different and more challenging than the first two parts."

I did not hear from her for a few days but then she sent me the following email:

"I've been reading the third part of your novel. Nissim, it's not easy reading I must say. I can only read a bit at a time and often I have to reread several times. Please be patient with me."

Another week passed without a word from Karen. I wondered how she was faring with my novel's philosophical and scientific disquisitions. When I first contemplated writing the part of my novel set in modern times I was uncertain how to present my complex ideas. I realized quickly I would need to write long dialogs. I would not be able to present these ideas within a strictly plot driven format. The first two parts of my novel are more plot oriented because they do not need to present these complex ideas that leverage modern scientific, philosophical and abstract fields. The first two parts are set in ancient times and therefore can only allude to these ideas. Only the perceptive reader already familiar with these ideas would be able to decipher these allusions.

Another week passed during which I did not hear from Karen and then I received the following email:

"I've finished reading it. I bet you were starting to think I'm a slow reader. I'll send you my impressions soon."

The next day I received her promised email. I have since then lost it so the following is my recollection, seasoned with embellishments that are nevertheless true to the spirit of her email.

First of all, let me offer you my sincerest condolences for your loss of your father. As a grief counselor I can tell you that the way you poured out your heart about your loss is the best way to heal. You captured your relationship with your father and your grief brilliantly in you novel. Really well done!

Now, on to your unusual and stunning novel. I hope you don't take this the wrong way but at times I was reminded of the Charlie Brown comic strip when I was reading your long and complex dialogs and philosophical digressions. You know, when Charlie Brown listens to his teacher talk and all he can hear is Wa Wa Wa. Now, I consider myself a reasonably intelligent woman. I have a psychology degree and I've thought English for a while. But I'm afraid after finishing your book my comprehension of your ideas is at best tenuous.

Don't take this as a knock on your ideas nor your writing abilities. Your skills as a writer are amazing. I just wish that you wrote the third part of your novel with that delicious and stunning poetic style that I so enjoyed when you wrote about Abraham. It makes me wish that one of Abraham's descendants wrote the remainder of your novel. I'm a romantic at heart. I can't help but prefer much more Abraham to Godel. What can I say?

Thank you very much for allowing me the privilege of reading your manuscript before it's published and remember me when you're a famous writer.

Karen

    I was disappointed and troubled that I could not reach Karen at an intellectual nor spiritual level. I was also puzzled at her remark about wishing the third part was written by one of Abraham's descendants. As a Jew am I not one of Abraham's descendants? Reflecting on the gist of her comments since she began reading my novel I realized she had mainly responded favorably to my novel for its story-telling aspects, for its interpersonal dynamics and for its poetic or lyrical passages. As a grief counselor she identified with my relationship with my father leading up to his death. She also felt Abram's anxiety at a visceral level when he struggled with his existential dilemma and ultimately caused his father's heartbreak and dispossession, not just of his property and land but also of his soul.
    "I felt Abram's heart-wrenching situation as though it's happening to me," she emailed. *"I felt the unfairness of fate in placing this dilemma in Abram's lap, he was still just a boy and should not have to struggle with such soul-wrenching decisions."*
    For the next few days I did not write. It was not in defeat, it was to immerse myself in deep reflection on my novel's agenda and my approach to achieving it. I wondered if I should change course. There is a passage in my novel where I write about the impact I want to have on my readers. This passage ends with the following:
    "...to then have the reader see the world, momentarily or for a life changed, through my eyes."
    Was I being unrealistic in expecting all my readers to understand my ideas so intimately? Or was the fault in my writing? After these days of navel gazing I had an epiphany. My dilemma was to teach every reader my ideas, but these very ideas were about an entity, a collective, emanating out

of its white-eyed parts. The emanating entity knows its parts but the parts do not know the entity. I realized my imperative was to teach the whole, not the parts. Not every reader would appreciate my ideas. Some readers, such as Karen, would only be turned on to the lyricism of my novel or to the psychological dynamics between its characters. These are the traditional offerings of a novel. But my overarching agenda was to teach the Civilization of Man and have it see the divine through my eyes.

When I emailed this epiphany to Karen she responded: *"Yes, I understand what you're saying but it would have been nice for me, as a lone person, to understand better what you were saying."*

I responded: *"You're right Karen. Even in light of my epiphany I can still stand to make my ideas more approachable to the individual person. I'm going to work on improving my Bachelors chapter where I lay out my ideas about the EBSP."*

For the following week, each day after work, I pruned and trimmed the chapter in my novel titled *The Early Years: Why Are All Bachelors Unmarried?* I excised over four-thousand words. Some of the casualties were too verbose sentences or trivial exchanges between my protagonist and the character named Carl who represents my friend Carmine. But the bulk of the words I sheared off were those elaborating on the relevance of the EBSP to Quantum Mechanics. I selected Quantum Mechanics as the editing victim because it has traditionally been the poster boy for the consciousness-creates-reality school of thought. I aimed to show in that chapter that even the Relativity theories and other fields point in that direction.

During my days of reflection that led to my epiphany I constructed a question that is the Litmus Test in determining if my ideas have percolated into my reader's mind and soul. The question is: After having read my novel do you now believe in god? If my reader had understood my ideas, be he atheist or believer, he or she would respond that god is no longer in the domain of belief. I had redefined god and placed it squarely in the domain of rational and scientific discourse. To reject my notion of god would be to reject my inductive and deductive arguments leveraging the ideas of Gödel Incompleteness and Chaos Theory. It would no longer be left to unreasoned faith. It is not a god operating as an external intelligence that creates as a watchmaker creates, but instead a creator manifest within the created, an I AM within an I AM within another.

***

I AM Done

Saturday, April 16th was my mother's seventy-third birthday. Pam and I took her for a late lunch to a restaurant at Kits beach named The Boathouse Restaurant. At 7:30 that evening we visited my sister Linda and her husband Avi at their apartment in the downtown district of Yaletown. Linda was still at her furniture store named L'Atelier Home which was within a ten minute walk.

As I plopped my two bottles of red wine on the kitchen counter I asked Avi: "Did you see my new book cover? I put it up on Facebook."

"No, I thought you already had a cover."

"I needed a new one."

I showed him the cover on my Facebook page.

He studied it for a few seconds with a blank expression. "It's very beautiful but that guy under the tree looks scary. Maybe you should just use the tree image."

I waved my right elbow. "No way, this is my cover, I'm not changing a thing."

"Looks to me maybe like the garden of Eden." He pronounced it in its original Hebrew: Aiden.

"Very perceptive, yes it is, at least it's what it means to me. The garden and the Tree of Knowledge of Good and Evil plays a central theme in my novel. Let me tell you, I spent months scouring the Internet for an image that is just perfect for what I need. When I finally saw this image I immediately knew I AM done."

"You just copied it from the Internet? It's free?"

"No way...you think I wanna get sued? I bought the rights to it from the artist. He's a polish guy living in Ireland."

"What's his name?"

"Tomasz Alen Kopera...Tomasz with a zed at the end. You should see his other stuff. It's breathtaking."

"Which reminds me," Pam said, "Ziva didn't you say Linda started painting pictures?"

"Oh yes," my mother said. "She's very talented."

"Ziva," Avi said, "how is it that you have a son who is a writer and a daughter that paints but what do you do?" Avi laughed.

"I just enjoy my life. I don't need anything complicated. That's it."

Avi poured the three of us a glass of wine and we sat on the large twenty-fifth floor patio with a view of BC Place stadium only a few blocks away. The previous few days had been sunny and hot but it had now cooled and the sun hid behind a billow of clouds. Music was blaring from inside

I AM Done

the apartment.

"Hey Avi, can you put on some Pink Floyd?"

"Why do you like it so much?"

"When I listen to Pink Floyd I see the face of god."

"But you do know what an Israel hater Roger Waters is?"

"Yes, unfortunately he is."

"So why do you listen to that creep?"

"You know, I used to think like that?"

"So what's your answer?"

"Because the inspiration necessary to compose soul-piercing beauty like that can only come from a source deeper than the veneer of our ego. To reject it based only on its veneer is to reject its true source."

"What source?"

"God. If I boycott the music of Pink Floyd I would not be boycotting Roger Waters. I would be boycotting god. Because it is the music of god being breathed into the human plane. I have a similar argument against Capital Punishment. The argument being the same as I already gave and the conclusion is that when you kill a man you are killing god."

"But is that too deep to be practical?"

"It's deep and practical. It's the deep becoming practical. It's god becoming man."

Linda came home to the music of Pink Floyd blaring from the speakers inside the apartment. We came in from the patio.

"You guys had your Floyd fix I see." She laughed.

"Don't get him started," Avi said. "But it reminds me, are you almost finished your novel?"

"Actually, I've started writing the last chapter just yesterday."

"So how are you going to end the novel?"

I took a sip of wine. "No, the chapter I'm writing now is not the last chapter in the book. It's the last chapter I'm writing. There's a difference."

"What do you mean?" Linda said.

"I've already completed the last chapter of the book a few months ago. The chapter I'm working on now will actually be the chapter just before the last chapter."

"Oh I see, gotcha," Avi said. "What's it about?"

"I'm writing now about one of my followers on Twitter who's read my manuscript a few months ago. But the chapter will end with my visit to my father's gravestone. I will write the final few sentences of my novel while sitting cross-legged in front of his gravestone."

"Wow, that's very emotional and poignant. But tell me, have you written most chapters out of order like that?"

"Probably a quarter of the chapters were written like that. And often I go back to chapters I've completed months or even years ago and add more stuff to them."

"I'm interested in understanding the mind of writers," Avi said. "Why do you write like that?"

"I follow inspiration which doesn't care about the final order of the chapters in the book. I've already written the last chapter because I had an epiphany months ago of how I wanted to end the book. I saw the last sentence of the book etched in my mind and I felt a compulsion to write it."

"So when you wrote that last chapter you started by writing its last sentence?" Linda said.

"Yes, I worked backwards."

"Interesting," Avi said. "I wonder how common that approach is with other writers. So listen, you got me curious now; what's this mysterious last sentence that got you so compelled to write it?"

"Hey, buddy, you're gonna have to read the book, Aaavi." Pam laughed.

"I'm not going to spoil it for you," I said. "Let me just say this last sentence captures the essence of the book in more ways that one. Not just because of its meaning at face value but also because it's positioned as the last sentence. That has a special meaning. But the readers will have to figure out the meaning of all this by themselves."

Linda plopped her lean frame on the chair across from me and put up her feet on the small leg-rest in front of her. She shut her eyes, took a deep breath and exhaled. She opened her eyes a few seconds later. "OK, now I can decompress."

She stretched her right arm to the side and grabbed a glass of red wine from Avi who had just then come out of the kitchen holding two glasses of wine.

"You do realize you'll need to market your book," Linda said. "It's not enough to write a great book. You need a marketing plan."

Her sudden return to discussing my book surprised me. "Of course, I know that. Over the last few years I've done a lot of research about not just the art of writing but also marketing."

"No doubt. You realize most great books never become successful, right?"

"Look, I know I have to market it, but I think my novel is something special. It doesn't need to follow the regular rules of marketing Fiction. It's not just another story about vampires romancing white American girls. My

I AM Done

novel's agenda is cataclysmic, it's about a new way of understanding god and about a new paradigm shift that will transform humanity."

"I don't care if you're the Messiah himself writing a novel. You still need a solid marketing plan."

"I think if the Messiah published a novel he would not need to follow the traditional rules of marketing."

"Well, you're not the messiah, Nissim. You're going to have to follow the normal marketing rules that apply to vampire romance novels or your novel."

"You know, I actually analyze the idea of messiah in my novel."

Linda rolled her eyes. "I don't believe the messiah is coming back."

"That's the Christian idea of the messiah."

"Well then, I don't believe he's coming at all."

"But what if the idea of a messiah just refers to a leader who will be associated with a paradigm shift that will change humanity? Just a regular guy, not some supernatural being."

"So now you're redefining what messiah means to suit your agenda? I don't believe in god. I don't believe the bible has any relevance to our times."

"What do you mean by god? You need to define what it is you don't believe in."

"That's one thing actually that always makes me really angry," Linda said, "when people start defining god in any way that suits them. They say cliché stuff like god is love or he is the whisper of the winds. Well, screw that nonsense. How can love or whispers split the Red Sea or raise a man from the dead? If you're gong to say you believe in god then stick to the script. You can't just redefine it according to your whims."

"Come on now, the idea of the divine has morphed throughout history. The ancient world believed in corporeal deities that were each associated with a specific aspect of nature and the universe. Monotheism was a sharp departure from that. But humanity still called it god. So why do we have to stick to the script? Why can't there be a new understanding of god? In my novel I explain god is not some entity floating somewhere out there and controlling the universe like a puppeteer controls a puppet. God is intrinsic to Existence."

"You see, that's what pisses me off. Why do you have to use the word 'god' then? What makes that a god in any sense at all? Why can't-"

"Because-"

"Wait, let me finish. You say you have a new insight into the origin of the universe. Well, why can't you just express it that way without the god stuff? Isn't all that contradicting what the idea of god means?"

"Can I speak now?"

"Sure."

"Guys, take it easy. No fighting," my mother said. "You're all talking about nonsense anyway."

I ignored her comment and addressed Linda's question. "Because I want to make a connection between what the ancient Hebrews conceived and what I've now conceived. I want to show that the Hebrew bible is not the Bronze Age nonsense atheists claim it to be. It's true, there are stories in the bible, especially the Torah, that are obviously not literally true. Moses didn't split the sea with his wand. Adam and Eve and the snake are not real characters."

"Well, I'm glad we agree on that."

"But you must understand the ancient Hebrews were thinking in a more abstract way. Their shift from polytheism to monotheism was not just a change in their belief system. It triggered a drastic change in their general way of thinking. One came with the other. That's why their scriptures would then depart from simplistic literalism, it became a multi-layered weave of metaphor."

"I still don't see why you need to use the word 'god'."

"Linda, do you guys remember that night we were with abba in the ICU and he was hooked up to all those tubes? You were there too, Avi."

"It was many nights," Avi said.

"It was the night I explained to you guys the meaning of YHVH. Do you remember I was writing on the white-board?"

I gave again the same explanation I gave that night. I explained the Hebrew letters have spiritual meanings and then I explained the meaning of YHVH via these meanings and the tautological feedback loop. I explained the correspondence of this meaning of YHVH to feedback loops in Chaos Theory and self-reference in Gödel Incompleteness. "So here we have to ask ourselves, is this pure coincidence or perhaps the writers of the Torah were inspired from some source below the strata of their identity as beings of space and time?"

"I think they were," Avi said.

"So that's why I use the word 'god', because what the ancient Hebrews called god turns out to be all of Existence itself as coded in YHVH. The word they used for god turns out quite fantastically to encode the deepest and most concise way to describe Existence."

"How did you ever come up with this idea?" Avi said.

"And it's not just the Hebrews, " I said.

I then explained how the meaning encoded in YHVH is also mirrored in the Bhagavad Gita. "And the fact a separate culture came up with the same idea adds another reason it's unlikely all this is a coincidence. There is a common source, a veiled well of knowledge, from where humanity is drawing these deep invigorating waters."

"I definitely can agree with that," Linda said.

"That's the H within YHVH. That's my redefined god. That's why I still use the word 'god'."

***

The next Friday my mother phoned me in the early afternoon. "What are you doing?"

"Just doing some writing."

"Good! That's very good."

I was surprised by my mother's sudden excitement about my writing.

"I showed Sandra your new book cover. She's asking me what your book is about. Wait...what?...hold on, Sandra is asking me a question."

Sandra is her best friend, a bon-vivant in her age group, fond of travel, fond of drink, fond of life's bedrock beneath its veneer. I heard a muffled conversation in the background and then my mother's voice speaking into the phone.

"Here, she wants to talk to you...wait..."

A second passed. And then I heard Sandra's peach-fuzz, dulcet tones. "Hello Dahling, I just saw your book cover. It's so beautiful. But mama wants to know, what is it about?"

"Hi Sandra. I'll tell you what it's about. Well...in a nutshell it's a novel about a new understanding of the divine and a new age that will soon dawn on humanity. My goal is to unify the magical realism and metaphor of religion and spirituality with the rationality of science and mathematics."

"Wow, you are brilliant. It's funny how we were just talking about that. Listen dahling, when is it going to be ready? Mama wants a copy."

"I'm very close, maybe a couple of weeks. I'll let you know."

"Good for you. OK honey, your mama now wants to talk to you."

I waited a few seconds and then I heard my mother's voice. "Good, how much until you are finished writing?"

"I think another couple of weeks.

"Very good. Then you can go back to work."

"Yes... yes, I'll start looking for something at that point."

I AM Done

After the phone call I again fell into the white-eyed embrace of my penultimate chapter. I wrote of a day that was the seventy-third birthday of my protagonist's mother. I wrote of a discussion he had with his sister. It was about god and messiah and of a new age that will soon dawn upon our bowed heads. And we will then bow as submission bows to its release. And then from Jerusalem, the city of Zion atop a hill, the temple will ripple out toward all humanity and shard itself into our core.

Each day I neared my novel's completion I felt vague pangs of existential despair I could not explain. But also each day its vagueness loosened and I could begin to see my source of discontent. It was a fear of my novel's impending finish and then of its release. And then a darting doubt flirted with me: *What will you do then?*

Aspiring for my novel had been my nobility, my identity. The next stage was a fearful mist to me. But I knew I had to engage it in the Wrestle and only then it would offer me the Dance.

A parent coddles her child within her protective embrace. She rues her child's impending release into worlds out yonder beyond the horizon of her warmth's embrace. But also she aspires for the release because only then the soul she daily breathes into her child will finally be exhaled into the mist.

And also each nearing day my novel whispered to me from within my nourishing womb and with its right hand index finger stabbing the heavens it heralded the good news of its imminent birth, and I then could no longer see it as the Chaos of words within me but of an entity with autonomy who will then wish to dance with me. But when I do finally exhale it out of me, I will then deny it the return.

It is April 28, 2016 at 4:54 PM. I'm sitting in my home-office writing these words while floating on the sounds of Enigma's *Le Roi est mort, vive le Roi!* and I'm overtaken by a feeling I'm truly just a funnel through which these words will come to you. Never have such words of semantic poetry flowed this effortlessly through me. As they pour out of me with untamed ferocity I fear to look at the face of their source because it would be to dance while locked in a gaze with the face of god.

And I know the time is just about done. It's been ten years of off and on writing. But this novel was continually on my mind and soul these ten years and the years before. I've mortgaged my software development career to express my spirit and reveal the soul to the Civilization of Man, and the creditors may soon come to repossess, but I'd have done so regardless.

I AM Done

Writing my novel has cost me more than a hundred thousand dollars of lost wages. There have been long periods during which I did not seek employment or I only sought part-time employment, otherwise I would not have been able to immerse myself in my writing and complete my novel to my satisfaction. But even when I worked full-time I devoted much of my extracurricular time to writing my novel and studying fields pertaining to it. I seldom furthered my software development knowledge. That too has cost me financially. To be a successful software developer one must continually study software development. It is a field like a river, never remaining in one spot. But despite these financial losses, I do not regret, for even one second, these sacrifices I have made. My novel is my spirit, and it is therefore the soul, and if it does not achieve success then I will nevertheless not regret my sacrifices. I have, to this day, squeezed almost all of my spirit into it. That alone can be my reward.

In the next few days I'll be breathing into my novel my last semantic breaths. My last such breath will be while sitting cross-legged looking onto my father's gravestone. Keep an eye on this here place once in a while so you won't miss the unfolding saga of these ultimate steps.

In the meantime I'll be going back to the other chapters and decide on which ones I'll squeeze the last remaining drops still within me. And even as I write these words I can't stop the gushing flow of semantic poetry falling out of the funnel and onto me. These are god's whispers to me.

Will this mighty whispering river that has burst out from the womb at my core and spent its fertility into me then become, after my last words, just a trickle merging back into its source?

Oh yes, I'll remind you now in case I forget to remind you the next time we meet, there's one more chapter still to come. I'll be taking you all the way back to that fertile time when legend will become blurred into fact. It's a time when I start wrestling with this unforgiving, exasperating, challenging, maddening and demanding novel. But it's also a time I start to dance. Another way I would have never wanted done.

***

Welcome back. I'm ecstatic for your return. Once again you're alongside me as I again write of these last few days; as they happen within my simultaneity. It is now May 2, 2016.

...
...
...

I AM Done

But suddenly the inspired words aren't coming to me. I've stared at the page for the last fifteen minutes and unable to write anything interesting. It's writer's block. I used to get this all the time when I was writing English essays in high school and university. But I wasn't trying very hard. Anyway, I'm trying to write something in my novel that's meaningful in a poetic way but my words just sound clunky and workmanlike. How come it came so easy to me last week when I wrote about... I'm stopping to write to see what I wrote on those previous pages of my novel... oh yes, I wrote about a mighty river whispering from me and, let's see...my last semantic breaths...hold on a minute while I look at all the other stuff on those pages.

...

...

...

Damn, sorry for the wait, it's amazing stuff. Who really wrote those words? I'll have what that guy is having. I hope the readers of my novel will forgive me for the paragraph I'm writing in my novel right now and the paragraph before it. They have clumsy prose and they're wordy and verbose and boring and just uninspired. But I keep writing like that for some unfathomable reason. If you could read these few paragraphs in my novel you'll definitely agree with me that their prose is unpolished and they just go on and on and on and on. They're not good. I need to get back my inspiration. I'll probably edit these paragraphs out later. I know there's no flowing poetry or a lyrical tempo. What I'll do is try to improve the remainder of the paragraph I'm currently writing in my novel. Maybe I'll just leave as is the previous paragraph and the current paragraph as it's so far and try to write better for the remainder of that paragraph. My readers will have to hold their noses until the paragraph gets good. But come to think of it, what I've just told you...well, I've decided to add these sentiments to my novel as well. As I'm telling you all this I'm actually writing it in my novel, so the message becomes the medium, that makes it interesting to my readers in a serpent-eating-its-own-tail kind of way, because by actually involving my readers in its banality instead of just telling them, it becomes very deep and interesting. But its only means of becoming interesting is by referring to its own banality. Something-interesting out of nothing-interesting, basically. Writers are advised: show don't tell. But I'll go to the final logical conclusion. I say BE, don't just show. Come to think of it, what I'm writing in my novel now reminds me of the Gödel self-negating sentence, the one asserting its own lie. It becomes interesting by referring to its own lack of anything interesting, but then because it becomes interesting it's no longer interesting. But enough of this banter. I'm looking with delight and wonder at that nearing day during which I'll be at my father's grave and write the final words in my novel. I told Pam of this early last week and she suggested she accompany me to that event and take pictures for posterity. At first I was excited to have her accompany me. But the next two days it occurred to me I'll need solitude during that event. I'll need to feel obligation and duty to none other than my novel. I'll need to crack open the veneer and only dance with my core. I've just now also written about this sentiment in my novel, and the more I wrote the more disillusioned I became with its conclusion. I feel shallow and dismissive because I've already told Pam that during this event I must dance alone. But I'm now seeing the errors of my thinking. That momentous occasion I have longed for all these years I should share with her. Her presence should not enforce the illusory separateness we the people perceive towards each other. Is love not the antidote that dispels this illusion? And then we see that we are each the Other and the Other is the Self. We are One.

The next we see each other may very well be the day we head to that cemetery. I'll write there the last paragraphs in my novel. In the meantime I'll finish its editing and polishing. I'll see you here soon my friend.

***

Welcome back, it's now May 3 and I'm sitting at my office desk again and writing the few remaining thoughts before the foray to the cemetery in the next few days. About two hours ago I made some enhancements to a chapter in the second part of my novel. The chapter is titled *The Navel Of Creation: A Loop In eternity*. I deepened the thoughts in the section where Abraham seals the covenant with the I AM. Abraham questions the I AM on why he is forbidden to reveal the mysteries he had seen that night and why he must not reveal the meaning of the name YHVH. I added to that section the idea it is precisely because the Hebrew people have not known the meaning of the name YHVH that the covenant unfolded according to original intent. Across the millennia the compulsive desire to know this meaning has compelled the Hebrews to visit semantic way-ports along their paths of discovery as they attempted to understand the meaning of YHVH. And in so doing they've launched realms of new thoughts, new ideas, and they shook humanity from its atavistic comforts. That's why the Hebrews are called the God Wrestlers.

But often when they visited the semantic way-ports of discovery they were under the misconception each such interim port was the final destination. They were unaware of their core's intended final destination - the meaning of YHVH.

After dealing with *The Navel Of Creation: A Loop In eternity* I've enhanced a paragraph much later in my novel. It doesn't matter which. Next I'll enhance yet another section in the second part of my novel. In the chapter where I describe the trial of Abram and his father I'll write of the blindness of the presiding judge to understand why Abram appropriates the term 'god' for his system of thought. In the judge's way of thinking the concept of god can only apply to a super-being within a polytheistic pantheon. I'll add this section as an allusion to the ridicule heaped on me by atheists and believers alike for thinking my own ideas point to something which can also legitimately be called god.

I hope to see you again here and I promise we will get to that cemetery very soon. Perhaps even the next time we meet.

***

Today is May 6, 2016. No, we're not going to the cemetery yet. I'm not in a visionary or poetic mood today for some reason. I feel simply like a biographer recording the last days of my novel's completion. I had a sudden urge today to email Paul Hamersky. As the writing of my novel winds down I am remembering people who played watershed roles in its writing. I have not communicated with Paul since the end of December 2014, but he has been on my mind many times since then. After I emailed him I revisited the chapter in my novel titled *The Story Unfolds* and I added there the story of how I first met him on Twitter in early 2014 and he agreed to be a beta reader for my early manuscript. I thought it would be inexcusable to omit him from the story of the gestation of my novel.

I am grateful that I have preserved my email correspondences with him. I included in that chapter verbatim excerpts of an email he sent me on April 3, 2014 in which he comments about my manuscript and specifically about the then new chapters about Abraham's later years. I have not changed his name in that chapter. My protagonist too has in his life a Paul Hamersky who has encouraged and emboldened him to complete his novel and to maintain a steely confidence in his ability to change the world.

Well, that's it for today.

***

I AM Done

Today is May 7th. I received an email reply from Paul:

Great to hear from you...of course I remember you. I look forward to reading it again and seeing the maturation of your personal evolution. Where SOD has gone, so have you. I am honored you have let me know. I'll be watching for it on Amazon.

Happy to hear you are planning to commit to print publishing, mainly because it will make you close the the back cover and send it out into the world to fend for itself. You have raised a child here...provided the seeds of inception, nurtured and fed it with your energy, perceptions and time(?:-) A stage is reached when a child must make their own mark on the world, for good or for bad. Congratulations Dr Frankenstein...it's alive.

I too have been evolving...because there is no other choice except to disappear. In what ways?...I am unable to be certain having come the realization that what evolves is our perceptions and interpretations of what surrounds us. Clean the lens of ones glasses and world becomes a more beautiful place. My world seems to be getting more beautiful and more ugly...again, without polarity there is no thing.

On a more practical note of the "what seems to be"....I was never able to fully embrace the social media thing so as you probably noticed, I disappeared from that arena. I'm still engaged in changing lives in dentistry :-)...orthodontics (which is like creating cover art on other peoples books) and have added the dental treatments for sleep apnea and snoring which does change lives. Sleep is an interesting "need" our physical presence requires....a lot like aging....no real cellular reason for it to be needed yet without it, we die.

Keep me in the loop....especially if the book tours gets anywhere near Denver :-) I'll reach out if anything would get me to the great north-west (SW from your perspective).

Stay well and a little insane...keeps one from being "normal"

All the best

Paul

I AM Done

I replied to his email:

Hi Paul

Yes, I do feel like I've raised a child, or more like I'm soon to give birth to a child. I use that metaphor towards the end of my novel. I've breathed into the novel gestating within my soul's womb and only when the novel is born then shall it exhale these breaths and it will become an autonomous entity. But now that the child's birth is imminent I will miss carrying it in my womb. These past years I've been longing for the day of this birth, but now I have mixed feelings. I'll miss writing my novel. I'll miss the delicious euphoria of breathing into it my soul.

But I'm looking forward with excitement to see what this child will accomplish in the world. I could not have given it birth without being constructively insane.

I'll keep you in the loop. By the way, do I have your approval to mention you in my novel? As you know, my novel uses self-reference. It is aware of itself.

Yours truly,

Nissim

Paul replied:

Approval given :-) Remember to breath and push. No one knows when the preborn is aware of itself but I believe that it is sooner than we might imagine, Just no memory capable of point of reference and therefore timeless.

P.

***

I AM Done

Today is May 12th. I've spent the last few days revisiting the chapter named *The Early Years: Why Are All Bachelors Unmarried.* I've tightened up my explanations and removed a few passages that did not serve the overall thesis.

That chapter examines the role of a principle I call the EBSP and shows its relevance to the Relativity theories as well as Quantum Mechanics. This principle is fundamental in my conclusion that there's but one consciousness at the root of it all. A few days ago I did more reading on the Special Theory of Relativity and I came across a discussion of Logical Positivism. I immediately realized its similarity to the EBSP. I heard of it many years ago at sixteen, when I read a biography about Einstein, but I have not read nor thought about it since then. I suspect all those years it lay just beneath my conscious awareness and it nourished the formation of my ideas. I added a short reference to it in the Bachelors chapters where Carl, who is a stand-in for Carmine, mentions its similarity to the EBSP.

***

Today, May 16th, is finally the day. The last few days I've suffered from extreme, throbbing pain in the big toe of my right foot and I could not walk. The pain is subsiding and I'll be able to limp to my father's gravestone. This temporary limp is unrelated to my permanent limp that I've had for the last ten years. I've a weakness below the knee of both legs which doctors have been unable to diagnose. My permanent limp isn't severe nor painful, but it's noticeable.

We'll be visiting my father at the cemetery and you'll be sitting with me, facing my father's gravestone, as I write the final words of my novel. These are the final words in real time, not the closing words of the final chapter. These final words appear at the end of the penultimate chapter in my novel and they tell the story of my protagonist's completion of his novel.

I began writing my novel in mid-April of 2006. That's ten years and one month ago. But I didn't write steadily for those ten years. After my separation from Jelene in July of 2006 I completely stopped writing. For one year I also stopped reading and thinking about the ideas I've breathed into my novel. I lost my passion.

After I met Pam during the last day of July, 2007 I gradually regained my passion. The whispers that fell silent the year before again started calling out to me from a place deep within. I could barely hear them at first, and at times I thought them to be empty echoes from my past. As the years passed they amplified, but still I didn't write. During those years I wondered if I'd ever complete my novel, and during times of severe doubt my heart ached and I became inconsolable.

During autumn of 2012 I resumed writing. My ambitions were modest at first. I aimed to publish only a novella on Amazon. But my passion for completing my novel was rekindled. It was like an exponential curve, slow and steady at first but then abruptly taking off. I tried to balance career and writing and I was initially successful but, gradually at first, I shifted my focus toward writing. These last few months I've only cared to complete my novel. I've been oblivious to all else.

Before we leave for the cemetery there's one more thing I want to write. I'll revisit a chapter in my novel named *My Manifesto* and have my protagonist defend his position that in the Third Age Judaism, along with all other religions, should and will fade. In that chapter he's in conversation with rabbi Flesher, who is a proxy for rabbi Fromeatsky. From 2005 to 2006 I was a member of a synagogue led by rabbi Fromeatsky, but I quit in 2006 when I could no longer tolerate the overbearing stench, like daggers in my nose, of its banal hatred toward Israel. Please wait for me while I write this, it will not take long.

I'm done adding my changes to *My Manifesto*. I'm leaving now for the cemetery. I'll meet you there. It's named Schara Tzedeck Cemetery - Hebrew for Gate Of Justice. The address is 2345 Marine Drive, New Westminster and is just a few minutes drive from South Burnaby. I'll see you there. My father's name is Shmuel Levy and his gravestone is a little west of a small shack. He's very close to the southern hedgerow and next to a narrow, paved walkway which runs north to south. Across from this walkway is an empty grassy field. In the next few years it too will be loaded with graves.

Well, here we are. I'm glad you joined me. Did you have difficulty finding my father's gravestone? Pamela couldn't join us because she's working. But she also insisted I should spend this time alone with my thoughts and my whispering companion. The cemetery is deserted during this overcast day. I hope it won't rain. The only people who might see me are the riders on the nearby Skytrains that pass by overground every minute or two. Are they seeing me? What must they be thinking when they see us sitting on top of his remains and with my laptop atop his gravestone. Let's meditate for a while. I need to hear the whispers. I need inspiration. I'm feeling flustered now because during such a momentous and anticipated event I'm not in command of the words that will satisfy the soul. I didn't want to contemplate what these words should be when I was home. I wanted this to be spontaneous.

The words are not coming to me. Perhaps I shouldn't be aspiring to write beautiful poetry. Perhaps I shouldn't be grasping for erudite words. I'm attempting to wrestle with this task but perhaps I should dance. My father plays a prominent role in my novel. Amidst its musings about Gödel and Chaos I've been compelled to show the world my father's heart. It's also my heart. Like him, I've also struggled with this world. He found his peace on that beach by disengaging from polite society. He also found it traveling the world on a shoestring. My way to peace and fulfillment is my novel. Nothing else has ever made sense in my life. Nothing else has inspired and motivated me. I crave to show humanity there's a new age coming. It's an age of peace and understanding of what god is.

I'm not seeking wealth. I'm not seeking adulation. But before I die I'm pleading with the I AM to grant me the knowledge that my novel has achieved what I intend for it. But I've been far from perfect. I've committed all the sins of the common man. Perhaps the I AM will not allow me to set foot on the promised land. But I want to be a better man. I want to let go of all the resentments and even hate that I feel for those who have wronged me throughout my life. But aspiring for enlightenment should never be motivated by a desire to feel smug about being enlightened. That is a contradiction. You should only better yourself for the sake of others. Do for others and then it will be done for you.

My womb's waters are breaking now. My novel is now being born. And once born it will exhale the breaths I've provided it within my womb. Go now into the world, my passion. I am sitting now on a grave which marks the end of my father's life. But my novel will now begin its life and go into the world from atop this grave. I AM done.

The Curtains Open: The Third Act

In mid-April 2006 Jenna and I invited Darnell to one of our Friday night rituals of television, red wine and spirited discussions. We had never before invited anyone else to these sacred Friday nights. Jenna met Darnell in the late 1980s when she worked as a receptionist at a major marketing agency in Vancouver. Darnell was wedged between two worlds: On the Left, the world we preached of social justice, compassion for the poor and disenfranchised, a spiritual quest for enlightenment and a governed Capitalism. On the Right, the world of his father, the founder of said marketing agency - a jet-setting world of wealth, high consumption, materialism and a Capitalism run amok.

Darnell was in his mid-thirties in those days, but he had never married and was perpetually single. He was a solitary sort, living within the confines of his introspections and spending many a solitary night and day working on his passions: sketching and painting. He is an alumni of the Emily Carr University of Art and Design on Vancouver's Granville Island - a quaint, tiny island with a large indoor food market, ocean themed businesses and an eclectic mix of bakeries, shops, art galleries, restaurants and coffee shops.

"Nini, Nini, I've been listening to you and Jenna for the last seven years filling my head with your ideas of enlightenment, but isn't that just pie-in-the-sky stuff? Well, to you for seven years. Jenna has been preaching to me far longer."

Nini was the name I bestowed upon myself when I was a toddler and could not pronounce my name. It had stuck since then with my family and my family's friends, and Darnell had taken a perverse liking to it.

"And you've savored every pearl of wisdom I've ever told you. Right, Darny baby?"

Darnell focused on me, ignoring, in jest, Jenna's comment. "You know, when I first met your wife she was like a bronzed goddess, a Nubian princess. She was belly-dancing in Middle Eastern restaurants around town, but somehow there was never any attraction. I never saw her as more than a friend or sister. Go figure because I always preferred the olive-skinned, dark-haired types, but still...nada...zilch."

"Could be because you couldn't handle an outspoken, opinionated bitch like me, couldja?"

"Maybe, but back to this enlightenment hocus-pocus crap. I can imagine a group of so-called enlightened people, each arguing they are the most enlightened of the bunch. Mirror, mirror on the wall, who's the most

The Curtains Open: The Third Act

enlightened one of all. You know, that kinda shit. I can imagine a society where the most enlightened get all the benefits and the unenlightened masses get nothing. So nothing has changed, it's still like uncontrolled Capitalism, but now the currency is enlightenment instead of money. It's not Capitalism, it's Enlightenmentism." Darnell laughed.

"Well then Darny baby, they aren't really enlightened then, are they?"

"Seems like the truly enlightened," Darnell said, "can't dwell on their enlightenment. Should they even know they're enlightened?"

"First of all," I said, "enlightenment is a journey, not a destination."

"Blah, blah blah, what does that even mean?"

"Hey Darnellio, where'd ya get that cynicism about all this spirituality stuff, from Freddie baby?" Jenna laughed. Fred is Darnell's father, the marketing mogul.

"Second of all," I continued, ignoring Jenna's and Darnell's retorts, "is there even anyone who's completely enlightened? No such person exists. That's why I say it's a journey. You never get there, you can only approach that elusive goal. To be truly enlightened is to see the face of god, and that is only achieved in death, and as a collective...not as you individually. What matters is that you head in the right direction."

"Hurry up and write your book already, for god's sake. You've been talking about it for years. You can explain all this in your book. You see Nini, I'm an artist and I do my art. If you're a writer then you should write."

"I haven't been ready all these years. I was still forming my ideas."

"I disagree, you should have started writing years ago."

"Hey hon, I can see the bottom of this bottle. Can you crack open another? Darnell, your glass looks very thirsty."

I went to the kitchen and uncorked another bottle of red.

"I'm good Nini," Darnell shouted to me when I was in the kitchen, "I shouldn't even have any. I'm still on my meds."

"I didn't know you're still on them," Jenna said.

"Yeah, well I was off them for a while, but then crazy shit between me, my dad and his bat-shit crazy wife has got me back on them."

I returned with the bottle of wine and refilled my and Jenna's glasses. Jenna took a sip. "Damn Darnell, her again? What's that coked-up nut up to this time?"

"I don't really want to go into it. She's driving me nuts, and my dad's just eating up her nonsense. Get this, a few months ago she bitched to my dad that he only bought her an $80,000 car for her birthday. I heard her actually say: 'Is that how shitty you treat your own wife, Fred?' Can you believe she said that? What a cow."

"Wow, talk about unfettered consumption," I said.

"So Nini, have you been writing already?"

I gave Darnell and Jenna a knowing smile. "I'm happy to say I've had a breakthrough and the time is now right for me to start writing my Magnum Opus."

"Magnum what? I'll take it that means your novel, right? I'm no English Major."

"Magnum Opus - it means Great Work in Latin," Jenna said.

"Hey hon, you didn't tell me about this."

"It happened a couple of weeks ago when you were staying at Penny's."

I told them the story of my epiphany during that Saturday when I decoded the meaning of YHVH.

When I finished, Darnell whistled in as much amazement as confusion. "That went too fast by me. I'm no Philosophy Major. I'll have to read your Magnum Opus." He snickered and gave me a wink. "What about enlightenment? Anything in your book about that crap?"

"Does a bear shit in the woods?" I laughed. "Of course there'll be a boat-load of stuff about enlightenment. One of the themes of my book will be that humanity is now at the dawn of a new spiritual and scientific awakening I call the Third Age."

"Global enlightenment? Pffft...Impossible. People are people. They're petty and scheming and greedy and selfish. Trust me, I know. That'll never change, for sure."

"I agree people don't change in that regard, but it's not at an individual level this change will occur, it's the emergent behavior from the collective that will change."

"The collective? The collective? If my dad heard you say that he'd cut out your liver with a dirty knife."

"Why?"

"He's a fan-boy of Ayn Rand. He doesn't believe in any of this collective Socialism crap. He believes in personal freedoms."

"Hey Darny baby, what he believes in is the right of the rich to do as they wish. Power makes right, n'est-ce pas?"

"Look, I'm not going to get caught in the middle of my dad's and your world-view again. What's wrong with personal freedoms?"

"Ayn Rand is the queen-bee of those who crap all over everything that's good and holy in order to appease their crass greed."

"That's what you and Jenna say."

"I once saw an old Donahue show she appeared on," I said. "Do you know what she said?"

"What Nini? Something about personal freedoms? My dad says she was big on that."

"Nonsense, she corrupted the intent of personal freedoms. We don't have the freedom to rape and pillage in order to satisfy our unquenchable lust for wealth and power. But that's what corporations do in her so-called free society. But on this occasion she said something that made the audience gasp."

"What hon? She musta stunk up the place."

"Donahue asked her if she's filled with wonder when she looks at the stars. She said she isn't and she doesn't like to look at them."

"That cow had no soul."

"When I heard that, I saw into her crass soul. The prophet Daniel spoke of the Abomination of Desolation that desecrates the temple of the Lord. I'm not a Christian but I find the book of Revelation intriguing because it expounds on this idea in the context of an Anti-Christ, just before the dawn of the Messianic Age. To me, the temple is a metaphor for all of Creation, the oceans, the forests, the dignity of the human soul, and, yes, the stars. These acolytes of Ayn Rand, these blasphemous Right Wing fascists, crap all over the temple of the Lord. For example, they deny Climate Change because they coddle the interests of big corporations whose earnings are generated by destroying the planet. And all this in the name of Ayn Rand's so-called free economy. They are shills for the plutocrats that twiddle their thumbs while the temple burns."

Jenna clapped short little claps while vibrating up and down on the sofa. "Bravo hon, bravo. Well said, well said."

"What Ayn Rand failed to realize is that in a free society government is itself an emanation from this freedom. Society organizes itself into public institutions of charity, of health services and so on. That is what government is. This is what the Civilization of Man is in its purest essence."

"My dad will say there's no such thing as civilization, only the actions of individuals, not this Socialist collective you talk about."

"First of all, I never condoned a restriction of personal freedoms. I'm talking about an emergent behavior, not the level of individual people."

"That's the Socialist collective."

"No it's not. Even a society ruled by complete anarchy will have an emergent collective behavior emanating out of it. It's got nothing to do with imposing restrictions at an individual level. After all, I'm talking about Order out of Chaos. The whole is greater than the sum of its parts."

"Oh for Christ's sake, I've been hearing that expression since I was a kid. What does that crap even mean? Isn't it just meaningless mumbo-jumbo that just sounds like you're saying something intelligent. But you're saying zilch, nada."

Jenna shot Darnell a dirty look. "Come on Darnell, that's not Nissim's style at all and you know it. So give your head a shake. When he says something you can bet he's thought it through. There isn't an ounce of hot air in his entire body." Jenna was becoming very invested in this discussion. She leaned forward from her slumped-back position on the couch, like a sports fan invested in every nuance and flavor of a sporting match.

"Look Darnell, I'll give you a few examples of what I mean. Exhibit A: the Renaissance, also known as the Age of Reason. Five-hundred years ago Europe was festering in superstition and ignorance. Then the Renaissance dawned and it was a great paradigm shift. Europe achieved great scientific breakthroughs. It no longer followed the pied-piper of superstition and ignorance. Now, do you think the character or intelligence of individual Europeans had improved? Of course not."

"Then how do you explain the change?"

"It's the emergent behavior, like an ant-hill, like fireflies synchronizing their blinking. When you learn a new skill do individual neurons in your brain get smarter?"

"You tell me, I'm no neuro-scientist."

"What changes is the network of communication between the neurons, not the neurons themselves. A skill learned is an emergent behavior that comes out of the feedback loops of communication between the neurons in your brain."

"So you're saying the Renaissance was an emergent behavior out of the network of communication between individual Europeans?"

"You got it Darnell."

"That's brilliant hon. You is soooo smart."

"So Nini, what's exhibit B?"

"The collapse of the Soviet Union."

"Hmm...interesting. I'm listening, I'm listening."

"If I had told you in the mid-Eighties that the Soviet Union would collapse within five or six years, what would you have said?"

"I don't know, I'm no political scientist."

"Well, I'll tell you what even experts would've said. They would've said I'm crazy, that things just don't change that fast. But it did collapse, and it collapsed fast, like an earthquake without a warning. No change forever and then, without warning, the ground shakes and splits open."

The Curtains Open: The Third Act

"So you're making an analogy between the collapse of the Soviet Union and the emergence of the Renaissance?"

"Yes, they are in fact manifestations of the same principle. They're both what's called Chaotic Phase Transitions. I'll give you another example. Evolution is another process governed by the laws of Chaos."

"But isn't Evolution a slow, gradual process? Where's the sudden change?"

"That's what people thought until recently, but in 1972 two paleontologists called Niles Eldridge and Stephen Jay Gould published a paper where they argued there are long periods where nothing changes, it's called stasis, and boom, suddenly many new species emerge. They called it Punctuated Equilibrium. Well, guess what? Evolution is a chaotic process governed by feedback loops. All Chaotic systems exhibit self-referencing behavior, and whenever you have that in just the right way then something amazing happens; a new entity emanates like a new being climbing out of the serpent hole. Imagine you're standing by that hole and nothing happens for ages, but then you see an arm jutting out, and it digs its fingers into the ground at the hole's edge and then a new being climbs out and it becomes independent of the hole, with its own Free Will."

"Damn hon, that's quite a visual. Don't take it the wrong way but I may have nightmares tonight." Jenna burst out laughing.

"Funny, too funny. But I've heard of Chaos Theory. The Butterfly Effect, right?"

"Yes, the Butterfly Effect is a picturesque way to show how a small change can snowball into a huge change."

"The flaps of the wings of a butterfly in Australia can eventually create a storm in North America," Darnell said.

"The fundamental principle is that in a system containing feedback loops, parts of the system communicate with each other, part A communicates with part B and this changes part B, but then part B communicates with part C and this imbues part C with an essence of part A because part B has been flavored with the essence of part A, so when part C now communicates with and changes part A, in effect part A is changing itself, and this process gets repeated over and over, faster and faster, back and forth, left and right, up and down and in all directions, it gets repeated across all the parts, each part with all the others, small groups communicating with other small groups and then the small with the large and the large with the small and then larger and larger sets, each subset a set of subsets, spiraling in and out, subsets piling atop subsets and within them and around and around, some wrestling with the others and some

The Curtains Open: The Third Act

dancing, some groups forming cohesive bonds and others dissolving in a roiling sea of self-referential turbulence, and the the entire system becomes a dense network that gets blanketed with these feedback loops across its entirety, and still faster and faster, like little vibrating springs, but they are subsets, and subsets of subsets, of the parts of the system that communicate with each other, like a stew cooking atop a fire, each ingredient flavoring all the others and getting flavored back with the essence of its own flavor mirrored back, and then, suddenly, critical complexity is achieved and the parts, and the subsets of the parts of ever spiraling complexity can no longer break away from their once temporary bonds...and without warning...boom...a new, autonomous entity finally explodes out of the turbulent sea."

Darnell and Jenna's mouths were hanging open. I was out of breath and I inhaled a shovelful of air.

"Hon, my head's spinning."

"Me too, Nini. I think I need a cigarette."

"Never mind, the point is these feedback loops are what create an emergent behavior which is unpredictable. It's called Pseudo Deterministic Chaos, also known as Free Will."

Darnell squinted his eyes. It was a sign of his deep reflection. "So you're saying the Renaissance is an emergent behavior in this insane sense?"

"Bingo. In my novel I'll be talking about what I call the Civilization of Man."

"Hon, isn't that kinda sexist?"

"I use the term Man, capital M, as a designation for all of humanity, and it's a reference to the word Adam in Genesis, which is a term that designates a template out of which humanity emerged out of Adama, the ground-of-being."

"I'm no theologian Nini, but-"

"Darnell, you don't seem to be much of anything according to your humble estimations." I laughed. "What are you Darnell?"

Darnell reflected on my question. He seemed stumped. "I'm not sure. I guess I'm someone trying to figure out what he is. I guess I'm just a poor schmuck trying to figure out my place in this fucked-up world."

"Then that makes you a philosopher," Jenna said.

"Let me tell you a story. In the Spring of 2004 we visited Rome. It was the first time for me, and of course Jenna had lived there for two years shortly before I met her. We went to the Coliseum, and as I was sitting on the steps I spotted the center stage where the emperors would sit and with an up or down thumb whimsically make life and death declarations. That

The Curtains Open: The Third Act

got me thinking about the nature of Empire and the coming Third Age. And then a thought flashed across my mind: The emergent resides in the people's seats, not the emperor's box."

"You never told me about that when we were there."

"I was still analyzing it, what it meant. I wasn't ready to share it."

"So Nini, what does it mean?" Darnell accentuated the word 'does'.

"It means the emergent comes from within the system, not from an external controller. God creates from the bottom up. It's a self-regulating system. But anyway, there you go. I've explained why it's not as inconceivable as you think, Darnell, that a monumental paradigm shift will completely transform the zeitgeist of humanity. The Civilization of Man is a Chaotic system subject to all the effects of such systems. This includes Chaotic Phase Transitions. And that's what the Third Age will be: A Chaotic Phase Transition, a Punctuated Equilibrium, a cataclysmic awakening within The Civilization of Man, and it will wash upon humanity like a thief in the night. It will make the Renaissance seem like just a dress-rehearsal."

"That sounds kinda apocalyptic. Is this the Messianic Age?"

"Why, yes it is. That's very astute of you. I thought you said you weren't a theologian." I winked playfully.

"And by the way, the very emergence of Existence from the H is itself a Chaotic Phase Transition. The Big Bang is a Chaotic Phase Transition." I waited for that to sink-in.

"Sounds like cocooned dolls," Jenna finally said, "Chaotic Phase Transitions within Chaotic Phase Transitions within Chaotic Phase Transitions."

"A mirror within a mirror within another. The self-referencing nature of Existence. It's the leitmotif by which the symphony of Existence is composed."

"And within an unremarkable corner of the world, you will be writing about these ideas? Why you, Nini? If this Third Age is such a sudden, unannounced change then how do you know about it?"

"Because I've always listened to the whispers emanating from a mysterious place inside me. Because I've invited YHVH at my bosom."

"That sounds like so much airy-fairy bull, really Nini. You're gonna have to give me a more rational explanation."

"You want rational, I'll give you rational. Humanity has had an obsession with understanding the divine, with interacting with the divine. This obsession has shaped much of history, more than the love of money, more than the lust for power, it has carved out empires, it has altered national boundaries, it has been the fire behind our political and sociological theories and institutions."

"But Marx was an atheist, Ayn Rand was also an atheist."

"Militant atheism is also a manifestation of our obsession with the divine. Don't kid yourself."

"I don't buy into your saying the quest for the divine has influenced civilization more than the lust for power or money."

"There are two reasons why this is so. One - our deep, inborn drive to understand Creation-"

"You mean science? I think sex is a far more powerful drive that shapes society. What's number two?"

"Hey Darny, you sound like a Freud fan-boy."

"Well, why not? I think Freud was one fucking smart Jew." Darnell winked at me.

I ignored his comment. "Two - our existential struggle to come to terms with our imminent death. The inborn yearning to understand ourselves as more than just meat with an expiry date."

"Hmmm...I can kinda agree with that actually. We cling to our ego and we can't come to terms with its inevitable demise for all eternity. Me personally, I don't give a fuck about dying."

"There were actually two forbidden trees in the garden of Eden. Did you know that?"

"I know about the apple tree, and after Adam and Eve ate it they knew the difference between good and evil and god gave them the boot."

"The other is the Tree of Eternal Life," Jenna said. "But initially only the Tree of the Knowledge of Good and Evil was forbidden, wasn't it?"

"You're right. It was only after Adam and Eve were banished that the Tree of Eternal Life was forbidden."

"Why did you bring that up?"

"You said you admired Freud's ideas and there's a tie-in with the two trees."

"This I gotta hear."

"The two trees correspond to Freud's Id and Ego. In Taoist terms they are the two Chis. In the body of ideas I've constructed I call it Dancing and Wrestling. One is an emanation and the other is a contraction."

"Which is which?"

"The Tree of the Knowledge of Good and Evil symbolizes Ego, Wrestling, Emanation, Order from Chaos. It's a creative energy. It's the abstract Feminine. When Adam and Eve ate from it they were banished from the Garden. This is an allusion to the emergence of space and time from a lower substrate of Existence."

The Curtains Open: The Third Act

"Exploding out of the Big Bang?"

"Yes."

"That's fucking deep."

"Fundamentally, our collective consciousness is space and time as a self-aware narrative. So the eating from the Tree of Knowledge symbolizes both the emergence of space and time and the emergence of our consciousness. These two are the same thing."

"So it's pure metaphor then," Darnell said.

"It's not just metaphor. If you understand that the Garden story is an abstraction, and if you then also understand that this abstraction is more fundamental than Physical Reality, then you'll understand that the Garden story is actually more real than what we ordinarily think of as real. If you get that then you'll also get how the Garden story is literally true in this abstract sense, because the physical emerges from a more fundamental abstract substrate."

"You should write that down. I'll need to reread that to have a hope of getting it."

"And then," Jenna said, "god placed an angel with a flaming sword that whirled left and right at the entry into the Garden, in order to bar our entry back, lest we eat from the Tree of Eternal Life and become like god."

"In order to prevent us," I said, "from eating the fruit of the Tree of Eternal Life and then collapsing this self-aware narrative back into the white-eyed womb of Existence. To eat from the fruit of knowledge is to be granted Free Will. To eat from the fruit of eternal life is to renounce Free Will and return to the white-eyed embrace of the Garden."

"But Adam and Eve fucked it all up and ate the god-damned apple, pun intended."

"But Darnell, we were created to be banished. We were setup. That has always been our sole purpose. That's why when we were in the Garden the Tree of Knowledge was never given the same protection that the Tree of Eternal Life was later given after we were banished. When we were in the Garden we were not barred from eternal life because we already had it."

"So where is this Garden then?" Darnell said.

"The Garden of Eden is within us," Jenna said.

"Like a mirror, within a mirror, within another."

"Wow, hon. That's sending shivers up my spine."

"So I'll tell you now why I'm seeing a seismic shift in the Civilization of Man. I'll tell you why I think we're at the dawn of the Third Age. And I'll tell you why I see it, and smell it, and taste it, and contemplate it, and meditate on it, and write about it more than anyone else. It's because my ideas are about a new understanding of what god is, an understanding that unifies the rational with the spiritual, an understanding that will cause an Existential Whiplash within humanity, precisely because humanity is obsessed with the divine and with impending death and with being at peace with impending death, and anything that will radically alter its understanding and its relationship with the divine will also radically change the character of civilization. And once these ideas are absorbed then a new resonance will strum between the two trees deep within our core. Once these ideas percolate into the bone marrow of humanity then a new zeitgeist is inevitable. It might take a while, but remember what I said about Chaotic Phase Transitions and Punctuated Equilibrium. It won't take anywhere as long as you might think."

"How long will it take? Within my lifetime?" Darnell said.

"I think so, yes."

"And what will that be? What are the changes we'll see?"

"Social justice like never imagined before. Religion as we know it will be no more. The distinction between atheism and belief will evaporate. The Catholic church will collapse. Islamic theocracies will crumble. Judaism will be no more because it will have served its mission of triggering this seismic shift. Secularism and divinity will merge. Abuses of power by corporations will no longer be tolerated by the zeitgeist. Empire will be no more. Empires have risen and fallen, waxed and waned, but it's not specific empires that will fall, it's the very template of empire that will be no more. And above all, we will have, once and for all, answered the deep questions about the nature of Existence, about the fabric of Reality. These are questions that have tugged at us since our emergence on the African Savannah. These are questions that have left us no peace because we craved to know the answers and we've created great religions and we have erected great universities, and we have built mighty machines that probe the depths of space and time and energy and matter, to answer these questions and we came successively close. But the closer we got, the further the answers to these questions seemed. It seemed we were chasing the horizon itself and it never got nearer. But in the coming Third Age we will finally exceed it."

"Darnell, what he's talking about is eschatology and it's huge, just huge."

"Do you believe it?"

"I do, I really do. I can feel it too."

***

The Curtains Open: The Third Act

"I have all the tools at my disposal. I have all the pieces of the Jigsaw puzzle."

"But now you have to put the puzzle together into one whole."

"And therein lies the rub. I don't know how. I'm flailing."

"What's the matter little Nini, suffering from a wee bit of writer's block, are we?"

Jenna was sounding like Darnell. I nodded in apparent resignation as I ran my right hand through my thick, curly hair. I needed a haircut. I knew her patronizing tone was meant in jest. "I haven't even written the first word of the novel yet. All I know is the title. The Third Age: A Quest For En Sof."

Jenna took a deep, satisfying drag of her cigarette as she was sitting on the ledge of the living room door leading to our fourth floor balcony. It was Sunday morning and she was soon to leave for church at St. James Anglican. "You have no idea? Surely you must have an inkling of how you want to start it."

It was a warm and sunny day during mid-April of 2006. Jenna had moved back home with me a couple of weeks before and we were trying to rebuild our fractured marriage. But I suspected the initiative was more mine than hers. We were due to vacation in Israel on May 1st. It is the land of my birth. A land on which I had not laid foot at that point for thirty years.

"I've been thinking of using a Midrashic approach to the first chapter."

"Midrashic?"

"A midrashic story is a take on some story arc in the Old Testament and-"

Jeniffer grimaced. "Hon, you know I hate that term. It's not like the Hebrew Testament is yesterday's stale pizza to be replaced by the piping hot and fresh Christian Testament...Christian testament...Hebrew testament... these are the names I live by."

"Point taken. You're the Christian and I'm the Jew?...ha ha. Let me continue though...where was I? Oh yes, OK. The biblical story arc is then embellished and shaped and crafted just so and...well the reason for this approach is to flesh out some theme or lesson in the Old... err I mean Hebrew Testament and expound on it and even add some new insights and speculations."

"And which story arc in the Hebrew Testament are you going all Midrashic on?" She emphasized the word 'Hebrew'.

I answered almost before she had a chance to finish her question. "The

The Curtains Open: The Third Act

story of Abraham as a child in the city of Ur, discovering monotheism and rejecting the idolatry of his family and his society."

"Well, that's a well defined start. That's what I do before I begin my writing. A well defined theme is a must before your first pen stroke, or keyboard tap. Listen, I've never written a novel but I find that approach very powerful when I write my articles and essays for the diocese."

"There's already a well known Midrashic tale about the young child Abraham smashing all the idols in his father's idol shop. His father was an idol merchant, you know?"

"Really, it's in the bible or just a Midrashic spin?"

"Spin I think. I don't know. I'll have to do an Internet search."

"Or you can just read the original, you know hon, the bible? Oy Vey." Jenna slapped her forehead in mock disgust and cackled. "Why are you going with this story arc? How does it shape your theme?"

"Well, you know I've been talking since I met you about the coming paradigm shift?"

"Ah yes, I remember our first date at Havana's. That was the first thing out of your mouth when I asked you to tell me something about yourself. 'I want to write a book that will change the world'. You know, I've come to believe in you since then."

Havana's is a Cuban restaurant in Vancouver's counter-culture Bohemian neighborhood of Commercial Drive. I lived only a few minutes walk from the Commercial Drive neighborhood in those days. It is the neighborhood were all the trees are well hugged. It is one of the neighborhoods in Vancouver that resonates with me.

"I'll start my novel with the shift from the First Age to the Second Age, from polytheism to monotheism. Young Abram's midrashic tale will epitomize that shift."

"And what of the Third Age?"

"That's the coming shift from monotheism to metatheism. A new relationship with the divine."

"Metatheism? Nice. I see you've already coined the term."

"I'll write a short midrashic chapter, maybe ten pages? And then the second chapter will leap four thousand years into the present times. I do know I want to give the novel a self-referential aspect."

"The novel will describe itself?"

"Yes, it will be basically about what happens in the world when the novel is released. It will slowly dawn on the reader that the book talked about in the novel is the very book he's holding in his hands and reading."'

"Brilliant. Like opening a 3D cutout book. It springs into the world from

The Curtains Open: The Third Act

the flat pages."

"Yes, or like infinite nested mirrors, each level having yet another level up above. The reader's world will become yet another level up above springing from the flat pages of the novel."

"You sure love that mirror metaphor, dontcha?" Jenna took one last, quick drag of her cigarette and put it out in the ashtray at her feet. She got up and brushed a few specs of cigarette ash off her flowing, knee length dress. "Gotta go hon. I think you're good to go. Will you be starting the novel today?"

I sighed. "Yes, I can't put this off any longer. I'm both ecstatic and terrified. I don't know what kind of writer I am really. What is my author's voice? Do I even have one? I don't know if I have the chops to pull this off. One thing's for sure, the time for talk is over, it's time to put up or shut up." I hoped to delay Jenna's departure.

"You're a good writer. I've read some of the stuff you've written on the forums, and you remember that short-story you wrote about Einstein meeting the Bat-Kol? It was really, really well done."

"Ah yes. I remember. But I never finished it. I've never had the discipline or the guts to finish anything I've ever started. Not school, not all the books I've wanted to read, not any of the subjects I've always wanted to master. Not anything."

"But Hon, those things weren't meant to be. It's not who you are. This novel you've been talking about it seems forever is your calling. You are exactly the kind of writer needed for the novel you so passionately want to write, nothing less and nothing more. I really believe that no one else can write it the way you have it in you to write it."

At that moment Jenna appeared to me like a Gypsy fortune-teller. Images of Zelda the Romanian Gypsy temptress danced in my head. Her dark, narrow eyes, her sharp, mocha features evoked in me a sense of an hypnotic ancient and unfathomable creative energy as intractable to science as to lore.

After Jenna left for the day I poured myself a generous amount of red wine from a half finished bottle left over from the previous night's get-together with Darnell. I sat in front of the computer, cleared my mind and invited the divine to speak to me from the semantic spaces of the soul. I sipped from the reverberating redness of the wine which, at that moment, became a proxy for my spirit's life-blood - my Adam's Dam (blood in Hebrew) emanating from Adama. But we all share the same soul, and so the wine became a proxy for space and time's collective soul. I pleaded for inspiration but my supplications were ignored. I fought my demons of

The Curtains Open: The Third Act

despair but I could not manage the resonance of the Wrestle.

I reminisced of a time long ago when I was only twenty years old. I was studying English 101 at the University Of British Columbia in the summer of Eighty-Four. It was at a summer session because I had failed English 101 two years before. A failure due more to my citizenship in a different realm than to the failings of my intellect, aptitude or the magnanimity of my core.

"You have such a poignant and evocative writing style," wrote my teacher on the top of the first page of the short-story I had submitted the week before, and she awarded me a B+.

"If only you would get your spelling errors under control I'd happily give you an A+," she wrote. Those were the days before spell-checking software.

I had written about a lonely sojourn on a desolate beach in the pregnant moment when sunset injures day's abandon and grants night the freedom to roam.

I had written about the mighty North Shore mountains, hoary with age and reverberating with an energy ineffable to the mind but savored by the soul.

I remembered how exhausting of mind, but above all of the soul, writing that short-story had been. I tried to reveal my spirit bare and exposed. I tried to destroy the ramparts and blow open the heavy gates shielding my secretive core.

But through my exhausting efforts I had only succeeded in weakening the facade between me and the world,

usually held at arm's length but through my story then,

only slightly nearer yet still remote.

There is an essence within everyone hidden in a chamber far beneath the veneer that encrusts our core.

We seldom allow it expression

beyond just its fractured shadows dancing on an external wall.

But if we all dig deep and reach into this secretive chamber we will, to our astonishment, discover we are all reaching into the same chamber, not a separate one for each within the all,

and then we will grasp each other's same-hand.

We all share the same soul.

I knew that in the novel of my compulsion I would have to expose this chamber,

ramparts and heavy gates destroyed once and for all.

And my novel would then cry out from this collective chamber and

speak for my left and for my right with one voice for all.
It would be the ineffable H reaching out to humanity from the navel of Creation,
proclaiming the dawn of a new age.
It would proclaim the sunset of the Second Age before the coming dawn,
a moment pregnant with change that will forever be remembered in the annals of the Civilization of Man.
It would herald a paradigm shift far greater than the Renaissance -
not just an age of reason, but of reason and divinity intertwined as an inseparable whole.
I envision the Third Age to be promoting
the two primordial dancers,
the abstract magical
and the other its complementary whole,
to engage in the Dance and thence
unshard into the Eternal garden
from whence they go forth.
They are in Eternity entwined,
but sharded by leitmotif into the realms
of space and time.
They are shards of the divine.
Would composing such a novel be an arduous journey, exhausting my body and above all my core?
Would I be as a drowning man, gasping for breath,
kicking and screaming while attempting to reach for the shore? But would every paragraph and page exhaust me,
yet also leave me yearning for more?
It would I am sure. This arduous compulsion will also uplift and invigorate me with waves of catharsis and frisson.
And I pray dearly for the same in my reader,
of soul-piercing joy.
If I fail to evoke the same in my audience then I would have failed to breach the ramparts and the gates shielding my innermost chamber,
our collective soul.
Only within this innermost shared sanctum can I truly touch someone's soul and by touching one I will be touching them all.

But I still did not know how to begin my novel. I knew the beginning, or even just the first paragraph, must set the tone and expose a theme I must

The Curtains Open: The Third Act

repeat at multiple levels of abstraction throughout the pages of my tome. I knew the heart and soul of my novel must not only emanate locally from its words, but also from the global self-referencing structure of its narrative. The medium is the message. The self-referencing nature of Gödel's Incompleteness theorems, and the infinitely hierarchical spaces of Chaos Theory, must be mirrored in the structure of my novel. The first sentence must be like a musical leitmotif, played at multiple levels of pitch, each pitch having a unique meaning but all such meanings emanating from the same polymorphic template, the inner chamber of my novel's source.

I sipped my red wine. Its flavor had mellowed since Friday night. I reflected on my life, on my struggles and my challenges from early childhood and until that point in time. I reflected on the vertigo I always felt, a nausea inducing state reminiscent of playing myself in a movie cameo, rather than in real life. I have always been an outsider, resonating to my own drummer, and no other, always a misfit in school, in the mating game, in the workforce and in life, always a dreamer and an outcast yearning to break the shackles tethering me to a world to which I cannot belong and to a zeitgeist with which I cannot resonate. But I always entertained feelings of manifest destiny to change the world rather than to abandon it. I wrestled with my existential angst rather than dancing, because I did not intend to abandon the world, I intended to nudge it as an anonymous butterfly nudges the weather into a new paradigm. I intended to flutter my tiny wings and effect huge change. But I now intended my novel, the instrument of my discontent, to be a real agent of change rather than, as the butterfly, merely symbolic. But it would not be my novel that changes the world, instead it would be as yeast leavening dough - scant in power but of great influence far beyond its size. No one person can change the world, it is simply a calling. It is the Civilization of Man singing a siren's song. It is the Civilization of Man, as an emergent entity, calling upon a shard of its divinity, but the change is orchestrated by the paradigm shift to be. The leaf can be the mother of the tree.

Since my recalcitrant youth I have engaged the whispers emanating from the semantic spaces within my core. Sometimes dancing with them but mostly wrestling. These whispers have always been louder to me than the loudest bellows of my teachers, my elders, society's intellectuals, traditionalists and even its progressives, now and yet to be. And it then dawned on me the leitmotif I have been seeking is plain to see. It is a leitmotif of being cast out into new worlds to be, and it is played across a wide swath of the musical scale. In A Major it is YHVH, Creation's Y cast out from the ineffable H. In B Major it is the Civilization of Man cast out

The Curtains Open: The Third Act

from the white-eyed Garden. In C Major it is the Hebrews, those who are cast out and cross over to new realms. Like the mirrors within a mirror within another, each a higher pitch of the same theme. And the principle, the polymorphic abstract template that gives rise to all these instantiations, is Gödel's Incompleteness which elucidates about theorems cast out and unfathomable from within.

I savored one more sip of my red wine's mellow. Each of its flavors wrestling with all the others. I was embarking on the first step in a journey intertwining the literary, scientific and divine, and if once the journey is completed I remain exhausted to the bone then I was joyfully prepared to pay the sweet price. "Yahvah," I cried out within the silent confines of my innermost chamber, "you are welcome to my comforts, even to my bones, if you would allow me to satiate my addiction, my compulsion and bring forth the convergence of my destiny." In the seeds of my exhaustion would reside my exhilaration.

I began typing my novel's opening sentence, its primordial words: a loop in Eternity.

Ever since I was a child I always felt like a citizen of a different realm...

Made in the USA
San Bernardino, CA
21 January 2020